50 GREAT MYTHS OF HUMAN SEXUALITY

D0874769

50 GREAT MYTHS OF HUMAN SEXUALITY

Pepper Schwartz
and
Martha Kempner

WILEY Blackwell

This edition first published 2015
© 2015 John Wiley & Sons, Inc.

Registered Office
John Wiley & Sons, Ltd, The Atrium, Southern Gate, Chichester,
West Sussex, PO19 8SQ, UK

Editorial Offices
350 Main Street, Malden, MA 02148-5020, USA
9600 Garsington Road, Oxford, OX4 2DQ, UK
The Atrium, Southern Gate, Chichester, West Sussex, PO19 8SQ, UK

For details of our global editorial offices, for customer services, and for information
about how to apply for permission to reuse the copyright material in this book please
see our website at www.wiley.com/wiley-blackwell.

The right of Pepper Schwartz and Martha Kempner to be identified as the authors
of this work has been asserted in accordance with the UK Copyright, Designs and Patents
Act 1988.

Library of Congress Cataloging-in-Publication Data
Schwartz, Pepper.
    50 great myths of human sexuality / Pepper Schwartz, Martha Kempner.
        pages cm
    Includes bibliographical references and index.
    ISBN 978-0-470-67433-8 (hardback) – ISBN 978-0-470-67434-5 (paper)
1. Sex–Miscellanea.   2. Sex customs–Miscellanea.   3. Man-woman relationships–
Miscellanea.   I. Kempner, Martha.   II. Title.   III. Title: Fifty great myths of
human sexuality.
    HQ21.S327 2015
    306.7–dc23
                                                        2014037290
A catalogue record for this book is available from the British Library.

Set in 9.5/11.5pt Sabon by SPi Publisher Services, Pondicherry, India
Printed and bound in Malaysia by Vivar Printing Sdn Bhd

1   2015

CONTENTS

PREFACE

Not so long ago, a member of the US House of Representatives said that he knew that a woman could not get pregnant if she was raped against her will. He explained that there was some sort of organic process in the body that would prevent conception under "legitimate rape" conditions. We can't imagine where he learned this. He claims doctors told him but unless they were lying or joking we can't imagine anyone who had gone to medical school actually believing it. It so ridiculous that it would never have occurred to us to include it as a myth in this book. And yet a grown, well-educated man—a member of Congress, no less—believed it firmly enough that he was comfortable repeating it as fact to a television reporter.

We don't think that this myth is sweeping the nation but it reminds us that there are some amazing misconceptions about human sexuality out there, many of which are certified by self-anointed "experts" and passed on as gospel, and some of which are even taught in our schools. Some are so misleading as to be dangerous while others may cause needless worry and anxiety.

We are all victims of swallowing a myth or two during some point of our lives; nobody gets all the right information, and sometimes early information sounds right until we learn it was actually quite inaccurate, but possibly not before we've told others what we first thought.

During Pepper's freshman year of college, she was in a suite with a number of women, most of whom were virgins when they arrived. One by one, most of the young women acquired boyfriends or entered into an intense dating relationship, and got physical. One of the girls got pregnant the first time. She was shocked. She was sure that "you could not get pregnant the first time you had sex," or that the odds against it were so great that she didn't need to worry. Like there was a sex-freebie, and after that things got serious. (That myth was very common in those days and still tossed around often enough that we did include it in the book along with the much newer myth that the soda Mountain Dew could prevent pregnancy when drunk in large quantities or used as a douche (see Myth # 25).

Myths have consequences. If we believe that a woman can't get pregnant the first time or during her period, some of us won't bother with contraception at those times. Even seemingly innocuous myths can change our behavior. If we believe, say, that red-haired girls are naturally hornier, some shy redhead is going to get come-ons that she doesn't like, and feel like she has to live up to expectations that she can't, or doesn't want to, fulfill.

It gets even more difficult because many beliefs about sexuality are based on personal or societal values and not scientific fact. And values changes. A couple of generations ago, mothers would tell their daughters to stay virginal until marriage because, as the saying went "He's not going to buy the cow if he can get the milk for free." That may not have been bad advice before the sexual revolution started to change women's behavior in the late 1960s and 1970s. It might not even be bad advice now, but it doesn't reflect today's reality in which virginity, not sexual experience, is often more of a cultural burden to women. Despite this reality and the fact that today's teens have sex earlier and get married later, the abstinence-only-until-marriage movement of the 1980s, 1990s, and early 2000s told young people in no uncertain terms that premarital sex was harmful. While some may continue to value premarital virginity and should be allowed to act on their beliefs, it is inaccurate to say that not doing so is harmful.

Other myths were just never true. Sometimes the facts are distorted because of political agendas. For example, some antiabortion activists have literally made up physical and emotional consequences for abortion (see Myth # 29) because they want to scare women enough so that they will not have an abortion. And still others have some basis in historical fact but are no longer true today. It is no longer true, for example, that young women and teens should avoid IUDs out of fear of their future fertility. The newest versions of this contraceptive method are safe for women of all ages.

For this book we picked 50 myths about sex. We admit it was hard to narrow them down. We picked them first if we thought that a lot of people believed them and might never know the truth unless we put them in this book. Second, we picked ones that had misinformation that was so dangerous that we were worried that people's reliance on them could seriously hurt them (emotionally or physically) or others (through discrimination). Finally, we picked ones that had good research to the contrary; we didn't want to be guilty of the same thing our book is trying to address! You can probably think of a lot more. And we'd be delighted if you wrote us and suggested others (there's always the second edition!).

We do want to address a few things before we delve into correcting misinformation. For the most part we focused on research from the United States and the cultural issues that are specific to this country. Attitudes about human sexuality are so different around the world that it would have been impossible to address each myth on a global scale. That said, we do include comparisons with other countries and cultures in some of our myths to help explain how variable beliefs can be and how societies can influence perceptions.

We also tried to be inclusive of same-sex couples wherever possible. Obviously, certain myths—like those about getting pregnant—are exclusive to heterosexual couples. Others are dedicated to correcting misunderstandings about gay, lesbian, bisexual, or transgender individuals and couples. Many myths, however, like those about faking orgasms or the importance of simultaneous orgasms, probably originated with heterosexual couples but can be applied to anyone. In these myths we tried to include research on same-sex couples wherever possible. Unfortunately, for many aspects of sexuality and sexual behavior, there has not been nearly enough research done on lesbian and gay couples. We are hopeful that as same-sex marriage and relationships become more open and accepted in our society, more researchers will begin to look closely at same-sex couples. (Perhaps that second edition we were talking about can include more information.)

Finally, we want to make sure that our readers understand that because beliefs on human sexuality are so often grounded in personal values and opinions, some of what you read will reflect our beliefs. Our opinions are grounded in science and we present that science to you throughout the book. Of course, we think it is only fair that you know that our opinions are also grounded in our collective years of experience working in the field of human sexuality, writing, researching, and teaching. And given this experience, sometimes we just couldn't help adding a little advice into our entries.

Ultimately, we hope these pages clarify, enlighten, and entertain you. Just because these are serious matters doesn't mean we can't have a little fun with them.

1 BODY PARTS

Who Has What and How It Works

Bigger Penises Are Better

How many jokes have we all heard about how much "size matters?" And how many retorts "It's not the meat, it's the motion?" There are so many penis jokes and so much bragging, it isn't funny. No, it really isn't. Because the fact is that men with smaller penises worry that they will not be virile enough, it may make them avoid sexual interaction or even peeing in a public urinal, and, even more importantly, some of those men will buy various fake products that will supposedly make them longer, stronger, or wider. Distraught men may even opt for surgery, and these implants can cause nerve damage and even impotence. Even if successful, these are serious operations which include cutting the suspensory ligament, followed by weeks of traction that include hanging weights on the penis (Vardi *et al.*, 2008). This results in added length, but only in the flaccid state! (So who is this operation really for? Could it be really to see other guys enviously ogle the longer penis in the men's room?) Attempts to add girth have even more problems, often resulting in uneven distribution of the added fat tissue which can have an overall lumpy effect. Most men who have the procedure are not happy with the result (Li *et al.*, 2006).

So How Big Are They Usually?

There are differences in penis size. There are wide ones that are short, long, and in between. There are long ones and short ones of different girth. The best study on penis size (Wessells *et al.*, 1996) found that the mean size of flaccid penises was about 3.5 inches and about 5.1 inches erect. When they measured against the pubic pad, it was about 6.2 inches. Mean circumference of the erect penile shaft was about 4.8 inches. Two-thirds of the men were within 1 inch of these measurements. Other studies also arrive at similar measurements (Templer, 2002). Interestingly, these studies found no correlation between the flaccid and erect state, so next time you sneak a glance at the guy at the next urinal just remember—you don't really know much.

There have been quite a few studies searching for whether a man's height has any positive correlation with penis size. Taller men certainly *think* their penises are bigger. An internet survey of 52,031 heterosexual men and women found taller men estimated they were larger while shorter men estimated they were smaller (Lever *et al.*, 2006). They may be right. Researchers in Iran actually studied the external genital dimensions of 1500 men and concluded that length had a significant positive correlation with height (Mehraban *et al.*, 2007). A study from the Department of Urology through the Athens Naval and Veterans Hospital measured 52 men under 40 and found that the penile shaft length, and total length, was correlated positively to height (Spyropoulos *et al.*, 2002).

Body mass also has had some correlation with penis size but most researchers feel that the correlation is because the penis of obese men retreats under the belly and so seems smaller than it is. Ultimately, researchers conclude that "fat level is a good predictor of when a man rates his penis as small versus large" (Lever *et al.*, 2006, p. 135).

People often joke that the larger the hand and feet the larger the schlong, but that doesn't seem to be the case. Urologists at St Mary's Hospital and the University College Hospital in London studied the stretched penile length of 104 men and found that there was not a "statistically significant relationship between stretched penile length and shoe size" (Shah and Christopher, 2002, p. 586). No one else has found such a link either.

While hands might not tell us anything, it turns out that the index finger can. The study of Iranian men found a positive correlation between the parameters of an index finger and the size of a man's penis (Mehraban *et al.*, 2007). Another study on a small sample of men found the same thing (Spyropoulos *et al.*, 2002). Voracek and Manning (2003) offered an explanation for this: "Homeobox (Hox) genes regulate limb development, including fingers and toes, as well as urogenital system development, including the penis. Therefore morphological patterns of the fingers may be related to morphological patterns of the external genitalia" (p. 201).

So there may in fact be some physiological continuities that can predict larger penis length. We think the better question, however, is why is everyone so interested? Are there really any differences between big penises and small when it comes to sexual satisfaction?

Does Size Really Affect Pleasure?

Well, there are two ways to look at this: what's in your head, and what's in your body. Physiological research refers to how effective different sized penises might be in terms of women's likelihood of orgasm and enjoyment of sex. Psychological factors refer to how mentally or emotionally or even aesthetically important size is for a woman's pleasure and/or likelihood of orgasm. A number of studies have taken a look at both. Let's look at heterosexual data first.

Masters and Johnson, the famous sex researchers whose work on sexual functioning in the late 1960s and 1970s jump-started the whole field of sexology and sex therapy, looked at hundreds (maybe thousands) of heterosexual sexual acts and concluded that size was irrelevant or a minor factor in women's sexual pleasure. Their research has been replicated numerous times (Masters and Johnson, 1966; Zilbergeld, 1999; Fisher *et al.*, 1983). The main reason they felt sexual arousal and orgasm were unrelated to penis size was because the vagina is such an accommodating space that, in general, the walls of the vagina grab the penis and conform to its size. The authors do note that women and men might not feel this grabbing at all times during sex because during the excitement and plateau phase of the sexual arousal cycle the bottom part of the vagina "balloons" (perhaps to capture semen more efficiently). At times of extreme arousal, the vagina could feel looser or the penis not quite as fulsome.

Though the popular media may suggest that women want bigger and wider penises, the research tells a different story and points to men being a lot more worried about penis size than women are. A large academic internet study found that while 55% of heterosexual men were happy with their penis size and/or girth, 84% of heterosexual women were happy with their partner's penis attributes. Only 14% wanted something bigger (Lever *et al.*, 2006). An older study by Zilbergeld was particularly conclusive about women's subjective opinion: out of 426 non-virginal women, not one mentioned that penis size was important (Fisher *et al.*, 1983).

More recent studies have also gathered some interesting results. Eisenman (2001) asked 50 women about the importance of penis size; 45% felt more width felt better, while only 5% responded positively to greater length. A European study asked a number of new mothers about their partner's penis size and sexual satisfaction and only 1% of them mentioned length as a positive addition to their enjoyment. The majority found penis length either unimportant (55%) or totally unimportant (22%). A number of women said that they thought length was less important than girth, but only 1% mentioned girth. On the other hand, an additional study by the same researchers did find that one out of three women mentioned size and/or length as being important (Francken *et al.*, 2002). In a 2006 article based on a 1998 study of 556 women in Croatia, girth was found to be more important than length but still only 12.8% of the sample rated either girth or length to be very important to them. However, when the authors limited their analysis only to the most sexually experienced women, a different story emerged as more of these women thought that penis size was important (Štulhofer, 2006).

Interestingly, how a penis appears was important to women in this study as 26.9% of sexually experienced women said that the appearance of their partner's penis was very important to them and 44.9% said that it was somewhat important. In fact, only 18.2% said aesthetics of the penis were totally unimportant. It is interesting that in these studies women have strong aesthetic preferences but lesser physiological ones.

Where does that leave us? Well, heterosexual men are clearly getting feedback that makes them worry about their penises. But, despite the pervasiveness of this myth, it seems rare that this feedback is truly based on size. Most importantly, there is certainly no credible information that penis size determines satisfaction in heterosexual relationships.

Is This Different for Gay Men?

Male sex workers advertise their wares according to size and gay male models in sexually explicit material seem to be chosen for the size and girth of their penises. In sexy gay cartoons, the guys are always hung. No wonder gay men worry about penis size—it seems to be a particularly widely held obsession in gay America. But does it matter in gay relationships?

Well, to some extent, what people believe to be real, is real in its consequences. (A saying first noted by W.I. Thomas, an early sociologist.) The aesthetics of penis size in the gay world has been so extolled that it would be odd if it didn't affect how a gay man felt about his equipment! But does it really make a difference in sexual satisfaction?

Certainly some men think it does. But are gay men who have partners with small penises more likely to stray or more likely to be sexually unfulfilled? We did not find any data on this topic in same-sex relationships so we are not sure if there is any consequence in a relationship one way or the other.

Why Do We Confuse Bigger Penises With Better Penises?

We think there are two reasons. First, the whole world seems to think bigger is better in just about everything from a hamburger to a house. Certainly, there are status points for having a big house—we know that it cost more and the person who builds or buys an elaborate estate is definitely trying to tell the world they are a big deal. Whether or not that house is pleasant to live in may be an entirely different matter. Bigger penises come from the same thought pattern. Of course we know that bigger isn't always better in everything. Look at the extraordinary weight gain that has accompanied larger bagels, enormous steaks, and super-sized French fries. In fact, a big penis may be painful to some women, dangerous in vigorous anal sex to either a homosexual or heterosexual partner, and may actually be softer because very big penises can have some problems distributing enough blood to be "rock hard."

The second reason we think bigger has been confused with better is because for the most part only huge penises are used in porno movies. We think they are used so that the male watcher can identify and feel powerful by association. But of course, another comparison may lurk in his head: "My penis doesn't look anything like that—maybe I am not capable of being that sexy!"

Obviously, individuals will have their preferences but the data swerve sharply toward penis size being irrelevant except for a small proportion of women who like the aesthetics of a larger penis and those gay men who are hooked on size as an erotic trigger. Most of us, however, are fine with the penis in front of us and get all the sexual satisfaction we need from other elements of our partner and our relationship.

References

Eisenman, R. (2001). Penis size: Survey of female perceptions of sexual satisfaction. *BMC Women's Health*, 1(1), 1. http://www.biomedcentral.com/1472-6874/1/1 (accessed July 17, 2014).

Fisher, W.A., Branscombe, N.R., and Lemery, C.R. (1983). The bigger the better? Arousal and attributional responses to erotic stimuli that depict different size penises. *Journal of Sex Research*, 19(4), 377–396. http://www.jstor.org/stable/3812063 (accessed July 17, 2014).

Francken, A.B., van de Wiel, H.B.M., van Driel, M.F., and Weijmar Schultz, W.C.M. (2002). What importance do women attribute to the size of the penis? *European Urology*, 42(5), 426–431.

Lever, J., Frederick, D.A., and Peplau, L. (2006). Does size matter? Men's and women's views on penis size across the lifespan. *Psychology of Men and Masculinity*, 7, 129–143.

Li, C.Y., Kayes, O., Kell, P.D., Christopher, N., Minhas, S., and Ralph, D. J. (2006). Penile suspensory ligament division for penile augmentation: indications and results. *European Urology*, 49(4), 729–733.

Masters, W.H. and Johnson, V.E. (1966). *Human Sexual Response*, vol. 1. Little, Brown & Co. Boston, pp. 223–276.

Mehraban, D., Salehi, M., and Zayeri, F. (2007). Penile size and somatometric parameters among Iranian normal adult men. *International Journal of Impotence Research*, 19(3), 303–309.

Shah, J. and Christopher, N. (2002). Can shoe size predict penile length? *BJU International*, 90(6), 586–587.

Spyropoulos, E., Borousas, D., Mavrikos, S., Dellis, A., Bourounis, M., and Athanasiadis, S. (2002). Size of external genital organs and somatometric parameters among physically normal men younger than 40 years old. *Urology*, 60(3), 485–489.

Štulhofer, A. (2006). How (un) important is penis size for women with heterosexual experience?. *Archives of Sexual Behavior*, 35(1), 5–6.

Templer, D.I. (2002). *Is Size Important*. CeShore, Pittsburgh, PA.

Vardi, Y., Harshai, Y., Gil, T., and Gruenwald, I. (2008). A critical analysis of penile enhancement procedures for patients with normal penile size: Surgical techniques, success, and complications. *European Urology*, 54(5), 1042–1050.

Voracek, M. and Manning, J.T. (2003). Length of fingers and penis are related through fetal Hox gene expression. *Urology*, 62(1), 201.

Wessells, H., Lue, T.F., and McAninch, J.W. (1996). Penile length in the flaccid and erect states: Guidelines for penile augmentation. *Journal of Urology*, 156(3), 995–997.

Zilbergeld, B. (1999) *The New Male Sexuality: the truth about men, sex, and pleasure*. Bantam Books.

Myth #2

Vaginas Are Dirty, Ugly, and Smell Bad

In the 1980s there was a series of television commercials that all began the same way; with a mother and her 20-something daughter going through some daily activity—like walking the dog or driving in a car. The daughter would suddenly become very serious, look at her mother intently, and say "Mom, do you ever get that not-so-fresh-feeling?" Despite the fact that the daughter never mentioned that this vague feeling had anything to do with her vagina, her mother would recommend a Massengill douche (or maybe it was Summer's Eve, we don't quite remember). The daughter would look relieved and invariably the clouds would part and the sun would shine. That "not-so-fresh-feeling" became the punch line of jokes for many years.

We haven't seen these ads for a while but there are certainly still commercials that advertise douches, special soaps, feminine hygiene wipes, and vaginal deodorant sprays. And maybe we haven't come that far as many of the current ads talk about embarrassing odors and the need for special products to take care "down there." These commercials are designed to sell products (products that nobody needs but we will get to that later) but in doing so they perpetuate the idea that the vagina is dirty and smells bad. Moreover, in doing so without ever using the words vulva or vagina, these ads perpetuate the idea that this is an area of the body that is so embarrassing, we can't even name it. (Unfortunately, in some ways this is true, many people—both men and women—can't name it because they don't know the right words or mix up which part is which.)

The end result of an industry that sells unneeded products and a society that can't or won't use proper language is that many women feel ashamed of their genitals, which can negatively impact their sex lives. Women have also begun to alter the appearance of their genitals; some by removing all or some of their pubic hair and others by undergoing painful reconstructive surgery to "normalize" the appearance of their genitals.

What's Where and What to Call It

Before we can successfully debunk the myriad of myths that surround the female genitals, we have to start by talking about the female genitals themselves. Forgive us if this is a repeat of something you've learned in an anatomy class or a human sexuality course (or, if we had our way, a fifth grade puberty class) but we think this bears repeating. The external female genitals are made up of a number of different parts. The *mons* or *mons pubis* is the pad of fatty tissue that covers the pubic bone and is naturally covered in pubic hair after puberty. The *labia majora* and *labia minora* are the outer and inner lips, respectively. The labia majora are also covered in pubic hair. When these lips are pulled apart they reveal the *clitoral hood*, the *clitoris*, the *urethral opening*, and the opening to the vagina. All of these parts together are referred to as the vulva (Kelly, 2011, p. 31).

The *vagina* is actually part of the internal reproductive anatomy as it is what connects the uterus (or womb) to the outside of the body. Though many people think of the vagina as like a tube or a tunnel—always open, just waiting for something to go in or come out—it is not. The vagina is made of muscles that can open up if something (like a tampon, a penis, or a sex toy) is inserted into it or something (like a baby) is being pushed out of it, but most of the time the walls of the vagina are touching each other. It is important to note that the walls of the vagina are very elastic and though they can stretch to accommodate a full-size infant during childbirth, they do not stay stretched out (Kelly, 2011, p. 34).

Taking Care of Vulvas and Vaginas

Though the marketing world seems to want women to believe that the vulva requires special lotions, soaps, and salves, and that the vagina must be frequently cleaned out—the truth is that the same soap and water techniques you use for the rest of your body are exactly what you need for your genitals.

The vulva has a lot of blood vessels and can get warm easily which is why it also has a lot of sweat glands; sweat helps the body cool off. Sweat also has smell and it is true that most vulvas do have a particular scent. Though they don't all smell the same, some people think the smell is a little salty, a little yeasty, or kind of like sour milk (Herbenick and Schick, 2011, p. 48). This is all normal and does not require any special deodorant soaps or sprays. As Martha's college professor, Dr. Goodenough, once said: "There is no reason that a woman's vulva should smell like a field of wild strawberries." Women should take note of the smell of their vulva because if it changes or becomes significantly stronger at any point this could be the sign of an infection, but other than that there is nothing to worry about. In fact, some people find the smell of a woman's vulva to be an integral part of sex and arousal.

As for the vagina—the internal part which can't be reached with soap in the shower—the good news is that it cleans itself. Yep, the vagina has self-cleansing mechanisms and a delicate balance of microorganisms that keep it healthy (Kelly, 2011, p. 35). Though the practice of douching—forcing water or other liquid into the vagina to clean it out—has been around for thousands of years, it has been proven time and time again to be harmful to women, increasing their risk of getting sexually transmitted infections (STIs) and other infections. A review of literature by Martino *et al.* (2004) found research confirming that douching has been associated with increased risk of pelvic inflammatory disease (PID), bacterial vaginosis (BV), cervical cancer, recurrent yeast infections, and HIV transmission. Douching has also been associated with infertility and having low birth weight or preterm infants. Several studies have also found an association between douching and chlamydia (a common STI) though others have not (Martino *et al.*, 2004, p. 1053).

Martino *et al.* do add a caution about seeing this as a direct cause and effect situation. They note that douching is more common in certain populations—African-Americans, people with low income, those with less education, and those who have more lifetime sex partners—who are already at higher risk for many of these outcomes including PID, BV, and STIs (Martino *et al.*, 2004, p. 1053). Still, douching is unnecessary and clearly risky.

The need for douching is one of the most stubborn myths about the vagina because, despite years of research showing that this is not healthy, many women still believe it is important and good for them. Ness *et al.* (2003) conducted a multisite study on douching habits and found that 66.5% of women who douched said it was to feel clean after menses, 43.6% said they did it for general hygiene reasons, 35.7% did it to cleanse themselves before or after sex, 26.9% did it to reduce vaginal odor, and 19.4% did it because they thought it was normal to douche (Ness *et. al.*, 2003, p. 72).

In their study of douching, Grimely *et al.* (2006) found that 70.3% of women who douched agreed with the statement "Douche products are safe to use; otherwise they wouldn't be on the market," Martino *et al.* looked at this very issue in their study and concluded:

> The FDA's [Food and Drug Administration's] role in regulation of the many vaginal douching products on the market is complex, as these products can be classified as drugs or cosmetics, depending on the type of claim made for the product and the type and strength of ingredients in the product. Although both cosmetic and drug products are required to prove safety, cosmetic products do not need to prove effectiveness as drug products do. The FDA also assesses the design and safety of any devices used to apply the douching solution. Our review suggests that current douching regulatory approaches are confusing at best and merit critical reassessment. (Martino *et al.*, 2004, p. 1054)

Additional oversight of these products seems wise as 90% of the women in Grimely *et al.*'s (2006) sample who douched had no intention of stopping (p. 303). Moreover, the women who douched were more likely to use other feminine hygiene products such as sprays (24% compared to 5.7% of nondouchers), cleansing wipes (30% compared to 14.5%), powder (21.5% compared to 6.6%), and cleansing bubble baths (20.5% compared to 6%). Interestingly, women who did not douche were more likely to use deodorant suppositories or tablets (19% of nondouchers compared to 12% of those who douche) (Grimely *et al.*, 2006, p. 307).

The myth that women's genitals need special attention and products in order not to smell bad is truly problematic. It has allowed industry to prey on women's insecurities and sell products that are not just unnecessary but potentially dangerous to their health.

Feeling Good About Girl Parts

In addition, it has perpetuated a cultural perspective that female genitals are something to fix and hide which has psychological implications for women as well.

Research has suggested that women who feel bad about their genitals are less likely to enjoy sex and more likely to participate in risky sexual behaviors. Morrison *et al.* (2005) found that more than one in five college students, for example, expressed dissatisfaction with the odor of their genitals. In an earlier study, Reinholtz and Muehlenhard (1995) found that negative perception about the smell and taste of one's genitals was linked to lower participation in various sexual activities (both as cited in Schick *et al.*, 2010, p. 401). More recently, as pornography has become more accessible, researchers have started to question how women feel about the appearance of their vulvas.

In a 2010 study, researchers at George Washington University used three separate measures to determine how young woman's perceptions of their vulvas impacted their sexual behavior and enjoyment. First, they measured "vulva appearance satisfaction," then they measured "genital image self-consciousness," and finally they measured "motivation to avoid risky sex, sexual esteem, and sexual satisfaction." As the authors had expected, the results indicated that "genital appearance dissatisfaction may have harmful consequences for both sexual satisfaction and sexual risk among college women due to its detrimental impact on genital image self-consciousness and self-esteem" (Schick *et al.*, 2010, p. 400). In a small study of older women, Berman *et al.* (2003) similarly found that "positive genital self-image was found to negatively correlate with sexual distress and depression and positively correlate with sexual desire." However, they found "no correlations between genital self-image and relationship health, perceived stress, overall sexual function, arousal, lubrication, orgasm, satisfaction, or absence of pain" (Berman *et al.*, 2003, p. 16).

Schick *et al.* go on to point out that genital appearance dissatisfaction is particularly disturbing among college students, many of whom are engaging in their first sexual experiences: "Reduced sexual satisfaction during these formative years may impinge upon the development of healthy sexual self-concept and set the stage for future difficulties and concerns." Moreover, they note that decreased motivation to avoid risky sex could leave this population even more vulnerable to STIs, including HIV/AIDS (Schick *et al.*, 2010, p. 400).

Vulvas Get (Unneeded) Makeovers

In our society it has become somewhat acceptable to change the appearance of body parts that we don't like. Women (and men) smooth out the natural wrinkles of old age with Botox, remove excess fat with liposuction, and use rhinoplasty to even out bumps and hooks and create that perfect ski slope nose. We also should not forget about the popularity of breast augmentations as an instant way to get the double D's that some members of our society seem to value. In their essay on the "Designer Vagina," Braun and Tiefer (2009) point out that, "Although genital distress is nothing new for women, women's genitalia were, until recently, largely excluded from the intense self-surveillance and improvement imperatives that cosmetic surgery culture mandates" (p. 1).

Today, there are a number of elective plastic surgery procedures that women can use to change the look and feel of their genitals. Some, such as "vaginal rejuvenation" and "revirginization" claim to tighten the vagina to make sex more pleasurable. Another procedure, called "G-spot amplification" is supposed to make it easier for women to take advantage of their G-spot, an area in the vagina said to have heightened sensation (see Myth #4 for a discussion of whether the G-spot exists in all or some women). Another procedure, called labiaplasty, changes the appearance of the vulva most often by reducing the size of the labia minora so that they do not extend beyond the edges of the labia majora. Some suggest that when a woman's labia minora are too long they can interfere with daily activities such as walking, wearing certain types of clothing, and exercising. Miklos and Moore (2008) argue that many women who seek to have labiaplasty do so because they are experiencing discomfort. They surveyed 131 women who had the procedure at one clinic over a 27-month period and found that 37% had strictly aesthetic reasons for it, 31% had strictly functional reasons for it, and 31% had a combination of functional and aesthetic reason for seeking the surgery.

The American College of Obstetrics and Gynecology (ACOG), however, says that these procedures are rarely if ever medically necessary. In its committee opinion on the topic, ACOG states:

> These procedures are not medically indicated, and the safety and effectiveness of these procedures have not been documented. Clinicians who receive requests from patients for such procedures should discuss with the patient the reason for her request and perform an evaluation for any physical signs or symptoms that may indicate the need for surgical intervention. Women should be informed about the lack of data supporting the efficacy of these procedures and their potential complications, including infection, altered sensation, dyspareunia, adhesions, and scarring. (ACOG, 2007)

Miklos and Moore also argue that most women (93.1%) sought the surgery for purely personal reasons while only a few (6%) were influenced by their male partners (2008, p. 1493). Some feminist theorists, however, would argue that we have to look at the context under which such choices are made to determine if they really are purely personal. In her article on Brazilian waxing, Piexota Labre (2002) points out that women may take pleasure in or even feel empowered by activities that objectify and sexualize the female body but this does not mean that they are actually in the position of power (2002, p. 127).

Tiefer describes two feminist arguments when it comes to the issue of choice particularly around cosmetic surgery. The first, she says, highlights the physical and psychological harms of cosmetic surgery and believes that participation in the beauty culture inevitably adds to the already oppressive environment and makes it that much harder for the next women to resist that intervention. These scholars believe that even if something, such as cosmetic surgery, is a solution for one individual it might still be wrong to allow it on a societal level because it increases gender inequality and limits the options of all women in the future. On the flip side, some feminist theorists suggest that all women have to live in our culture that is saturated with images of perfection and that sufferers deserve relief even if it takes the form of something as extreme as cosmetic surgery (Tiefer, 2008, p. 474).

Taking It (Pubic Hair, That Is) All Off

Cosmetic surgery on one's genitals is extreme and the question of whether women have, or should have, the choice to change a perceived problem with the appearance of their vulva may be harder to answer when dealing with something so drastic, painful, and permanent. We doubt that many of our readers will ever even consider elective plastic surgery on their genitals. We bet, however, that most of our readers (especially the women) have already considered removing—and many have already removed—some or all of their pubic hair. This is not all that drastic (hair grows back) but it can be painful and it does alter the natural appearance of the vulva—which, post-puberty, is meant to be covered with hair.

A recent study of adolescents at a Texas health clinic found that 70% routinely shaved or waxed their pubic hair (Bercaw-Pratt, et al., 2012). In a larger study, Herbenick et al. (2010) surveyed 2451 women about their pubic hair grooming practices and found that overall most women had some hair on their genitals but this varied by age. Among the youngest participants, aged 18–24, 20.1% reported being typically hair-free in the previous month compared to 12.1% of those aged 25–29, 8.6% of those aged 30–39, 6.5% of those aged 40–49, and 2.1% of those aged 50 or older. The percentage of women who had removed all of their pubic hair at least once in the past month was slightly higher for all ages; 18–24 years (38%), 25–29 years (32.2%), 30–39 years (23.2%), 40–49 years (16%), and 50 or over (9.1%). Even more women partially removed their pubic hair one or more times during the past month. Still, the authors conclude that the majority of women typically have some pubic hair (Herbenick et al. 2010).

These findings contradict other findings in research as well as mainstream media reports that suggest that hairlessness is the new norm for vulvas. In her article, "The Brazilian wax: New hairlessness norm for women?," Peixota Labra, a native Brazilian, discusses this purely American phenomenon and fears that women are getting sucked into a practice that is not necessary, in part because of the media's fascination with and lack of criticism for this technique. According to Peixota Labre (2002), the Brazilian wax—which involves removing all (or almost all) of the hair from the mons and the labia as well as any hair a woman has, well, between her butt cheeks—started not in Rio but at a New York City salon. The procedure became a darling of women's magazines which often featured first-hand accounts by reporters, and was made infamous by an episode of *Sex and the City* which brought the expression "landing strip" (to describe one stripe of hair artfully left behind) into common parlance. The media acknowledges that waxing hurts (we can still hear the screams of Steve Carrel when he waxed his chest in *The Forty-Year-Old Virgin*) but few conclude that it is not worth the pain.

Peixota Labre notes the gradual social acceptance of removing body hair from other areas such as the underarms and legs. She writes "most women first started to remove body hair to conform to social norms but later continued to do so for reason related to femininity and attractiveness" (p. 116). She suggests that "the removal of female body hair, particularly in the genital area, can be viewed as a component of the objectification of women and construction of women as objects designed to attract male attention and provide men with sexual pleasure" (p. 124). She, too, blames advertising and other media for perpetuating the idea that women in their natural state are less than ideal: "As a result, body hair, which is both natural and normal, has been constructed as a revolting enemy against which women must continuously wage battle" (p. 124).

Interestingly though, Herbenick *et al.* found that even after controlling for other factors, those women who were typically hair-free or sometimes hair-free in the previous month scored significantly higher on their genital self-image scale, meaning that these women had more positive images of their own genitals than the women who had not removed any or all of their pubic hair in the previous month (Herbenick *et al.*, 2010, p. 3325).

It is possible that these women were more comfortable with their vulvas before taking off the pubic hair which is what allowed them to put in that effort to begin with or it is possible that they felt better about their genitals at the time of the study because they had "conformed" to a new societal standard.

We are not going solve the ongoing debate around how women's beauty choices get made and whether they can ever be truly personal in our society, especially when it comes to issues of the vulva. What we can tell you is that neither genital surgery nor removing pubic hair is medically necessary and as such should not be done without giving it careful thought (and in the case of surgery discussing it with one or more health care professionals).

We also want to throw in one word of caution from a study that came out while we were writing this chapter. It found that the incidence of pubic hair grooming accidents that are bad enough to land people in the emergency room are going up. It seems almost comical, but the report by scientists at the University of California, San Francisco found that cuts, scrapes, and burns to the urogenital area increased fivefold between 2002 and 2010 with an estimated 2500 injuries in 2010. The majority of these injuries (57%) were in women but no small number (43%) occurred in men. And these figures are likely an underestimate given how many people may not seek help. The primary culprit was the razor (83%) but scissors factored into 22% of injuries and hot wax into just over 1% (Glass *et al.*, 2012). We are not taking a position on whether anyone should wax, pluck, tweeze, shave, or grow some kind of pubic hair Mohawk; just be careful.

A Do Nothing Policy

To wrap up our rant on vulvas here, we just want to make sure that everyone understands the basics which are simple: the vulva is outside, the vagina is inside. The vagina cleans itself and the vulva just needs regular showers with soap and water to stay fresh. Neither part needs to be deodorized, powdered, made smaller, made bigger, or in any other way altered. Instead, we suggest enjoying them the way they are.

References

American College of Obstetrics and Gynecology (ACOG) Committee on Gynecologic Practice. (2007). Vaginal "rejuvenation" and cosmetic vaginal procedures, Committee Opinion, Number 378. http://www.acog.org/Resources_And_Publications/Committee_Opinions/Committee_on_Gynecologic_Practice/Vaginal_Rejuvenation_and_Cosmetic_Vaginal_Procedures (accessed July 17, 2014).

Bercaw-Pratt, J.L., Santos, X.M., Sanchez, J., Ayensu-Coker, L., Nebgen, D.R., and Dietrich, J.E. (2012). The incidence, attitudes and practices of the removal of pubic hair as a body modification. *Journal of Pediatric and Adolescent Gynecology*, 25(1), 12–14.

Berman, L.A., Berman, J., Miles, M., Pollets, D., and Powell, J.A. (2003). Genital self-image as a component of sexual health: Relationship between genital self-image, female sexual function, and quality of life measures. *Journal of Sex and Marital Therapy*, 29(Suppl. 1), 11–21.

Braun, V. and Tiefer, L. (2009). The 'Designer Vagina' and the pathologisation of female genital diversity: Interventions for change. *Radical Psychology: A Journal of Psychology, Politics, and Radicalism*, 8(1).

Glass, A.S., Bagga, H.S., Tasian, G.E., Fisher, P.B., McCulloch, C.E., Blaschko, S.D, et al. (2012). Pubic hair grooming injuries presenting to U.S. emergency departments. *Urology*, 80(6), 1187–1191.

Grimley, D.M., Annang, L., Foushee, H.R., Bruce, F.C., and Kendrick, J.S. (2006). Vaginal douches and other feminine hygiene products: Women's practices and perceptions of product safety. *Maternal and Child Health Journal*, 10(3), 303–310.

Herbenick, D., and Schick, V. (2011). *Read My Lips: A Complete Guide to the Vagina and Vulva*. Rowman & Littlefield Publishers.

Herbenick, D., Schick, V., Reece, M., Sanders, S., and Fortenberry, J.D. (2010). Pubic hair removal among women in the United States: Prevalence, methods, and characteristics. *Journal of Sexual Medicine*, 7(10), 3322–3330.

Kelly, G.F. (2011). *Sexuality Today*, 10th edn. McGraw-Hill.

Martino, J.L., Youngpairoj, S., and Vermund, S.H. (2004). Vaginal douching: Personal practices and public policies. *Journal of Women's Health*, 13(9), 1048–1065.

Miklos, J.R., and Moore, R.D. (2008). Labiaplasty of the labia minora: Patients' indications for pursuing surgery. *Journal of Sexual Medicine*, 5, 1492–1495.

Morrison, T.G., Bearden, A., Ellis, S.R., and Harriman, R. (2005). Correlates of genital perceptions among Canadian post-secondary students. *Electronic Journal of Human Sexuality*, 8, 1–22.

Ness, R.B., Hillier, S.L., Richter, H.E., Soper, D.E., Stamm, C., Bass, D.C., et al. (2003). Why women douche and why they may or may not stop. *Sexually Transmitted Diseases*, 30(1), 71–74.

Peixoto Labre, M. (2002). The Brazilian wax: New hairlessness norm for women? *Journal of Communication Inquiry*, 26(2), 113–132.

Reinholtz, R.K., and Muehlenhard, C.L. (1995). Genital perceptions and sexual activity in a college population. *Journal of Sex Research*, 32(2), 155–165.

Schick, V.R., Calabrese, S.K., Rima, B.N., and Zucker, A.N. (2010). Genital appearance dissatisfaction: Implications for women's genital image self-consciousness, sexual consciousness, sexual esteem, sexual satisfaction, and sexual risk. *Psychology of Women Quarterly*, 34(3), 394–404.

Tiefer, L. (2008). Female genital cosmetic surgery: Freakish or inevitable? Analysis from medical marketing, bioethics, and feminist theory. *Feminism and Psychology*, 18(4), 466–479.

Myth #3 Male Circumcision Is Dangerous and Completely Unnecessary

Despite the fact that this is only the third myth out of 50—and many issues in sexuality are the subject of debate—we are going to make a prediction that this will be the most controversial entry in the whole book. Public opinion of male circumcision—an age-old practice of removing the foreskin (or prepuce) from the head of the penis—has swung wildly throughout history. While it was once primarily a religious practice for Muslim and Jewish men, it became an accepted medical procedure that was more common than not in the United States and parts of Europe during the twentieth century. In recent years, however, the percentage of male infants who are circumcised has been dropping and a heated debate has been taking place between those who believe this is a medically beneficial (or even a medically necessary) procedure and those who see it as an immoral form of bodily mutilation without consent.

The debate is so heated that even the science becomes controversial, with those who want to see an end to circumcision casting doubt on the research methods and even the motives of the researchers.

We don't believe that we can solve this debate within the confines of this entry, nor is that our goal. Instead, we will attempt to explain it thoroughly so that you have the best information and thinking on the topic. Our aim is to fairly represent all sides of the debate. That said, we are not neutral on the topic, as sexual health educators we naturally put a lot of weight on the science of public health—especially those studies that show circumcision reduces the risk of contracting and/or transmitting STIs, including HIV. We believe that as of now the scientific evidence on the benefits and risks of male circumcision is strong enough to suggest that this practice is neither dangerous nor completely unnecessary.

The Scientific Debate Over Circumcision

Medical science has been in favor of male circumcision since the Victorian era though the earliest rationales for it were less scientific and more, well, ridiculous. (This is no doubt part of the reason that some people are suspect of today's research.) At the end of the nineteenth century, doctors suggested that circumcision would cure everything from "masturbation to epilepsy to bed-wetting" (DeLaet, 2009, p. 418). By the mid-twentieth century, however, medicine was focusing on more reasonable benefits such as a reduction in certain kinds of cancers.

Interestingly, Dr. Abraham Ravich, Martha's great grandfather, was among the physicians who began making these arguments. Ravich was a urologist in Brooklyn starting in the 1920s. Many of his patients were Jewish immigrants from Eastern Europe who were circumcised because of their religion. He noted that these men had fewer incidences of penile cancer, prostate cancer, and venereal disease (VD , or what we now refer to as sexually transmitted infections, STIs). He published his results in a book, *Preventing V.D. and Cancer by Circumcision*, in the early 1970s. In our research, we have found that some anticircumcision activists (who like to call themselves intactivists) refer to Ravich as a zealot who invented his research to advance the practice of circumcision.

There are similar complaints about even the most recent research. Some say that the studies are unreliable because of their retrospective design, the small sample sizes, the indirect approach to obtaining data, and the reliance on self-report to determine if participants were, in fact, circumcised. Others argue that the results of studies about HIV in Africa are irrelevant to babies born in the United States because the HIV epidemic here (not just the incidence of HIV but the ways in which it is commonly transmitted) are so very different.

The American Academy of Pediatrics (AAP) released a new committee opinion on circumcision in 2012. In order to develop this opinion, AAP created a task force of experts to review the research that had been published between its last review in 1995 and 2011. The task force assigned each article an evidence rating of "excellent," "good," "fair," or "poor" based on the methodology used and how well it was applied. In writing their review of the research—and ultimately developing the committee's decision—the task force took these ratings into account (AAP, 2012, p. e761). Though we understand that some in the medical world do not agree with the task force's findings, we believe that the technical report represents a comprehensive and thoughtful look at the research and are relying on it in our summary of what the research says.

Low Risk Procedure

In determining the cost–benefit of an invasive procedure, the first thing to understand is whether the procedure itself has risks or complications and how serious those are. The AAP points to two large hospital-based studies with good evidence that the risk of significant acute complications is very low, 0.19–0.22%, and most were not serious. Acute complications mean those that happen right away: bleeding, infection, and penile injury. There are other complications that can happen later, such as adhesions, but these are also quite rare (AAP, p. e771). The complication rate may be slightly higher if the procedure is performed by a traditional or ritual provider outside of the hospital but there are few data about this. The complications are also higher when circumcision is performed after the newborn period (AAP, p. e773).

One of the complaints that those opposed to circumcision have is that the procedure is painful and that it has historically been carried out with no pain medication. In the past, infants were just given a sugar-covered pacifier. The AAP acknowledges that this is not sufficient pain management, even for an infant, and suggests that "adequate analgesia" be used (p.770).

Health Benefits of Circumcision

According to the AAP, the current research suggests that newborn circumcision can help prevent urinary tract infections (UTIs), penile cancers, HIV, human papillomavirus (HPV), and other STIs.

- *Urinary tract infections:* there is good evidence from two studies that the task force describes as "well-conducted" that newborn circumcision reduces the incidence of UTIs in boys under the age of 2 years. The results of another study suggest that 7–14 out of 1000 uncircumcised boys will develop a UTI during their first year of life compared to 1–2 out of 1000 circumcised boys. UTIs are not usually serious though they are uncomfortable and can require a visit to a physician, medication, and possibly even a hospital stay or an invasive procedure (AAP, 2012, p. e767).
- *Penile cancers:* there is some evidence that circumcision prevents penile cancer and even more evidence that it prevents the most invasive form of penile cancer. However, penile cancer is so rare in the United States that it would take 990 circumcisions to prevent one case of penile cancer (p. e767). Some would argue that this negates any prevention benefit when it comes to penile cancer because 990 circumcisions would likely lead to two complications.
- *HIV:* some of the best evidence on the health benefits of circumcision comes from studies in areas where HIV rates are high. The AAP task force states: "Review of the literature revealed a consistently reported protective effect of 40 percent to 60 percent for male circumcision in reducing the risk of HIV acquisition among heterosexual males in areas with high HIV prevalence due to heterosexual transmission (i.e. Africa)" (p. e764). There is less research on the protective effect in the United States where the overall HIV rate is lower and transmission is more common among men who have sex with men. A recently released study from the Centers for Disease Control and Prevention (CDC), however, put the findings from these African studies into mathematical models and suggested that male circumcision before sexual debut would reduce the lifetime risk of HIV transmission by 15.7% for all males (Samson *et al.,* 2010). This projection takes into account that circumcision seems less likely to protect men who have sex with men (MSM) from HIV transmission. The task force explains: "It is not known to what extent circumcision may be protective against HIV transmission from MSM who practice insertive sex versus for those who engage in receptive sex" (p. e765).

Researchers also offer an explanation of how circumcision protects men against HIV. One possible reason is that the inside surface of the foreskin is easily torn especially during sex and this could provide an entry point for HIV (and other germs). The foreskin also contains "a high density of HIV target cells (i.e., Langerhans cells, CD4 T cells, macrophanges) which facilitates HIV infection of host cells." And, finally, germs may get trapped under the foreskin giving them more time to replicate (p. e764).

- *HPV and cervical cancer:* this last explanation has been shown to be a possibility in HPV infection as well. As a reminder, HPV is the virus that causes genital warts. It also causes cervical cancer in women. HPV is one of the most common STIs in the United States. The task force found two studies with good evidence of 30–40% reduction in risk among circumcised men. There are four other studies that provide fair evidence of risk reduction. A study by Australian researchers found that the foreskin can provide a reservoir for HPV cells (a place for them to collect) (Ladurner Rennau *et al.*, 2011). However, the authors of that study caution that just because those cells are there does not mean they're transmissible.

  Still, there is good evidence that circumcision reduces the rate of male-to-female transmission of high risk HPV (the types of the virus that are most likely to cause cervical cancer) from men who were not infected with HIV. Moreover, there is some evidence (rated as fair) that male circumcision has a protective effect against cervical cancer for female partners as well if the man has multiple female partners (AAP, 2012, p. e768).

- *Other STIs:* finally, there is evidence that circumcision is protective against syphilis, herpes, chancroid (a rare bacterial infection), and BV (a bacterial infection of the vagina that is not necessarily sexually transmitted). The evidence suggests that circumcision provides no protection against chlamydia or gonorrhea.

Impact on Sex

One of the claims of those who are opposed to male circumcision is that it negatively impacts sexual function and reduces sexual pleasure. As most males are circumcised as infants (long before they become sexually active), it is hard to measure the direct impact of the procedure on sensitivity or function.

Some studies have looked at the impact on sexual satisfaction for men who are circumcised as adults. The AAP task force found two good quality studies of these men. In the first study of 5000 Ugandan men, circumcised men reported significantly less pain on intercourse than uncircumcised men and 2 years after the procedure the men's sexual satisfaction remained the same as it had been at baseline (98.4% compared to 98.5%). Interestingly, the satisfaction level in the control group went up from 98% at baseline to 99.9% 2 years later. The second study looked at men in Kenya and found that 64%

reported greater sensitivity after the procedure and that 55% of circumcised men reported having an easier time reaching orgasm than they did before the procedure (though this change was not statistically significant; AAP, 2012, p. e769).

According to the AAP, a study of Korean men found fair evidence of decreased pleasure from masturbation after adult circumcision. For the most part, though, studies have failed to show any evidence that circumcision decreases sexual sensitivity compared to uncircumcised penises. Most evidence suggests that there is no difference in sexual sensation and satisfaction for men regardless of whether they are circumcised (AAP, 2012, p. e769).

As with the task force's conclusion on health benefits, many disagree with its conclusions on sexual pleasure and function. Christopher L. Guest, the co-founder of Children's Health & Human Rights Partnership, writes in his rebuttal to the AAP report: "the foreskin is richly innervated, erogenous tissue which enhances sexual pleasure and it also provides a unique, linear gliding mechanism during sexual intercourse." He points out that, in 2009, the College of Physicians and Surgeons of British Columbia stated "the foreskin is rich in specialized sensory nerve endings." In 2010, the Royal Australian College of Physicians stated "the foreskin is a primary sensory part of the penis, containing some of the most sensitive areas of the penis" and, in the same year, the Royal Dutch Medical Association concluded "the foreskin is a complex erotogenic structure that plays an important role in the mechanical function of the penis during sexual acts" (Guest, 2012).

The Ethical Debate over Circumcision

It is clear that the debate over circumcision is very heated and growing more so. Georganne Chapin, the executive director of the anticircumcision group Intact America, said this about the practice: "About a million people a year, newborn babies, lose a normal, healthy, functional, pleasurable, protective body part without their consent" (Bristol, 2011, p. 1837).

Chapin and other anticircumcision activists dismiss the AAP task force's report as being biased and profit-driven. She suggests that the report represents "a trade association agenda that desperately seeks to justify and secure reimbursement for a medically-unnecessary surgery that harms children and violates their basic human rights" (Chapin, 2012). She further dismisses the science suggesting that the African studies on HIV are being used as "an after-the-fact justification for a custom that is increasingly being rejected by those who see it as violating children's rights to bodily autonomy and their own future freedom of religion" (Chapin, 2012).

After dismissing the current science, those who oppose circumcision frequently argue that the procedure is unethical because infants cannot give informed consent, infants are not at immediate risk if they do not get circumcised, and as such parents are unfairly imposing their cultural values on children in a way that cannot be revoked. They also suggest that those in the

Western world who support circumcision—including the medical community—are blinded by their own cultural values that see female circumcision as an abhorrent, primitive ritual but see no moral parallels when boys are subjected to a similar procedure.

Informed Consent and Immediate Risk

One of the basic premises in the practice of medicine is physicians cannot perform any procedure on a patient without first getting his/her informed consent. To do this, health care providers must clearly explain the risks and benefits before getting the patient's explicit permission. There is widespread agreement that children are not capable of giving consent and as such their parents or guardians are in charge of their health throughout childhood and adolescence. Those who oppose circumcision, however, argue that parents should not have the right to permanently alter their child's body unless it is immediately necessary for their health and well-being.

Certainly, many people would agree that it would be inappropriate for a parent to consent to a nose job for their 10-year-old; that since the procedure is not immediately (if ever) medically necessary, the decision should be deferred until the child is old enough to decide for him or herself. The issue is not as clear-cut when children are born with facial deformities or even large birthmarks in visible areas—many parents find it morally acceptable to consent to certain plastic surgery procedures (even those that are for purely aesthetic reasons) if they feel it will improve their child's quality of life.

Circumcision presents an additional complication because the procedure cannot necessarily be postponed. Delaying circumcision makes it more complicated, more painful, more risky, and more psychologically difficult. So, while ideally surgical procedures would wait until the infant grew and was able to make his own decisions, this is not really possible with circumcision.

Moreover, the health benefits of circumcision, though not immediate, may only be seen if the procedure is done at an early age. From a public health perspective it is important that protective measures against STIs, such as vaccines for HPV and hepatitis B, be given before an individual is sexually active and subject to exposure. Chapin and others argue that even if the studies of HIV in Africa are scientifically valid, they are irrelevant to infants in the United States who are not and will not be sexually active for more than a decade. While this is true, parents make decisions not just for their children's current health, but for their future health as well. Vaccines are actually a good example; children may not be at risk for the measles at the moment they receive the measles, mumps, and rubella (MMR) inoculation but parents choose the shot anyhow to protect them throughout their lives. Moreover, parents vaccinate infants in order to protect not just their own children but their communities as vaccinations are most effective when the majority of the "herd" is vaccinated (Benatar and Benatar, 2003). The same may be true of circumcision as widespread circumcision is being promoted as a way to reduce HIV in areas with a high prevalence of the disease (Wamai et al., 2011).

In truth, even the ethical arguments about circumcision hinge on the science and research. If you believe the science that finds circumcision to be low risk and high benefit, then these arguments about informed consent are not issues—parents have always been allowed to consent to medically necessary procedures for their minor children. If you do not believe the procedure is beneficial, or worse you think it is harmful, then your answers to these ethical questions will likely be different.

Role of Culture, Religion, and the Comparison to Female Circumcision

Male circumcision began as a cultural and religious ritual rather than a medical procedure. Many people continue to choose it for their boys not because of the medical benefits but because of the cultural significance. In fact, some argue that male circumcision is morally acceptable simply because of its cultural and religious roots. However, this is not sufficient reason to justify any practice. Benatar and Benatar point out that "simply because a practice is culturally valued does not mean it is morally acceptable" (2003, p. 43). If the procedure is harmful, for example, then the cultural value is morally overridden. The case in point for this side of the argument is actually female circumcision which is often called female genital mutilation (FGM).

FGM refers to a wide range of practices which the World Health Organization (WHO) has put into four categories. The first is the removal of the prepuce or outer skin of the clitoris. This procedure is the least invasive and most common form of FGM worldwide and is the most similar to male circumcision. The second involves the removal of the clitoris and may also involve the removal of all or part of the inner vaginal lips (the labia minora). This procedure is much more invasive than male circumcision. Moreover, it prevents clitoral stimulation and may prevent all orgasms in many women. The third category is called infibulation and is the most extreme and invasive form of FGM. It involves the total or partial removal of the external genitalia as well as stitches in the vagina to narrow the vaginal opening. Infibulation is common in two countries (Sudan and Eritrea) but not common in the rest of the world though it is often what we think of when we hear the term FGM. Finally, the fourth category is labeled "unclassified" by the WHO and encompasses some of the least invasive forms of FGM (such as ritual nicking of the clitoris) and the most damaging forms (such as putting a caustic substance inside the vagina) (DeLaet, 2009).

The argument over FGM pits those who say these procedures are integral parts of certain cultures and that women who don't have them will be shunned by their communities against those who say FGM impinges on basic human rights (DeLaet, 2009 p. 414). Though some women's rights advocates suggest that certain minimally invasive forms of ritual FGM should be acceptable, there is a large worldwide campaign to eradicate the practice completely.

Many opponents of male circumcision question why there is not the same moral outrage to this procedure. DeLaet acknowledges that "male circumcision as typically practiced is not the physical or moral equivalent of infibulation, and it is not difficult to understand why either defenders of male circumcision or critics of female genital mutilation would resent the comparison" (p. 415). The most common form of FGM, however, involves the removal of the prepuce which is analogous to the foreskin on the penis. The procedure is not all that different from male circumcision but the reaction to each procedure is worlds apart. DeLaet notes that, "Critics of the disparate treatment of male and female circumcision argue that it reflects a "Western" double standard in which human rights activists in the West disregard sexual mutilations performed on boy children in their own societies" (DeLaet, 2009, p. 414).

This is an interesting double standard and we agree that people see the world through their own cultural lenses. It is likely that our opinion on circumcision is colored by our own backgrounds and by growing up and raising our own children in a culture and a religion that supports male circumcision and condemns the practice on women.

Ultimately, however, we believe that everything comes down to whether the procedure is harmful or beneficial. There is no research to suggest that FGM is beneficial and a great deal of research suggesting that especially the more invasive forms are harmful. Though disagreements remain, today's research suggests a certain degree of benefit from male circumcision.

Conclusions

As of now, no major medical organizations are suggesting that all newborn infants be circumcised for health reasons. Instead, the view is that the procedure should be available to any family that wants it and should be reimbursed by insurance. Both AAP and the CDC suggest that parents need to be carefully educated about the benefits and risks of the procedure and the ways to make it as safe and painless as possible if they choose it.

We agree that more education about circumcision is necessary as parents should understand the existing science (including the criticisms of this science) and make the best choice for their child. We understand that this is an area that people—both in favor of and opposed to newborn circumcision—feel very strongly about and we hope that a healthy and respectful debate continues.

References

American Academy of Pediatrics (AAP) Task Force on Circumcision. (2012). Male Circumcision. *Pediatrics*, 130(3), e756–e785. http://pediatrics.aappublications.org/content/130/3/e756.full.pdf+html (accessed July 17, 2014).

Benatar, M. and Benatar, D. (2003). Between prophylaxis and child abuse: The ethics of neonatal male circumcision. *American Journal of Bioethics*, 3(2), 35–48.

Bristol, N. (2011). Male circumcision debate flares in the USA. *Lancet*, 378, 1837.

Chapin, G. (2012). First do no harm. *The Huffington Post* (October 4). http://www.huffingtonpost.com/georganne-chapin/circumcision-task-force-report_b_1919711.html (accessed July 17, 2014).

DeLaet, D.L. (2009). Framing male circumcision as a human rights issue? Contributions to the debate over the universality of human rights. *Journal of Human Rights,* 8(4), 405–426.

Guest, C.L. (2012). Revised male infant circumcision policy: A disservice to Americans. *American Academy of Pediatrics Online* (September 22). http://pediatrics.aappubli cations.org/content/130/3/585/reply#pediatrics_el_55044 (accessed July 17, 2014).

Ladurner Rennau, M., Buttazoni, A., Pichler, R., Schlenk, B., Klinglmair, G., Richter, E., *et al.* (2011). Prevalence of human papillomavirus infection of the inner foreskin in men without clinical symptoms. *Journal of Urology,* 185(4), e570.

Sansom, S.L., Prabhu, V.S., Hutchinson, A.B., An, Q., Hall, H.I., Shrestha, R.K., *et al.* (2010). Cost-effectiveness of newborn circumcision in reducing lifetime HIV risk among US males. *PLoS One,* 5(1), e8723.

Wamai, R.G., Morris, B.J., Bailis, S.A., Sokal, D., Klausner, J.D., Appleton, R., *et al.* (2011). Male circumcision for HIV prevention: Current evidence and implementation in sub-Saharan Africa. *Journal of the International AIDS Society,* 14(1), 49.

Myth #4 The G-spot Is the Most Orgasmic Part of a Woman's Body

There are definitely proponents of the G-spot who extol it as a special site for orgasm and pleasure inside the vagina. And there are women who believe they have a G-spot and want to protect their firm sense of the reality of their own body. But there are skeptics with some pretty convincing evidence to the contrary. This topic is hotly debated and if you voice skepticism to the believers, especially the "re-discoverers," they are likely to bite your head off. But we're brave.

Let's start with the hardest part.

What Is the G-spot?

In the 1940s, Ernest Graftenberg located a spot inside the vagina that he felt had different tissue and was related to the urethra. Not too much was made of this until the publication of *The G Spot and Other Recent Discoveries About Human Sexuality* by Alice Kahn Ladas, Beverly Whipple and John D. Perry in 1982. These authors did some experiments on women and felt that Graftenberg had located an uncelebrated erotic spot and, moreover, that it was the locus of vaginal orgasms and not related to the clitoris. They named it the G-spot after its discoverer and wrote a number of scientific papers about it in addition to the book. The research was dismissed by many sexual medicine specialists but the original authors and other researchers continued to defend—and extend—their initial assertions.

Jannini *et al.* describe the debated area this way:

> The G-spot is a sensitive area felt through the anterior wall of the vagina about half-way between the back of the pubic bone and the cervix, along the course of the urethra. It is easiest to feel the G-spot with the woman lying on her back. If one or two fingers are inserted into the vagina, with the palm up, using a "come here" motion, the tissue that surrounds the urethra will begin to swell.

When the area is first touched, the woman may feel as if she needs to urinate, but if the touch continues for a few seconds longer, it may turn into a pleasurable feeling" (2010, p. 27).

For many women, however, finding this spot has proved elusive. They can't just stick their fingers in and feel for an easily identifiable location. This has created doubt about the very existence of the G-spot and sent the original researchers and others who have followed them back to the lab to try to demonstrate its exact construction.

Quite recently, a Polish researcher did some work on cadavers and found that "the G-spot appeared as a well-delineated sac with walls that…resembled erectile tissues. The superior surface of the sac had bluish irregularities visible through the coat. From the distal tail, a rope-like structure emerged, which was seen for approximately 1.6 mm and then disappeared into the surrounding tissue" (Ostrzenski, 2012, p. 1355). His findings are still being debated.

Are G-spot Orgasms Better?

Most enthusiasts claim that the spot, when stimulated, not only creates exquisite sexual sensitivity but also a different kind of orgasm, "Barry R. Komisaruk, Professor at the Department of Psychology, Rutgers, wrote that the G-spot was a different orgasmic pathway than the clitoris even though the area is a bundle of overlapping nerves that include the clitoris" (Jannini et al., 2012, p. 958). A paper from some of the members of the original research team further states: "Some women describe experiencing orgasm from stimulation solely of the G-spot. The orgasm resulting from stimulation of the G-spot is felt deep inside the body, and includes a bearing-down sensation" (Jannini et al., 2010, p. 27).

The researchers who resurrected the discussion of a G-spot also believe that they have evidence that the brain reacts differently to stimulation from this spot from clitoral excitement:

> Because the vaginal and the cervical self-stimulation activated sensory cortical regions that are distinctly different from the region activated by clitoral self-stimulation, this refutes the possibility that awareness of vaginal or cervical stimulation is simply a consequence of indirect clitoral stimulation…This is further evidence that vaginal and cervical stimulations generate their own unique sensory input to the brain that is separate and distinct from clitoral sensory input, and adequate to activate orgasm. (Jannini et al., 2012, pp. 960–961)

So Why Doesn't Everyone Believe the G-spot Exists?

This all sounds pretty convincing and there are certainly many women who will attest to the unique sensitivity of their G-spot. It is even described as fact in quite a few textbooks. Yet, there is a large group of scientists who do not believe that a special tissue or area of sexual excitation exists that is separate from the clitoral nerves that surround the entrance to the vagina. And there are many women who search for the spot inside their vagina, to no avail. Even the G-spot research team says, "Women have reported that they have difficulty locating and stimulating their G-spot by themselves, except with a dildo, a G-spot vibrator, or similar device...(but they have no difficulty identifying the erotic sensation when the area is stimulated by a partner)" (Jannini *et al.*, 2010, p. 27).

The ongoing debate is really focused on whether or not the G-spot is separate from the rich network of clitoral nerves that surround it. Masters and Johnson were the first to determine that the clitoral structures surround and extend along and within the labia. They filmed and analyzed orgasms from both clitoral stimulation and vaginal intercourse and concluded that all orgasms originated in some kind of direct or indirect clitoral arousal (Masters and Johnson, 1966).

More recent research has concurred. Tim Spector, who co-authored a 2009 study on the topic, also hypothesized the tissue in the G-spot area may be part of the clitoris and is not, as argued, an unaffiliated sexual zone (Archer and Lloyd, 2002, pp. 85–88). Urologist Helen O'Connell also did anatomic studies and wrote that the G-spot is indeed clitoral tissue and therefore even though excitation may be sourced in the vagina, it is clitoral nerves creating the sensation. O'Connell used magnetic resonance imaging (MRI) scans and felt that there was conclusive evidence that the "legs" of the clitoris accounted for the G-spot's erectile tissue. To quote her, "The vaginal wall is, in fact, the clitoris...If you lift the skin off the vagina on the side walls, you get the bulbs of the clitoris" (O'Connell *et al.*, 2005, pp. 1185–1195).

An interesting secondary discovery for O'Connell in examining female cadavers was that some women seemed to have more extensive clitoral nerves than others. She felt this may account for ease—or difficulty—of having an orgasm or needing direct versus indirect stimulation of the clitoral area. Her work has been replicated by the French team of Odile Buisson and Pierre Foldes who used imaging technology to come to their conclusions. They also showed how the clitoral system surrounds and stimulates the vagina and is therefore responsible for "vaginal" orgasms. Basically, the authors conclude that the vaginal and clitoral system are so intertwined that it is ridiculous to try and separate their interaction (Buisson and Foldes, 2009, pp. 1223–1231).

A recent study by a team of researchers hypothesized that the G-spot is an extension of the clitoris and clitoral nerve system and that the friction against these nerves is the cause of vaginal orgasms as opposed to them being caused by a distinctly different anatomical structure. In an influential article, the lead author, Kilchevsky, stated unequivocally that because the clitoris is essentially the same biological structure as the penis (the latter enlarged by male hormones), there is no reason evolution would create two separate apparatus for orgasms. He lambasts porn providers and sex toy makers for what he believes to be the mythology of a G-spot (Kilchevsky *et al.*, 2012).

In fact, these authors were convened as part of a panel in 2010 and again in 2012 by the *Journal of Sexual Medicine* in an effort to get a definitive answer on this subject. The panel was tasked with examining dozens of papers written on the G-spot, and, ultimately, they discounted them. The panel concluded, "Reports in the public media would lead one to believe the G-Spot is a well-characterized entity capable of providing extreme sexual stimulation, yet this is far from the truth" (Kilchevsky *et al.*, 2012).

Where Does This Leave Us?

We think skepticism about the G-spot is warranted. The samples of women who have been investigated are small, a small group of investigators are primarily responsible for most of the writing on the topic, and the density of clitoral nerve endings in the area makes the demarcation of a morphologically unique area hard to support. Furthermore, like some of the scientists who have failed to find the G-spot or define it as a special area of sexual function, we are worried that women who cannot find it (perhaps because it doesn't exist) will now feel they are sexually deficient in yet another way!

If the G-spot is still disputed territory, perhaps we can find a compromise on this issue from the work of Rutgers professor Barry Komisaruk who did some of the MRI studies in which brain scans showed that stimulating the clitoris, vagina, and cervix lit up separate areas in women's brains. He concluded: "I think that the bulk of the evidence shows that the G-Spot is not a particular thing. It's not like saying, 'What is the thyroid gland?' The G-Spot is more of a thing like New York City is a thing. It's a region, it's a convergence of many different structures" (Komisaruk *et al.*, 2011).

However, we do not want our readers to take our skepticism as reason not to do some personal experimentation on themselves or their partners. In fact, we urge you to follow the instructions above and see what you find and how it feels. We bet that if it feels good and leads to a really intense orgasm, none of you will really care if it's a separate anatomical structure or a cluster of clitoral nerves.

References

Archer, J. and Lloyd, B. (2002). *Sex and Gender*. Cambridge University Press.

Buisson, O. and Foldès, P. (2009). The clitoral complex: a dynamic sonographic study. *Journal of Sexual Medicine*, 6(5), 1223–1231.

Jannini, E.A., Rubio-Casillas, A., Whipple, B., Buisson, O., Komisaruk, B.R., and Brody, S. (2012). Female orgasm(s): One, two, several. *Journal of Sexual Medicine*, 9(4), 956–965.

Jannini, E.A., Whipple, B., Kingsberg, S.A., Buisson, O., Foldès, P., and Vardi, Y. (2010). Who's afraid of the G-spot? *Journal of Sexual Medicine*, 7(1), 25–34.

Kilchevsky, A., Vardi, Y., Lowenstein, L., and Gruenwald, I. (2012). Is the female G-spot truly a distinct anatomic entity? *Journal of Sexual Medicine*, 9(3), 719–726.

Komisaruk, B.R., Wise, N., Frangos, E., Liu, W.-C., Allen, K., and Brody, S. (2011). Women's clitoris, vagina, and cervix mapped on the sensory cortex: fMRI evidence. *Journal of Sexual Medicine*, 8(10), 2822–2830.

Ladas, A.K., Whipple, B., and Perry, J.D. (1982). *The G Spot and Other Recent Discoveries About Human Sexuality*. Holt, Rinehart, and Winston, New York.

Masters, W. H. and Johnson, V.E. (1966). *Human Sexual Response*, Vol. 1. Little, Brown & Co., Boston, pp. 223–276.

O'Connell, H.E., Sanjeevan, K.V., and Hutson, J.M. (2005). Anatomy of the clitoris. *Journal of Urology*, 174(4), 1189–1195.

Ostrzenski, A. (2012). G-spot anatomy: A new discovery. *Journal of Sexual Medicine*, 9(5), 1355–1359.

Myth #5   Testosterone Is the Main Predictor of Sex Drive in Men, and You Can Always Add More

There is no doubt that testosterone, an androgen, or male hormone, plays a part in sexual arousal and appetite. Though this hormone does have an impact in both men and women, the fact is that sexual appetites are highly mediated by mood, values, beliefs, experience, relationships, physical complications, medications, and a host of other conditions. Teasing out how much of a role testosterone really has can be difficult. But we're up to the challenge and in this myth we look at the research for both men and women.

Testosterone in Men

Testosterone is a sex hormone that is produced by both the testes in men and the ovaries in women as well as the adrenal glands in both men and women. It is responsible for secondary sex characteristics in men such as facial hair, body hair, and deep voice. Testosterone has an activating effect on sexual desire for both men and women (Kelly, 2011).

For men, androgens are a core part of the erectile system. Studies of erectile dysfunction have found that low levels of free testosterone correlates with impaired ability of the cavernous endothelia and corporeal smooth muscle cells to deliver enough blood for the penis to become rigid (Aversa *et al.*, 2000, p. 517). Further, several studies have shown that low testosterone levels will correlate with lower sexual desire (Aversa *et al.*, 2000). It is not true, however, that having high testosterone levels will always correlate with more sexual activity or better erections (Anderson *et al.*, 1992; Bagatell *et al.*, 1994). Erection and arousal issues may have an organic origin but unless lower than normal levels of free testosterone are found, or there is some injury to the genitals, the primary causes of lack of arousal or erection are thought to be mostly due to psychological issues with sex, performance fears, relationship woes, or lack of attraction (Aversa *et al.*, 2000, p. 519; Buvat and Lemaire, 1997).

The part that testosterone plays in sexual drive is actually a controversial subject among researchers. A number of studies have indicated that total testosterone was related to erectile ability but not sex drive, except among aging men where less bioavailable testosterone was present (Gades *et al.*, 2008, p. 2209). Another study also found correlations to erection but not sex drive (Ahn *et al.*, 2002). The long-running Massachusetts Male Aging study found no correlation with either total or bioavailable testosterone and erectile functioning (Gades *et al.*, 2008). These findings, however, were somewhat modified by a meta-analysis of 17 trials by Boloña *et al*; they felt that testosterone had a direct effect on erections and a modest effective on sex drive (Boloña*et al.*, 2007). In addition, a study of Korean sex offenders who were chemically castrated using drugs to inhibit testosterone came to the conclusion that testosterone was the mediating agent for sexual arousal. However, the authors did say they could not be positive about their results because of a small sample, the fact that there was no placebo/control group, and the possibility that the offenders were not being honest in their self-reports (Koo *et al.*, 2013, p. 565).

Even more controversial than the role low testosterone level has in sex drive is the question of what to do about it. If a low testosterone level is truly present, many doctors recommend testosterone therapy which is used to help increase sexual interest and create better erectile function (Bancroft and Wu, 1983; Kwan *et al.*, 1983; Cunningham *et al.*, 1990; Rakic *et al.*, 1997; Aversa *et al.*, 2000). In a recent article, Ronald Swerdloff, chief of the division of endocrinology and metabolism at the UCLA School of Medicine, stated "Men who have repeatedly tested low for testosterone concentrations in their blood and who also have symptoms consistent with testosterone deficiency are reasonable candidates for treatment" (Nutrition in Action, 2014a, p. 10). But testing is difficult. Swerdloff goes on to say, "Some men may have a low level on one day, but a week or a month later, they may be back to a completely normal level"(Nutrition in Action, 2014a, p. 10).

There are some interesting and subtle factors of how the mind influences the body that suggest that testosterone deficiencies themselves as well as reduced blood flow to the penis might actually be due to stress factors or, often, relationship factors. Difficulty or hostility at work, in the family, or in a relationship, for example, may cause decreased testosterone levels. To quote one group of investigators, "Present data show that, in subjects consulting for sexual dysfunction, deterioration of the couple's relationship may be associated with impairment in sexual activity, which, in turn, can lead to a mild hypogonadism"(Corona *et al.*, 2009, p. 2597). In other words, it's not just sex drive and erections that are influenced by psychological factors, testosterone levels themselves are highly influenced by emotions (Aversa *et al.*, 2000; Corona *et al.*, 2009).

Researchers are also concerned about the long-term effects of adding testosterone. Some believe that there is not enough information available yet to know whether potentially dangerous side effects come with long-term use of replacement therapy (Gades *et al.*, 2008, pp. 2210–2013; McKinlay, 2006).

Testosterone in Women

If you think the action of testosterone is a controversial topic concerning men, it is nothing compared to the friction in the medical and behavioral science communities over the function of testosterone in women—and the dangers that hormone drug therapy may present to women. At issue are various kinds of testosterone treatments: oral testosterone, transdermal testosterone, testosterone patches, sublingual testosterone, intramuscular, subcutaneous, pellets, gels, and creams (Hubayter and Simon, 2008, pp. 187–188).

Here, we start with rats (sorry ladies). Researchers looking for a medical way to reduce or change what they consider to be low sexual desire in women (or what women and/or their partners consider a lack of ability to want or enjoy sex) first started to see if they could arouse female rats. One study used looked at vardenafil, a PDE5 inhibitor similar to that found in Viagra, in combination to see if they could produce some horny rodents. Neither testosterone injected under the skin nor an oral version of vardenafil worked on their own, but when they put the two together female rats became more receptive to male mounting behavior and also sought out the males for sexual activity (Snoeren *et al.*, 2011, p. 989).

Other studies have carried out similar tests on human females. Van der Made *et al.* (2009) applied the combination of testosterone and vardenafil to women patients who said they had extremely little or no sexual desire and concluded that the combination enhanced desire and was demonstrated by more sexual arousal when they watched erotic images.

A few double-blind studies on women with deficient hormonal levels found that being treated with estrogen produced some changes in sexual desire (Mulhall *et al.*, 2004; Bain *et al.*, 2007). Other approaches included using testosterone with estrogens in women who no longer had functioning ovaries. This was deemed to improve sexual interest (Snoeren *et al.*, 2011, p. 991). Stephanie Page, a researcher at the University of Washington, has written that "some good trials show a small benefit for sexual function in women who have undergone surgical menopause or who are naturally menopausal" (Page *et al.*, 2005).

A batch of studies, some of them with very small samples, have looked at women's natural peaks of testosterone around ovulation and found correlation with sexual gratification when intercourse or other sexual activity occurs at that time. One study of 11 couples found that high baseline testosterone, but not daily testosterone, was related to women's positive evaluation of their sexual experience (Persky *et al.*, 1978, p. 157).

While all researchers admit that there is not enough research on the use of testosterone alone as a mediator of female sexual interest, there is a lot of "off-label" use. "Off label" use means the drug has been approved by the Food and Drug Administration (FDA), which has demanding standards, but not for the use it is currently being applied to. So, when synthetic testosterone which was approved for erectile problems in men is used for sexual arousal in women without being tested for efficacy and safety, that use is referred to as "off label." Nonetheless, some doctors feel the use of testosterone in various hormonal combinations for women who are upset about the loss of sexual interest is appropriate. For example, Estratest, a common hormonal combination, is FDA approved to help women suffering from extreme post-menopausal discomforts (sleeplessness, hot flashes, headaches, and other problems) but is being used "off label" as a way to increase sexual interest in women. Research suggests that the combination of estrogen and testosterone increases blood flow to the vaginal area, clitoral sensitivity, and rates of orgasm. As a result it increases sexual desire and behavior. It can also prevent vaginal atrophy among older women or women who have had their ovaries removed (Lobo *et al.*, 2003; Hubayter and Simon, 2008, p. 183).

Advocates of testosterone therapy admit certain possible negative side effects such as increased skin oiliness, acne, deepened voice timbre, changes in personality such as increased hostility, weight gain, and hair loss. Other side effects include elevated liver function, lower HDL levels (high density lipo-protein, the good cholesterol), and even carcinoma (a type of cancer) (Hoeger and Guzick, 1999; Redmond, 1999; Snoeren *et al.*, 2011). A particularly trou-bling study published in the *New England Journal of Medicine* found that when 209 men with low testosterone levels were involved in a study that gave some men testosterone and others a placebo, the men who received additional testosterone were five times more likely to have a heart attack or other heart problems. This was so worrisome that the researchers cancelled the research (Nutrition in Action, 2014b). Still, there are clearly clinicians who feel that the chances of these side effects are slight and the benefits may be worth it.

The presence of these side effects is not a minor issue to a large group of critics who are fighting the legitimization of testosterone therapy for women. They believe women's bodies have been used as experimental laboratories for a lot of drugs (for example, high dose contraceptive pills). Perhaps the angri-est commentary on testosterone therapies comes from a group of feminist researchers and clinicians who feel that the whole concept of low sexual desire for women has been invented. Chief among these critics is psychologist Lenore Tiefer (2001), who, with a number of other therapists, clinical profes-sionals, and researchers, feels that the definition of "low" desire is highly biased because it is based on male standards and male needs. They argue that an arbitrary standard of sexual desire has been created and that the attenua-tion of desire in women may be "natural" and appropriate and should not be problematized. Instead of telling women that a certain level of desire is "nor-mal" and anything different from that is a problem that needs to be fixed, they suggest that we normalize the continuum of desire that clearly exists among women, especially post-menopausal women.

So Why All the Fuss About Testosterone?

Testosterone has received much attention in many ways because it seems like a potentially quick fix. Unfortunately, the role of testosterone in sexual arousal and behavior is anything but straightforward and while looking for medical answers to a lack of sexual interest is reasonable and may have worthy outcomes, the fact is that at present we do not have a simple explanation for lower sexual desire or difficulties with arousal. While we know testosterone has a role, we can't pinpoint it precisely, which means we can't simply say add some more and all will be fine. Most sex therapists believe that except for severe hormonal deficiencies (which may need a medical answer), the answer for most sexual issues will be found by looking more closely at psychological, emotional, and relationship issues.

References

Ahn, H.S., Park, C.M., and Lee, S.W. (2002). The clinical relevance of sex hormone levels and sexual activity in the ageing male. *BJU International,* 89(6), 526–530.

Anderson, R.A., Bancroft, J., and Wu, F.C. (1992) The effects of exogenous testosterone on sexuality and mood of normal men. *Journal of Clinical Endocrinology and Metabolism,* 75, 1503–1507.

Aversa, A., Isidori, A.M., De Martino, M.U., Caprio, M., Fabbrini, E., Rocchietti-March, M., *et al.* (2000). Androgens and penile erection: Evidence for a direct relationship between free testosterone and cavernous vasodilation in men with erectile dysfunction. *Clinical Endocrinology,* 53(4), 517–522.

Bagatell, C.J., Heiman, J.R., Rivier, J.E., and Bremner, W.J. (1994) Effects of endogenous testosterone and oestradiol on sexual behavior in normal young men. *Journal of Clinical Endocrinology and Metabolism,* 78, 711–716.

Bain, J., Brock, G., Kuzmarov, I; International Consulting Group (2007). Canadian Society for the Study of the Aging Male: Response to health Canada's position paper on testosterone treatment. *Journal of Sexual Medicine,* 4, 558–566.

Bancroft, J. and Wu, C.W. (1983) Changes in erectile responsiveness during androgen replacement therapy. *Archives of Sexual Behavior,* 12, 59–66.

Boloña, E.R., Uraga, M.V., Haddad, R.M., Tracz, M.J., Siderao, K., Kennedy, C.C., *et al.* (2007). Testosterone use in men with sexual dysfunction: A systematic review and meta-analysis of randomized placebo-controlled trials. *Mayo Clinic Proceedings,* 82, 20–28.

Buvat, J. and Lemaire, A. (1997) Endocrine screening in 1022 men with erectile dysfunction: Clinical significance and cost-effective strategy. *Journal of Urology,* 158, 1764–1768.

Corona, G., Mannucci, E., Lotti, F., Boddi, V., Jannini, E.A., Fisher, A.D., *et al.* (2009). Impairment of couple relationship in male patients with sexual dysfunction is associated with overt hypogonadism. *Journal of Sexual Medicine,* 6(9), 2591–2600.

Cunningham, G.R., Hirshkowitz, M., Korenman, S.G., & Karacan, I. (1990) Testosterone replacement therapy and sleep-related erections in hypogonadal men. *Journal of Clinical Endocrinology and Metabolism,* 70, 792–797.

Gades, N.M., Jacobson, D.J., McGree, M.E., St Sauver, J.L., Lieber, M.M., Nehra, A., *et al.* (2008). The associations between serum sex hormones, erectile function, and sex drive: The Olmsted County Study of Urinary Symptoms and Health Status among Men. *Journal of Sexual Medicine,* 5(9), 2209–2220.

Hoeger, K.M. and Guzick, D.S. (1999). The use of androgens in menopause. *Clinical Obstetrics and Gynecology,* 42, 883–894.

Hubayter, Z. and Simon, J.A. (2008). Testosterone therapy for sexual dysfunction in postmenopausal women. *Climacteric: the Journal of the International Menopause Society,* 11(3), 181–191.

Kelly, G.F. (2011). *Sexuality Today: The Human Perspective,* 10th edn. McGraw Hill.

Koo, K.C., Shim, G.S., Park, H.H., Rha, K.H., Choi, Y.D., Chung, B.H., *et al.* (2013). Treatment outcomes of chemical castration on Korean sex offenders. *Journal of Forensic and Legal Medicine,* 20(6), 563–566.

Kwan, M., Greenleaf, W.J., Mann, J., Crapo, L., and Davidson, J.M. (1983) The nature of androgen action on male sexuality: A combined laboratory–self-report study on hypogonadal men. *Journal of Clinical Endocrinology and Metabolism, 57, 557–562.*

Lobo, R.A., Rosen, R.C., Yang, H.M., Block, B., and Van Der Hoop, R.G. (2003). Comparative effects of oral esterified estrogens with and without methyltestosterone on endocrine profiles and dimensions of sexual function in postmenopausal women with hypoactive sexual desire. *Fertility and Sterility, 79(6), 1341–1352.*

McKinlay, J.B. (2006). Should we begin a large clinical trial of testosterone in men? "Not yet." *Journal of Men's Health and Gender, 3, 33–35.*

Mulhall, J.P., Valenzuela, R., Aviv, N., and Parker, M. (2004). Effect of testosterone supplementation on sexual function in hypogonadal men with erectile dysfunction. *Urology, 63, 348–352.*

Nutrition in Action Health Letter (2014a) Who really needs testosterone? pp. 10–11.

Nutrition in Action Health Letter (2014b) Summary of article in the *New England Journal of Medicine* 363, 109, 2010.

Page, S.T., Amory, J.K., Bowman, F.D., Anawalt, B.D., Matsumoto, A.M., Bremner, W.J., *et al.* (2005). Exogenous testosterone (T) alone or with finasteride increases physical performance, grip strength, and lean body mass in older men with low serum T. *Journal of Clinical Endocrinology and Metabolism, 90(3), 1502–1510.*

Persky, H., Lief, H.I., Strauss, D., Miller, W.R., and O'Brien, C.P. (1978). Plasma testosterone level and sexual behavior of couples. *Archives of Sexual Behavior, 7(3), 157–173.*

Rakic, Z., Starcevic, V., Starcevic, V.P., and Marinkovic, J. (1997) Testosterone treatment in men with erectile disorder and low levels of total testosterone in serum. *Archives of Sexual Behavior, 26, 495–504.*

Redmond, G.P. (1999). Hormones and sexual function. *International Journal of Fertility and Women's Medicine, 44, 193–197.*

Snoeren, E.M., Bovens, A., Refsgaard, L.K., Westphal, K.G., Waldinger, M.D., Olivier, B., *et al.* (2011). Combination of testosterone and vardenafil increases female sexual functioning in sub-primed rats. *Journal of Sexual Medicine, 8(4), 989–1001.*

Tiefer, L. (2001). A new view of women's sexual problems: Why new? Why now? *Journal of Sex Research, 38(2), 89–96.*

van der Made, F., Bloemers, J., Yassem, W.E., Kleiverda, G., Everaerd, W., van Ham, D., *et al.* (2009). The influence of testosterone combined with a PDE5-inhibitor on cognitive, affective, and physiological sexual functioning in women suffering from sexual dysfunction. *Journal of Sexual Medicine, 6(3), 777–790.*

Myth #6 Everyone Is Born Either Male or Female

Sometimes it seems like every television show and movie we watch has to have a birth scene in it. Whether it's an hour-long hospital drama (remember *Grey's Anatomy's* Bailey refusing to push because her husband was having brain surgery down the hall), a network sitcom (poor *How I Met Your Mother's* Lily went into labor while her husband was falling down drunk in Atlantic City), a Disney channel half-hour comedy made for tweens (the mom on *Good Luck Charlie* has now been seen giving birth twice), or the climax of a blockbuster movie (who can forget the famous crotch/crowning shot in *Knocked Up*), women are constantly giving birth on the big and little screen.

The scene in the hospital room (or the car or the elevator—because fictional babies always seem to come super-fast and at the worst moments) plays out differently depending on whether the goal is to mimic real life drama or go for the cheap laughs, but it always ends the same way with someone happily proclaiming: "It's a Boy!!!" (Okay, sometimes it ends with "It's a Girl!" But you get our point.)

In Hollywood, this big moment is simple; the doctor peeks between the baby's legs and makes the all-important proclamation and the parents are always surprised (even though many of today's parents know the sex months before delivery through prenatal tests) and delighted (that is after the dad who dreamt of a son melts the first time he holds his daughter).

For some parents in real life, however, it not possible for the doctor to proclaim boy or girl just by looking at their infant.

Ultimately, our gender is based on *biological sex* which is determined by our chromosomes, hormones, and internal and external genitalia. As we grow, we learn how males and females are expected to behave (known as *gender roles*), decide how we want to present our gender to the world (*gender expression*), and develop our own internal sense of whether we are male or female (*gender identity*). Though much of society—from the media, to the fashion industry, to every modern toy store—would like us to believe that there are only two choices, many think that gender rests on a continuum with male and female at either end and many (if not most) people residing somewhere in between.

In this entry, we are going to focus on variations of *biological sex* and what happens when someone's biological sex is not firmly male or female. Later in the book (Myth #9) we cover gender roles and gender identity in more detail and look at what happens when a person is transgender, which means that their internal sense of gender identity does not match their biological sex or the gender roles society expects of them. Though these two issues are inextricably linked for some people, we believe it is important to look at them separately.

Variations in Biological Sex

As we often do when addressing a long-standing myth in human sexuality, we have to start this entry with a review of basic biology. We apologize if we are repeating things you learned in ninth grade but we are pretty sure that you didn't hear it all back in high school.

Sperm and ova (eggs) are known as gametes. They each carry 23 individual chromosomes that, when they come together, become the 23 pairs of chromosomes that make up our unique genetic identity. One of those pairs of chromosomes determines our biological sex. Ova always (or almost always—more on that later) carry one X chromosome while sperm typically carry either an X or a Y chromosome. When they come together and everything goes according to plan, an embryo with XX chromosomes develops into a female while one with XY chromosomes develops into a male.

All fetuses start out with two undifferentiated gonads and certain homologous structures that can become either male or female sex organs. There is a specific section of the Y chromosome (called the TDF or testes-determining factor region) that sends a signal to the gonads telling them to develop into testes. The testes in turn begin to produce testosterone which sets the rest of the fetal development on a path toward becoming male. This means that homologous structures in the fetus (structures that start out the same) will turn into the internal reproductive system (such as the Cowper's gland, prostate gland, seminal vesicles) and the external male genitalia (the penis and scrotum).

Without TDF, the gonads become ovaries and produce estrogen instead of testosterone. The fetus then develops along a female path meaning that these homologous structures will become a uterus, fallopian tubes, and a vagina internally, and externally they will develop to form the labia minora, labia majora, clitoris, and the vaginal opening. (Since we are reviewing here, let us remind you that these are not all of the internal and external parts in either male or female reproductive systems.)

Though the majority of babies born will have followed one of these two paths, there are many points along the way where things can diverge from these paths.

Chromosomal Anomalies

Like life itself, these anomalies can start with the egg or the sperm. Though each gamete is supposed to have only one sex chromosome, things can happen during meiosis (the process of cell separation) that cause them to have more than one or none. This means that an embryo can begin to develop with too many or too few sex chromosomes. These are some of the more common conditions that can result.

- **Turner syndrome**, XO, develops when either the egg cell or the sperm cell does not have a sex chromosome at all. Individuals who are born with Turner syndrome have external female genitalia and internal female reproductive organs (ovaries, uterus, and fallopian tubes) but the ovaries are not functional and do not produce estrogen during development. Females with Turner syndrome are usually short, have a broad chest with the nipples way out to the sides, and have low ears. They may have congenital heart defects as well. They will not develop secondary sex characteristics on their own. They are often given human growth hormone during childhood to help them grow taller and estrogen therapy after puberty to increase their development of secondary sex characteristics (Mader, 1992, p. 17).
- **Klinefelter syndrome**, XXY, happens when an egg with two X chromosomes is fertilized by a sperm with a Y chromosome or an egg with an X chromosome is fertilized by a sperm with both an X and a Y. These individuals will appear male when born but some abnormalities including small testes, a female pattern of pubic hair, poor muscle development, and a lack of facial hair may begin to be noticed as the individual reaches puberty (Mader, p. 19). Males with Klinefelter syndrome tend to have long limbs, broad hips, and some learning

disabilities (especially in verbal skills). These men are also infertile. In fact, many men with the condition find out they have it as adults because they are having trouble conceiving. Those who find out at birth or during puberty can be treated with testosterone to help bring on secondary sex characteristics (Kelly, 2010, p. 101).

- **Supernumerary Y syndrome**, XYY, happens when an egg with one X chromosome is fertilized by a sperm with two Y chromosomes. These males are usually taller than average but have no other outward symptoms. Most males with XYY syndrome have normal sexual development and are fertile. However, males with XYY may be at higher risk for learning disabilities, including delayed development of speech and language skills. They may also face delayed development of motor skills, weak muscle tones, hand tremors, and other motor tics. The syndrome has also been associated with behavioral and emotional difficulties (Kelly, p. 101). It was once suggested that these males had higher aggression and were more likely to be in prison than other males but that theory has since been disproven (Mader, p. 19).

- **Triple X syndrome, also known as meta-females,** XXX, develops when an egg cell that has two X chromosomes is fertilized by a sperm cell with an X chromosome of its own. Individuals with three X chromosomes may never know it as they most often have no physical abnormalities. However, they might have menstrual irregularities, suffer from fertility issues, and go through menopause at an early age (Mader, p. 19).

There are other variations as well. A fetus could have XO/XY which would mean it will develop either male or female genitals or some combination but likely have no other issues. The fetus could also have both XX/XY which would mean that it could develop some combination of ovaries and testes and would likely have a uterus. The external genitals could be male or female or some combination. At puberty, individuals with XX/XY usually grow breasts and begin to menstruate (Kelly, p. 101). It is important to note that there is no syndrome from embryos with YO sex chromosomes because at least one X is required for survival. Any embryo that has just a Y chromosome will result in a spontaneous abortion or miscarriage.

Hormonal Anomalies

While chromosomes set a fetus on the path toward its biological sex, how the fetus develops is also very much controlled by the hormones it is exposed to while *in utero* (and after birth) and how the body processes these hormones. Again, there are many things that can go differently during development but these are some of the most common.

- **Androgen insensitivity syndrome (AIS)** occurs when the body cannot process male sex hormones (known as androgens). When this happens in someone who is genetically male (XY), the process of developing a male reproductive system and male genitalia is interrupted. The TDF region will tell the undifferentiated gonads to become testes and the testes will produce testosterone but, because the body cannot process this hormone, the fetus will develop along a female path and will appear female when born with their external genitalia appearing as labia. The internal reproductive organs, however, will not have developed completely. The baby will be born with a shortened vagina and will not have a uterus (Blonna and Levitan, 2005, p. 119). The baby will also have testes which will most often be located somewhere in the abdomen. After puberty, individuals with AIS are often given estrogen replacement therapy to help develop female secondary sex characteristics. They may also have to have their testes removed as these can become cancerous (Kelly, p. 105). Though people with AIS are genetically male, most identify as female.

- **Congenital adrenal hyperplasia (CAH)** is a disorder of the adrenal glands (there is one adrenal gland located on each of our kidneys) which causes a buildup of androgens in a fetus and infant. If this happens in someone who is genetically male it can cause sex characteristics to appear too early. Males with CAH may have a deepening voice, an enlarged penis (though normal testes), pubic hair, armpit hair, and well-developed muscles before puberty. Genetic females (XX) with some forms of CAH will usually have normal internal reproductive systems (ovaries, uterus, and fallopian tubes) but may have an enlarged clitoris at birth. In some instances the clitoris may be so large that it is mistaken for a penis. They may also develop pubic hair and armpit hair before puberty and may develop facial hair as well. There is also evidence that females with CAH tend to develop a male gender identity (Kelly, p. 105).
- **DHT deficiency** is a problem that affects genetic males (XY). *In utero* these males do not produce enough of a hormone called dihydrotestosterone (DHT) which has a critical role in male sexual development, including the development of the external genitalia. Many people with this deficiency are born with external genitalia that look female, others are born with external genitalia that appear male but are unusually small (sometimes called a micropenis). Still others will be born with what is called ambiguous genitalia where it is hard to tell whether they are male or female just by looking. During puberty, people with this condition often develop male secondary sex characteristics such as increased muscles, deeper voices, and pubic hair. Their penis and scrotum often grows larger as well. Despite the fact that many have been raised as females, they do not develop breasts or other secondary sex characteristics (Kelly, p. 105).

Evolving Language

In the old days, anyone born with ambiguous genitals of any kind would have been called a hermaphrodite. The medical definition of a true hermaphrodite, however, means someone who has both ovaries and testes. Most people with the conditions mentioned above do not fit into that category. Some medical professionals make the distinction of pseudohermaphrodites noting that someone with testes (but no ovaries) and some female genitalia would be a male pseudohermaphrodite and someone with ovaries (but no testes) and some male genitalia would be a female pseudohermaphrodite.

In 1993, Anne Fausto-Sterling, a biologist who frequently writes about gender, wrote an article for *The Sciences* magazine in which she suggested we should recognize five biological sexes. In addition to males and females, she suggested adding "herms" (named after true hermaphrodites), "merms" (named after male pseudohermaphrodites), and "ferms" (named after female pseudohermaphrodites). In a follow-up essay, she admits that her "tongue was planted firmly in cheek" when she suggested these names but that her point was clear; the two-sex system that is so deeply embedded in our culture is not sufficient to "encompass the full spectrum of human sexuality" (Fausto-Sterling, 2000, p. 19).

Though the concept of five sexes might seem crazy to some of us, other cultures have been more open to recognizing those who do not fit into the male and female categories. There is a village in the Dominican Republic, for example, where a genetic mutation has meant that many babies are born with DHT deficiency. These babies have genitals that look female during childhood but once exposed to testosterone during puberty they develop male secondary sex characteristics. Villagers have given these men the name *guevedoche*, which means "balls at twelve." They are also sometimes referred to as *machi-embra* (male-female) (Herdt, 1990). The important part is that over the generations they have been accepted at least to some degree as a third sex. The Sambia tribe of Papua New Guinea also has a similar genetic mutation and has seen many children born with genitals that appear to be female at birth but eventually develop male secondary sex characteristics. These individuals are assigned the name *kwolu-aatnwik* and are not expected to take on either male or female gender roles in the society. They are allowed to become spirit doctors or shamans (Kelly, p. 97).

In the Western world there is no real agreement even now as to what we should call an individual whose biological sex is not easily categorized. The same year that Fausto-Sterling suggested five sexes, activists founded the Intersex Society of North America (ISNA). According to its website: "The Intersex Society of North America (ISNA) is devoted to systemic change to end shame, secrecy, and unwanted genital surgeries for people born with an anatomy that someone decided is not standard for male or female." As its name suggested, the ISNA proposed using the term intersex as "general term used for a variety of conditions in which a person is born with a reproductive or sexual anatomy that doesn't seem to fit the typical definitions of female or male." While this terminology became popular for a number of years some still found it to be "pejorative to patients" and "confusing to practitioners and parents alike" (Lee *et al.*, 2006, p. e.488).

New guidelines put out by experts in the field and supported by the ISNA (which has now closed its doors) propose using the term "disorders of sex development" (DSD) and defining this as "congenital conditions in which the development of chromosomal, gonadal, or anatomic sex is atypical" (Lee *et al.*, p. e488). Not everyone is happy with this language either, primarily because it begins with the term disorders. Some activists and people living with DSD believe that this further marginalizes their identities.

Evolving Treatment

If we don't have the language to even talk about those born with disorders of sex development, imagine how hard it must be for parents of these infants to figure out what to do. In the United States there has historically been a rush to fix that which is not "normal." In many cases this has meant that parents are told that their infant needs to have surgery to make their genitals appear more like an average clitoris or penis. In truth though, it has always been much easier to create labia and a vagina than it has been to create a penis (especially one that functions). Most of the time, therefore, doctors would recommend that parents surgically create female genitalia and begin to raise the infant as a girl regardless of the chromosomal sex or what hormones the infant was exposed to *in utero*.

This is what happened to Cheryl Chase, the founder of ISNA. She was born in 1956 with ambiguous genitalia—she had what could have been an enlarged clitoris or a micropenis and something that appeared to be a vaginal opening. At first doctors recommended that she be brought up as a boy so she went home from the hospital with the name Charlie. But her parents were concerned about the appearance of her genitals and consulted another team of experts when she was 18 months old. Based on the fact that she had a fairly normal vagina, these experts recommended surgery to make her external genitals look more female. She underwent a clitoridectomy and was sent home as Cheryl. Her parents never told her what had happened and she remembers many unexplained surgeries and genital exams during her childhood. She also remembers not fitting in with the other girls: "I was more interested in guns and radios and if I tried to socialize with any kids, it was generally boys, and I would try to best my brother" (Colapinto, 1997).

Fausto-Sterling notes the case of Max Beck who was born with disorders of sex development and was surgically assigned female. Though comfortable in that identity through her teens, Max first came out as butch lesbian in her twenties and then in his mid-thirties became a man. He is now married to a female partner and they have had children (through reproductive technologies).

Interestingly, the most famous test case of gender reassignment in children did not involve someone who had a disorder of sex development at all. Instead, the case involved identical twin boys who were born in 1965 with identifiably male sex organs. At 8 months old they underwent circumcision because they were suffering phismosis (a condition in which the foreskin will not pull back). There was a serious accident during the procedure and one twin essentially lost his penis. His parents had few choices and little hope as the doctors they saw all said they could not rebuild a penis that would either look normal or function properly.

The parents then found out about a doctor at Baltimore's Johns Hopkins Hospital who was researching and performing sex reassignment surgeries. Dr. John Money was a pioneer in the field of gender and had a theory that gender was a purely cultural concept that came from how kids were raised especially early in their lives. He believed that infants are born as blank slates and it is not until their parents and society imprint them with gender that they begin to see themselves as either male or female.

Money met with the parents of the infant (then named David) and assured them that if they allowed surgeons to construct external female genitalia and then raised the child as a girl, "she" would be capable of growing into a well-adjusted young women. Money was particularly interested in this case because as an identical twin David came with a control group. If "she" could be successfully raised as a female while her brother (who had her exact genetic make-up) was successfully raised as a male, it would go a long way toward proving Money's blank slate theory.

The parents took Money's advice, the surgery was carried out, and they proceeded to raise David as Brenda. Money followed the case, which he always referred to as "John/Joan," and repeatedly published articles about its success in which he described "Joan" as a happy, well-adjusted girl who had easily adopted more female roles and characteristics. In 1973, *Time* magazine pointed to Joan saying, "This dramatic case provides strong evidence for a major contention of women's liberationists: that conventional patterns of masculine and feminine behavior can be altered. It casts doubt on the theory that major sexual difference, psychological as well as anatomical, are immutably set by genes at conception" (Colapinto, 1997).

It is unclear if Money failed to notice the truth or deliberately ignored it but Brenda's family tells a very different story. Her brother tells it this way: "I recognized Brenda as my sister but she never, ever acted the part. She'd get a skipping rope for a gift, and the only thing we used it for was to tie people up, whip people with it." He went on to say, "When I say there was nothing feminine about Brenda, I mean there was nothing feminine. She walked like a guy. She talked about guy things, didn't give a crap about cleaning house, getting married, wearing makeup" (Colapinto, 1997). Brenda's mother claims that the very first time she put a dress on her, the little girl tried desperately to pull it off.

Everyone describes a miserable childhood of feeling different and not fitting in anywhere. Brenda realized early on that she was not a girl in many ways starting perhaps with her preference for peeing standing up. When Brenda imagined her future, she pictured herself living as a man married to a woman.

Though she reluctantly began taking hormones as a young teenager and as a result grew breasts, Brenda refused to see Dr. Money any more and began to be treated by doctors and psychologists closer to home. One day when she was 14, she met with a doctor who was trying to convince her to have the surgery that would be needed to finish creating a vagina but Brenda kept refusing. The doctor asked in exasperation "Do you want to be a girl or not?" Brenda answered, loudly, "No." The doctor then told her parents that he thought it was time to tell Brenda the truth.

David remembers hearing the story from his father that afternoon and feeling a number of conflicting emotions, the overwhelming one, however, was relief. He instantly changed his name back to David and began the process of going back to living as a boy. He had his breasts surgically removed and then had a rudimentary penis constructed right before he turned 16. Another operation in his twenties created a better looking and more functional penis.

When the real result of John/Joan's case became public in the mid-1990s, David was 31, married to a woman, and raising the children she had from previous relationships as his own. He said he was happy living as a man but acknowledged that getting there was not easy and that he had even contemplated suicide a number of times. Unfortunately, the happiness did not last; in 2004 David Reimer took his own life (Colapinto, 2004).

Today's Thinking

Based on cases like Cheryl Chase and John/Joan, the prevailing wisdom today suggests that rushing into surgery—which has permanent repercussions—for purely cosmetic reasons is a bad idea. Some conditions do require early surgery for functional reason (such as separating the vagina from the urethra) or safety (such as removing testes located within the abdomen as they can become cancerous. ISNA helped to convene an International Consensus Conference on Intersex. One of the major outcomes of the conference was a consensus document written by the Lawson Wilkins Pediatric Endocrine Society in the United States and the European Society for Pediatric Endocrinology.

The overall advice is to take it slow and not treat the situation as a medical emergency that requires immediate intervention. The consensus statement suggests that health care providers should avoid making any gender assignment before an expert evaluation is conducted and that such an evaluation should be made at a center with an experienced multidisciplinary team (ideally that team would include pediatric endocrinologists, surgeons, urologists, psychologists, gynecologists, geneticists, and neonatologists who have experience with DSD). The team will make a diagnosis based on anatomy, genetics, imaging (such as ultrasound or MRIs), and measurement of various hormone levels.

In a culture that instantly categorizes everyone based solely on appearance and doesn't even have the proper pronouns to talk about someone without referring to gender, the task of raising a child without an identified gender is practically impossible and unadvisable as it can be troubling to the family and the child. Instead, the guidelines suggest that every infant be assigned a gender. This assignment should be made based on the diagnosis, genital appearance, surgical options, need for lifelong replacement therapy (such as estrogen shots), potential for fertility, and the views of the family and culture.

However, the idea is that this gender assignment can change if it turns out to be inconsistent with how the baby feels as he or she grows up. The consensus statement explains that atypical gender behavior is common in those born with DSD and should not be seen as an indicator that the gender was wrongly assigned or should be changed. That said, if affected children or adolescents report "significant gender dysphoria" (a sense that their gender identity does not match the gender they've been assigned), they should be given a comprehensive psychological evaluation and an opportunity to explore gender issues with a qualified professional over time. "If the desire to change genders persists, the patient's wish should be supported and may require the input of a specialist skilled in the management of gender change" (Lee, p. e493).

These new guidelines recognize that the process of developing a gender identity (even for people born with a clear biological sex) is complicated and ever evolving. The approach that they are recommending therefore is one of caution which leaves all irrevocable decisions to be made by the individual when he/she has developed an internal sense of who they are.

These guidelines represent a major step forward in how we think about biologic sex and how we handle differences. Nonetheless, we are still a society that tries to categorize people as male or female and masculine or feminine. While we certainly tolerate more variations in gender roles and expressions than we once did, we still hold onto many stereotypes about how an individual should look and behave. As we see later in the book when we explore gender roles, gender identity, and transgender issues more closely, we still have a lot of work to do in dispelling myths about what makes someone a man or a woman. This much is clear—it is more than just what is between someone's legs.

References

Blonna, R. and Levitan, J. (2005). *Healthy Sexuality*. Thomson Wadsworth, New York.

Colapinto, J. (1997). The true story of John/Joan. *Rolling Stone* (December 11), pp. 54–97.

Colapinto, J. (2004). What were the real reasons behind David Reimer's suicide? *Slate* (June 3). http://www.slate.com/articles/health_and_science/medical_examiner/2004/06/gender_gap.html (accessed July 18 2014).

Fausto-Sterling, A. (2000). The five sexes, revisited. *The Sciences (New York)*, 40(4), 18–25.

Herdt, G. (1990). Mistaken gender: 5-alpha reductase hermaphroditism and biological reductionism in sexual identity reconsidered. *American Anthropologist*, 92(2), 433–446.

Kelly, G.F. (2010). *Sexuality Today*, 10th edn. McGraw Hill, New York.

Lee, P.A., Houk, C.P., Ahmed, S.F., and Hughes, I.A. (2006). Consensus statement on management of intersex disorders. *Pediatrics*, 118(2), e488–e500.

Mader, S. (1992). *Human Reproductive Biology*, 2nd edn. William C. Brown, New York.

2 ORIENTATION AND IDENTITY

Who We Are and Who We Want

You Can Tell If Someone Is Gay Just by Looking at Him/Her

You may have heard the popular term "gaydar." A pithy combination of radar and gay, gaydar refers to someone's ability to distinguish homosexual individuals from heterosexual individuals using indirect cues. Many people truly believe that they can spot a gay person from a mile away, possibly because in the past they have successfully guessed who was gay and who was not. Of course, what they don't know is how many people were gay who they never noticed and how many people they labeled as gay who were not.

We could write an entire separate entry analyzing why people feel the need to decide if a person is gay or straight upon meeting them. It's not necessarily a mean-spirited game—a single straight woman might use her "gaydar" to prevent embarrassing herself by coming on to a handsome man who turns out to be gay, for example. But often the game is played simply because we as a culture love to categorize people based on some outward characteristics or behavior—he's gay, she's fat, he's had plastic surgery. We love to jump to conclusions but the truth is we are often wrong and we can only see what people are showing us.

For this entry, we examined the nature of "gaydar signals"—the cues people are seeing as an indication that another person is gay—as well as the accuracy of gaydar and the implications it has for how we relate to others. Before we continue, however, we thought it important to remind you of one key point—sexual orientation, gender identity, and gender expression are not the same. Sexual orientation—whether someone is gay, straight, or bisexual—refers to who they are attracted to and fall in love with. Gender identity is a person's internal sense of being male or female. And, gender expression is

50 Great Myths of Human Sexuality, First Edition. Pepper Schwartz and Martha Kempner.
© 2015 John Wiley & Sons, Inc. Published 2015 by John Wiley & Sons, Inc.

how a person chooses to show this identity to the world through his or her appearance and behavior. We note this here because the research suggests that the cues used to identify someone as gay often more accurately reflect his/her gender identity or expression than sexual orientation. (We talk more about these issues in Myths # 8 and 9.)

My Gaydar Is Stronger Than Yours

To believe that you can tell whether a man or women is gay (though gaydar is most often used in discussing gay men, people do think they can spot a lesbian as well), you have to believe that there are distinctive aspects to the appearance or behavior of gays and lesbians that gives them away. Some researchers have tried to pinpoint exactly which traits are most commonly perceived as "gay." Most research seems to suggest that not conforming to typical gender roles is the basis for the majority of initial judgments. And, to some extent this does work. One research team carried out two studies that asked people to judge sexual orientation from pictures, short videos, and sound recordings. Sexual orientation assessment had high, but imperfect, outcomes (Rieger *et al.*, 2010, p. 124). Interestingly, two studies have found that observers were best able to determine sexual orientation by looking at video clips or computerized images that only showed body shape and movement (Ambady *et al.*, 1999). Freeman *et al.* (2010) found that the masculinity and femininity of facial features are also common cues that perceivers use to infer sexual orientation.

One common mistake respondents in studies made when asked to guess sexual orientation was to only label those people with gender-atypical facial or other mannerisms as gay or lesbian, which meant they missed all of the homosexual people who did not display these traits. Of course, the opposite was also true, heterosexuals whose gender behaviors were atypical were invariably classified as gay (Freeman *et al.*, 2010, p. 1327–1328).

And, lest we think that gays and lesbians are immune to these mistakes, studies have shown that they only have a modest advantage when it comes to their gaydar (Berger *et al.*, 1987; Ambady *et al.*, 1999). A study of speech patterns found that fellow homosexuals were slightly better at judging sexual orientation for gay men but this advantage did not extend to identifying lesbians (D. Sylva, L. Sell, and J.M. Bailey, 2007, unpublished data). Other studies have found no major difference between heterosexual and homosexual respondents (Rieger *et al.*, 2010, pp. 125–126).

The real problem is that gaydar is merely picking up signals of attributes linked to masculinity and femininity but there's an "imperfect" linkage of these attributes and sexual orientation (Rieger *et al.*, 2010, p. 136). And this linkage is different in different cultures because what is considered "masculine" or "feminine" varies widely (Ross, 1983). Some researchers have suggested that sexual orientation is able to be perceived across many different cultures, at least in so far as men display behaviors, speech, or mannerisms that do not fulfill normative expectations of masculinity (Rule *et al.*, 2011, p. 1500). In a survey study, however, Ross (1983) suggested that cultures less accepting of homosexuality may be less tolerant of gender-variant behavior. This could mean a heightened sensitivity in labeling people who don't conform as gay or lesbian. This idea was confirmed in a study that found Americans were more vigilant about cues than Japanese or Spanish "raters." This may indicate that Americans think more about the topic, or that American gay men are more likely to display behaviors that identity themselves to other gay men or are more at ease displaying counter-normative behaviors than men in more restrictive and homophobic cultures. It may also mean that Japan or Spain allows a much wider group of behaviors to be perceived as within average masculinity than America does (Rule *et al.*, 2009).

There may also be very specific cultural variations in the perception of traits. For example, some research indicates that Americans are much more likely than people from Japan to believe that individuals have fixed and stable traits, as opposed to situational ones, and therefore are more likely to make sweeping judgments about someone based on things like mannerisms and speech patterns (e.g., Dweck and Leggett, 1988; Choi *et al.*,1999).

The fact that gaydar can be true some of the time but not all of the time has implications for how people are treated. As Ambady *et al.* (2000) pointed out in their review of evaluations of thin slices of behavior, initial impressions can influence subsequent actions. People frequently assume sexual orientation on the basis of norms of masculinity and femininity and, depending on their personal values about sexual orientation, may act more or less positively to that person.

Researchers have also questioned whether gaydar is more in the eyes of the beholder than in whomever those eyes happen to see. Are people extra-vigilant and judgmental when they are uncomfortable with homosexuality and/ or any gender-variant behavior? There seems to be some evidence for this. One study found, for example, that conservatives were much more likely to note differences in gay men than liberals, and were more likely to assume that someone they saw as less masculine was gay (Stern *et al.*, 2013, p. 521).

An Imperfect Measure

In the end we are left with the idea gaydar works sometimes but not all the time, because it is almost entirely based on identifying "feminine" or "masculine" characteristics. The problem with this method is that an individual's sexual orientation is not tied to his/her own gender but to the gender of the people to whom he/she is attracted. So while not conforming to society's expectations for how a man or a woman should dress, act, or talk is often perceived as a statement of sexual orientation, it more accurately reflects a person's gender identity.

Don't get us wrong, there are certainly some gay men and lesbians who you can spot a mile away because they conform to all of the stereotypes that society has set for them. For many, this is an important part of their identity and a way to show the world who they are. The next time you want to test your gaydar, however, just remember that there are as many if not more gay men and lesbians who exhibit no "tell-tale" traits and there are plenty of heterosexual men and women who don't conform to our definition of masculine or feminine. The ultimate answer may be that you can tell someone is gay just by looking at them when, and only when, he/she wants you to.

References

Ambady, N., Bernieri, F.J., and Richeson, J.A. (2000). Toward a histology of social behavior: Judgmental accuracy from thin slices of the behavioral stream. *Advances in Experimental Social Psychology*, 32, 201–271.

Ambady, N., Hallahan, M., and Conner, B. (1999). Accuracy of judgments of sexual orientation from thin slices of behavior. *Journal of Personality and Social Psychology*, 77, 538–547.

Berger, G., Hank, L., Rauzi, T., and Simkins, L. (1987). Detection of sexual orientation by heterosexuals and homosexuals. *Journal of Homosexuality*, 13, 83–100.

Choi, I., Nisbett, R.E., and Norenzayan, A. (1999). Causal attribution across cultures: Variation and universality. *Psychological Bulletin*, 125, 47–63.

Dweck, C.S. and Leggett, E.L. (1988). A social-cognitive approach to motivation and personality. *Psychological Review*, 95, 256–273.

Freeman, J.B., Johnson, K.L., Ambady, N., and Rule, N.O. (2010). Sexual orientation perception involves gendered facial cues. *Personality and Social Psychology Bulletin*, 36, 1318–1331.

Rieger, G., Linsenmeier, J.A.W., Gygax, L., Garcia, S., and Bailey, J.M. (2010). Dissecting "gaydar": Accuracy and the role of masculinity–femininity. *Archives of Sexual Behavior*, 39, 124–140.

Ross, M.W. (1983). Femininity, masculinity, and sexual orientation: Some cross-cultural comparisons. *Journal of Homosexuality*, 9, 27–36.

Rule, N.O., Ambady, N., and Hallett, K.C. (2009). Female sexual orientation is perceived accurately, rapidly, and automatically from the face and its features. *Journal of Experimental Social Psychology*, 45, 1245–1251.

Rule, N.O., Ishii, K., Ambady, N., Rosen, K., and Hallett, K. (2011). Found in translation: Cross-cultural consensus in the accurate categorization of male sexual orientation. *Personality and Social Psychology Bulletin*, 37(11), 1499–1507.

Stern, C., West, T.V., Jost, J.T., and Rule, N.O., Annual meeting of the International Society of Political Psychology (2013). The politics of gaydar: Ideological differences in the use of gendered cues in categorizing sexual orientation. *Journal of Personality and Social Psychology*, 104(3), 520–541.

Myth #8   No One Is Really Bisexual

Poor bisexuals! No one wants to believe in them (Mayfield and Carrubba, 1996; Eliason, 1997). Men who say they are bisexual are written off by both gay and straight male peers. Gay men are prone to saying that these are just men who are too scared to come out (Blumstein and Schwartz, 1977, p. 30; Rust, 1995; Udis-Kessler, 1996). Heterosexuals have their own version of disbelief. Perhaps fueled by homophobia, heterosexuals will generally code a man who has had even one same-sex experience as gay regardless what that man calls himself (Mohr and Rochlen, 1999, p. 353).

People don't believe women who claim to be bisexual either but for different reasons. Some believe they just haven't come out yet while others dismiss same-sex relationships as a phase or experimentation (gay until graduation). This plays into beliefs and stereotypes we have about female sexuality which say that women who make love to other women (whether in porn or in real life) are hot and view "girl on girl" sex as primarily performed to feed male fantasies rather than as displaying the women's real preference. In fact, even lesbianism is often considered part of female sexual flexibility and written off as a phase (unless and until it lasts a lifetime). In cases where a woman has previously been heterosexual and then enters into a same-sex relationship, the presumption is that she will someday "change back" to being heterosexual (Hutchins, 1996; Ochs, 1996).

Sexual behavior and sexual orientation or identity are different. There are men who identify as gay but sometimes sleep with women, women who are straight but sometimes sleep with women, and every other permutation you can imagine. And then there are bisexuals—men and women who are attracted to, have sex with, and may fall in love with a person of the same gender or one of the opposite but whose identity remains the same regardless of who they are with at the time.

The Search for the "True" Bisexual

As with much of sex research, we can start with Kinsey. In his pathbreaking book, Kinsey unequivocally stated that sexual attraction and behavior was on a continuum rather than locked into dichotomous categories (Kinsey *et al.*, 1948). He found that "37 percent of the total male population had had at least some overt homosexual experience to the point of orgasm between adolescence and old age." Additional research by Kinsey and his team found that somewhere between 8 and 20% of females (depending on marital status) had experienced some kind of homosexual contact between the ages of 20 and 35 (Kinsey *et al.*, 1953). Yet when asked how they identified only 4% of the males and 1–3% of the females considered themselves homosexual from the beginning of their adolescence. The Kinsey data made it clear that bisexual behavior and fantasy is not at all uncommon yet some people still question bisexuality as an identity (Blumstein and Schwartz, 1977, p. 31–32).

More recent surveys have suggested that bisexual identification may be more common than we thought. The 2010 National Survey of Family Growth found that 7–8% of the population identified as lesbian, gay, or bisexual but same-sex experiences were far more common (2010). The Pew Research Center (2013) surveyed 1174 adults who identified as LGBT. Of them, 40% identified as bisexual compared to 36% who said they were gay, 16% who said they identified as lesbian, and 5% who said they were trans. There were more women who identified as bisexual than men, which is often the case.

Despite the numbers of people who say they are bisexual, skepticism that this is a "real" identity and not just indecision, runs rampant. In attempts to prove scientifically that some people are (or are not) bisexual, researchers have carried out lab experiments in which they measure arousal to same-sex and opposite-sex images. A study found that regardless of whether they identified as straight or lesbian, most women were genitally aroused by both male and female pornography. They used these data to confirm the idea that women are more bisexually orientated and have more fluid sexuality (Chivers *et al.*, 2004). The team's follow-up study made waves when it concluded that bisexual men responded in the same way as homosexual men when measuring genital arousal (Rieger *et al.*, 2005). This research gave credence to the stereotype of bisexual men as just gay men who were afraid to come out. For example, a *New York Times* headline at the time read "Straight, gay, or lying? Bisexuality revisited" (Carey, 2005).

At the urging of some bisexual advocates, however, some of the same authors agreed to rerun the study and to use different recruiting methods. Instead of advertising in gay magazines and letting men contact them, this team specifically contacted men who placed ads online looking for a sexual experience with both members of an opposite-gender couple. To be in the study these men had to have had romantic relationships with both men and women in the past. This new study had different findings. The arousal patterns of these men seemed to confirm their self-identity as bisexual (Rosenthal *et al.*, 2011).

Reaching an Identity

There is no one way to be bisexual nor is there one route to identifying as bisexual. There is no "typical" family background, no specific times of the life cycle where the "change" happens, and for that matter no uniform consistency of identity (Blumstein and Schwartz, 1977, p. 37).

There seem to be a number of ways people come to label themselves as bisexual as opposed to just having had sexual experience with both sexes but still preferring to call themselves hetero- or homosexual. The paths to bisexuality include being labeled in adolescence as bisexual or gay, recognizing a continuing attraction for both genders, having fallen in love with individuals of both genders over time (this was particularly true for women), being in a group of peers that supported the idea they were bisexual and encouraged sexual experimentation with three ways, and, finally, having or developing an ideology that supported bisexuality such as a belief that all people are inherently bisexual (Blumstein and Schwartz, 1977, pp. 40–43).

Research shows that men who are predominantly heterosexual are more nervous about same-sex attraction much less same-sex behavior than women who adopt a heterosexual identity. Women often felt that becoming sexual with another woman was an understandable extension of close friendship and female affection (Blumstein and Schwartz, 1976, p. 171). While the experience might have been shocking, they were less likely to use it as a pivotal point of self-identification whereas men, after having one same-sex experience, often felt compelled to redefine who they were (Blumstein and Schwartz, 1977, p. 43). For example, a 10-year study followed 79 women who self-identified as lesbian or bisexual or chose not to label themselves. Over time, two-thirds of the women changed the identities they held at the beginning of the study and one-third changed their identity twice. Interestingly, bisexuality was the identity that was one of most stable over time. The author felt that "the distinction between lesbianism and bisexuality [was] a matter of degree rather than kind." The overall conclusion was that indeed, many women's sexual self-labeling, and behavior, has a great degree of fluidity (Diamond, 2008, p. 5).

Most studies have not found the same degree of fluidity in men although more changes in men's biographies occur than is commonly presupposed (Diamond, 2008, p. 5). A quite large, non-random study found that up to 40% of homosexual men adopted a bisexual identity but eventually labeled themselves as gay (Lever, 1994). Another study saw a similar shift but also noted that a number of the bisexual men became more heterosexual over time (Stokes *et al.*, 1997).

One of the issues is that many people don't come out as bisexual because they fear that neither heterosexuals nor homosexuals will accept them. Robyn Ochs, who travels the country as a bisexual speaker and activist, told the *New York Times* that she was reluctant to come out as bi in college because the lesbian community on her campus would not be supportive:

> They said that bisexuals couldn't be trusted, that they would inevitably leave you for a man. Had I come out as a lesbian I could have be welcomed with open arms, taken to parties, invited to join the softball team. The lesbian red carpet, if you will. But for me to say I was a lesbian would have required that I dismiss all of my previous attractions to men as some sort of false consciousness. So I didn't come out. (Denizet-Lewis, 2014)

This lack of support for bisexuals takes its toll. Research has found that bisexuals report higher rates of depression, anxiety, substance use, victimization by violence, thoughts of suicide, and sexual health concerns (Dodge and Sandfort, 2007).

Redefining Sexual Categories

It has become clear that the same set of behaviors can lead different people to different conclusions about their own sexual orientation. Researchers have begun to discuss how over-simplified our ideas of sexual attraction and identity have been all these years (Diamond, 2005; Savin-Williams, 2001; Weinrich and Klein, 2002; Rust, 1992; Golden, 1996). Even Kinsey and colleagues, in their work over 50 years ago, argued that sexual orientation was not an either/or proposition. Today the Kinsey scale, which rates people on a continuum of 0 (exclusively homosexual) to 6 (exclusively heterosexual) is well known. Using the scale, individuals can score themselves based on behaviors. Other sexologists have added layers to the Kinsey scale over the years to reflect preferences for romance and friendship among others. In addition, some argue that the scale is more accurate if individuals are asked to look at the past, present, and future.

There is also a big generational shift. Young people—those in their teens and twenties—have begun to discuss more personal options and latitude both in terms of what they do sexually and how they define themselves. People are realizing that sexual identity is not just about what you have done or who you have done it with but also your fantasies, your romantic attractions, and your friendship preferences. Some of the terms that younger generations now use include 'bi-curious" or pansexual, or queer, and sometimes polyamorous, indicating a desire to live in romantic and sexual situations with both men and women (Diamond, 2005; Golden, 1996; Thompson and Morgan, 2008, p. 15; Gammon and Isgro, 2006).

We might not even have to say this but, just in case, we believe that bisexuality exists because we know people who identify as bisexual and we believe not only that sexuality identity is and must be a matter of personal choice, but that we all have to respect that choice.

References

Blumstein, P. and Schwartz, P. (1976). Bisexuality in women. *Archives of Sexual Behavior*, 5(2), 171–181.

Blumstein, P. and Schwartz, P. (1977). Bisexuality: Some social psychological issues. *Journal of Social Issues*, 33(2), 30–45.

Carey, B. (2005). Straight, gay or lying: Bisexuality revisited. *New York Times* (July 5).

Chivers, M.L., Rieger, G., Latty, E., and Bailey, J.M. (2004). A sex difference in the specificity of sexual arousal. *Psychological Science*, 15(11), 736–744.

Denizet-Lewis, B. (2014). The scientific quest to prove bisexuality exists. *New York Times* (March 20).

Diamond, L.M. (1993). Homosexuality and bisexuality in different populations. *Archive of Sexual Behavior*, 22(4), 291–310.

Diamond, L.M. (2005). A new view of lesbian subtypes: Stable versus fluid identity trajectories over an 8-year period. *Psychology of Women Quarterly*, 29, 119–128.

Diamond, L.M. (2008). Female bisexuality from adolescence to adulthood: Results from a 10 year longitudinal study. *Developmental Psychology*, 44(1), 5–14.

Dodge, B. and Sandfort, T.G (2007). A review of mental health research on bisexual individuals when compared to homosexual and heterosexual individuals. In Firestein, B.A. (ed.) *Becoming Visible: Counseling Bisexuals Across the Lifespan*. Columbia University Press, New York, pp. 28–51.

Eliason, M.J. (1997). The prevalence and nature of biphobia in heterosexual undergraduate students. *Archives of Sexual Behavior*, 26, 317–326.

Gammon, M. and Isgor, K. (2006). Troubling the canon bisexuality and queer theory. *Journal of Homosexuality*, 52, 159–184.

Golden, C. (1996). What's in a name? Sexual self-identification among women. In Savin-Williams, R.C. and Cohen, K.M. (eds) *The Lives of Lesbians, Gays and Bisexuals: Children to adults*. Harcourt Brace, Fort Worth, TX, pp. 229–249.

Hutchins, L. (1996). Bisexuality: Politics and community. In Firestein B.S. (ed.) *Bisexuality: The Psychology and Politics of an Invisible Minority*. Sage, Thousand Oaks, CA, pp. 420–462.

Kinsey, A.C., Pomeroy, W.B., and Martin, C.E. (1948). *Sexual Behavior in the Human Male*. W.B. Saunders, Philadelphia, PA.

Kinsey, A.C., Pomeroy, W.B., Martin, C.E., and Gebhard, P.H. (eds) (1953). *Sexual Behavior in the Human Female*. Indiana University Press, Bloomington, IN.

Lever, J. (1994). Sexual revelations: The 1994 Advocate survey of sexuality and relationships: The men. *The Advocate*, pp. 18–24.

Mayfield, W.A. and Carrubba, M.D. (1966). Validation of the attitudes toward bisexuality inventory. *Poster presented at the 104th Annual Convention of the American Psychological Association*, Toronto, Canada.

Mohr, J.J. and Rochlen, A.B. (1999). Measuring attitudes regarding bisexuality in lesbian, gay male and heterosexual populations. *Journal of Counseling Psychology*, 46(3), 353–369.

Ochs, R. (1996). Biphobia: It goes more than two ways. In Firestein B.A. (ed.) *Bisexuality: The Psychology and Politics of an Invisible Minority*. Sage, Thousand Oaks, CA, pp. 217–239.

Pew Research Center (2013). A survey of LGBT Americans attitudes, experiences and values in changing times. http://www.pewsocialtrends.org/files/2013/06/SDT_LGBT-Americans_06-2013.pdf (accessed July 19, 2014).

Rieger, G., Chivers M.L., and Bailey J.M. (2005). Sexual arousal patterns of bisexual men. *Psychological Science*, 16(8), 579–584.

Rosenthal, A.M., Sylva, D., Safron, A., and Bailey, J.M. (2011). Sexual arousal patterns of bisexual men revisited. *Biological Psychology*, 88(1), 112–115.

Rust, P. (1992). The politics of sexual identity: sexual attraction and behavior among lesbian and bisexual women. *Social Problems*, 39(4), 366.

Rust, P. (1995). *Bisexuality and the Challenge to Lesbian Politics: Sex, Loyalty and Revolution*. New York University Press, New York.

Savin-Williams, R.C. (2001). A critique of research on sexual-minority youths. *Journal of Adolescence*, 24(1), 5–13.

Savin-Williams, R.C. and Cohen, K.M. (1996). *The Lives of Lesbians, Gays, and Bisexuals: Children to Adults*. Harcourt Brace, TX.

Stokes, J.P, Damon, W., and McKirnan, D.J. (1997). Predictors of movement toward homosexuality: A longitudinal study of bisexual men. *Journal of Sex Research*, 34, 304–312.

Thompson, E.M. and Morgan, E.M. (2008). "Mostly straight" young women: variations in sexual behavior and identity development. *Developmental Psychology*, 44(1), 15–21.

Udis-Kessler, A. (1996). Challenging the stereotypes. In Off Pink Collective (eds) *Bisexual Horizons: Politics. Histories. Lives*, Lawrence and Whishart, London, pp. 45–57.

Weinrich, J.D. and Klein, F. (2002). Bi-gay, bi-straight, and bi-bi: Three bisexual subgroups identified using cluster analysis of the Klein Sexual Orientation Grid. *Journal of Bisexuality*, 2(4), 109–139.

Myth #9 Most Transgender Individuals Get Surgery

Throughout our lives we are constantly asked whether we are male or female. Our parents may have asked that question during a sonogram or in the delivery room (depending on the year we were born). Little kids may ask their parents if they see us walking down the street and they can't make a snap judgment (right or wrong) by themselves based on our hair or clothes or makeup. Every form we ever fill out from entry into kindergarten to college application, from marriage license to driver's license, and at every doctor's office we go to, asks us to check a box: M or F.

For most of us this is an easy question to which no one (ourselves, our parents, our doctors) gives a second thought but for some it can get complicated.

The answer to the question, are you male or female, lies in both our biological sex and our gender identity. Biological sex is relatively simple. It is made up of body parts and chromosomes. Under most circumstances a person who has two X chromosomes will also have ovaries, a uterus, a vulva, a vagina, and breasts and will be biologically female. A person with XY chromosomes will have a penis and testicles and will be biologically male. In some instances, chromosomal anomalies occur and individuals have other combinations such as XO, XXY, or XYY which affect how their internal and external genitalia develop and appear. In other cases, people have normal sex chromosomes but something happens during fetal development that means their internal or external genitalia do not develop along a typical male or female route. All of these issues are referred to as disorders of sex development and individuals born with them may be called intersex. (Myth # 6 discusses these biological issue in more detail.)

Here we focus on the other element of the answer to the ultimate M/F question—our gender identity, which is a person's internal sense of being male or female. For most people this internal feeling matches their biological sex but for some it does not. This entry looks at some basic facts and long-held myths about what it means to be transgender.

Gender Expression

As we just mentioned, gender identity is someone's internal sense of being male, female, or somewhere in between. Gender expression then is how an individual chooses to announce this identity to the world. Society has relatively rigid rules for how males and females *should* be different even as small children. These rules apply to outward appearance, speech patterns, and behaviors. Girls are supposed to dress in pink, be pretty and shy, and play with dolls. Boys should gravitate towards blue, be rough and outgoing, and prefer trucks. We all notice when a young girl dresses in "boy's" clothing and even more so when a young boy wants to dress "like a girl." In fact, gender expression is the one aspect of gender that others can see automatically (biological sex is hidden under clothes and gender identity is a feeling).

Most people conform to expected gender expression often without really thinking about it. The cultural scripts that tell us how to behave are so ingrained in our society that it is often hard to discern what is a conscious decision to do what society says—does the 3-year-old girl want to wear a dress out of some natural drive to seem female, as a result of the images and influences she has been exposed to in her young life, or is it out of a desire to please adults around her who will undoubtedly tell her how pretty she looks? Teich (2013) points out that we really don't let our children choose their gender expression, at least not when they are young. We dress babies, for example, so that the world can know instantly whether these tiny beings with unformed facial features and bald heads are male or female (p. 10).

As people grow, and become more aware of their own internal sense of gender, they may be more likely to choose how they want to express it to the world. Gender nonconformity is a generalized term for people who do not express themselves in the typical way that they "should" based on their biological sex. The man who wears makeup and high heels or the woman who cuts her hair short and wears tailored men's suits are not conforming to society's views of gender. This does not mean, however, that these individuals are transgender. They may be completely comfortable with their biological sex but simply prefer the outward appearance associated with the opposite gender.

It's also worth noting that some people object to our binary system of classifying gender in which people only have two choices—male or female. In general we do not allow for variations that might fall somewhere between the two. Some have argued that gender belongs on a continuum and people should be allowed to fall at any place between the two points. Individuals who feel they do not identify as either male or female sometimes refer to themselves as genderqueer (National Center for Transgender Equality, 2009). (Given the history of the word queer as a derogatory term for gay people, this is not a term we suggest using to describe anyone unless the person has told you that's how they identify themselves. Still, it is good to know.)

Gender Identity Is Not Sexual Orientation

In years past, people would look at a woman who presented a masculine image and say "Oh, well, she's clearly a butch lesbian" or see an effeminate man and assume he was gay. This may be the result of cultural misunderstandings about sexual orientation that led people to believe that because gay men wanted to have sex with men their ultimate goal was to be a woman. As Teich points out, this is a very heteronormative way of looking at the world— a vision in which feminine women marry masculine men and anything other than that is seen as somehow abnormal (Teich, 2013). Fortunately, as a result of the gay rights movement and the work advocates have done, much of society now has a better understanding of sexual orientation.

An individual's sexual orientation is not tied to his/her own gender but to the gender of the people to whom he or she is attracted. Individuals who are attracted to someone of the same sex are considered homosexual, individuals attracted to someone of the opposite sex are heterosexual, and individuals who are attracted to either a same-sex or opposite-sex partner are bisexual. The fact that gender and sexual orientation are different means that a person who was born male but feels female and is attracted to women can identify both as a transwoman and as a lesbian—she is a woman attracted to women. Similarly, the biological female who now lives as a male and is dating a woman would identify as heterosexual (Coleman *et al.*, 1993).

So What Is Transgender?

Transgender is an umbrella term for a person who feels that their gender identity and biological sex do not match. Often when we use this term we are talking about a biological male who has always felt trapped in his body because he feels like a girl or a female who wants to live as a man. These specific examples may also be used as definitions for transsexual, an older term that describes a person who identifies as the opposite gender than the one they were assigned at birth. Though the term is still used, some don't like it because of the emphasis on sex instead of gender (National Center for Gender Equality, 2009).

There are a myriad of other terms that fall under the umbrella of transgender and more accurately describe some people's identity. For example, transman, transgender man, female-to-male, or FTM are all terms used to describe someone who was assigned female at birth but has transitioned to male. Transwomen, transgender woman, male-to-female, or MTF would all describe the opposite case. (Language is continually evolving but for now the term transman or transwoman is preferred.)

Transitioning refers to the time when a person begins living as the gender with which they identify rather than the gender they were assigned at birth. This often includes changing his/her name; telling family, friends, and coworkers; and changing his/her appearance. Though some transmen and transwomen may have always had a gender expression that didn't match their biological sex, during their transition they often take this expression further so that they are not just presenting to the world as feminine, for example, but as a woman (Teich, 2013).

Once a person has transitioned and is living his/her life as the opposite gender to the one assigned at birth, he/she may want to drop all of these labels and just be a man or be a woman. Using male pronouns and referring to a transman in the way you would any other man is part of showing respect.

We also want to mention some terms that sometimes fall under the genre of transgender but may cause confusion. Cross-dressers, for example, are men or women who occasionally dress in the clothing expected of the opposite gender. Cross-dressers generally accept the biological sex they were assigned at birth and have no plans to live as the opposite gender but enjoy dressing that way once in a while. Cross-dressers used to be called transvestites but many think that word is derogatory at this point. Finally, drag queens and drag kings are performers who dress as the opposite gender as part of their act. Again, most do not have any desire to be or live as the opposite gender but do enjoy the performance of it (National Center for Transgender Equality, 2009).

Transition Does Not Always Mean Surgery

One of the things people are most interested in when they learn that someone is transgender is what's going on under his or her clothes. We have a fascination with genitals and a curiosity about all that is different so often we can't help but wonder and even ask. Television host Katie Couric recently raised the ire of the transgender community when she asked transwoman and model Carmen Carrerra whether her "private parts" were different now. Had

Carrerra been born a woman, it is unlikely that Couric would have asked about her vagina on national television. But Couric knew her audience's interest would be piqued and she pressed on, asking the question again, despite her guest's discomfort (Cooper, 2014).

The truth is that when you meet transgender people you don't know what steps they have taken to transform their outward appearance or their genitals. The good news is that today there are options to help change bodies to match how transgender people feel. The bad news is that these options are often prohibitively expensive and not covered by insurance.

Some transgender individuals choose hormone therapy. Those transitioning from male to female have to start by suppressing testosterone because this male hormone is very strong. They can then add estrogen, which is one of the primary sex hormones in women. It is available as a pill or patch. Transwomen on estrogen therapy can expect some breast growth though it may take a few years and will not result in particularly large breasts. Estrogen also helps redistribute fat in a more feminine pattern so that instead of holding it all in the middle like many men do (think beer belly), it will be distributed to the hips, butt, and thighs. Though the hormone does reduce the production of body hair, it often doesn't stop the growth of facial hair. Transwomen may have to use other means such as laser hair removal to get rid of their beards. Estrogen also does not change a woman's voice—once someone has gone through puberty as a male, the deeper voice is there to stay. Transwomen may choose to work with a voice coach to train themselves to speak in a higher pitch with a more feminine cadence (Teich, 2013).

Transwomen may also find that estrogen lowers their libidos. Moreover, transwomen who use hormone therapy but choose not to change their genitals will find that estrogen lowers the amount of ejaculate during orgasm and may affect sperm production as well.

For transmen, hormone therapy begins with testosterone which can cause many of the same changes that boys see at puberty: their voices will get lower, they will get more body hair, including facial hair, and their body fat will redistribute into a male pattern. (Speaking of male pattern, they may start to notice typical male baldness too.) Testosterone may also enlarge the clitoris and increase libido. And, notably, it will stop menstruation. Hormone therapy, however, does not typically decrease breast size.

Many transmen and transwomen stop medical interventions at hormone therapy either because they feel this is sufficient for their transition or because they do not want or cannot afford surgery. Those who do choose surgery have a number of options. What was once called a "sex change" operation is now better known as gender reassignment surgery though some prefer the term gender affirming surgery because the purpose isn't to change a person's *gender* but to change his/her body to match it. Whatever you call it, it usually involves more than one surgery and transmen and transwomen can choose which and how many they want.

For transwomen, the surgeries could include breast augmentation to make the breasts larger, facial feminization surgery to make the face appear more feminine, and a trachea shave to make the Adam's apple less prominent. Transwomen who choose to have genital surgery may have a vaginoplasty which creates a vagina by turning the penis inside out. In some procedures, surgeons use the glans (the head of the penis) to create a clitoris which can be successful because this is the most sensitive part of the penis. This is accompanied by an orchiectomy, the removal of the testicles. The scrotal sac is then used to make the labia majora (Teich, 2013).

Transmen have a harder time with genital surgery because while surgeons have become very good at making vaginas out of penises, the reverse is much more difficult. Gender reassignment surgery for transmen often starts with removal of the breasts in a mastectomy. This is sometimes referred to as top surgery and may be the only surgery a transman chooses. Others may also choose to have their internal reproductive organs—the uterus, ovaries, and fallopian tubes—removed (Monstrey *et al.*, 2011).

For those who want to alter their genitals surgically to be more masculine, the first option is a metoidioplasty and is for transmen who have taken testosterone and seen enlargement of their clitoris. If the clitoris is large enough, the surgeon can free it from the clitoral hood and reroute the urethra through it so it resembles a small penis. The surgeon can then close the vagina, make a scrotal sac out of existing tissues, and put testicle implants in the sac (Teich, 2013).

The other option is a phalloplasty in which the surgeon creates a penis out of skin and tissue from elsewhere in the body, lengthens the urethra, attaches the nerves, and then attaches the new penis in its proper place. Though ideally this is done in one surgery, for many transmen it takes a few surgeries and there is a risk of scarring and loss of sensation. Once sensation has returned to the tip of the penis, which usually takes about a year, the surgeon can implant a penile prosthetic, which can help the man become erect, as well as prosthetic testicles (Monstrey *et al.*, 2011).

Make Room for Variation

We can't say for sure what percentage of transpeople have surgery because no statistics exist on how many transpeople there are in the population let alone the choices they make. The truth is that unless you are the loved one, close friend, or partner of a transman or transwoman it shouldn't really matter what they choose to do. Everyone is entitled to determine their own gender expression and gender identity and, if this does not match their biological sex, they are entitled to make whatever changes they feel necessary to their appearance, behavior, life, and body. Those around them can seek to know what they have gone through (as long as it comes from a place of empathy and understanding and not just curiosity and voyeurism) but the most important thing is that we respect their choice.

Transgender individuals face huge obstacles in all aspects of their lives when transitioning—social (family and friends who refuse to accept the change), legal (trying to change birth certificates or driver's licenses can seem impossible in some places), medical (hormones can have side effects and surgeries can be painful), and financial (insurance does not cover many of the medical expenses and some face discrimination on the job and even job loss). Moreover, transgender individuals also face increased discrimination and violence (Grant *et al.*, 2011).

We need to work together to ensure that all people regardless of gender can live free of discrimination and violence. We think that one place to start actually involves stopping—we have to curb our instinct to categorize people and expect or demand that they fit neatly into our categories. We have to let people choose their own categories, make their own labels, and even decide to have none at all. And we have to stop focusing on (and wondering about) what's in between somebody's legs. It's not really any of our business and most of the time (unless we are planning on getting intimate), it really doesn't matter.

References

Coleman, E., Bockting, W.O., and Gooren, L. (1993). Homosexual and bisexual identity in sex-reassigned female-to-male transsexuals. *Archives of Sexual Behavior*, 22(1), 37–50.

Cooper, T. (2014). What not to say to a transgender person. *CNN*. http://www.cnn.com/2014/01/15/living/transgender-identity/ (accessed July 19, 2014).

Grant, J.M., Mottet, L.A., and Tanis, J.T. (2011). *Injustice at Every Turn: Report of the National Transgender Discrimination Survey*. National Center for Transgender Equality and National Gay and Lesbian Task Force, Washington DC. http://www.endtransdiscrimination.org/PDFs/NTDS_Report.pdf (accessed July 19, 2014).

Monstrey, S.J., Ceulemans, P., and Hoebeke, P. (2011). Sex reassignment surgery in the female-to-male transsexual. In: *Seminars in Plastic Surgery*, vol. 25, no. 3. Thieme Medical Publishers, p. 229.

National Center for Transgender Equality (2009). Understanding transgender: Frequently asked questions about transgender people. http://transequality.org/Resources/NCTE_UnderstandingTrans.pdf (accessed July 19, 2014).

Teich, N.M. (2013). *Transgender 101: A Simple Guide to a Complex Issue*. Columbia University Press, New York.

Myth #10 Homosexuality Can Be Cured

In 2005, a 16-year-old named Zack Stark used his Myspace page (remember Myspace?) to tell the world about his experience at Refuge, a fundamentalist Christian camp which "exists to be a Christ-centered ministry for the prevention or remediation of unhealthy and destructive behaviors facing families, adults, and adolescents." Stark's parents had sent him to Refuge in the hope of changing his sexual orientation from gay to straight. The program was described as lasting 2–6 weeks. During the day, participants attended sessions in a "park-like setting." At night, they were sent to a hotel with a legal guardian. In an email to his parents, the leaders of the program described details including "solitary confinement, isolation, and extreme restrictions of attire, correspondence, and privacy sanctioned by biblical quotations." Using the newly evolving social media to tell his story to the world, Stark wrote: "Even if I do come out straight, I'll be so mentally unstable and depressed it won't matter" (SIECUS, 2005).

Stark's experience is unfortunately not that unusual. Throughout the 1980s and 1990s, in response to the growing acceptance of gays and lesbians, there was a movement that clung to the idea that homosexuality was an illness and promised to cure it. Called reparative therapy or conversion therapy, it often employs extreme methods (such as administering electric shocks if patients show signs of arousal when viewing same-sex images). Supporters of reparative therapy sometimes call their patients "ex-gays" and claim that these men (and women, though mostly men) are now happily living as heterosexuals. Former ex-gays, however, tell a different story.

In fact, in recent years many of those who started and supported the movement have announced their opposition to it, saying it does more harm than good. Major medical and mental health associations agree and suggest that this approach is potentially dangerous.

What we have to remember, however, when reading about reparative therapy and efforts to "cure" same-sex attraction, is that until 1973 even mainstream medical organizations considered homosexuality as a mental disorder.

Starting With Freud

Sigmund Freud, an Austrian neurologist in the 1900s, is largely considered to be the father of modern psychology. He pioneered the practice of psychoanalysis and presented numerous theories about how the mind and psyche develop including a number of theories about sexuality. Though he never focused too heavily on homosexuality, Freud seemed to be tolerant for his time. In the 1930s he signed a statement calling for the decriminalization of homosexual acts in Germany and Austria. He believed that everyone had some homosexual component within them but that "normal" people were able to sublimate it. He saw homosexuality as the "unconflicted expression of an infantile sexual wish" (Drescher, 1998, p. 9). He did not believe that curing homosexuality was truly possible and his one attempt to do so within his own practice failed completely. In the case of a young woman who had fallen in love with an older woman, he writes:

> In general to undertake to convert a fully developed homosexual into a heterosexual does not offer much prospect of success than the reverse, except for good practical reason the latter is never attempted. (Freud, 1920, p. 150, as cited in Drescher, 1998, p. 10)

Those who followed Freud through the 1940s, 1950s, and 1960s continued to believe that homosexuality was a problem of the psyche and many began to search both for the cause, and unlike Freud, the cure. Bieber and his colleagues believed that parents were to blame. Socarides wrote in 1968 that, "The family of the homosexual is usually a female-dominated environment wherein the father was absent, weak, detached, or sadistic (Socarides, 1968, p. 38, as cited in Drescher, 1998, p. 14). (Ironically, Socarides' own son came out as gay in the 1990s; Drescher, 1998, p. 14). Others at the time believed that homosexuality was caused by a phobia of taking on the expected gender role. They suggested that behavioral therapy used to cure other phobias could be adapted to cure homosexuality. Ovesey believed that the cure for homosexuality was quite simply heterosexual intercourse. He acknowledged that most patients would be resistant to the idea but that it was the therapist's role to push him gradually through dating women and then "necking," "petting," and eventually going further. If the patient continued to resist, however, the therapist might have to give him an ultimatum by threatening to terminate treatment (Dresher, 1998, p. 15).

Others who were devoted to sexual orientation change efforts (SOCE), as they are sometimes called in the professional literature, used aversion treatments "such as inducing nausea, vomiting, or paralysis; providing electric shocks, or having the individual snap an elastic band around the wrist when the individual became aroused to same-sex erotic images or thoughts" (American Psychological Association, 2009, p. 22).

A Change in Thinking

While these practitioners were trying to alter the behavior (and some would say the very essence) of their patients, others were beginning to question whether homosexuality was really an illness in the first place. In 1957, psychologist Evelyn Hooker studied a nonclinical sample of homosexual men and compared them with matched heterosexual men. She found no difference in how well-adjusted they were. Up until that point much of the research had been carried out on people who presented to psychologists and psychiatrists asking for or needing help. Similar research a year later found similar results among homosexual women. Over the next decade, research into sexual orientation proliferated and continually found few differences between homosexuals and heterosexuals. Moreover, research failed to support the theories that family dynamic, problems with gender identity, or early trauma caused homosexuality (American Psychological Association, 2009, pp. 30–31).

This was also when the gay rights movement was gaining momentum and activists began arguing that it was time for the American Psychiatric Association to remove homosexuality from its official list of mental disorders known as the DSM (Diagnostic and Statistical Manual of Mental Disorders). In the early 1970s, some of these activists heckled a talk being given by Dr. Robert Spitzer, a psychiatrist and professor at Columbia University. Spitzer, who describes himself as always being drawn to conflict, sat down with the hecklers to hear why they believed homosexuality should not be considered an illness. He was intrigued by their arguments. He was also a junior member of a committee that was in the process of rewriting the DSM. He organized a symposium on the issue and entered into heated debates with some colleagues (including Socarides) who remained committed to seeing homosexuality as a mental disorder. In the end, the committee and the American Psychiatric Association sided with Spitzer and voted to drop homosexuality as a disorder and replace it with "sexual orientation disturbance," a diagnosis designed to identify people whose sexual orientation, gay or straight, caused them distress (Carey, 2012).

The Rise of Religious Reparative Therapy

Some psychiatrists and psychoanalysts, chief among them Socarides, remained firmly opposed to this decision. They continued to argue that homosexuality needed to be cured and as the mainstream professional organizations began to see it differently, they set out to create a new organization. Socarides, together with Joe Nicolosi, a leader in the reparative therapy movement, and others formed NARTH (National Association for Research and Therapy of Homosexuality). NARTH was founded on the "assumption that obligatory homosexuality is a treatable disorder." The goal of the organization was to study homosexuality but it was not open to the suggestion that its founding doctrine was flawed: "NARTH officers may opt to deny or remove membership when an individual's written statements or public speeches show clear antipathy to this position" (Drescher, 1998, p. 20).

NARTH was not the only organization that promoted reparative therapy but the others came mostly from a religious rather than a scientific background. In 1976, Exodus International formed as an umbrella organization for religious ministries that were practicing reparative therapy. The mission of Exodus, at one point boasting 260 ministries around the world, was to "[mobilize] the body of Christ to minister grace and truth to a world impacted by homosexuality." The organization described itself as "the leading global outreach to churches, individuals and families offering a biblical message about same-sex attraction" (Exodus International).

Exodus and other ex-gay ministries became quite vocal in the 1990s. In 1998, Exodus was one of 15 prominent conservative groups that paid for a million-dollar ad campaign telling people they could "pray away the gay" (Bessen, 2010). One ad starred the future president of Exodus, Alan Chambers, a self-proclaimed ex-gay, and his wife. That same year, Focus on the Family began its traveling road show "Love Won Out," which was designed "to educate and equip Christians on how to respond to the issue of homosexuality in a biblical way" (Truth Wins Out). The event catered to parents and young people, and explained that homosexuality is the result of bad parenting but that it can be overcome. The website Truth Wins Out, however, says that attendees are treated to information designed to paint homosexuality in the worst light possible. It quotes one of the event's speakers as saying: "I'm telling you homosexuality, homosexual impulse, is always prompted by an inner sense of emptiness. It's not about sex" (Truth Wins Out).

Proponents argued that many individuals, especially those whose religion disapproved of homosexuality, were deeply conflicted and that they were offering these people (mostly men) a lifeline. Jeffrey Ford, a psychologist who both underwent and provided reparative therapy before breaking with the movement, likens it to a strict religious cult: "The followers are sincere and devout; they believe what they are saying with their heart, mind, and soul" (Ford, 2002, p. 72). He explains that, in the beginning, finding the ex-gay ministry gave him hope and a forum for acknowledging what he had been going through all his life: "To move from feeling isolated and alone into a community where others have shared similar life experiences is overwhelming. It's right up there with falling in love or tasting chocolate for the first time" (Ford, 2002, p. 71).

But the honeymoon eventually wore off. Ford was subjected to aversive shock therapy that left him with burns on his forearm the size of quarters. He was also encouraged to imagine a very stimulating same-sex encounter and then, when he became aroused, was guided into a scenario that was frightening or repulsive, such as having the person he imagined himself with vomit all over him. Looking back, he writes: "The process, in my opinion, was barbaric and abusive. I felt ashamed and embarrassed waiting in the outer office with patients of other therapists. I would try to hide my arm or wear long-sleeved shirts so others wouldn't see the burn marks as I left" (Ford, 2002, p. 78). Worse yet, it didn't work, as the homosexual feelings and fantasies kept coming back. In fact, during his work in an ex-gay ministry, Ford fell in love with a man and had his first homosexual experiences. This kind of sexual "acting out" was apparently not uncommon within the movement (Ford, 2002, p. 82).

Despite this, people within the movement, like Socarides and Nicolosi, continued to publish articles and books exalting the success of efforts to change sexual orientation but as insiders they lacked credibility within the scientific and medical community. In a recent *New York Times* article, Drescher described the movement: "People with a shared worldview basically came together and created their own set of experts to offer alternative policy views" (Carey, 2012). In fact, in many ways the ex-gay movement became synonymous with efforts to deny gays and lesbian their civil rights, especially the right to marry.

Then the movement found some scientific legitimacy from the most unlikely source. Dr. Robert Spitzer, the psychiatrist who argued vehemently for the changes to the DSM in 1973, decided he was curious about whether reparative therapy really could work. To study the issue, he recruited 200 men and women who were set to receive reparative therapy at centers across the country including those run by Exodus and NARTH. In in-depth telephone interviews he asked them about their sexual urges and feelings before and after therapy and rated their answers. He then compared the scores. In a paper which was released at a meeting in 2001 before being published without peer review in the *Archives of Sexual Behavior*, he concluded that most of the participants had successfully changed their sexual orientation (Carey, 2012).

Those involved in the reparative therapy movement hailed this as a major victory and seized on Spitzer's reputation and career history as proof that he wasn't biased. They used this study to argue for everything from removing Gay Straight Alliances from schools to banning gay marriage and civil unions. Many of Spitzer's colleagues, on the other hand, jumped on this study as bad science, noting that it didn't test any particular method of conversion therapy (some of the participants weren't even in therapy but had simply done independent bible study) and that it relied on self-reported feelings. They argued that the participants may have been lying not just to Spitzer but to themselves.

A Movement Begins to Crumble

Even as supporters of reparative therapy were reveling in their new found legitimacy, the movement itself was besieged by a series of scandals. In 2000, John Paulk, a Focus on the Family employee and board member of Exodus North America, was placed on probation by Exodus after being photographed in a well-known gay bar in Washington, DC (Evangelical Press, 2000). In 2003, an actor whose photographs were used in the "pray away the gay" ads because he claimed to have been cured of homosexuality was found to be meeting men on the internet (Bessen, 2010).

Then, in 2006, Michael Bussee apologized for his role in the ex-gay movement saying "to those I may have harmed by my involvement in EXODUS, I am truly sorry." Bussee had helped found Exodus International in the early 1970s. Despite his commitment to reparative therapy, however, he fell in love with Gary Cooper, another anti-gay counselor, whom he met while traveling the country for the ministry. The men later left the agency and their wives and married each other in 1982. In his public apology he describes growing up hating his gay feelings and beginning a search for his own cure as young as 12. His search took him to the church where he was told "If I had enough faith, I would eventually be 'set free.' I wanted it more than anything and sincerely believed it would come true" (Bussee, undated).

He explained that he and a friend founded the first ex-gay ministry, EXIT, to help other people in their positions because they wanted more than anything for faith to cure them. Eventually though he realized that: "Not one of the hundreds of people we counseled became straight. Instead, many of our clients began to fall apart—sinking deeper into patterns of guilt, anxiety, and self-loathing." Bussee now describes himself as an "evangelical Christian and a proud gay man" (Bussee, undated).

Other ex-gays also came forward saying that their sexual orientation had not been changed despite years of reparative therapy. John Smid, the former director of Exodus affiliate Love in Action, told MSNBC host Chris Matthews that he is gay and that it is actually impossible to change one's sexual orientation (*Huffington Post*, 2011). And others got caught. In 2010, the national media seized on the story of George Rekers, an anti-gay "expert" who co-founded the conservative political group, the Family Research Council, and was frequently called to testify on why same-sex couples should not be allowed to adopt children. Rekers was found on vacation with a male escort he had hired on RentBoy.com. Rekers rather lamely claimed that he had hired the young man to lift his heavy luggage. In a later statement, Rekers tried to explain further: "I deliberately spend time with sinners with the loving goal to try to help them" (*Huffington Post*, 2010).

The Science

Still, the biggest blow to the ex-gay movement may have come in the form of science. In 2009, a special committee of the American Psychological Association released a report finding that there was no evidence that sexual orientation can be changed through therapy. The committee looked at 83 peer-reviewed studies conducted between 1960 and 2007 and found that most had serious methodological problems and none were based on "credible scientific theory as these ideas have been directly discredited through evidence or rendered obsolete" (American Psychological Association, 2009, p. 82). As for the type of therapy practiced by Exodus International and similar groups, the task force concluded that it is grounded in religious beliefs that see homosexuality as sinful and as such are "not based on theories that can be scientifically evaluated" (American Psychological Association, 2009, p. 92). Though some research subjects appeared to have learned how to ignore or not act on their homosexual feelings it was unclear how long these behavior changes lasted. Moreover, the task force concluded that this did not amount to changing actual sexual orientation: "The results of scientifically valid research indicate that it is unlikely that individuals will be able to reduce same-sex sexual attractions or increase other-sex attractions through SOCE" (American Psychological Association, 2009, p. 92).

Even more damning, the report concluded that SOCE was potentially harmful. The task force said it had concerns about the safety of SOCE and the unintended harms noted by some participants including "loss of sexual feeling, depression, suicidality, and anxiety" (American Psychological Association, 2009, p. 83).

The task force was even more forceful when it came to inpatient treatment of adolescents such as the program that Zack Stark was forced to attend. It wrote: "We found that serious questions are raised by involuntary and coercive interventions and residential centers for adolescents due to their advocacy of treatments that have no scientific basis and potential for harm due to coercion, stigmatization, inappropriateness of treatment level and type, and restriction of liberty" (American Psychological Association, 2009, p. 86).

The American Psychological Association is not the only organization to condemn the practice of reparative therapy. The Pan-American Health

Organization said in a statement released in 2012: "Services that purport to 'cure' people with non-heterosexual sexual orientation lack medical justification and represent a serious threat to the health and well-being of affected people." It went on to say "'Conversion' or 'reparative' therapies and the clinics offering them should be denounced and subject to adequate sanctions" (Pan-American Health Organization, 2012).

The American Medical Association "opposes the use of 'reparative' or 'conversion' therapy that is based upon the assumption that homosexuality per se is a mental disorder or based upon the a priori assumption that the patient should change his/her homosexual orientation" (American Medical Association, undated).

The American Psychiatric Association says "Psychotherapeutic modalities to convert or 'repair' homosexuality are based on developmental theories whose scientific validity is questionable. Furthermore, anecdotal reports of 'cures' are counterbalanced by anecdotal claims of psychological harm. In the last four decades, 'reparative' therapists have not produced any rigorous scientific research to substantiate their claims of cure. Until there is such research available, [the American Psychiatric Association] recommends that ethical practitioners refrain from attempts to change individuals' sexual orientation, keeping in mind the medical dictum to first, do no harm" (American Psychiatric Association, 2000).

The American Academy of Pediatrics, notes: "Therapy directed specifically at changing sexual orientation is contraindicated, since it can provoke guilt and anxiety while having little or no potential for achieving changes in orientation" (Frankowski and Committee on Adolescence, 2004).

The Future of Reparative Therapy

In May of 2012, Robert Spitzer apologized to the gay community for his role in endorsing reparative therapy and the ex-gay movement. He admitted that he agreed with his critics—the study he had published on the success of reparative therapy was flawed. As he told the *New York Times*, "The simple fact is that there was no way to determine if the subject's accounts of change were valid." He went on to apologize:

> I believe I owe the gay community an apology for my study making unproven claims of the efficacy of reparative therapy. I also apologize to any gay person who wasted time and energy undergoing some form of reparative therapy because they believed that I had proven that reparative therapy works with some "highly motivated" individuals. (Carey, 2012)

Even more shocking than this better-late-than-never apology was the announcement that came from Alan Chambers, the president of Exodus International, just a few months later. At the organization's annual meeting, Chambers explained that there is no cure for homosexuality and that reparative therapy offered false hopes and could even be harmful. The group, he said, would no longer practice it. In the media blitz that followed, Chambers told the *Associated Press*:

> I do not believe that cure is a word that is applicable to really any struggle, homosexuality included. For someone to put out a shingle and say, "I can cure homosexuality"—that to me is as bizarre as someone saying they can cure any other common temptation or struggle that anyone faces on Planet Earth. (Condon, 2012)

To the *New York Times* he said that virtually every "ex-gay" he has ever met still harbors homosexual cravings, himself included. He went on to say that gay Christians like himself face a lifelong spiritual struggle to avoid sin and should not be afraid to admit it (Eckhols, 2012).

A year later, Chambers made another shocking announcement; Exodus International was closing its doors for good. In a statement Chambers said:

> "Exodus is an institution in the conservative Christian world, but we've ceased to be a living, breathing organism. For quite some time we've been imprisoned in a worldview that's neither honoring toward our fellow human beings, nor biblical. The board voted unanimously to close the agency" (Kempner, 2013).

As the practice continued to fall out of favor, two states, California and New Jersey, passed laws that prohibit reparative therapy for minors. As we write this, the New Jersey law is being challenged in court but other states are nonetheless considering similar laws.

Though there will always be those who believe homosexuality is a sin and seek to change it, and there are still organizations like NARTH that take a hard line, for the most part reparative therapy is looked at as a discriminatory practice that lacks any legitimacy.

References

American Medical Association (AMA) (undated). AMA polices on GLBT issues: H160.991 Health care needs of the homosexual population. http://www.ama-assn.org/ama/pub/about-ama/our-people/member-groups-sections/glbt-advisory-committee/ama-policy-regarding-sexual-orientation.page (accessed July 19, 2014).

American Psychiatric Association (May 2000). Position statement on therapies focused on attempts to change sexual orientation (reparative or conversion therapies). http://web.archive.org/web/20110110120228/http://www.psych.org/Departments/EDU/Library/APAOfficialDocumentsandRelated/PositionStatements/200001.aspx (accessed July 19, 2014).

American Psychological Association (APA) Task Force on Appropriate Therapeutic Responses to Sexual Orientation. (2009). *Report of the Task Force on Appropriate Therapeutic Responses to Sexual Orientation*, American Psychological Association, Washington, DC. http://www.apa.org/pi/lgbt/resources/therapeutic-response.pdf (accessed July 22, 2014).

Bessen, W. (2010). Ex-gay group should repent not revel. *Huffington Post* (June 17). http://www.huffingtonpost.com/wayne-besen/ex-gay-group-should-repen_b_616197.html (accessed July 19, 2014).

Bussee, M. (undated). *Statement of apology by former exodus leaders.* Retrieved March 23, 2013 from Beyond Ex-Gay website. http://www.beyondexgay.com/article/busseeapology. html (accessed August 11, 2014).

Carey, B. (2012). Psychiatry giant sorry for backing gay cure. *New York Times* (May 18). http://www.nytimes.com/2012/05/19/health/dr-robert-l-spitzer-noted-psychiatrist-apologizes-for-study-on-gay-cure.html?pagewanted=1&_r=2& (accessed July 19, 2014).

Condon, P. (2012). Exodus International, "ex-gay" Christian group, backs away from reparative therapy. *Associated Press.* http://www.huffingtonpost.com/2012/06/27/exodus-international-ex-gay-christian-group-reparative-therapy_n_1630425.html (accessed July 19, 2014).

Drescher, J. (1998). I'm your handyman. *Journal of Homosexuality*, 36(1), 19–42.

Eckhols, E. (2012). Rift forms in movement as believe in gay 'cure' is renounced. *New York Times* (July 6).http://www.nytimes.com/2012/07/07/us/a-leaders-renunciation-of-ex-gay-tenets-causes-a-schism.html?pagewanted=all&_r=0 (accessed July 19, 2014).

Evangelical Press (2002). Ex-gay leader disciplined for bar visit. *Christianity Today* (October 1). http://www.christianitytoday.com/ct/2000/octoberweb-only/53.0.html (accessed July 19, 2014).

Exodus International (undated). *About Us.* http://exodusinternational.org/about-us/ (accessed March 23, 2013).

Ford, J.G. (2002). Healing homosexuals: A psychologist's journey through the ex-gay movement and the pseudo-science of reparative therapy. *Journal of Gay and Lesbian Psychotherapy*, 5(3–4), 69–86.

Frankowski, B.L. and Committee on Adolescence (2004). American Academy of Pediatrics: Sexual orientation and adolescents. *Pediatrics*, 113(16), 1827–1832. http://pediatrics. aappublications.org/content/113/6/1827.short (accessed July 19, 2014).

Huffington Post (2010). George Rekers, anti-gay activist, caught with male escort 'rentboy.' *Huffington Post* (July 5). http://www.huffingtonpost.com/2010/05/05/george-rekers-anti-gay-ac_n_565142.html (accessed July 19, 2014).

Huffington Post (2011). John Smid, former 'ex-gay' leader says he is gay and changing sexual orientation is impossible. *Huffington Post* (October 21) [Video file]. http://www.huffingtonpost.com/2011/10/20/john-smid-former-ex-gay-minister-sexual-orientation-_n_1022417.html (acccessed July 19, 2014).

Truth Wins Out (undated). Love Won Out. http://www.truthwinsout.org/love-won-out/ (accessed July 19, 2014).

Kempner, M. (2013). 'Pray Away the Gay' No More: 'Ex-Gay' Ministry Closes, Leader Apologizes to Gay Community. *RH Reality Check* (June 20). http://rhrealitycheck.org/article/2013/06/20/pray-away-the-gay-no-more-ex-gay-ministry-closes-leader-apologizes-to-gay-community/ (accessed July 19, 2014).

Pan-American Health Organization (2012). "Therapies" to change sexual orientation lack medical justification and threaten health.http://new.paho.org/hq/index.php?option=com_content&view=article&id=6803&Itemid=1926 (accessed July 19, 2014).

SIECUS (2005). Community Advocacy Update: Tennessee moves to investigate ex-gay camp. http://www.siecus.org/index.cfm?fuseaction=Feature.showFeature&featureid=1262&pageid=483&parentid=478 (accessed July 19, 2014).

Myth #11 Same-Sex Relationships Are Inherently Different from Those Between One Man and One Woman

For many years there was an overriding belief in our society that gay and lesbian couples were inherently different from heterosexual ones. A man and a woman were meant to get together, get married, and have kids. This was the foundation of our society. When a man and a man did that (or a woman and a woman), it was considered unusual, different, not normal. And, given the discrimination gays and lesbians face in all aspects of their lives, it's not surprising that the assumption was these relationships were lesser—less committed, less serious, less important. This belief was used by many to justify denying same-sex couples marital rights.

Though gay marriage is just beginning to see widespread support among politicians and the public, researchers have known for decades that when we compare heterosexual with same-sex couples, they are much more alike than different. Moreover, those differences that do exist, do not support the notion that "same-sex" couples are "less" anything—in fact, in many areas same-sex couples have relationship advantages.

More Similarities

The first really big comparative study of same and opposite-sex couples was carried out by Blumstein and Schwartz (yes, our very own Pepper Schwartz, one of the authors of this book) in the late 1970s and early 1980s. It was a large study funded by the National Science Foundation of over 12,000 people or 6000 couples. The goal was to compare married heterosexual couples, cohabiting heterosexual couples, gay male couples, and lesbian couples. The general findings could be summed up by saying that married couples and same-sex couples (both lesbian and gay) were more like each other than all three of them were like cohabiting heterosexual couples (mostly because the latter had much more variable commitments to each other). The gender similarities were also striking: gay males were more like cohabiting and married heterosexual males than they were like lesbians or cohabitating or married heterosexual women. And lesbians were more like cohabiting and married women than they were like anyone else in the study. Gender socialization, attitudes, and behaviors were extraordinarily similar regardless of a person's sexual orientation (Blumstein and Schwartz, 1983).

The research also found that all four kinds of couples share some relationship characteristics when it comes to sex. Regardless of type of relationship, couples had higher satisfaction if they had higher sexual frequency. In addition, equality of initiation and refusal of sex was also associated with higher satisfaction in all four kinds of couples.

The biggest sexual difference was that committed gay male couples were more likely to openly negotiate nonmonogamy and were more able to tolerate nonmonogamy without hurting the relationships than the other couples (Blumstein and Schwartz, 1983). Other studies have found that gay male couples may also have particular issues with the impact of a long relationship and aging on the couple's physical relationship (Peplau and Fingerhut, 2007).

One of the enduring myths about same-sex couples is that their relationships are solely about sex. Obviously, this isn't true. Like every other couple, same-sex partners have to deal with job demands, housework, lifestyle, and often children. There is a large and interesting base of literature on similarities and differences between how same-sex and opposite-sex couples handle the day-to-day aspects of life together.

A longitudinal study by Kurdek compared both partners from same-sex couples without children with both partners from heterosexual married couples with children. He looked at five central measures of relationship health and found that for half of the comparisons, gay and lesbian partners were similar to heterosexual partners. There were, of course, some differences but, interestingly, they concluded that the majority of these differences (78%) "reflected better adaptations on the part of the same-sex relationships than the heterosexual relationships." Specifically, the author analyzed interaction patterns with family and friends, conflict management, and the way each partner filtered information about the relationship. He concluded:

> Relative to heterosexual partners, partners from gay couples and partners from lesbian couples do not function in ways that place their relationships at risk for distress. In particular, there is no evidence that gay partners and lesbian partners were psychologically maladjusted, that they had high levels of personality traits that predisposed them to relationship problems, that they had dysfunctional working models of their relationships, and that they used ineffective strategies to resolve conflict. (Kurdek, 2004, p. 896)

In fact, gay and lesbian couples are often better at conflict management and communication. A study of 75 gay, 51 lesbian, and 108 heterosexual couples who had no children looked at how couples handled conflicts in six areas that were common to all couples: reactions to excessive critical statements; differences on politics and social issues; bringing up personal failings like drinking or smoking too much; lack of trust or lying; intimacy and sex; and lack of time together due to job or school or other commitments. There were some differences about which issues predominated between couples. Heterosexual couples, for example, argued more frequently about social issues than lesbian or gay male couples, and same-sex couples argued more frequently about trust issues (Kurdek, 1994, pp. 931–932). Still, the couples were more alike than different and frequency of overall conflict was similar. Issues about intimacy, personal failings, power, and emotional distance were most important for all couples. These results are similar to those found by numerous researchers over time (e.g. Bryant and Demian, 1994; Storaasli and Markman, 1990; Blumstein and Schwartz, 1983).

In addition to the issues being the same, the study also found that couples had similar reactions to the frequency with which they argued. All couples had a decrease in satisfaction over a year's time if they continued to argue about issues pertaining to personal power and influence in the relationship (Kurdek, 1994, p. 923).

Some studies have found that same-sex couples have advantages over heterosexual ones in how they communicate and function. A study that compared 92 childless gay male couples with 226 childless heterosexual couples and 312 couples living with children, found that the highest levels of relationship satisfaction and functioning as measured by various assessment instruments was in lesbian couples. Lesbian and gay male partners have consistently shown higher levels of expressiveness in the relationship which seems to be a key factor in communication and satisfaction with communication (Kurdek, 1987; Miller *et al.*, 2003; Gottman *et al.*, 2003; Kurdek, 2008, pp. 708–709). (There is some literature, however, that finds lesbians can be too expressive, and that this intense engagement over every little thing within a relationship can engender claustrophobic feelings; Clunis and Green, 1988.)

Given these advantages it's not surprising that in the study of same-sex and opposite-sex couples both with and without children, the most decline in satisfaction over 10 years was among the heterosexual couples with children (Kurdek, 2008, p. 701). This is a common finding in other studies as well (Twenge *et al.*, 2003).

Another area in which same-sex couples have a slight advantage is in the division of labor such as household chores or childcare. Sharing duties gives couples a sense of solidarity and improves relationship satisfaction, and studies have found that same-sex couples are more equal in their division of labor (Goldberg, 2010; Johnson and O'Connor, 2002). Blumstein and Schwartz (1983) found that gay males and lesbians were more egalitarian in their households. While some of them delegated all of household management to one partner, this pattern was relatively rare. A later study by Carrington (1999) examined the negotiation of these chores and described how they were divided in ways that did not follow gender traditions. In contrast, heterosexual couples show a less egalitarian, more gender-based division of labor which causes strife (Coltrane, 2000; Farr and Patterson, 2013, p. 1236).

Part of household management is about decision making whether in terms of the relationship itself, the housework, or the finances. Blumstein and Schwartz (1983) found that arguing about money management lowered satisfaction in all kinds of couples as did unequal decision making power. Interestingly, financial equality was particularly important for gay couples. A study by Kurdek and Schmidt (1986) questioned if decision making in general was more shared in cohabitating same sex and opposite-sex couples compared with married couples, reasoning that the former would be more egalitarian. However, they found this was only greatly true among lesbians. This was also found to be the case in the Blumstein and Schwartz study. What was true in this study was that the more shared decision making there was, the happier all couples seemed to be.

Another study looked at tactics of decision making, comparing different kinds of couples. It found that styles varied by gender as well as by type of relationship (Howard *et al.*, 1986, p. 102). Both heterosexual women and gay men were more likely to use manipulation and supplication to get their way rather than direct confrontation. The authors felt that this similarity might exist because these tactics worked better on male partners (Howard *et al.*, 1986, p. 107). The authors also found that gay men, heterosexual men, and heterosexual women were more likely than lesbians to use disengagement strategies (stop listening, leave the room, etc.) to get their way (Howard *et al.*, 1986, p. 108). Still, overall, the authors concluded that there "was no obvious way that homosexual couples differed from heterosexual couples on their use of influence tactics."

Comparisons of Gays and Lesbians as Parents

Because there have been many custody disputes as well as struggles over the right to adopt children or serve as foster parents, the parenting qualifications of gay men and lesbians, and the effects on children, have been studied by a multitude of researchers. We focus on this in the next entry (Myth # 12) but suffice it to say that, while there have been a few outlier studies, the majority of the research shows that same-sex parenting compares favorably with opposite-sex parenting.

Social Support

Unfortunately, there is one area in which same-sex couples fare less well than their heterosexual peers and it is ultimately out of their control. Kurdek (2004) explains: "The only area in which gay and lesbian partners fared worse than heterosexual partners was in the area of social support: Gay partners and lesbian partners received less support for their relationships from family members than heterosexual parents did" (2004, p. 896). Other research has also shown that same-sex couples get less support from family and friends than married couples and even cohabiting heterosexual partners get more support (Kurdek and Schmitt, 1986, p. 718).

This may reflect discomfort with same-sex relationships on the part of family or friends or could be a result of the couple attempting to keep a low profile because of fear of disapproval by family or society. We can't underestimate the difficulty that this lack of support causes nor can we forget about the legal and financial obstacles that laws prohibiting same-sex marriage have created for these couples. Such impediments take their toll on relationships.

As gay marriage becomes more accepted in our society and as more states pass laws legalizing same-sex marriage, we can only hope that these couples get the support they need from family, friends, and community.

References

Blumstein, P. and Schwartz, P. (1983). *American Couples: Money, Work, Sex*. Morrow, New York.

Bryant, A.S. and Demian. (1994). Relationship characteristics of American gay and lesbian couples: Findings from a national survey. *Journal of Gay and Lesbian Social Services*, 1, 101–117.

Carrington, C. (1999). *No Place Like Home: Relationships and Family Life Among Lesbians and Gay Men*. University of Chicago Press, Chicago.

Coltrane, S. (2000). Research on household labor: Modeling and measuring the social embeddedness of routine family work. *Journal of Marriage and Family*, 62, 1208–1233.

Clunis, D.M. and Green, G.D. (1988). *Lesbian Couples*. Seal Press, Seattle, WA.

Farr, R.H. and Patterson, C.J. (2013). Coparenting among lesbian, gay, and heterosexual couples: Associations with adopted children's outcomes. *Child Development*, 84(4), 1226–1240.

Goldberg, A.E. (2010). *Lesbian and Gay Parents and Their Children: Research on the Family Life Cycle.* American Psychological Association, Washington, DC.

Gottman, J.M., Levenson, R.W., Swanson, C., Swanson, K., Tyson, R., and Yoshimoto, D. (2003). Observing gay, lesbian, and heterosexual couples' relationships: Mathematical modeling of conflict interaction. *Journal of Homosexuality*, 45, 65–91.

Howard, J.A., Blumstein, P., and Schwartz, P. (1986). Sex, power, and influence tactics in intimate relationships. *Journal of Personality and Social Psychology*, 51(1), 102–109.

Johnson, S.M., and O'Connor, E. (2002). *The Gay Baby Boom: The Psychology of Gay Parenthood.* New York University Press, New York.

Kurdek, L.A. (1994). Areas of conflict for gay, lesbian, and heterosexual couples: What couples argue about influences relationship satisfaction. *Journal of Marriage and the Family*, 56(4), 923–934.

Kurdek, L.A. (1987). Sex role self schema and psychological adjustment in coupled homosexual and heterosexual men and women. *Sex Roles*, 17, 549–562.

Kurdek, L.A. (2004). Are gay and lesbian cohabiting couples really different from heterosexual married couples? *Journal of Marriage and Family*, 66(4), 880–900.

Kurdek, L.A. (2008). Change in relationship quality for partners from lesbian, gay male, and heterosexual couples. *Journal of Family Psychology*, 22(5), 701–711.

Kurdek, L.A. and Schmitt, J.P. (1986). Relationship quality of partners in heterosexual married, heterosexual cohabiting, and gay and lesbian relationships. *Journal of Personality and Social Psychology*, 51(4), 711–720.

Miller, P.J.E., Caughlin, J.P., and Huston, T.L. (2003). Trait expressiveness and marital satisfaction: The role of idealization processes. *Journal of Marriage and Family*, 65, 978–995.

Peplau, L.A. and Fingerhut, A.W. (2007). The close relationships of lesbians and gay men. *Annual Review of Psychology*, 58, 10.1–10.20.

Storaasli, R.D. and Markman, H.J. (1990). Relationship problems in the early stages of marriage: A longitudinal investigation. *Journal of Family Psychology*, 4, 80–98.

Twenge, J.M., Campbell, W.K., and Foster, C.A. (2003). Parenthood and marital satisfaction: A meta-analytic review. *Journal of Marriage and Family*, 65, 574–583.

Myth #12 Children of Same-Sex Parents Have Psychological Issues and Usually End Up Gay

In 2011, a college student made national headlines when he testified in front of state lawmakers in Iowa who were considering a constitutional amendment that would ban gay marriage. Like so many debates on this topic, one question comes up over and over again: what about the children? Zach Wahl, then a student at the University of Iowa, was there to tell legislators that he was raised by two mothers and he was just fine.

In his 3-minute testimony which quickly went viral and landed him on both Letterman and the *Ellen DeGeneres Show*, Wahl said that his family was like every other family—they ate together, went to church, and fought. They had happy times and struggles like the health of his biological mother who was diagnosed with multiple sclerosis in 2000 and is confined to a wheelchair. Working through the hard times so that they could get to the good ones, he said, is what makes him, his sister, and his mothers, a family. At one point, he addressed the chairman of the committee directly:

> I score in the 99th percentile on the ACT. I'm an Eagle Scout. I own and operate my own small business. If I was your son, Mr. Chairman, I believe I'd make you very proud. I'm not so different from any of your children. (Wahl, 2011)

Wahl finished his testimony, powerfully, by saying:

> In the next two hours, I'm sure we're going to hear a lot of testimony about how damaging having gay parents is on kids. But not once have I ever been confronted by an individual who realized independently that I was raised by a gay couple. (Wahl, 2011)

Wahl was no doubt correct about what followed his testimony. Opponents of same-sex marriage often argue that growing up in a household with two mothers or two fathers instead of the typical mother and father will have harmful effects on children. Nature, they say, obviously intended children to grow up with a male and a female, after all, only heterosexual couples can have kids on their own.

These opponents suggest that there is no way that children of gay and lesbian couples can do as well as those who grow up in traditional heterosexual relationships. Instead, children of gay or lesbian couples, they argue, will face psychological damage, poor parent relationships, stigmatization from peers, and increased rates of sexual abuse. There is also the fear that these children will be confused about gender identity and/or grow up to be homosexual themselves. These arguments have been around for decades and have been used as reasons why same-sex couples should not be allowed to marry or adopt children as well as why a parent who comes out as gay or lesbian should not get custody of his/her biological children.

There is actually a good deal of research that has looked at the children of gay fathers and/or lesbian mothers and almost all of it comes to the same conclusion: these kids are no different from their peers with heterosexual parents.

Before we delve into this research more closely, however, there are a few words of caution. In order to get a true understanding of whether the gender and sexual orientation of parents matter, an ideal study would compare children in same-sex families with children in similar heterosexual families. An ideal study would also have a large sample size that was representative of same-sex families across the country in order to be able to generalize the results.

For many reasons these studies don't exist. Until recently, many same-sex parents kept a low profile in order to avoid stigma and discrimination. The census did not track same-sex cohabiting couples until 2000 which would have made finding a large sample of families to study quite difficult. The studies that do exist on the topic are, for the most part, quite small and use convenience samples. The results, therefore, are not necessarily generalizable to the entire population of same-sex families. Still, researchers believe that these studies are telling. In a recent commentary, Mark Amato, a sociologist at the University of Pennsylvania said: "If growing up with gay or lesbian parents were catastrophic for children, even studies based on small convenience samples would have shown this by now" (Pappas, 2012).

Another problem, at least for those who want to use the research to prove that same-sex marriage is either a good or a bad idea from the point of view of the children, is that for the most part the existing research does not look at children who were brought up in such relationships because the laws granting same-sex marriage rights are simply too new. While contemporary studies have looked at children being raised by committed same-sex couples, much of the available research focuses on children who grew up with divorced lesbian mothers (those who had previously been in a heterosexual marriage) and compared them with children of divorced heterosexual mothers. Few studies looked at children with gay fathers, most likely because these fathers often did not end up with custody of their children.

Finally, it is important to remember as you read through the results that no family exists in a vacuum. The psychosocial development of children is impacted not just by what goes on in their own homes, but by what goes on in their communities and beyond. The stigma faced by gays and lesbians and their children is an important component of how young people fare.

After all of those caveats, we repeat our summary of many decades of research: there is no discernible difference between kids raised by heterosexual parents and those raised by same-sex parents.

Gays and Lesbians Can Be Good Parents

The fears about same-sex couples raising children may stem from outdated and stereotypical views of lesbians and gay men themselves and the discriminatory belief that they're simply not fit to raise children. Remember, historically it was not that long ago that homosexuality was believed to be a mental illness. Moreover, the clichés about lesbians suggests that they are not as feminine or nurturing as heterosexual women and gay men are often looked at as irresponsible and unable to settle into a monogamous relationship. These traits, some argue, make gay men and lesbians bad candidates for parenthood.

Sweeping generalizations about any group of people are usually wrong and this is no exception. A review of research on same-sex parenting conducted by the American Psychological Association (APA) in 2005 concluded that "beliefs that lesbian and gay adults are not fit to be parents have no empirical foundation" (Patterson, 1995). Studies have found, for example, that lesbian women and heterosexual women are not particularly different when it comes to either their overall mental health or their approach to child rearing. Other research suggests that lesbian and gay parents may actually have superior parenting skills to those of matched heterosexual couples. Gay and lesbian couples, for example, have been found to be less likely to report physical punishment of children and more likely to report positive parenting techniques such as reasoning (Patterson, 1995).

Their Children Are Smart, Happy, and Have Good Relationships with Their Parents

Though opponents would like us to believe that these children suffer unduly because of their parents' relationship, this theory is not supported by the research. A 2008 meta-analysis of studies published since the 1970s found that across 26 measures of psychological well-being, the children of same-sex couples were similar to those of opposite-sex couples. There was also no difference between the cognitive development of children of same-sex couples and that of their peers (Crowl *et al.*, 1998). The APA review also suggests that there is no difference between these children and their peers in a number of categories, including separation/individuation, psychiatric evaluation, behavior problems, personality, self-concept, school adjustment, and intelligence (Patterson, 1995).

In fact, the only statistically significant difference that has been found suggests that lesbian and gay parents were more likely to report a positive parent–child relationship than heterosexual parents. Interestingly, however, while the parents reported better relationships their children did not. The children's perception of the parent–child relationship did not vary between same-sex and opposite-sex families (Crowl *et al.*, 1998). The authors suggest that gay and lesbian parents may feel very protective of their children, who they fear will be subject to homophobia, and as such perceive a closer relationship than heterosexual parents.

There are actually some data to suggest that lesbian parents do better than opposite-sex couples. Biblarz and Stacey point out that: "Lesbian coparents seem to outperform comparable married heterosexual, biological parents on several measures, even while being denied the substantial privileges of marriage" (Biblarz and Stacey, 2010).

The Kids Are Not Likely to Be Victims of Sexual Abuse

One of the fears that the APA looked into in its review revolved around sexual abuse and the assertion that children of same-sex parents were more likely to be victims. This outrageous assumption is likely based on a completely inaccurate belief that gay men and lesbian women are more likely to sexually abuse children (see Myth # 13 for more on this erroneous belief). Children of gay men and lesbians are more likely to know other gay adults which, if you believed this train of thought, would increase their risk of abuse.

In truth, sexual abuse by adult women (whether lesbian or heterosexual) is extremely rare. Most abuse is perpetrated by men, and gay men are no more likely to abuse children than heterosexual men.

The APA review concluded that "fears that children in the custody of lesbian and gay parents might be at heightened risk for sexual abuse are without basis in the research literature" (Patterson, 1995).

The Kids Do Not Have Gender Issues

Arguments against gay and lesbian parents have suggested that kids will grow up not knowing appropriate gender roles and will have problems with their own gender identity.

As we've discussed in other entries, gender roles refer to the ways society *expects* men and women to act and the ways in which men and women are *supposed* to be different. Some people may fear that a young man growing up in a house without a father or a young woman growing up without a mother would not have anyone to model the behavior of their own gender. We should note that children grow up in households without either a mother or a father for many reasons (divorce, death, and desertion) that have nothing to do with sexual orientation. These children, like those in same-sex families, may find role models of their own gender outside their immediate family whether it's a relative, a teacher, or a coach.

More importantly, though, children learn gender roles not just from their families, but from all aspects of society—television shows and movies constantly tell us how men and women should and should not act; magazines are aimed at women or men (but rarely both); and toy stores divide their content into a boy section and a girl section.

It shouldn't come as a surprise, therefore, that children of same-sex couples are no more likely to have issues with gender roles than their peers. The APA review points to over 10 studies that have found that children of lesbian mothers "fall within typical limits for conventional sex roles" (Patterson, 1995). (This is one of the places where there is no research on children of gay men.)

We think these concerns about the children's gender have another origin as well—stereotypes that suggest lesbians are not real women and gay men are not real men. It's not just that these children will grow up with two women and no men (or vice versa), it's the idea that the women or men they do grow up with have gender issues of their own and will not model *appropriate* gender roles. This is an unfair categorization. Sexual orientation is not about one's own internal sense of maleness or femaleness (that's gender identity) or outward appearance as male or female (that's gender expression). Just because a man or a woman is in a same-sex relationship does not mean that he or she doesn't otherwise conform to traditional gender roles and expressions. While some gay men may seem feminine, many don't. Similarly, just like heterosexual women, some lesbians are more masculine than others but many are quite feminine.

So, again, it should come as no surprise that the meta-analysis carried out it 2008 found no statistically significant differences in the gender identity of children brought up by same-sex parents when compared with children of heterosexual couples (Crowl *et al.*, 2008). The APA reports on research that found that children of lesbian couples are happy with their gender and had no wish to be a member of the opposite gender. Again, there are no similar studies of children with gay fathers (Patterson, 1995).

Most Kids Grow Up to be Heterosexual

We find this myth about young people who grow up with two mothers or two fathers to be particularly upsetting because it is predicated on the belief that homosexuality is a bad thing. The fear alone seems to suggest that if we discovered that most of these young people grew up to be homosexual like their parents we would have proof that same-sex couples should not raise children. We think that a child's sexual orientation is far less important than his/her overall psychological well-being.

That said, it's always nice to take the wind out of the sails of a ridiculous argument and the research does that for us here. The APA review looked at over 10 studies and found that the great majority of offspring of both gay fathers and lesbian mothers described themselves as heterosexual (Patterson, 1995). A 1995 study, for example, found that 90% of adult sons of gay fathers were heterosexual (Bailey *et al.*, 1995, as cited in Patterson). A 1997 study that compared 25 young adults with lesbian mothers with 21 young adults with divorced heterosexual mothers found that the offspring of lesbians were no more likely to describe themselves as being attracted to people of the same sex than those with heterosexual moms. There was one difference, however. Among the young adults who did describe same-sex attractions, kids with lesbian moms were more likely to both consider entering into a same-sex relationship and to have actually done so than kids with heterosexual moms (Golombok *et al.*, 1997, as cited in Patterson).

Social Stigma

It is clear from the current debate over same-sex marriage that while the needle is moving, same-sex couples still face stigma and may feel ostracized from their families or communities. It is not unreasonable, therefore, to question what impact this has on the children of these couples.

A 1998 study compared children born via artificial insemination to lesbian mothers with children born via artificial insemination to heterosexual mothers. This study found that all of the children developed in a normal fashion and their "adjustment was unrelated to structural variables such as parental sexual orientation or the number of parents in the household."

The early research again focuses mostly on the children of lesbian mothers and finds that they did not fare worse than their peers whose heterosexual mothers were divorced. A number of studies have found that they have similar friendships with peers and that their early romantic relationships are not different from those of their peers. One study did find that they were likely to have heard anti-gay remarks but noted that: "young adult offspring of divorced lesbian mothers did not recall being the targets of any more childhood teasing or victimization than did the off-spring of divorced heterosexual mothers" (Gatrell *et al.*, 2000, as cited in Patterson, 2005).

Here we think it is important to remember that if these young people were to be subject to more teasing than other kids and suffered as a result, it would not be their fault nor would it be the fault of their parents.

A Controversial Study

In the summer of 2012, a study was published in the journal *Social Science Research* that contradicted all of the previous research and suggested that children of gay and lesbian parents were more likely to have negative outcomes as adults including being on public assistance, in therapy, or unemployed (Regnerus, 2012a).

In an opinion piece published on Slate.com, Mark Regnerus argued that his results showed that parents who had same-sex relationships represented an unstable environment for children. Contrary to prior research that claimed lesbian parents might actually have a leg up on heterosexual couples, he found mothers who had same-sex relationships to be the least stable and suggested that their children were most likely to have been in foster care at some point. Regnerus writes:

> On 25 of 40 different outcomes evaluated, the children of women who've had same-sex relationships fare quite differently than those in stable, biologically-intact mom-and-pop families, displaying numbers more comparable to those from heterosexual stepfamilies and single parents. (Regnerus, 2012b)

In explaining (or defending) why his results were so very different from the decades of research before it, he claimed that he had a larger sample and better research methods.

Social scientists, however, were quick to point out that the study was deeply flawed and the results did not actually say anything about stable same-sex couples. While the study was based on a survey of almost 3000 18- to 39-year-olds, most participants had been raised by heterosexual parents and only a small number qualified as children of same-sex parents. In fact only 175 participants said their mother had at one point been in a lesbian relationship and another 73 had a father who had been in a relationship with another man. They represented less than 2% of the sample (Pappas, 2012).

Moreover, these respondents were not, in fact, raised by same-sex couples. Only two respondents in the whole study reported living with one parent and his/her same-sex partner for their entire childhoods. As such the study cannot really determine how children raised in a same-sex marriage would really fare and should not be interpreted as trumping or dismissing all of the positive research that came before. The rest of the participants in the same-sex parent category came from families that were not intact for reasons that the study did not examine. It is unfair to compare these children with those from "biologically-intact mom-and-pop families" and then blame the outcome on the fact that one parent had a same-sex relationship at some point in his/her life.

The Same-Sex Parenting Debate

As we write this, same-sex marriage is being heavily debated in the United States. The Supreme Court recently struck down certain parts of a federal law known as the Defense of Marriage Act (DOMA). DOMA was passed in 1996 and specified that the federal government will not recognize any marriage that is not between a man and a woman regardless of the law of the state in which the marriage took place. In declaring the law unconstitutional, the majority noted, among other things, that DOMA "humiliates tens of thousands of children now being raised by same-sex couples" and "makes it even more difficult for the children to understand the integrity and closeness of their own family and its concord with other families in their community and in their daily lives" (*United States v. Windsor*).

This decision means that the federal government has to recognize same-sex marriages performed in states that have legalized such unions. It does not, however, mean that all state have to make same-sex marriage legal or that no state can choose to ban the practice forever. There is still a lot of legal wrangling going on as lower courts across the country hear challenges both to laws making same-sex marriage legal in certain states and to attempts to ban same-sex marriage in others. It is likely that the US Supreme Court will have to hear some of these cases and make another ruling on same-sex marriage within the next few years.

Though much progress has been made recently, the debate about same-sex marriage in the United States is far from over and questions about how children of same-sex couples fare are still openly debated.

More research needs to be done on children growing up in same-sex families in order to know if there are any differences in their outcomes compared with their peers in similar, heterosexual families. It will be especially interesting to watch this first generation of children with married same-sex parents grow and determine what, if any, changes to their overall well-being occur as a result of both increasing support for same-sex marriage rights and the actual laws that recognize and legitimize their families.

References

Bailey, J.M., Bobrow, D., Wolfe, M., and Mikach, S. (1995). Sexual orientation of adult sons of gay fathers. *Developmental Psychology*, 31, 124–129.

Biblarz, T.J. and Stacey, J. (2010). How does the gender of parents matter? *Journal of Marriage and Family*, 72(1), 3–22.

Crowl, A., Ahn, S., and Baker, J. (2008). A meta-analysis of developmental outcomes for children of same-sex and heterosexual parents. *Journal of GLBT Family Studies*, 4(3), 385–407.

Gartrell, N., Banks, A., Reed, N., Hamilton, J., Rodas, C., and Deck, A. (2000). The National Lesbian Family Study: 3. Interviews with mothers of five-year-olds. *American Journal of Orthopsychiatry*, 70(4), 542–548.

Golombok, S., Tasker, F.L., and Murray, C. (1997). Children raised in fatherless families from infancy: Family relationships and the socioemotional development of children of lesbian and single heterosexual mothers. *Journal of Child Psychology and Psychiatry*, 38, 783–791.

Johnson, S. M. and O'Connor, E. (2002). *The Gay Baby Boom: The Psychology of Gay Parenthood*. New York University Press, New York.

Pappas, S. (2012). Gay parents study suggesting downside for kids draws fire from social scientists. *Huffington Post* (June 12). http://www.huffingtonpost.com/2012/06/12/gay-parents-study-kids-social-scientists_n_1589177.html (accessed July 21, 2014).

Patterson, C.J. (1995). *Lesbian and Gay Parenting*. American Psychological Association Public Interest Directorate, 8.

Regnerus, M. (2012a). How different are the adult children of parents who have same-sex relationships? Findings from the New Family Structures Study. *Social Science Research*, 41(4), 752–770.

Regnerus, M. (2012b). Queers as folk: Does it really make no difference if your parents are straight or gay. *Huffington Post* (June 11). http://www.slate.com/articles/double_x/doublex/2012/06/gay_parents_are_they_really_no_different_.single.html (accessed July 21, 2014).

United States v. Windsor, 570 U.S. 12 (June 26, 2013), (Docket No. 12-307).

Wahl, Z. (2011). *Testimony: What Makes A Family?* http://www.zachwahls.com/?page_id=273 (accessed July 21, 2014).

Myth #13 Most Child Molesters Are Gay Men

One of the scare tactics that has been used to prejudice people against homosexual men is the message that they are dangerous to children. This belief has been so widespread that in many places in the world—and even some institutions in the United States—gay men (and in some cases, lesbians) are barred from working with children in the capacity of nannies, teachers, or scout leaders. Certainly, there have been cases of molestation of children by gay men, but the truth is that by far most molestation of children has been committed by heterosexual men.

We hear so many stories, however, about young boys being molested by adult men that the idea that most perpetrators are heterosexual sounds somewhat counter-intuitive. After all, if a man molests a male child, is it not, by definition, a homosexual act? The answer is complex but, as we will show in this discussion, despite the stories that make headlines most cases of child molestation involve heterosexual men and young girls. Moreover, pederasts (adults who sexualize children) are most often attracted by a child's immature body and not necessarily picky about gender. There are certainly cases of young boys molested by gay men—but that is only a small part of a much larger, sadder, and scarier picture.

Who Molests Children?

Studies indicate there are two kinds of child molesters: most common is the situational child molester who would prefer to have sex with an adult but will use a child if no other opportunities are available. Somewhat rarer are adults who actually prefer children to adult partners and who use child pornography and other aids that objectify children for sexual arousal. The offenders who prefer very young children are generally unlikely to differentiate between boys and girls (Roesler and Poyer, 1994, p. 43). If the person sexualizes older, post-pubescent children, however, he is likely to prefer one sex or the other.

Men (and it is primarily men) who prefer children have been labeled as "fixated" by some researchers, and the general understanding is that these kind of offenders have been sexually attracted to young children since adolescence. While they may have sex with peers or even partners who are older than themselves, those adult sexual acts are happenstance because their fixation is never replaced by age-appropriate sexual partners (Groth and Birnbaum, 1978, p. 176). They are attracted to immature bodies. Some are slightly more attracted to boys than girls, but studies indicate they prefer boys who have a "feminine" presentation, such as having no facial hair, body hair, or muscles (Groth and Birnbaum, 1978).

In contrast, other men primarily have sex with adults but find themselves desiring younger children when they are stressed in their primary adult relationship. These offenders are almost always heterosexually attracted (Groth and Birnbaum, 1978).

Innumerable Studies

Child sexual abuse is a much underreported crime because victims are often scared to come forward. Even when reported it can be hard to convict sex offenders. For this reason, statistics on child sexual abuse are difficult to calculate and the details of any one case can be hard to determine. Still, innumerable studies over the years have found that most abuse is enacted by heterosexual males. This is not a new or startling finding. (Balsam *et al.,* 2005; Turner *et al.,* 2007; Peter, 2009; Putnam, 2003; Shusterman *et al.,* 2005; Zink *et al.,* 2009).

In fact, one study found the rates of pedophilia so low among homosexuals that the authors hypothesized, "The possibility emerges that homosexuality and homosexual pedophilia may be mutually exclusive" (Groth and Birnbaum, 1978, p. 175). They go on to say, "the child offender who is also attracted to and engaged in adult sexual relationships is heterosexual. It appears, therefore, that the adult heterosexual male constitutes a greater sexual risk to underage children than does the adult homosexual male" (Groth and Birnbaum, 1978, pp. 180–181).

One study used an innovative design to determine who was more likely to abuse children. It looked at the medical records of children evaluated for sexual abuse at a hospital. The cases included 276 girls and 76 boys. The mean age of the children was 6 years old but the range went as young as an infant and as old as 17. Abuse was judged not to have occurred at all in 35 of the cases. Another 74 cases involved children who were abused by peers or teenagers less than 18 years old. Of the remaining 269 cases, only two abusers were identified to be gay or lesbian. In 83% of the cases, the presumed offender was the heterosexual partner of someone in the child's family.

In another study of 136 convicted child molesters, over 80% had been in a committed adult heterosexual relationship at the time of the victimization and at trial (Roesler and Poyer, 1994, p. 43). The authors concluded that if this sample were typical, "a child's risk of being molested by his or her relative's heterosexual partner is over 100 times greater than by someone who might be identifiable as being homosexual, lesbian, or bisexual" (Roesler and Poyer, 1994, p. 44).

Researchers have also noted that children living with same-sex couples experience less abuse than their peers. An in-depth longitudinal study of kids, aged 17, who had grown up in a lesbian household asked 39 girls and 39 boys if they'd ever been physically, sexually, or mentally abused at home. None of these adolescents indicated any kind of abuse by either a parent or caretaker (Gartrell *et al.*, 2011, p. 1199). In fact, all studies (with the exception of those sponsored by ideological anti-gay groups) have found that kids in a same-sex parent household are unlikely to be abused (Bos *et al.*, 2007; Bos and Sandfort, 2010; Gartrell and Bos, 2010; Gartrell *et al.*, 2005; Golombok, 2007; Perrin, 2002; Tasker, 2005; Vanfraussen *et al.*, 2002).

Witch Hunts

Given the data, we have to ask ourselves why homosexuals are tagged with such a hideous reputation for child abuse. Certainly, homophobia and discrimination in general are at the root. But the myth persists, even as same-sex marriages become more accepted and discrimination against gays and lesbians begins to wane. We believe there are a few explanations for this.

First, there are splinter groups of men, some of whom are gay, who wish to legitimize the sexual predation of young people. Some of these "man-boy-love" groups publish propaganda on the internet about why adult–child sexual liaisons are "good" for adolescent boys. These men are disowned by the vast majority of gay men and women but their existence has been utilized by anti-gay groups to prove that molestation is a gay phenomenon (Brongersma, 1991).

Another big issue over the last 10 years or more has been the stories of Catholic priests across the United States who were found to have abused young boys for years without ever being punished (Clark, 2006, p. 1). These revelations, deeply disturbing to Roman Catholics and to the public at large, received a great deal of publicity and much was made of the fact that Catholic priests have to be celibate. Media pundits, religious scholars, and sexologists were forced to speculate about whether the priesthood attracts men who are conflicted about their sexual orientation (the Church does not, after all, accept homosexuality) and whether it is this conflict that culminates in the abuse of young boys. Given how widespread the problem within the Church is, one could argue that the priesthood selects for a larger than chance number of men who force themselves on boys and abuse the trust that the Church, families, and children had granted them, but we don't yet understand why.

While the stories that came to light illuminated a hidden horror in many young boys' lives, they do not represent the reality of the usual ratio of heterosexual to homosexual child sexual abuse. Unfortunately, they have reinforced the erroneous notion that gay men pose a danger to children.

Based on these beliefs, there have been modern attempts to legally forbid gay men and women from working with or caring for children. For example, a Colorado initiative in the early 1990s made a point of linking homosexuality with pedophilia. At that time a group called Colorado for Family Values put out a patently false statement asserting that gay people were responsible for 50% of all child molestation (Brongersma, 1991; Roesler and Poyer, 1994, p. 41).

These kind of false statistics have fueled fights in many states over whether gay and lesbian couples can become foster or adoptive parents. In some states, lawyers representing same-sex couples who want to become foster parents or adoptive parents have successfully argued against constraints on gay parenting, in part by presenting voluminous data on why homosexuals are actually less likely to be abusive than heterosexuals. But other states continue to see gay and lesbian couples as unfit to be adoptive or foster parents (Arkansas Department of Human Services, 2010; Falk, 1989; Ford, 2010; Golombok and Tasker, 1994; Patterson, 1992).

This witch hunt that accuses gay men of being likely pedophiles has also played out in schools. Administrators, eager to protect themselves against accusations of child endangerment, seem to focus on the widely reported cases in which teachers or coaches have molested a boy, and forget about the dozens of cases more that involved a heterosexual teacher's victimization of a girl, not to mention the increasing number of reported cases that involve sexual relations between young female teachers and male high school students. Their selective memory then affects hiring and firing practices. In 2014, an administrator in a Catholic high school in Seattle, Washington married his same-sex partner, and when the administration of the high school found out, the man was immediately fired. Parent groups protested and asked for the administrator to be reinstated, but he was not. In this case religious values interacted with values about child protection—and of course, the church was super-sensitive about homosexuality for many reasons, not the least of which was their recent experience with predatory priests.

The Boy Scouts have also made headlines for the organization's long-standing policy that prohibited gay and lesbian parents from being scout leaders as well as openly gay boys from being members. Under intense pressure both from inside and outside the organization, there was a vote on this rule which resulted in a positive change. As of January 2014, the scouts will allow gay members. However, the vote stopped short of changing the policy for adults, so gay and lesbian parents of boy scouts are still prohibited from serving as troup leaders (Boy Scouts of America, 2013).

It does seem like change is in the air—unfortunately, the misperceptions about homosexuals as likely child molesters linger and progress has been far too slow.

References

Arkansas Department of Human Services. (2010). *Cole v. Arkansas.* https://www.acslaw. org/acsblog/all/arkansas-dept.-of-human-services-v.-cole (accessed August 11, 2014).

Balsam, K.F., Rothblum, E.D., and Beauchaine, T.P. (2005). Victimization over the lifespan: A comparison of lesbian, gay, bisexual, and heterosexual siblings. *Journal of Consulting and Clinical Psychology,* 73, 477–487.

Bos, H.M.W., van Balen, F., and Van den Boom, D.C. (2007). Child adjustment and parenting in planned lesbian-parent families. *American Journal of Orthopsychiatry,* 77, 38–48.

Bos, H.M.W. and Sandfort, T.G.M. (2010). Children's gender identity in lesbian and heterosexual two-parent families. *Sex Roles,* 62, 114–126.

Boy Scouts of America (2013). The Boy Scouts of America Statement. http://www.scouting. org/MembershipStandards/Resolution/results.aspx (accessed August 11, 2014).

Brongersma, E. (1991). Boy-lovers and their influence on boys: Distorted research and anecdotal observations. *Journal of Homosexuality,* 20, 145–173.

Clark, S. (2006). Gay priests and other bogeymen. *Journal of Homosexuality,* 51(4), 1–13.

Falk, P.J. (1989). Lesbian mothers: Psychosocial assumptions in family law. *American Psychologist,* 44, 941–947.

Ford, C. (2010). Family First worth fighting. Australian Broadcasting Corporation. http:// www.abc.net.au/unleashed/stories/s2979646.htm (accessed July 21, 2014).

Gartrell, N. and Bos, H.M.W. (2010). The US National Longitudinal Lesbian Family Study: Psychological adjustment of 17-year-old adolescents. *Pediatrics,* 126, 1–9.

Gartrell, N.K., Bos, H.M.W., and Goldberg, N.G. (2011). Adolescents of the U.S. National Longitudinal Lesbian Family Study: Sexual orientation, sexual behavior, and sexual risk exposure. *Archives of Sexual Behavior,* 40(6), 1199–1209.

Gartrell, N., Deck, A., Rodas, C., Peyser, H., and Banks, A. (2005). The National Lesbian Family Study: 4. Interviews with the 10-year-old children. *American Journal of Orthopsychiatry,* 75, 518–524.

Golombok, S. (2007). Research on gay and lesbian parenting: An historical perspective across 30 years. *Journal of GLBT Family Studies,* 3, xxi–xxvii.

Golombok, S. and Tasker, F. (1994). Children in lesbian and gay families: Theories and evidence. *Annual Review of Sex Research,* 4, 73–100.

Groth, A.N. and Birnbaum, H.J. (1978). Adult sexual orientation and attraction to underage persons. *Archives of Sexual Behavior,* 7(3), 175–181.

Patterson, C.J. (1992). Children of lesbian and gay parents. *Child Development,* 63, 1025–1042.

Perrin, E. C., and American Academy of Pediatrics, Committee on Psychosocial Aspects of Child, Family Health (2002). Technical report: Coparent or second-parent adoption by same-sex parents. *Pediatrics,* 109, 341–344.

Peter, T. (2009). Exploring taboos: Comparing male- and female-perpetrated child sexual abuse. *Journal of Interpersonal Violence,* 24, 1111–1128.

Putnam, F.W. (2003). Ten-year research update review: Child sexual abuse. *Journal of the American Academy of Child and Adolescent Psychiatry,* 42, 269–278.

Roesler, T.A. and Poyer, K.L. (1994). Are children at risk for sexual abuse by homosexuals? *Pediatrics,* 94(1), 41–44.

Shusterman, G., Fluke, J., McDonald, W.R., and Associates. (2005). Male perpetrators of child maltreatment: Findings from NCANDS. United States Department of Health and Human Services. http://aspe.hhs.gov/hsp/05/child-maltreat/ (accessed July 21, 2014).

Tasker, F. (2005). Lesbian mothers, gay fathers and their children: A review. *Journal of Developmental and Behavioral Pediatrics,* 26, 224–240.

Turner, H.A., Finkelhor, D., and Ormrod, R. (2007). Family structure variations in patterns and predictors of child victimization. *American Journal of Orthopsychiatry*, 77, 282–295.

Vanfraussen, K., Ponjaert-Kristoffersen, I., and Brewaeys, A. (2002). What does it mean for youngsters to grow up in a lesbian family created by means of donor insemination? *Journal of Reproductive and Infant Psychology*, 20, 237–252.

Zink, T., Klesges, L., Stevens, S., and Decker, P. (2009). Trauma symptomatology, somatization, and alcohol abuse: Characteristics of childhood sexual abuse associated with the development of a sexual abuse severity score. *Journal of Interpersonal Violence*, 24, 537–546.

3 SEXUAL STATS

Who Has Sex? How Often? How Hot?

Single People Have the Best Sex Life Since They're Not Tied Down

There is something to this myth: all the research says that younger people have more sex than older people and single people tend to be younger. But that's about as far as the facts go just because single people are free doesn't mean they have partners and it doesn't mean that when they find a partner, they have quality sex.

It's debatable which kind of relationship offers the best sex, but there is no indication from the data that single men and women who are racking up the numbers are having the "best" sex.

Sex, Singles, and the Media

Magazines, especially magazines that conceive of themselves as "men's magazines" or "women's magazines," seem to flash singles' "hot sex" on every cover. But once people get out of the early to mid-twenties the majority of young singles maintain partnered sex either in serious dating relationships or in cohabitations.

Perhaps the myth comes either from the fantasies married people have of how great hooking up must be or it may have all started during the late 1960s and 1970s when singles broke the no-sex-before-marriage rule with a vengeance. More young men and women went to school after high school and the age of first marriage started on its upward trend into the twenties for both men and women. The proportion of young adults who didn't marry also

50 Great Myths of Human Sexuality, First Edition. Pepper Schwartz and Martha Kempner.
© 2015 John Wiley & Sons, Inc. Published 2015 by John Wiley & Sons, Inc.

increased, and those who did marry experienced an increased divorce rate (Laumann and Michael, 2001).

But this is true in a number of countries and many studies have compared what makes people most sexually satisfied by looking at singlehood versus couplehood (married or unmarried) and found that "swinging singles" aren't winning the satisfaction sweepstakes. One reason that singles may have less sexual satisfaction is that depression is higher in single and divorced people and is incompatible with high sexual satisfaction (Michael and O'Keane, 2000; Bruce and Kim, 1992; Pedersen and Blekesaune, 2003).

Laumann *et al.* felt that their data showed more sexual satisfaction among people in monogamous, committed relationships than dating ones, because there was more time, and more incentive, to learn what pleased a long-term partner than a short-term one (Laumann *et al.*, 1994). However, other researchers, using the same data, had different explanations for the difference in satisfaction. Waite believed that satisfaction was only higher for married women than married men, and concluded that women functioned better sexually in secure relationships (Waite and Joyner, 2001a, b). A study by Meadows (1997) adds support to his conclusion because it found that older women reported more sexual satisfaction the longer they were in a relationship.

When it comes to men, the findings are mixed. Sprecher (2002) found that the unmarried men in her study were actually more likely than the unmarried women to be more sexually satisfied when the quality of the relationship they were in was high. But in Waite's research, the men who expressed high sexual satisfaction were more likely to be in what they considered a permanent relationship than a cohabiting or dating one. Waite went on to pen a quite provocative book stating that just about everything was better in marriage, and that cohabiters (not to mention people who were dating) had less highly rated sex lives than married couples (Waite and Gallagher, 2000).

Is Marriage Better?

This theme of the benefits of marital commitment and mutual trust has been echoed in numerous publications. In fact, a flood of research has lauded marital happiness in contrast to any other kind of status—single or cohabiting (Brown, 2000; Brown and Booth, 1996; Lee *et al.*, 1991). Treas and Giesen (2000) studied cohabiters and married couples and noted that cohabiters exhibited lesser commitment and less sexual loyalty. One reason for satisfaction in marriage is security and less fear of infidelity (Forste and Tanfer, 1996; Laumann *et al.*, 1994; Pedersen and Blekesaune, 2003; Glass and Wright, 1992). Most people want, and demand, monogamy.

However, some scholars feel that Waite, and other researchers, have been too sweeping in their praise of marriage over other forms of sexual relationships. Warehime and Bass felt that marriage should be looked at more closely, to see which marriages are more satisfying than others, and to determine if "'intimacy beliefs and perspectives at multiple states of life' might make it clearer about when sexual satisfaction was highest." They also felt that research should be done to see if singles who had been previously married experienced sexual satisfaction differently from people who had never been married (Warehime and Bass, 2008, pp. 247–248).

Others also point out that while sexual satisfaction may be higher in marriage, long-term relationships do take their toll on sexual satisfaction (Liu, 2000; Gatzeva and Paik, 2011). Most research indicates less frequency over the life cycle of a relationship and high sexual frequency is associated with greater satisfaction (Northup et al., 2013). Habit, routine, and boredom become the enemy of eroticism over time (Sprecher and Regan, 1998; Haavio-Mannila and Kontula, 1997; Pedersen and Blekesaune, 2003). In addition, as marriages go on, couples are more likely to have children which is known to have a negative effect on couples' sexual lives. (Brown, 2004; Doss et al., 2009).

The duration of the relationship and subsequent boredom, however, is not only an issue in marriage. A longitudinal population-based sample in Norway found that men and women who had been dating a while showed decreasing sexual satisfaction over time (Pedersen and Blekesaune, 2003, p. 179).

So Who Has the Best Sex?

In the end, it appears that being single is no sexual nirvana. While singles have some advantages over married couples, married couples have some advantages over them (like always having a partner). We think that individual relationships are far more important than categories and the research backs us up. It turns out that people who are having more sex, and frequent orgasms with their partner, are more sexually satisfied, no matter what kind of relationship they are in (Carpenter et al., 2009; Parish et al., 2007; Haavio-Mannila and Kontula, 1997; Edwards and Booth, 1994; DeLamater, 1991).

References

Brown, S. L. (2000). The effect of union type on psychological well-being: Depression among cohabitors versus marrieds. *Journal of Health and Social Behavior*, 41, 241–2555.

Brown, S.L. and Booth, A. (1996). Cohabitation versus marriage: A comparison of relationship quality. *Journal of Marriage and the Family*, 58, 668–678.

Bruce, M.L. and Kim, K.M. (1992). Differences in the effects of divorce on major depression in men and women. *American Journal of Psychiatry*, 149, 914–917.

Carpenter, L.M., Nathanson, C.A., and Kim, Y.J. (2009). Physical women, emotional men: Gender and sexual satisfaction in midlife. *Archives of Sexual Behavior*, 38, 87–107.

DeLamater, J. (1991). Emotions and sexuality. In McKinney, K. and Sprecher, S. (eds) *Sexuality in Close Relationships*. Lawrence Erlbaum Associates, Inc., Hillsdale, NJ, pp. 49–92.

Doss, B.D., Rhoades, G.K., Stanley, S.M., and Markman, H.J. (2009). The effect of the transition to parenthood on relationship quality: An 8-year prospective study. *Journal of Personality and Social Psychology*, 96, 601–619.

Edwards, J.N. and Booth, A. (1994). Sexuality, marriage, and well-being: The middle years. In Rossi, A.S. (ed.) *Sexuality Across the Life Course*. University of Chicago Press, Chicago, pp. 233–259.

Forste, R. and Tanfer, K. (1996). Sexual exclusivity among dating, cohabiting, and married women. *Journal of Marriage and the Family*, 58(3), 3–47.

Gatzeva, M. and Paik, A. (2011). Emotional and physical satisfaction in noncohabiting, cohabiting, and marital relationships: The importance of jealous conflict. *Journal of Sex Research*, 48(1), 29–42.

Glass, S. and Wright, T. (1992). Justifications for extramarital relationships: The association between attitudes, behaviors, and gender. *Journal of Sex Research*, 29, 361–387.

Haavio-Mannila, E. and Kontula, O. (1997). Correlates of increased sexual satisfaction. *Archives of Sexual Behaviour*, 26, 399–419.

Laumann, E.O., Gagnon, J., Michael, R.T., and Michaels, S. (1994). *The Social Organization of Sexuality: Sexual Practices in the United States*. University of Chicago Press, Chicago.

Laumann, E.O. and Michael, R.T. (2001). *Sex, Love and Health in America: Private Choices and Public Policies*. University of Chicago Press, Chicago.

Lee, G.R., Seccombe, K., and Shehan, C.L. (1991). Marital status and personal happiness: An analysis of trend data. *Journal of Marriage and the Family*, 53, 839–844.

Liu, C. (2000). A theory of marital sexual life. *Journal of Marriage and the Family*, 62, 363–374.

Meadows, M. (1997). Exploring the invisible: Listening to mid-life women about heterosexual sex. *Women's Studies International Forum*, 20, 145–152.

Michael, A. and O'Keane, V. (2000). Sexual dysfunction in depression. *Human Psychopharmacology*, 15, 337–345.

Northrup, C., Schwartz, P., and Witte, J. (2013). *The Normal Bar: The Secrets of Extremely Happy Couples*. Crown/Random House, New York City, NY.

Parish, W.L., Luo, Y., Stolzenberg, R., Laumann, E.O., Farrer, G., and Pan, S. (2007). Sexual practices and sexual satisfaction: A population based study of Chinese urban adults. *Archives of Sexual Behavior*, 36(1), 5–20.

Pedersen, W. and Blekesaune, M. (2003). Sexual satisfaction in young adulthood: Cohabitation, committed dating or unattached life? *Acta Sociologica*, 46, 179–193.

Sprecher, S. (2002). Sexual satisfaction in premarital relationships: Associations with satisfaction, love, commitment, and stability. *Journal of Sex Research*, 39(3), 190–196.

Sprecher, S. and Regan, P.C. (1998). Passionate and compassionate love in courting and young married couples. *Sociological Inquiry*, 68, 163–185.

Treas, J. and Giesen, D. (2000). Sexual infidelity among married and cohabiting Americans. *Journal of Marriage and the Family*, 62, 48–60.

Warehime, M.N.P. and Bass, L.E.P. (2008). Breaking singles up: Sexual satisfaction among men and women. *International Journal of Sexual Health*, 20(4), 247–261.

Waite, L.J. and Gallagher, M. (2000). *The Case for Marriage: Why Married People are Happier, Healthier, and Better Off Financially*. Doubleday, New York.

Waite, L.J. and Joyner, K. (2001a). Emotional satisfaction and physical pleasure in sexual unions: time horizon, sexual behavior, and sexual exclusivity. *Journal of Marriage and the Family*, 63, 247–264.

Waite, L.J. and Joyner, K. (2001b). Emotional and physical satisfaction with sex in married, cohabiting, and dating sexual unions: Do men and women differ? In Laumann, E.O. and Michael, R.T. (eds) *Sex, Love, and Health in America: Private Choices and Public Policies*. University of Chicago Press, Chicago, pp. 239–269.

Married Sex Is Boring, and Boring Sex Is Bad

Most of the jokes about sex in marriage are kind of lame because they are all the same—without fail they poke fun at how boring marital sex is. It seems that everyone (both the jokes' writers and the audience who laughs) assumes that after a long passage of time it's inevitable that marital sex won't be that hot.

Wrong. While it is truth it may not be as rough and tumble as the first years of over the top infatuation, the deeper truth is that the majority of married men and women have quite a bit of sex and like their sex lives.

That said, the frequency of sex does diminish as we get older, not necessarily because we are less attracted to our partners but because of the burdens of age, work, mundane relationship issues, and other life challenges (Northrup *et al.*, 2013). And there is a sizeable minority of people who become disinterested in sex within their marriage.

Many Married People are Satisfied With Their Sex Lives

A national study of adults found that only 23% of men and women felt their sexual relationship was often or always "routine." On the flip side, 38% said sex was never or hardly ever routine. The rest seemed to mix routine sex with something a little spicier (Kaiser Family Foundation, 1998). A more recent study (which had a large sample but not one picked randomly) found that the majority of couples thought of their sex lives as satisfying. Interestingly, this was almost uniformly true of couples that described themselves as "extremely happy" (Northup *et al.*, 2013, p. 13).

Good communication skills seem to be very important for a happy sex life because in order to have a good sex life couples need to, well, talk to each other (Bograd and Spilka 1996; Kaslow and Robinson 1996; Robinson and Blanton, 1993; Mackey *et al.*, 2004, p. 129). Other research has indicated that sexiness in long-term couples is related to the quality of communication, the importance of sexual relations to the couple, physical affection, and psychological intimacy (Mackey *et al.*, 2004, p. 124). Sex lives within marriage "ebb and flow" over the course of the relationship. Studies have also found that on days when couples feel positively about each other, lust was also high (Ridley, 2006). Most researchers agree that if good communication exists in the couple, sex will stay interesting, relatively frequent, and fulfilling (Hyde and DeLamater, 2011).

What is perhaps most important is that couples know how to ride out the times when sex is a little boring without letting it affect their happiness or their commitment. Happy couples know that sex doesn't always have to be passionate to be fulfilling and that if they continue to communicate and maintain psychological intimacy, any periods of sexual boredom will eventually be punctuated by more memorable moments of sexual intensity.

But Doesn't Sex Get Dull In Marriage?

Of course it does—though we would argue that this is not unique to marriage or even long-term relationships. Not every act of sex is going to be earth shattering. Some are going to be great, others okay, and others a little dull. For many people even dull sex is better than the other ways they could be spending their time, like watching mindless television, surfing the internet, or cleaning the house.

We wonder if some of the fears and stereotypes about married sex have actually come from experts who want to help couples get over this problem before they even have it. Listen to some expert advice and you'd expect everyone was dreaming up new ways to paint their walls rather than enjoying passionate sex. One self-help book put it this way:

> [Sex] is the most natural thing in the world, a logical result of romantic love, the physical expression of a more symbolic union. But sex with someone that you love can also be as routine and dull as brushing your teeth. It can be a cause of shame and misery. (Litvinoff, 1999, p. 67)

Wow, that makes it sound like sex in marriage is not only a downer, but almost tragic. Another expert says:

> It's a lot easier to introduce sexual novelty and undisclosed aspects of eroticism in one-night stands or an affair than in your marriage. It's a greater challenge to your sense of self when you're with a spouse. That's why sexual boredom (and affairs) are so prevalent. We demand stability in marriage—and when we get it, we complain that things are always the same. The resulting boredom contributes to low desire. (Schnarch, 1997, p. 151)

But just because stability and eroticism may conflict, that doesn't mean committed couples aren't having fun in bed. Maybe they are not having as much fun as they did in a tumultuous and ultimately doomed taboo relationship—but most people would not sign up for that relationship again, and they would overwhelmingly sign up for being married to the same person they married years and years ago (Northrup *et al.,* 2013).

Some therapists worry that this whole subject has been overtherapized. They posit that fears of inadequacy in marital sex lives will actually cause anxiety and dissatisfaction, and lead to the inadequacy that was feared in the first place. After all, everything is relative and what we compare ourselves to makes a difference. It is possible that as a society intent on talking about how married sex is boring and boring sex is bad, we have upped the ante so much that expectations for sexual frequency and passion have become unrealistic and what is now perceived of as sexual boredom would not have been considered an issue in the past (Tunariu, 2004, p. 68).

But Men Really Do Get Bored, Right?

There is a good deal of research that indicates that men have a higher need for variety and novelty than women do, not just when it comes to sex but in all aspects of their lives (Vodanovich and Kass, 1990; Sundberg *et al.*, 1991; Watt and Blanchard, 1994; Watt and Ewing, 1996). Researchers found that men scored higher than women on a Boredom Proneness Scale which assessed an individual's need for challenge, excitement, and variety (Watt and Ewing, 1996; Watt and Vodanovich, 1999). Boredom with sex with the same partner has also been found to affect men more than women (Symons, 1992).

It is often referred to by psychologists as the "Coolidge Effect." This may be apocryphal, but President Coolidge is said to have responded to his wife's praise for the ardent nature of a rooster they saw by saying the rooster must be so randy because he had so many hens from which to choose. In more professional language the Coolidge Effect is used to describe how a sexually bored male could be revitalized with the addition of a new female to sexual life (see Dewsbury, 1981 for a review). Socio-biologists think this preference for variety is part of a larger male reproductive strategy to impregnate as many women (or hens, or bears, or horses) as possible. The famous evolutionary biologist Edmund Wilson (1988, p. 65) believed that men would inevitably have a "satiation effect" (lower sexual interest) if restricted to monogamy. Other researchers have been less sure about the impact of sexually exclusive relationships, but many agree that a variety of sex partners is more desired by men than women (Apt and Hurlbert, 1992; Greer and Buss, 1994; Laumann *et al.*, 1994). Furthermore, some researchers have found that men value physical attractiveness more than women do when selecting a lifetime partner (Frazier and Esterly, 1990), are more likely to engage in extra-marital sexual behavior (Hurlbert, 1992), and are more likely to justify sexual desire on the basis of its pleasure potential than as an outcome of emotional attachment (Hill and Preston, 1996).

There is an ongoing debate about the origin of these tendencies. Many of the authors who note these differences also note the cultural conditions that helped create them (Regan and Berscheid, 1999). However, others are more apt to agree with Wilson that the desires are innate. Popular discourse at this point seems to support a biological explanation more than a cultural one— even though changing cultural practices (such as growing acceptance of women who "hook up" with men) would belie the idea that these differences are necessarily biologically driven.

So, Can the Sexual Sparks Still Fly?

Research indicates that sexual passion feeds on novelty, mystery, and uncertainty—including physical and psychological distance, and even danger and conflict (Person, 1999). Familiarity does modify sexual passion but we have to remember that passion is not the same as sexual satisfaction (Schwartz, 1994; Plaud *et al.*, 1997; O'Hanlon, 1981; Perkins and Hill, 1985; Dyer-Smith and Wesson, 1997).

Part of the problem may be that the most common way in which researchers ask about sexual vibrancy in long-term couples is to measure frequency of sex. But quantity is not the same as quality. It is certainly easier to find out about how many times a couple had sex than how each of those sex acts felt to each of the members of the couple, but we think this information is equally as important, if not more so.

Another measurement problem is that both members of a couple may not necessarily feel the same way about their sex life. More often than not, couples have different sexual appetites and have different satiation points (Clement, 2002, p. 243). This complicates the work of gauging what kind of sparks, or fulfillment, a given relationship might have. Therapists often work to help a couple find a common "sexual denominator" so that they can create a pace and intensity that recognizes the couple's differences (Clement, 2002, p. 245). However, Clement, a well-respected sex therapist in Germany, feels that compromising desires often produces a much more boring sex life for a couple. He thinks that finding a pattern in which each person can exercise their erotic potential in their own way will keep the relationship sexy (Clement, 2002, p. 245).

We think the trickier question is what couples do to experience their sex life as worthwhile, once they realize that some of the time there will be sex that is more bread and butter than chocolate decadence (Tunariu, 2004, p. 88). Couples who understand this and are able to remain emotionally close even when sex is boring are in the best position to have an overall satisfying sex life.

References

Apt, C. and Hurlbert, D.F. (1992). The female sensation seeker and marital sexuality. *Journal of Sex and Marital Therapy*, 18(3), 15–324.

Bograd, R. and Spilka, B. (1996). Self-disclosure and marital satisfaction in mid-life and late-life remarriages. *International Journal of Aging and Human Development*, 42 (3), 161–172.

Clement, U. (2002). Sex in long-term relationships: A systematic approach to sexual desire problems. *Archives of Sexual Behavior*, 31(3), 241–246.

Dewsbury, D.A. (1981). Effects of novelty on copulatory behaviour: The Coolidge effect and related phenomena. *Psychological Bulletin*, 89, 464–482.

Dyer-Smith, M.B.A. and Wesson, D.A. (1997). Resource allocation efficiency as an indicator of boredom, work performance and absence. *Ergonomics*, 40(5), 515–521.

Frazier, P.A. and Esterly, E. (1990). Correlates of relationship beliefs: Gender, relationship experience and relationship satisfaction. *Journal of Social and Personal Relationships*, 7, 331–352.

Greer, A.E. and Buss, D.M. (1994). Tactics for promoting sexual encounters. *Journal of Sex Research*, 31, 185–201.

Hill, C.A. and Preston, L.K. (1996). Individual differences in the experience of sexual motivation: theory and measurement of dispositional sexual motives. *Journal of Sex Research*, 33, 27–45.

Hurlbert, D.F. (1992). Factors influencing a woman's decision to end an extramarital sexual relationship. *Journal of Sex and Marital Therapy*, 18, 104–113.

Hyde, J. and DeLamater, J. (2011). *Understanding Human Sexuality*, 11th edn. McGraw Hill, New York, NY.

Kaiser Family Foundation (1998). *Sex in the Nineties: 1998 National Survey of Americans on Sex and Sexual Health*. Menlo Park, California, publication number 1430.

Kaslow, F. and Robinson, J. (1996). Long-term satisfying marriages: Perceptions of contributing factors. *American Journal of Family Therapy*, 24 (2), 153–170.

Laumann, E.O., Gagnon, J.H., Michael, R.T., and Michaels, S. (1994). *The Social Organization of Sexuality: Sexual Practices in the United States*. University of Chicago Press, Chicago.

Litvinoff, S. (1999). *The Relate Guide to Sex in Loving Relationships*. Vermilion, London.

Mackey, R.A., Diemer, M.A., and O'Brien, B.A. (2004). Relational factors in understanding satisfaction in the lasting relationships of same sex and heterosexual couples. *Journal of Homosexuality*, 47(1), 111–136.

Northrup, C., Schwartz, P., and Witte, J. (2013). *The Normal Bar: The Secrets of Extremely Happy Couples*. Crown/Random House, New York City, NY.

O'Hanlon, F. (1981). Boredom: Practical consequences and theory. *Acta Psychologica*, 49, 53–82.

Perkins, R.E. and Hill, A.B. (1985). Cognitive and affective aspects of boredom. *British Journal of Psychology*, 76, 221–234.

Person, E.S. (1999). *The Sexual Century*. Yale University Press, New Haven and London.

Plaud, J.J., Gaither, G.A., Henderson, S.A., and Devitt, M.K. (1997). The long-term habituation of sexual arousal in human males: a crossover design. *Psychological Record*, 47, 385–399.

Regan, P.C. and Berscheid, E. (1999). *Lust: What We Know About Human Sexual Desire*. Sage, California.

Ridley ,C.A. (2006). The ebb and flow of marital lust: A relational approach. *Journal of Sex Research*, 43, 144–153.

Robinson, L. and Blanton, W. (1993). Marital strengths in enduring marriages. *Family Relations*, 42, 38–45.

Schnarch, D.M. (1997). *Passionate Marriage: Sex, Love, and Intimacy in Emotionally Committed Relationships*. Norton, New York.

Schwartz, P. (1994). *Peer Marriage*. Macmillan, New York.

Sundberg, N.D., Latkinc, A., Farmer, R., and Saoud, J. (1991). Boredom in young adults: Gender and cultural comparisons. *Journal of Cross-Cultural Psychology*, 22, 209–223.

Symons, D. (1992). On the use and misuse of Darwinism in the study of human behaviour. In Barkow, J.H., Cosmide, L., and Tooby, S.J. (eds) *The Adapted Mind: Evolutionary Psychology and the Generation of Culture*. Oxford University Press, Oxford, pp. 137–162.

Tunariu, A. (2004). Men in love: Living with sexual boredom. *Sage Family Studies Abstracts*, 26(2).

Vondanovich, J. and Kass, S.J. (1990). Age and gender differences in boredom proneness. *Journal of Social Behavior and Personality*, 5, 297–304.

Watt, J.D. and Blanchard, M.J. (1994). Boredom proneness and the need for cognition. *Journal of Research in Personality*, 28, 44–51.

Watt, J.D. and Ewing, J.E. (1996). Toward the development and validation of a measure of sexual boredom. *Journal of Sex Research*, 33, 57–66.

Watt, J.D. and Vodanovich, S.J. (1999). Boredom proneness and psychosocial development. *Journal of Psychology*, 333, 303–308.

Wilson, G.D. (1988). The sociobiological basis of sexual dysfunction. In Cole, M. and Dryden, W. (eds) *Sex Therapy in Britain*. Open University Press, Buckingham, pp. 49–68.

Myth #16 Grandma Doesn't Have Sex (and I Doubt that Mom Does Either)

There is no doubt that the idea of parents, much less grandparents, having sex has a certain "Ewwwh" factor for most of us—regardless of whether we are children or adults ourselves. Somehow, at least in Western culture, we prefer to think of our parents as asexual, or at least only interested in sex for reproduction. The problem is that this discomfort in thinking of our parents as sexual extends to all older people and leads to a generalized assumption that sex is only for the young. This is simply ridiculous.

For one thing, sex is a life-long gift and it would be a shame if people started shutting their instincts and desires down just because they thought they had gotten too old to be sexually active. For another, this is at odds with reality. Studies indicate that if people are in a relationship, they are likely to be having sex until health or loss of a partner intervenes. And satisfaction is high—75% of women and 80% of men over age 75 that were having sex, said they got great pleasure from it (Waite *et al.*, 2009). It looks like the view of sex among the aging has been changing in recent years; one study found that while in 2004, 60% of people over the age of 50 thought there was "too much attention to sex" in the world, only 20% agreed with that statement in 2009 (Fisher, 2009). Being older today is not the same as being older just a short time ago, and sex plays a big part in why.

The Good News

Recent attention to sex and aging means we have some good data on what lies in store for those of you who are a bit under 50, including information from a large national randomized study (Fisher, 2009) and a much larger cyber study (Northrup *et al.*, 2013).

Affection

Two-thirds of men over 50 and about half of the women say they still hug and kiss their partner in public and 78% say they still hold hands at least some of the time (although this does get less common with age and duration of the relationship). But if we confine ourselves to the happiest couples, 73% still can't keep their hands off of one another, 74% exchange passionate kisses at least once a week, and 85% say "I love you" to their partner at least once a week. Not surprisingly, the numbers are not as good for couples who do not claim extreme happiness—38% of couples over 50 who describe themselves as unhappy to moderately happy never kiss passionately (Northrup *et al.*, 2009).

Intercourse

Studies vary quite a bit on what the actual frequency of intercourse is for couples over 50 and it is important to divide their numbers by decade since there are changes over time. While sex is in most older people's lives, there is no doubt that increasing age has an impact on desire and behavior. Frequency starts to go down somewhat at age 50, decreases slightly in the sixties, and then takes a dive for both men and women in the seventies (Fisher, 2010). Still, a study of 80- to 102-year-olds who were in good health found that

62% of the men and 30% of the women still had sexual intercourse. And even more reassuring, 8 out of 10 respondents said they usually or always were orgasmic during intercourse (Bretschneider and McCoy, 1988). Overall, sexual happiness was likely if an older person had a partner, had good health, and had a partner with good health (Fisher, 2009).

Playful Sex

Even more good news—old people are not unimaginative in bed. In one study, 60% of women over 50 and 40% of the men said they used sex toys. That makes sense both because sex toys have gone mainstream and are easy to buy these days on- and off-line, but also because as people age into their eighties and nineties, partners become less accessible and sexual aids are more and more useful.

Body Parts

While women do have less lubrication as they age, the clitoris—the prime site for orgasm—stays intact and is not much bothered by aging. Men start to have more erectile issues as they age, but most do not have severe problems until into their seventies. Even better, most of those are correctable with drugs or other interventions. Men do take longer to have an orgasm later in life, but most women don't complain about that (Hyde and DeLamater, 2011).

The Sobering News

The rates of intercourse after 70 really does go way down. There is also some indication that sex gets a little humdrum as relationships age. When people who were in a relationship of more than 21 years were asked if they felt their partner often had sex with them out of a sense of obligation, almost 50% said yes (Northrup *et al.*, 2013). This may be because the spark has gone out of the relationship, but perhaps it is just a courtesy that long-time partners do for one another when one person is interested and the other is not.

However, there are several things that interfere with some older women's and men's sexual desire and/or ability.

Menopause and Beyond

The climacteric is the general name for the period of time in the forties and fifties when there are significant hormonal changes in men and women. The female version is called peri-menopause (the beginning of the end of menstruation) and menopause (the stopping of menstruation). Hormones change gradually, over a period of years—not a sudden aha moment. Menopause is stressful for some women, and a moderate event for others. The change in hormones gives some women night sweats, mood swings, sleeplessness, and even crankiness. This can be caused artificially in young women when endometriosis, cancer, or some other problem requires removal of the uterus and, more important, the ovaries. These operations send a woman into menopause—but because it's not gradual the effects can be temporarily dramatic. Unhappily, some women have a decade or more of symptoms.

But menopause in women is not necessarily an opponent of sexual desire, and most women contend with the changes without losing sexual interest. Research indicates that while some of the hormones that have a direct impact on sexual arousal do decrease (though not necessarily disappear since the adrenal glands continue to secret androgens) other factors, like the desirability of the relationship, mental health, and general health play a much greater role in whether or not women are still very interested in sexual contact (Hayes *et al.*, 2008).

An issue that many older women contend with is vaginal dryness. During and after menopause, the hormones that control the production of vaginal secretions during sexual arousal diminish. This can mean that sex is painful and intercourse feels abrasive. The good news is that two-thirds of women do not experience severe vaginal problems (Agency for Healthcare Research and Quality, 2005). Some women use estrogen therapy to increase lubrication but they can also use any number of commercially available lubricants. One has to assume that these products wouldn't be such big sellers if older women were uninterested in sex.

Men Go Through a Change Too

Men also have hormonal changes for which they have to compensate. Testosterone levels decrease gradually over the years (Schiavi, 1990). Testosterone is known to account for at least some of our sexual appetite and a decrease in this male hormone can lead to a decrease in desire. Both men and women are sometimes prescribed additional testosterone but there is debate as to whether this is overprescribed (Chu and Lobo, 2004; Warnock *et al.*, 1997). Some significant research indicates that "low T" is really only present in 1 in 20 men in their seventies and extremely rare in younger men (Wu *et al.*, 2010). (See Myth # 5 for an in-depth discussion of testosterone.)

There is no doubt, however, that as men age, the blood flow to the penis decreases to some degree (which is different in different men) and erections are no longer as hard as they once were (Waite *et al.*, 2009). By age 70, 56% of men have erectile problems (Fisher, 2009). Erectile dysfunction drugs have come to the rescue for most men—and for men who cannot take these drugs there are a variety of other ways to get hard, including implants and painless shots. (We know it's hard to believe the shots are painless, but that is what the men who have had them assure us.)

While there clearly are some physical issues, research suggests that overall satisfaction has to do with a combination of physical and psychological issues. A 2007 study that used a randomized sample of people aged 45 and over found reasons for cessation of or limited sex included the impact of medications, arthritis, stroke, and heart problems but also depression, attitudes about sexuality in general, and lack of a partner (DeLamater and Moorman, 2007). A study by Schiavi *et al.* (1994) of men aged 45–74 found that those in good relationships were highly satisfied with their sexual life; however, there were moderating forces such as erectile dysfunction and lack of good information about sex. While some people have great sexual lives into very old age, there are physical problems that can really start compromising enjoyment or ability and, to add insult to injury, the medications for these problems may affect arousal. Only one-quarter of men and women over 70 indicate extreme satisfaction with their sex lives (Fisher, 2009).

Cultural Issues

Personal and cultural attitudes about sex also seem to affect older people more than younger ones. Take our obsession with young bodies as the standard for sexual attractiveness. This can affect both men and women's feelings and enjoyment of their sexuality. A study found that middle-aged women's desire for sex, frequency of orgasm, and frequency of sexual behavior was dependent on how attractive they felt rather than anything to do with menopause (Koch *et al.*, 2005). Some social scientists believe older people are victims of a contrast effect—being bombarded with images of young, good-looking people all the time can make older individuals feel worse about themselves (Kenrick and Gutierres, 1980). Still, a study indicated that 53% of women over age 75 and 63% of men the same age said they were strongly attracted to their partner (AARP, 1999).

We think that as new images of sexiness for older men and women appear (think of the Viagra and Cialis ads), and as medical advances increase healthy lifespans, the frequency of and satisfaction with sex will continue to increase for older people.

A Better Longer Life

If you love your grandma, you want her to have sex. Research indicates that she will be happier, healthier, and live longer if she has orgasms (Persson, 1980, Davey Smith *et al.*, 1997). This is true for grandpa too. In fact, one longitudinal study of men correlated having at least one orgasm a month with a significantly higher survival. And, men who had two orgasms a week were the big winners in the longevity sweepstakes (Davey Smith *et al.*, 1997). Further, a study of older men found that those who had sex at least twice a week were the least likely to have heart attacks (Hall *et al.*, 2010). Sex brought both physical and psychological benefits—participants said that sex made them feel more wanted, needed and that, like the rest of us, they craved the exchange of affection that occurs during sexual moments.

Of course, there is one caveat to all of this which is that age does not provide any protection against STIs and older people need to practice safer sex as well. Older adults grew up before this phrase even existed and many who find themselves divorced or widowed at the end of a long relationship are unprepared for a world in which STIs are so common. So, before grandma or grandpa starts dating, someone ought to take her/him aside and discuss the importance of condoms.

We believe that the numbers on older adults and sex will continue to go up both in terms of frequency and satisfaction. Cultural and personal factors affect sexuality and aging enormously, and as we mentioned at the beginning of this chapter, our culture is not just becoming more sex positive but becoming more comfortable with the fact that we are all sexual well into our senior years.

References

Agency for Healthcare Research and Quality (2005). Management of menopause related symptoms. http://archive.ahrq.gov/clinic/epcsums/menosum.htm (accessed August 12, 2014).

AARP (1999). AARP/Modern Maturity Survey. Prepared by NFO Research for AARP. http://assets.aarp.org/rgcenter/health/mmsexsurvey.pdf (accessed August 12, 2014).

Bretschneider, J. and McCoy, N. (1988). Sexual interest and behavior in healthy 80–102 year olds. *Archives of Sexual Behavior*, 109–130.

Chu, M. and Lobo, R. (2004). Formulations and use of androgens in women. *Journal of Family Practice*, 53, s3.

Davey Smith, G., Frankel, S., and Yarnell, J. (1997). Sex and death: Are they related? Findings from the Caerphilly Cohort study. *British Medical Journal*, 315, 1641–1644.

DeLamater, J. and Moorman, S. (2007). Sexual behavior in later life. *Journal of Aging and Health*, 19, 921–925.

Fisher, L.L. (2010). *Sex, Romance and Relationships: AARP Survey of Midlife and Older Adults*. AARP, Washington DC. http://assets.aarp.org/rgcenter/general/srr_09.pdf (accessed August 12, 2014).

Hall, S., Shackelton, R., Rosen, R.C., and Araujo, A.B. (2010). Sexual activity, erectile dysfunction, and incident cardiovascular events. *American Journal of Cardiology*, 105, 192–197.

Hayes, R.D., Dennerstein, L., Bennett, C.M., Sidat, M., Gurrin, L.C., and Fairley, C.K. (2008). Risk factors for female sexual dysfunction in the general population: Exploring factors associated with low sexual functioning and sexual distress. *Journal of Sexual Medicine*, 5, 1681–1693.

Hyde, J. and DeLamater, J. (2011). *Understanding Human Sexuality*, 11th edn. McGraw Hill, New York.

Kenrick, D.T. and Gutierres, S.E. (1980). Contrast effects and judgments of physical attractiveness: When beauty becomes a social problem. *Journal of Personality and Social Behavior*, 38, 131–140.

Koch, P., Mansfield, P., Thurau, D., and Cary, M. (2005). Feeling frumpy: The relationship between body image and sexual response changes in middle aged women. *Journal of Sex Research*, 42, 215–223.

Northrup, C., Schwartz, P., and Witte, J. (2013). *The Normal Bar: Secrets of Extremely Happy Couples*. Crown, Random House, New York.

Persson, G. (1980). Sexuality in a 70-year-old urban population. *Journal of Psychosomatic Research*, 24(6), 335–342.

Schiavi, R. (1990). Sexuality in aging men. *Annual Review of Sex Research*, 1, 227–250.

Schiavi, R.C., Mandeli, J., and Schreiner-Engel, P. (1994). Sexual satisfaction in healthy aging men. *Journal of Sex and Marital Therapy*, 20(1), 3–13.

Waite, L.J., Laumann, E.O., Das, A., and Schumm, L.P. (2009). Sexuality: Measures of partnerships, practices, attitudes and problems in the National Social Life, Health and Aging Study. *Journal of Gerontology: Social Sciences*, 64B, 156–166.

Warnock, J., Bundren, J., and Davod, W. (1997) Female hypoactive sexual desire disorder due to androgen deficiency: Clinical and psychometric issues. *Psychopharmacology Bulletin*, 33, 761–766.

Wu, F.C., Tajar, A., Beynon, J.M., Pye, S.R., Silman, A.J., Finn, J.D., *et al.* (2010). Identification of late onset hypogonadism in middle-aged and elderly men. *New England Journal of Medicine*, 363, 123–135.

Myth #17   Young People Are Sexually Wild, Promiscuous, and Irresponsible

Not so long ago a study of teen sexual behavior was released by the Centers for Disease Control and Prevention (CDC) that contained a ton of information about what young people aged 15–24 were doing in the bedroom (or perhaps in the backseat of a car). Those of us who work in sexual health were pretty excited to get these data because, though our society is obsessed with the idea of teen sexual behavior, we tend to be afraid to ask young people what they're really doing. (Some parents even protest surveys about teen sex out of fears that asking the questions will give their kids new ideas that they just might try.) This particular survey asked about oral, vaginal, and anal sex; contraception use; same-sex behavior; and even attitudes toward sex, pregnancy, and birth control. But the media seized on just one thing—a statistic that found that the number of teens who had not engaged in any type of sexual behavior with another person had gone up.

Headlines proclaimed "More teens waiting longer to have sex," "More teens delay," and, our favorite from a British publication, "No Sex Please, We're Americans." The journalists and experts interviewed for these articles seemed to agree that this was good news and that adults, parents in particular, should be pleased. In his *New York Times* editorial on the importance of monogamy, Ross Douthat (2011) went so far as to say that this statistic was good news for all conservatives.

The report, *Sexual Behavior, Sexual Attraction, and Sexual Identity in the United States: Data from the 2006–2008 National Survey of Family Growth* (hereafter referred to as *Sexual Behavior 2006–2008*), found that 29% of females and 27% of males aged 15–24 reported that they had never had sexual contact with another person. This was a small but statistically significant change from 2002 when it was 22% for both males and females. It is important to note, however, that this small change was only statistically significant when looked at for the whole group of 15- to 24-year-olds. When looked at in two separate groups—15–19 and 20–24 years—it was no longer significant (and let's face it when it comes to how we feel about young people and sex there are worlds between a 16-year-old and a 23-year-old). More importantly, this statistic only refers to those young people who had never had *any* sexual contact (by which the researchers meant oral, anal, or vaginal sex) with another person; the percentage of young people who had had vaginal sex, for example, was unchanged from 2002, and we have no idea whether the "virgins" were kissing, caressing, or otherwise canoodling (Chandra *et al.*, 2011).

It is true that the young people who fit into this no-sexual-contact-of-any-kind category are protected from sexually transmitted infections (STIs) and pregnancy. But we don't think this is why the media zeroed in on this finding or why one expert declared it "extraordinary progress on a social issue that many once considered intractable." When it comes to teen sexual behavior, our society seems to be stuck on the idea that no sex is the *only* acceptable finding.

To support this idea—that sexual behavior among teens is inherently bad—our society has painted a picture of young people as hormone-soaked risk-takers who cannot be trusted to make any good decisions about sex. And while it is true that teens are more likely to take risks in life than fully formed adults, this vision of them as utterly irresponsible when it comes to sex is simply a myth.

A deeper look at this study and others shows that many teens and young adults are making responsible decisions; they delay sex, have relatively few partners, enter into real relationships, and use contraception. And yet, we adults give them so little credit for behaving, in many ways, better than us.

So What Are They Doing?

According to *Teenagers in the United States; Sexual Activity, Contraceptive Use, and Childbearing, National Survey of Family Growth 2006–2008*, another report based on NSFG data, 42% of never-married females and 43% of never married-males have had vaginal sex in their lifetime. This number is not changed from 2002; however, leading up to 2002 there had been a steady decline with the percentage of never-married females aged 15–19 who had had vaginal intercourse dropping from 51% in 1988, to 49% in 1995, to 46% in 2002. Similarly, for never-married males the percentage who had had vaginal sex dropped from 60% in 1988, to 55% in 1995, to 45% in 2002 but did not drop again (Martinez *et al.*, 2011).

There are lots of theories about why the number of young people having sex began to drop during that time. Some argue that this is when society started becoming highly aware of the risk of HIV and that a life-threatening STI was a game changer for teenagers. Others credit sexuality education while still others undoubtedly credit abstinence-only-until-marriage programs. One mother of a teenager that we spoke to jokingly argued that it was all because of video games—if teens are really logging 30 hours a week of screen time, when would they possibly have time to have sex?

Others have suggested that teens are simply having different kinds of sex (oral and anal) instead. *Sexual Behavior 2006–2008* found that anal sex is relatively rare (11% of females and 10% of males aged 15–19 report engaging in anal sex with an opposite-sex partner and 1% of males that age report doing so with a partner of the same sex). That same study found that oral sex is quite common—27% of 15-year-old boys and 23% of 15-year-old girls have ever had oral sex with an opposite-sex partner and, by ages 18 and 19, these numbers jump to 70% for boys and 63% for girls. In addition, 7% of females and 2% of males aged 15–19 report oral sex with a same-sex partner.

Journalists and experts have spouted many theories about this rise in oral sex among teens; most of them negative. Some say that teens are using oral sex to avoid vaginal sex and, therefore, prevent pregnancy *and* live up to society's hopes that they stay virginal. Others suggest that oral sex now has a certain cachet and teens are using it to gain popularity and prestige. And still others have referred to it (with fear in their voices we imagine) as a "gateway" to vaginal sex.

But this is rampant speculation. We don't even know if there is a real rise in this behavior because we just started asking about it; 2002 was the first time questions on oral sex were included in the NSFG and there has been no statistically significant change since then. As for the theory that teens are having oral sex instead of vaginal sex to preserve their chastity, the numbers don't seem to support it as only 7% of girls aged 15–19 and 9% of males aged 15–19 reported having had oral sex but not vaginal sex. In fact, only 50% of young people aged 15–24 reported having had oral sex before vaginal sex.

It will likely not come as a surprise to anyone that that the most common sexual behavior among teens is solo masturbation. The National Survey of Sexual Health and Behavior (NSSHB), for which researchers at Indiana University surveyed a representative sample of individuals aged 14–94 about a wide range of sexual behavior, found that 48% of teens aged 14–17 had engaged in solo masturbation in their lifetime compared to 22% who had given oral sex, 19% who had received it, 23% who had had vaginal intercourse, and 5% who had had anal intercourse (Fortenberry *et al.*, 2010).

When Do They Start?

Part of the myth about teenagers behaving badly in the bedroom is the idea that they're starting to have sex at younger and younger ages. We've all heard the stories about 12-year-olds being caught having sex in school, which send shivers down the spines of middle school parents everywhere, but for the most part it is not the youngest teens who are doing it. *Sexual Behavior 2006–2008* found that the proportion of females who had engaged in vaginal sex rose steadily as they aged; 23% of 15-year-olds, 34% of 16-year-olds, 44% of 17-year-olds, and 62% of 18- to 19-year-olds. The numbers are similar when it comes to oral sex which (as mentioned earlier) jumps from 23% among 15-year-old girls to 63% among females aged 18 and 19. Males also become more experienced with age. The percentage of males who have had vaginal intercourse jumps from 21% at 15 to 66% at 18 and 19, and whereas 27% of 15-year-old boys have had oral sex, by the time they are 18 and 19, 70% have done so.

Though there are some people who believe sex is never appropriate outside of marriage regardless of age, when it comes to societal acceptance of sexual behavior we set very different standards for a 15-year-old than we do for even an 18-year-old. *Teenagers in the United States* suggested that teenagers themselves agreed with those standards: 68% of male teenagers and 60% of female teenagers agreed that it was okay for unmarried 18-year-olds to have sex if they have strong affection for each other, but only 39% of males and 27% of females said the same about 16-year-olds. (To give teens credit for behaving true to their beliefs, the percentages of teens that are having vaginal intercourse at 16 match these numbers pretty well.)

Who Are Their Partners?

While today's teens are often portrayed as unable or unwilling to really bond with another person and as interested in sex but not relationships, once again the data suggest otherwise. In fact, only 14% of females and 25% of males described their first partner as "just friends" or someone they had just met. And, according to *Teenagers in the United States*, the most common first partner for vaginal intercourse (reported by 72% of females and 56% of males) is someone with whom they were "going steady." According to the NSSHB, more than two-thirds of females aged 14–17 reported that the last time they had received oral sex, given oral sex, or had penile–vaginal intercourse their partner had been a boyfriend/girlfriend. A substantial proportion of males (49%), however, did report receiving oral sex from a partner other than a boyfriend/girlfriend.

They're not out looking for somebody new every weekend either. *Teenagers in the United States* (which limited its data to vaginal intercourse) found that many teenagers (26% of females and 29% of males) had had two lifetime partners and that only a few (14% of females and 16% of males) had had more than four partners in their lifetime. The number of partners does not increase drastically when you take oral and anal sex into account. *Sexual Behavior 2006–2008* found that 23% of 15- to 19-year-olds had one lifetime oral sex partner, 8% had two, 16% had three to six partners, 4% had between seven and 14 partners, and only 1% had more than 15.

How Often Are They Getting Some?

It turns out that young people aren't having sex all that frequently. *Sexual Behavior 2006–2008* found that while 42% of never-married teens had ever had vaginal intercourse, only 30% had done so in the 3 months prior to the survey, and only 25% had done so in the prior month. The NSSHB had similar findings: 21% of all teenagers aged 14–17 had engaged in vaginal intercourse in their lifetime but only 14% had done so in the 90 days prior to the study.

Okay, But Are They Using Protection?

One could argue that even if teens are not out there boffing like bunnies, they are opening themselves up to risks every time they do have sex. It's true that all sex carries the potential risk of pregnancy and STIs but the good news is that many teens are taking appropriate precautions. In fact, when it comes to protecting themselves from pregnancy and disease young people tend to behave better than their adult counterparts.

Teenagers in the United States found that 84% of sexually active, never-married female teenagers used contraception at their most recent intercourse; 55% used a condom, 31% the pill, and 21% used both a condom and a hormonal method (the pill, the shot, the patch, and the contraceptive ring are all hormonal methods). Sexually active, never-married males reported even better rates of contraceptive use; 93% used some method at last intercourse with 79% using condoms, 39% the pill, and 35% both a condom and a hormonal method.

The data on contraceptive use at first intercourse were also encouraging as 79% of sexually active, never-married females and 87% of their male peers used some form of contraception the first time they had vaginal intercourse. This is a particularly important statistic because research has shown that using a contraceptive method at first sex is a good indicator of future use. In fact, *Teenagers in the United States* found that teen females are almost twice as likely to have a birth before reaching age 20 if they did not use a contraceptive method at their first sex.

The news on condom use is also good; 95% of sexually active, never-married teenagers report having used a condom at some point and it is the most common contraceptive used both at first intercourse and most recent intercourse. Use of a condom at first intercourse among sexually active, never-married males actually increased from 71% in 2002 to 82% in 2006–2008. Perhaps the most impressive statistic about condoms, however, is among those never-married males who had had sex within the month prior to the survey: 71% of males used condoms 100% of the time. Obviously we would want that number to be closer to 100% of males 100% of the time (and we definitely want to see improvement in this for their female counterparts only 51% of whom could say the same thing), but this is a good start.

That said, there were no significant changes in the percentage of teenaged females or males using contraception at first intercourse or most recent intercourse. In fact, the increases in contraceptive use that had been seen between 1995 and 2002 did not continue. One has to wonder if our unique and seemingly single-minded emphasis on getting teens to avoid (or delay) sexual activity has gotten in the way of encouraging teens to be responsible when they do become sexually active.

Keep Proving This Myth Wrong

The myth of teens as wild, sex-crazed, and irresponsible is just that—a myth—and a dangerous one as we would never want a teen to sink to society's negative and ill-informed vision of him/her. To those of you reading this book who are between the ages of 15 and 24, let us take a moment to say congratulations for behaving better than most adults believed or expected you would, and while we're at it, congratulations for behaving better than many adults.

That said, we also have to take a moment to remind you that that our country still has ridiculously high rates of unintended pregnancy (among both teens and adults) and STI. We believe that you can do even better—especially when it comes to condoms and other forms of contraception which have to be used consistently (every time) and correctly (the right way)—and prove, once and for all, that adults have it all wrong: teens are not wild and crazy sex maniacs, they're thoughtful and responsible individuals entering into mature and healthy sexual relationships.

References

Brown, D. (2011). A sweeping survey of Americans' sexual behavior. *The Washington Post* (March 4).

Chandra, A., Mosher, W.D., Copen, C., & Sionean, C. (2011). Sexual behavior, sexual attraction, and sexual identity in the United States: Data From the 2006–2008 National Survey of Family Growth. *National Health Statistics Reports*, 36. http://www.cdc.gov/nchs/data/nhsr/nhsr036.pdf (accessed July 22, 2014).

Douthat, R. (2011). Why monogamy matters. *New York Times* (March 6).

Fortenberry, J. D., Schick, V., Herbenick, D., Sanders, S.A., Dodge, B., and Reece, M. (2010). Sexual behaviors and condom use at last vaginal intercourse: A national sample of adolescents ages 14 to 17 years. *Journal of Sexual Medicine*, 7(s5), 305–314.

Martinez, G., Copen, C.E., and Abma, J.C. (2011). Teenagers in the United States: sexual activity, contraceptive use, and childbearing, 2006–2010 National Survey of Family Growth. *National Center for Health Statistics, Vital Health Stat*, 23(31). http://www.cdc.gov/nchs/data/series/sr_23/sr23_031.pdf (accessed July 22, 2014).

Myth #18   Anal Sex is Not Normal

The anal passage has its biological purpose as part of the body's waste management system. Nonetheless, its proximity to the genitals, its walls that are tight but allow entry of a finger, penis, or dildo, and its rich network of nerve endings, encourage an auxiliary purpose as an erotic part of the body.

For some people, just the knowledge that other people enjoy anal sex produces a "yuck" response. For others, homophobia intensifies their negative reaction because they assume only gay men engage in anal sex. They also assume that all gay men have anal intercourse. In truth, a large number of people (gay and heterosexual) have at least experimented with anal sex and a significant number do it as a regular part of their sexual life.

Let's take a look at what really goes on.

Heterosexual Anal Sex

Anal sex is common in many countries where it has been seen as a way to have intercourse without risking a pregnancy as well as a way to maintain "technical virginity" in countries and cultures where this is essential for marriageability. It is a common practice throughout Latin America, South America, Southern Europe, the Middle East, and Mexico (Sanders and Reinisch, 1999).

Here in the United States, we have done a lot of research on anal sex. Not because we are particularly fascinated by this kind of eroticism, but rather because we often take a public health/disease prevention approach to thinking about sexual behavior and we have feared that anal sex carries a higher risk of sexually transmitted infections (STIs), including HIV. While the anal canal can easily accommodate a penis, the anus does not naturally lubricate and abrasions can cause tears in the anal wall meaning that infected semen can more easily enter the bloodstream. So public health researchers and clinicians want good information about who is doing what to whom. The data, however, are often in conflict with one another. It is an awkward question to ask since many people, even those who have had anal sex, see it as a taboo subject, with some shame attached and don't want to talk about it.

Laumann *et al.* (1994) found that 5% of women aged 18–44 found receptive anal sex to be either a "very appealing" or "somewhat appealing" practice. That may sound small but remember 5% of all sexually active women represents approximately 4 million people in the United States. Other researchers, unimpressed with traditional methodologies and fearing this was an underestimate, made more intrusive inquiry into anal sex habits and got higher numbers. A study by Boiling *et al.* indicated that 72% of subjects had at least experimented with anal sex and that 23% regularly engaged in anal intercourse. Boiling's methodology was studied in a paper by Voeller (1991) who found that Boiling was more persistent than other researchers in terms of following up a first denial of anal sexual behavior. Boiling found at first inquiry that patients commonly denied engaging in anal intercourse and only at the second or third interview would they acknowledge and discuss this sexual act. Part of the reason for this reticence (or even lying) may have been not wanting to seem at risk for AIDS. And in fact, this underreporting (or denial) may have affected many if not most studies on heterosexual anal sex (Erickson *et al.*, 1995; Laumann *et al.*, 1994; Voeller, 1991; Halperin, 1999).

Newer numbers come from a random sample population survey of 3545 Californians. The survey found 8% of men and 6% of women reported having had heterosexual anal intercourse at least monthly throughout the previous year. Younger respondents and those who were not married were even more likely to report this practice. For example, 13% of males aged 19 and 20 reported anal intercourse at least monthly. Although most respondents who had had anal sex said they did so between 1 and 5 times a month, 10% of those who had had anal sex said they did it between 6 and 30 times per month (Bogart *et al.*, 2005). Another study of Californians concluded that about 1 in 14 heterosexual people in the state regularly engaged in anal sex (Erickson *et al.*, 1995; Halperin, 1999).

The most recent nationally representative data comes from the National Survey of Sexual Health and Behavior (NSSHB) which was published in 2010. It found that 5% of men aged 16–19, 11% of men aged 20–24, more than 20% of men aged 25–49, and 11% of men aged 50 and older had had insertive anal sex in the last year. The numbers for women are remarkably similar with 4% of women aged 14–17, 18% of women aged 18–19, more than 20% of women aged 20–39, and 4% of women aged 50 and older reporting anal sex in the past year (Herbenick *et al.*, 2010).

The lifetime numbers are also similar with 40% of men aged 25–49 and 40% of women aged 20–49 reporting having engaged in anal sex at some point (Herbenick *et al.*, 2010). Other studies have also looked at lifetime incidence of anal sex and found that 35% of women and 40% of men aged 25–44 in the United States have had anal sex at some point (Baldwin and Baldwin, 2000).

These may be underestimates because there is still a real stigma attached to anal sex which can make honest answers hard to get. A study that investigated the underreporting of sensitive behaviors, with a particular interest in abortion, found that participants were more willing to admit to having an abortion than to engaging in anal intercourse (Smith *et al.*, 1999).

Heterosexual Anal Sex Among Specific Populations

As it is hard to get an overall picture as to how many heterosexual Americans have anal sex, it can be helpful to look at specific populations that may have higher rates of anal sex.

Much of the research on anal sex has focused on AIDS transmission and as such much of it has concentrated on populations uniquely at risk. In a study of sexual behavior among 146 partnered male intravenous drug users, 38% reported engaging in anal sex. In another national survey of 1368 women intravenous drug users, 37% reported practicing anal intercourse within the previous year. Other studies of drug users in the United States have identified rates of anal sex ranging from 30 to 74% (Lewis *et al.*, 1990; Rosenblum *et al.*, 1992; Voeller, 1991; Erickson *et al.*, 1995; Forquera and Truax, 1997; Halperin, 1999, p. 220).

Adolescents and college students have also been the subject of many studies on anal sex because they too are considered to be "at risk." Again, however, the results are all over the map. As mentioned earlier, the NSSHB found that only 5% of adolescents (14–19) had had anal intercourse (Herbenick *et al.*, 2010). A study of 793 adolescents aged 13–21 conducted at a New York City clinic revealed that 26% of female clients had already engaged in anal sex. A self-administered anonymous questionnaire survey of female adolescents in a northern California rural area found that 12% of Hispanic and 10% of white young women reported a history of anal intercourse. Using a similar methodology, a New York City study of predominately Hispanic and

African-American female adolescents found that 9% of the 13- to 15-year-olds, 25% of 16- to 18-year-olds, and 38% of 19- to 21-year-old young women had engaged in anal sex. Moreover, 68% of the adolescents who had anal sex had done so at least once in the preceding 3 months (Hein *et al.*, 1995; Kegeles *et al.*, 1990; Jaffe *et al.*, 1988; Halperin, 1999).

Not surprisingly, college students are having anal sex as well. Surveys at North American college campuses have identified fairly high prevalence rates for anal sex. Of 3400 undergraduate students surveyed at the University of Maryland, for example, 25% reported having practiced heterosexual anal intercourse (Kotloff *et al.*, 1991; MacDonald *et al.*, 1990; Gilbert and Alexander, 1998; Halperin, 1999). A survey in the early 1990s at a Midwestern university found that 17% of male and 18% of female students reported having anal sex (Reinisch *et al.*, 1995; Halperin, 1999).

There is also some research to suggest higher rates of anal sex among Hispanics than non-Hispanics in the United States, though these numbers are somewhat confusing because far more men than women say they engaged in heterosexual anal sex. In the University of Chicago survey, 34% of Hispanic men said they had practiced heterosexual anal intercourse in their lifetime—twice what was reported by Hispanic women. When asked just about the last year, 19% of Hispanic men reported anal sex compared with 12% of Hispanic women. In addition to Latino cultural patterns where men are more likely to have anal (and other types of) sex with secondary or tertiary partners, part of this gender discrepancy may be due to Hispanic women being less likely to report, even in an anonymous telephone interview, this form of sexual activity. Others have also suggested that some Hispanic males may be having anal sex with male partners but reporting it as heterosexual for fear of being labeled gay (Erickson *et al.*, 1995; Laumann *et al.*, 1994; Voeller, 1991; Brody, 1995; Halperin, 1999).

Anal Sex Among Gay Men

Though anal sex may be automatically associated with gay men, it is important to remember that not all men who have anal sex are gay (they may identify as bisexual or even heterosexual but occasionally have sex with another man) and not all gay men have anal sex.

Research indicates that 2–10% of males in the United States have had a same-sex adult sexual experience, but only a small minority regularly engages in receptive anal intercourse (Binson *et al.*, 1996; Fay *et al.*, 1989; Halperin, 1999, p. 720). It is estimated that approximately half to at most two-thirds of sexually active men who have sex with men in the United States regularly engage in receptive anal intercourse (Edward Laumann, Eric Rofes, personal communications, September 1999). For example, according to an unpublished 1996–1998 study of sexual behavior in the four large urban centers (New York City, San Francisco, Los Angeles, Chicago), 51% of men who have sex with men reported having receptive anal intercourse during the previous 12 months (Lance M. Pollack, personal communication, September 1999).

The consensus of most researchers is that roughly 1% to at most 1.5% of adult males (or approximately 1 million men in the United States) regularly practices receptive anal sex (Edward Laumann, Eric Rofes, personal communications, September 1999). This is decidedly lower than the estimate of women's anal sex behavior (Erickson *et al.*, 1995; Laumann *et al.*, 1994; Turner *et al.*, 1995; Catania *et al.*, 1992; Holmberg, 1996; Binson *et al.*, 1996; Halperin, 1999).

Is Virginity the Motive?

As we have mentioned, preservation of virginity is the motivation for large numbers of women who have anal intercourse, especially in places where virginity is highly prized or even required (Sanders and Reinisch, 1999). This question has come up here in the United States many times, especially during the rise of the abstinence-only-until-marriage movement when many students were taught that the ultimate goal was to remain a virgin until your wedding night. Researchers and educators wondered if this emphasis on virginity pushed young people toward alternative behaviors such as oral sex.

Sanders and Reinisch found that 19% of their sample of college students did not consider anal intercourse to be "sex." This would allow for an individual who engages in anal intercourse but abstains from vaginal sex to still label herself a "virgin." Few published studies explore virginity as a motivating factor for anal sex; however, a study of urban high school students in grades 9 through 12 *who identified as virgins* found that 1% of the sample had engaged in heterosexual anal intercourse during the previous year (Schuster *et al.*, 1996). A review of several studies concluded that "virginity" may have a role in the occurrence of anal intercourse among adolescents (McBride and Fortenberry, 2010, p. 130; Halperin, 1999).

In general, however, there are few data to support the idea that young people are having anal sex to preserve their virginity as few adolescents have anal sex (or even oral sex for that matter) before they have vaginal sex.

Do We Like It?

Recently, it seems that more people are talking about anal sex—television shows from *Sex And the City*, to *Entourage*, to *Girls* have depicted characters discussing it, worrying about, and even trying it. But the question still looms, do people (especially women) really like it?

Research shows that men find it more pleasurable than women do (Pinkerton *et al.*, 2003, Wilson and Medora, 1990), but is mixed on what percentage of women find it pleasurable. A study of college students found that 45% of women said that they had engaged in anal receptive penetration with a finger or sex toy (e.g., butt-plug, dildo, or vibrator), and the authors felt the motivation for these activities was seeking pleasure (McBride and Fortenberry, 2010). But another study found that the majority of the 47% of a female sample who had anal sex reported it as a negative experience (Rogala and Tyden, 2003). Some of this negative reaction may be due to the fact that in some of these instances coercion, violence, or roughness may have occurred (McBride and Fortenberry, 2010). We know even less about the context and pleasure of receptive anal sex of men whose female partners use dildos to penetrate them. Studies document receptive anal sex behaviors, both oral–anal and manual–anal contact, occurring in heterosexual men who report having only had female sexual partners but don't determine how much the men enjoyed these activities (McBride and Reece, 2008; McBride et al., 2008).

We should not discount pleasure or the possibility of pleasure during anal sex. The fact that many people are engaging in this act regularly suggests that it has the potential to be extremely pleasurable. As with everything, we suggest that people who are interested talk with their partner and experiment. Possibly starting slow—say inserting a finger a few times before trying a dildo or a penis—can alleviate fear and increase pleasure. Lubrication is also very important for anal play because the skin around the anus is very sensitive and does not lubricate itself at all. And, of course, we'd be remiss if we didn't remind our readers that anal sex carries the risk of STIs—a risk that can increase if there is any tearing—which makes lubrication more important and condoms very important as well.

For people who are interested in experimenting with anal sex, there are a number of books—such as *Anal Pleasure and Health: A Guide for Men, Women and Couples* by Jack Morin or *The Guide to Getting it On* by Paul Joannides—that can help you get ideas on how to have the best and most pleasurable experience. There are also books written specifically for women, lesbian women, and gay men. We suggest finding a guide that you like so that you (and your partner) can decide if anal sex works for you.

References

Baldwin, J.L. and Baldwin, J.D. (2000). Heterosexual anal intercourse: An understudied, high-risk sexual behavior. *Archives of Sexual Behavior*, 29, 357–373.

Binson, D., Moskowitz, J., Mills, T., Anderson, R., Paul, J., Stall, R., et al. (1996). Sampling men who have sex with men: Strategies for a telephone survey in urban areas of the United States. *Proceedings of the Section on Survey Research Methods*, American Statistical Association Meetings, 68–72.

Bogart, L.M., Kral, A.H., Scott, A., Anderson, R., Flynn, N., Gilbert, M.L., et al. (2005). Sexual risk among injection drug users recruited from syringe exchange programs in California. *Sexually Transmitted Diseases*, 32, 27–34.

Brody, S. (1995). Lack of evidence for transmission of human immunodeficiency virus through vaginal intercourse. *Archives of Sexual Behavior*, 24, 383–393.

Catania, J.A., Coates, T.J., Stall, R., Turner, H., Peterson, J., Hearst, N., et al. (1992). Prevalence of AIDS-related risk factors and condom use in the United States. *Science*, 258, 1101–1106.

Erickson, P.I., Bastani, R., Maxwell, A.E., Marcus, A.C., Capell, F.J., and Yan, K.X. (1995). Prevalence of anal sex among heterosexuals in California and its relationship to other AIDS risk behaviors. *AIDS Education and Prevention*, 7, 477–493.

Fay, R.E., Turner, C.F., Klassen, A.D., and Gagnon, J.H. (1989). Prevalence and patterns of same-gender sexual contact among men. *Science*, 243(4889), 338–348.

Forquera, M.A. and Truax, S.R. (1997). Risk factors for HIV seropositivity in women accessing publicly-funded HIV testing sites in California. *California HIV/AIDS Update*, 10, 21–25 (California Dept. of Health Services Office of AIDS).

Gilbert, L. and Alexander, L. (1998). A profile of sexual health behaviors among college women. *Psychological Reports*, 82(1), 107–116.

Halperin, D.T. (1999). Heterosexual anal intercourse: Prevalence, cultural factors, and HIV infection and other health risks, part I. *AIDS Patient Care and STDs*, 13(12), 717–730.

Hein, K., Dell, R., Futterman, D., Rotheram-Borus, M.J., and Shaffer, N. (1995). Comparison of HIV+ and HIV− adolescents: Risk factors and psychosocial determinants. *Pediatrics*, 95, 96–104.

Herbenick, D., Reece, M., Schick, V., Sanders, SA, Dodge, B., and Fortenberry J.D. (2010). Sexual behavior in the United States: Results from a national probability sample of men and women 14 to 95. *Journal of Sexual Medicine*, 7(Suppl 5), 255–265.

Holmberg, S.D. (1996). The estimated prevalence and incidence of HIV in 96 large US metropolitan areas. *American Journal of Public Health*, 86, 642–654.

Jaffe, L.R., Seehaus, M., Wagner, C., and Leadbeater, B.J. (1988). Anal intercourse and knowledge of acquired immunodeficiency syndrome among minority group female adolescents. *Journal of Pediatrics*, 112, 1005–1007.

Kegeles, S., Greenblatt, R., Cardenas, C., Catania, J., Ontiveros, T., and Coates, T.J. (1990). How do Hispanic and white adolescent women differ in sexual risk behavior and in their antecedents? *International Conference on AIDS*, 6, 264 (Abst no. F.C. 733).

Kotloff, K.L., Tacket, C.O., Wasserman, S.S., Bridwell, M.W., Cowan, J.E., Clemens, J.D., *et al.* (1991). A voluntary serosurvey and behavioral risk assessment for human immunodeficiency virus infection among college students. *Sexually Transmitted Diseases*, 18, 223–227.

Laumann, E.O., Gagon, J.H., Michael, R.T., and Michaels, S. (1994). *The Social Organization of Sexuality: Sexual Practices in the United States*. University of Chicago Press, Chicago.

Lewis, D.K., Waiters, J.K., and Case, P. (1990). The prevalence of high-risk sexual behavior in male intravenous drug users with steady female partners. *American Journal of Public Health*, 80, 465–466.

MacDonald, N.E., Wells, G.A., Fisher, W.A., Warren, W.K., King, M.A., Doherty, J.A.A., *et al.* (1990). High-risk STD/HIV behavior among college students. *Journal of the American Medical Association*, 263(23), 3155–3159.

McBride, K.R. and Fortenberry, J.D. (2010). Heterosexual anal sexuality and anal sex behaviors: A review. *Journal of Sex Research*, 47(2), 123–136.

McBride, K.R. and Reece, M. (2008). Heterosexual anal sex behaviors among men: Implications for STI risk. *Paper presented at the 51st Annual Meeting of the Society for the Scientific Study of Sexuality*, San Juan, Puerto Rico.

McBride, K.R., Reece, M., Herbenick, D., Sanders, S., and Fortenberry, J.D. (2008). Heterosexual anal sex research: Using mixed methods to understand sexual behavior. *Poster at the 136th Annual Meeting of the American Public Health Association*, San Diego.

Pinkerton, S.D., Cecil, H., Bogart, L.M., and Abramson, P.R. (2003). The pleasures of sex: An empirical investigation. *Cognition and Emotion*, 17, 341–353.

Reinisch, J.M., Hill, C.A., Sanders, S.A., and Ziemba-Davis, M. (1995). High-risk sexual behavior at a Midwestern university: A confirmatory survey. *Family Planning Perspectives*, 27, 79–82.

Rogala, C., and Tyden, T. (2003). Does pornography influence young women's sexual behavior? *Women's Health Issues*, 13, 39–44.

Rosenblum, L., Darrow, W., Witte, J., Cohen, J., French, F., Sikes, K., *et al.* (1992). Sexual practices in the transmission of hepatitis B virus and prevalence of hepatitis delta virus infection in female prostitutes in the United States. *Journal of the American Medical Association*, 267, 2477–2481.

Sanders, S.A. and Reinisch, J.M. (1999). Would you say you'd "had sex" if...? *Journal of the American Medical Association*, 281, 275–277.

Schuster, M.A., Bell, R.M., and Kanouse, D.E. (1996). The sexual practices of adolescent virgins: genital sexual activities of high school students who have never had vaginal intercourse. *American Journal of Public Health*, 86(11), 1570–1576.

Smith, L.B., Adler, N.E., and Tschann, J.M. (1999). Underreporting sensitive behaviors: The case of young women's willingness to report abortion. *Health Psychology*, 18, 37–43.

Turner, C.F., Danella, R.D., and Rogers, S.M. (1995). Sexual behavior in the United States, 1930–1990: Trends and methodological problems. *Sexually Transmitted Diseases*, 22, 173–190.

Voeller, B. (1991). AIDS and heterosexual anal intercourse. *Archives of Sexual Behavior*, 20, 233–276.

Wilson, S.M., and Medora, N. (1990). Gender comparisons of college students' attitudes toward sexual behavior. *Adolescence*, 25, 615–628.

4 PERFORMANCE
Lights, Camera, Orgasm

Myth #19 The First Time You Have Sex Is One of the Best and Most Meaningful Events of Your Life

Rose petals are strewn across the floor, candles flicker on every available surface bathing the room in a yellow glow, and soft music plays in the background as you and your partner (whom you love deeply and feel completely at ease with) fall gracefully onto the bed, effortlessly remove each other's clothes, and proceed to make passionate, pleasurable (and, of course, protected) love. No one finds themselves squirming to free a pinned armed, no one screams "ouch" because the other person has accidentally kneed them in the groin or sat on their hair, no one fears their upper lip is too sweaty or worries that the angle is unflattering to their stomach, thighs, or butt. At no point does anyone doubt that they are doing it right or utter the question "Is it all the way in?" Nobody farts. All moans are elegant (more song than grunt). And, everybody has an earth-shattering orgasm.

Sound like your first time? We doubt it.

People tend to put a lot of emphasis on the first time they have sex. It's a rite of passage. It's the first time a person risks pregnancy or sexually transmitted infections (STIs). It's something almost everyone does eventually. As Laura Carpenter (2001) explains: "Societal concerns about sexuality often crystalize around virginity loss, both because it is widely perceived as one of the most significant turning points in sexual life and because of the emphasis public health and policy professionals place on first coitus and sexual initiation" (p. 127). It is also a sexual experience that most people remember years, even decades, later (which can't be said of all sexual experiences). But is it really one of the most meaningful events in your life? Should it be?

50 Great Myths of Human Sexuality, First Edition. Pepper Schwartz and Martha Kempner.
© 2015 John Wiley & Sons, Inc. Published 2015 by John Wiley & Sons, Inc.

In this entry we explore our fascination with the first time and try to understand why societies put so much emphasis not just on this one event but on virginity itself. We also examine historical changes to these views about virginity and try to figure out how young people really feel about losing it.

Historical Views on Virginity

In many cultures virginity has historically been tied to purity and morality, especially for women. Virginity was, for example, crucial for a woman's marriageability. Some traditions even required proof of premarital virginity—such as blood on the marriage sheets (Tsui and Nicoladis, 2004). While this remains true in some cultures today, the view of virginity in the United States has shifted considerably in modern history. Carpenter (2001) provides a brief history of virginity in this country in which she explains that our views have always been rooted in Christian tradition. In the mid-to-late nineteenth century, the view of virginity as a source of, or proof of, a woman's purity and morality held strong and loss of virginity was seen as an "irrevocable loss of innocence." Moreover, it was assumed that unmarried women were virgins. If a woman lost her virginity outside of marriage it might signify "the onset of moral corruption, madness, and even death" (p. 128).

In the early 1900s, however, this view began to change. Though virginity was still seen as valuable to women, more young women were more willing to have sex outside of marriage—especially within the context of a relationship that was heading toward marriage. In fact, from the 1920s to the 1960s a pattern began to emerge in which young men and women had sex before marriage but with the person they planned to marry (Brumberg, 1997, as cited in Carpenter, 2001).

We think of the 1960s as the start of the sexual revolution and indeed things did start to change during that decade as more young people began engaging in premarital sex with multiple partners most of whom they were not planning on marrying. Women's perception of their virginity shifted as well. Rather than seeing it as something of value, they began to think of it more in the ways that men historically had—as something that was neutral at best and undesirable at worst (Carpenter, 2001). As these views changed, so did behaviors and women began to lose their virginity with similar frequency and at similar ages to men (Carpenter, 2001).

The 1990s were also an interesting time for views on virginity. For many men and women, the idea of virginity as a stigma—something to get rid of—seemed prominent. Though it wasn't released until the end of the decade, the movie *American Pie* which focuses on the efforts of a few boys to lose their virginity seems to epitomize this view. At the same time, however, the Religious Right was arguing that we had strayed too far from modesty and chastity and that it was time to put the sexual revolution behind us and go back to the days when virginity was a virtue. They put a lot of political capital into this and got the federal government to back "chastity" education through the Adolescent Family Life Act (AFLA) and then abstinence-only-until-marriage programs through both Title V and the Community-Based Abstinence Education (CBAE) funding streams. At their height, these programs received a total of $176 million per year (SIECUS, 2010a). Programs funded with this money were required to adhere to a strict definition of abstinence education which, among other things, told young people that sex was only appropriate in a mutually monogamous relationship in the context of marriage and that sex outside of marriage was likely to have harmful physical and psychological effects (SIECUS, 2010b).

Programs funded by these grants often focused heavily on the importance of virginity, suggested it was a precious gift that could only be given once, and implied that teenagers who were not virgins were somehow lacking in character. They also frequently exaggerated the consequences of premarital sex which could apparently cause everything from loss of reputation, to problems with your parents, to bad grades, to winding up in jail. At the same time, however, sex within marriage was said to have no risks at all (Kempner, 2001). A number of these programs ended with young people signing virginity pledges in which they promised to remain abstinent until their wedding day. Some young people also participated in virginity pledge events—such as those sponsored by True Love Waits or the Silver Ring Thing. These events were often religious in nature with readings from the Bible and an ultimate pledge to God. Certain virginity pledge ceremonies took on the feel of wedding ceremonies in which a young woman was given a ring—most often by her father—that symbolized their commitment to staying abstinent until marriage. That ring would then be removed by her father as part of her actual wedding ceremony (Kempner, 2003).

Research on virginity pledges showed mixed results. Under certain circumstances they did help some young people delay sex for an average of 18 months. While far short of marriage, this could be considered a public health success as it represents a year and a half in which these kids had no risk of STIs or pregnancy. That said, the majority of pledgers (88%) did have sex before marriage and, in a disturbing finding, these young people were less likely than peers who hadn't pledged, to use condoms or other contraception when they did become sexually active (Bearman and Brückner, 2001).

Despite this research, the media picked up on this renewed interest in virginity and suggested that young people were changing their tune and "staying pure." A 1994 *Newsweek* article, entitled Virgin Cool, suggested:

> A lot of kids are putting off sex, and not because they can't get a date. They've decided to wait, and they're proud of their chastity, not embarrassed by it. Suddenly, virgin geek is giving way to virgin chic. (Ingrassia, 1994)

The data on teen sexual behavior does show some drop in sexual behavior throughout the 1990s. The Centers for Disease Control and Prevention (CDC) began its Youth Risk Behavior Survey (YRBS) in 1991. The survey is designed to ask about all sorts of risk behavior from using alcohol and tobacco, to wearing seatbelts and bicycle helmets, to having sex. In 1991, the first year of the study, 54.1% of high school students reported ever having had sex. This number dropped steadily over the next decade hitting a low of 45.6% in 2001. It has been unchanged ever since (Kann *et al.*, 2014).

All of this is to say that in modern history, society has had some pretty conflicting views on virginity. These views impact how individuals feel about their own first time.

Individuals' Views on Their Virginity

Laura Carpenter has done extensive work on individuals' views of their virginity, publishing a number of articles and a book, *Virginity Lost: An Intimate Portrait of First Sexual Experiences* (2005). Carpenter identifies three common frames through which most young people view their virginity. The first harkens back to the understanding of virginity as holding intrinsic value, especially for women. This view uses the metaphor of virginity as a gift that one partner gives and the other partner takes. She explains:

> Perceiving virginity as a very valuable gift, not least because of its nonrenewable nature, these women and men were concerned primarily with finding partners who would appreciate the worth of their gift and, more important, reciprocate with a gift of similar value (typically the recipient's own virginity or increased commitment to the relationship). (Carpenter, 2001, p. 133)

A second way that many people viewed their own virginity or more specifically their virginity loss was as part of a process. According to Carpenter, "These men and women believed that virginity loss, like social transitions in general, would increase their knowledge (about sexuality and themselves) and leave them feeling transformed" (2001, p. 133).

Finally, some people viewed their virginity as a stigma or something they wished to get rid of as soon as possible. These young people, "typically emphasize the importance of not incurring additional stigmas, such as a reputation for sexual ineptitude, during the campaign to lose virginity" (Carpenter, 2001, p. 133).

These frames are important not just because they help to highlight the various notions that society has of virginity, but because they directly impact how individuals feel about their first sexual experience as well subsequent ones. She writes: "Importantly, some metaphors for virginity loss are more conducive to emotional and physical well-being—before during and after virginity loss than others" (Carpenter, 2005, p. 13).

In her 2001 study, Carpenter found that those who saw virginity as a gift were most likely to be proud of their virginity beforehand, to lose it to someone they were in a serious relationship with, and to use contraception when they did have sex for the first time. On the flip side, however, they were also more likely to feel ashamed of having lost their virginity especially if their partner failed to reciprocate the gift in some way, such as by becoming more committed to the relationship. In contrast those who saw it as part of a process tended to be "best equipped to work through physically and emotionally negative experiences by talking with their partners in ways that helped ensure more positive sexual experiences later on" (p. 135). Finally, those who saw virginity as a stigma were less likely to be honest with their partners about it in advance, therefore preventing open communication. Some of these young people were devastated when their status as a virgin was discovered by the partner. These respondents were most likely to lose their virginity to a temporary partner and least likely to use contraception when they did so. They were, however, typically satisfied by whatever first experience they did have.

Though most studies on virginity and the first time are limited to heterosexual participants, Carpenter's studies include some individuals who identified as gay, lesbian, or bisexual. She found that gay and lesbian respondents were much more likely to view virginity through the process frame (73% compared with 46% of heterosexuals). She suggested that this was particularly true of gay and bisexual respondents in part because the process included both virginity loss and coming out (Carpenter, 2001). She also noted that while 54% of heterosexual respondents had seen virginity as a gift at least at some point in their lives this was only true of 31% of their gay and lesbian counterparts (Carpenter, 2001). Some other studies have determined that young women who first have sex with other women appear to enjoy greater control over the experience than women whose first partners are men (Brumberg, 1997 and Thompson, 1995, as cited in Carpenter, 2002).

How People Feel About Their First Time

Over the years, many researchers have asked individuals to consider how they felt about their first sexual experience either right away or in hindsight. The results suggest that pretty much no one had the candles and rose petals scene we described at the beginning or, even if they did, they didn't enjoy it.

A 2010 study, for example, looked at data from almost 2000 college students around the United States to determine whether they experienced physiological and/or psychological satisfaction the first time they had intercourse. (This study, like most, was limited to heterosexual intercourse.) The study also asked them about various emotions they felt at the time as well as relationship characteristics (Higgins *et al.*, 2010). It found that the mean age of first intercourse was 16.6 and the majority of respondents were in a "committed love relationship" or a "steady dating relationship." When asked about physiological satisfaction, only 17.3% reported being extremely satisfied, 22.8% were considerably satisfied, 21.9% were moderately satisfied, 16.9% were slightly satisfied, and 21% of all respondents said they were not at all physiologically satisfied by their first intercourse experiences. These results, however, varied largely by gender with 42.7% of black men and

30.7% of non-Hispanic white men reporting being extremely satisfied compared with just 9.2% of black women and 6.5% of non-Hispanic white women. The results at the opposite end of the spectrum were similar with only 8.0% of black men and 3.6% of non-Hispanic white men saying they were not at all physiologically satisfied compared with 34.4% of black women and 29.8% of non-Hispanic white women (Higgins *et al.*, 2010, p. 388). (Though the results are presented broken down by race, the authors note there was little racial variation.)

When it came to psychological satisfaction the numbers were very similar with 18.5% of the whole sample experiencing extreme satisfaction and 17.8% experiencing none. Everyone else fell somewhere in the middle. Women were also less likely than men to report psychological satisfaction though the numbers were not quite as striking as they were for physical satisfaction. Among both men and women guilt was a somewhat common emotion with 20.6% of the sample saying they experienced extreme or considerable guilt and 13.2% saying they felt moderate guilt. Anxiety was even more common with 41.3% of all respondents reporting extreme or considerable anxiety and another 22.4% reporting moderate anxiety (Higgins *et al.*, 2010, p. 388).

The authors concluded that women still have a lot of ground to gain as men continue to be much more likely to be satisfied with their early sexual experiences (Higgins *et al.*, 2010).

Higgins *et al.* note that their findings for men were similar to an earlier study of Canadian students conducted by Tsui and Nicoladis (2004) but they differed when it came to women. In that study, men were significantly more likely to report feeling physically satisfied after first intercourse (62% versus 35%) but there was almost no difference between the genders when it came to emotional satisfaction (56% for men and 54% for women). Men and women also had similar overall assessments of the experience with 72% of men and 61% of women saying it was either perfect, very good, or good in contrast to 11% of men and 13% of women who thought it was bad or very bad (Tsui and Nicoladis, 2004, p. 100). There were some notable differences between the genders, however, with 5% of men experiencing pain compared with 52% of women. In addition, 76% of men reported experiencing an orgasm compared with just 12% of women (Tsui and Nicoladis, 2004, p. 99).

In attempts to get young people to put off having sex we often caution them that bad things will happen after the first time—he'll never want you again, she'll leave you, you'll regret it, you'll get pregnant. In this study, however, most of the participants (87% of men and 89% of women) reported having sex with the same partner again, 83% of men and 86% of women reported staying as or becoming a couple after first sex, and none of them reported a pregnancy. Moreover, 76% of men and 72% of women said they had no regrets about the experience, and 63% of men and 65% of women said they had been the "right age" (Tsui and Nicoladis, 2004, p. 100).

These positive results have not been found in other studies, specifically those of young men and women in the United States where regret is common and many seem to wish they had waited. For example, a study surveyed teen-agers aged 12–17 in the spring of 2001 and followed up again in 2002 and 2004. The survey asked about their experience with intercourse and their feelings afterward with questions such as "Do you wish you had waited longer to have sex for the first time?" "Were you personally ready for sex? "Was your relationship at the right point to have sex?" and "Were you with the right person to share your first sexual experience?" (Martino *et al.*, 2009).

The researchers found that 46% percent of respondents (61% of females and 39% of males) who first had sex after the initial survey in 2001 wished they had waited longer to have sex. Of teens who wished they had waited, 70% said they weren't ready, 76% said their relationship was not in the right place, and 65% said they had not been with the right person (Martino *et al.*, 2009, p. 96).

These feelings are closely echoed by a periodic survey by the National Campaign to Prevent Teen and Unplanned Pregnancy that consistently finds close to 60% of young people wish they had waited (Albert, 2010, p. 20). This statistic gets a great deal of press attention and is often fodder for abstinence-only-until-marriage proponents who want to use it as proof that we need to stress the importance of virginity until marriage. Whenever we see it, however, we wonder if some of this regret is superimposed onto the event in retrospect simply as a result of being asked "Do you wish you had waited?" Is it possible that a teen wasn't actively feeling regret but believed this to be the socially acceptable answer to an adult's question? We don't know but we do know that the mixed messages in our society tell teens—especially young women—that they should be interested in sex, act sexy, but stop short of actually wanting sex. We worry that these mixed messages also suggest that it is okay to have sex as long as you feel a little guilty about it afterward.

Education Ahead of Time

Perhaps instead of asking young people how they felt in retrospect, we should work to educate them about sexuality and first sexual experiences before they have them. We can tell them that it probably won't be rose petals and candles, it's usually awkward and messy and that's okay. We can tell them that it should feel good and that it's okay to stop if it doesn't and enjoy it if it does. (We can tell young women that while pain at first intercourse is not unusual, a little lubricant can go a long way toward eliminating it.) We can tell them that it carries risks and they should be safe. And, we can tell them that while it is not the most important moment in their lives, it is one that they will undoubtedly remember better than many, if not most, other sexual experiences and as such they should be sure that they are ready, they have the right partner, and are in the right relationship. Because even if it's not perfect (and trust us, it rarely is), we hope it is an experience that everyone is able to look back on fondly.

References

Albert, B. (2010). *With One Voice 2010: America's Adults and Teens Sound Off About Teen Pregnancy A Periodic National Survey.* National Campaign to Prevent Teen and Unplanned Pregnancy.

Bearman, P.S. and Brückner, H. (2001). Promising the future: Virginity pledges and first intercourse. *American Journal of Sociology,* 106(4), 859–912.

Carpenter, L.M. (2001). The ambiguity of "having sex": The subjective experience of virginity loss in the United States. *Journal of Sex Research,* 38(2), 127–139.

Carpenter, L.M. (2002). Gender and the meaning and experience of virginity loss in the contemporary United States. *Gender and Society,* 16(3), 345–365.

Carpenter, L.M. (2005). *Virginity Lost: An Intimate Portrait of First Sexual Experiences.* New York University Press, New York.

Higgins, J.A., Trussell, J., Moore, N.B., and Davidson, J.K. (2010). Virginity lost, satisfaction gained? Physiological and psychological sexual satisfaction at heterosexual debut. *Journal of Sex Research,* 47(4), 384–394.

Ingrassia, M. (1994). Virgin cool. *Newsweek,* 124(5849), 58–69. http://www.newsweek.com/virgin-cool-189654 (accessed August 12, 2014).

Kann, L., Kinchen, S., Shanklin, S.L., Flint, K.H., Kawkins, J., Harris, W.A., *et al.* (2014). Youth risk behavior surveillance: United States, 2013. *Morbidity and Mortality Weekly Records Surveillance Summaries,* 63(Suppl 4), 1–168.

Kempner, M. (2001). *Toward a Sexually Healthy America: Abstinence-only-until-marriage Programs that Try to Keep Our Youth "Scared Chaste."* Sexuality Information and Education Council of the United States (SIECUS).

Kempner, M. (2003) A controversial decade: 10 years of tracking debates around sexuality education. *SIECUS Report,* 31(6), 33–48.

Martino, S.C., Collins, R.L., Elliott, M.N., Kanouse, D.E., and Berry, S.H. (2009). It's better on TV: Does television set teenagers up for regret following sexual initiation? *Perspectives on Sexual and Reproductive Health,* 41(2), 92–100.

SIECUS (2010a). A brief history: Abstinence-only-until-marriage funding. http://www.nomoremoney.org/index.cfm?pageid=947 (accessed July 22, 2014).

SIECUS (2010b). What programs must teach. http://www.nomoremoney.org/index.cfm?pageid=948 (accessed July 22, 2014).

Tsui, L. and Nicoladis, E. (2004). Losing it: Similarities and differences in first intercourse experiences of men and women. *Canadian Journal of Human Sexuality,* 13(2), 95–106.

Myth #20 Good Sex Always Ends With Simultaneous Orgasms

The idea that good sex ends with each partner climaxing at exactly the same time is not an invention of R rated movies or women's magazines. It actually has been around a lot longer than that. *Ideal Marriage,* an international best-selling marriage manual published in 1932, perpetuated the idea. The author, gynecologist Theodoor Hendrik Van de Velde, opined: "In normal and perfect coitus, mutual orgasm must be almost simultaneous" (p. 181). Simultaneous penetrative orgasm would, according to Van de Velde, contribute to the attachment and well-being of the partnership.

This opinion seems to be born directly from Freudian psychiatry which treats any orgasm except one achieved during intercourse as "immature" and accords simultaneous orgasm during intercourse "a special harmony"

(Brody and Weiss, 2012). The problem with this view is that it does not reflect the reality for many women and couples. Many women report having better orgasms from clitoral stimulation than vaginal penetration, and most couples admit that perfectly timed orgasms are rare. What's more, striving for simultaneous orgasms during intercourse may put so much pressure on couples that they don't enjoy the sexual experience and might not be able to orgasm at all.

Simultaneous orgasms may be a happy accident—but aiming for them every time (or even sometimes) can undermine sexual pleasure.

Why Do We Think Simultaneous Orgasms Are Better?

Clearly, many men and women do believe that coming at the same time is best. For example, one study found that simultaneous orgasm was considered important by 41% of the men and 30% of the women surveyed (Colson *et al.*, 2006, p. 124). The question now is why they believe this.

There are several origins for the myth of the superior pleasures of simultaneous orgasm. Today, we can blame pseudo-science and self-help websites that tell of the sublime nature of perfectly timed mutual orgasms. And, while we're at it, we should probably throw a little blame at movie and television portrayals of sex in which we commonly see couples falling apart under the sheets satisfied after what we can only imagine is two well-timed orgasms. (Oddly, porn is probably more accurate since it is actually able to show the orgasm and not just the basking afterward.)

However, the truth is that first we have to blame the experts. Researchers and writers like Van de Velde have suggested for a long time that having an orgasm during intercourse at the same time creates greater physiological and emotional satisfaction. The fact that there were no legitimate studies to back up this assertion didn't seem to make a difference—experts continued to say that simultaneous orgasms were the goal. In fact, there is a companion myth that emerges from time to time that suggests that mutually timed orgasms are also more likely to result in conception. This rather difficult trick was actually certified in marriage manuals and textbooks of the 1950s. (It is, by the way, totally unfounded.)

And yet simultaneous orgasms still have their expert fans who not only do research and writing on the supremacy of vaginally experienced orgasms but downgrade any other experience. They associate women's orgasms during intercourse (rather than other kinds of sexual stimulation), with greater relationship satisfaction and even mental and physical health (Brody, 2007; Brody and Costa, 2008; Costa and Brody, 2010; Brody and Weiss, 2010; Brody and Weiss, 2012). Or, to quote one set of authors, "there is support for the concept that vaginal orgasms concurrent with the man's PVI (penis in vagina, simultaneous orgasm) has benefits even beyond those of vaginal orgasm" (Brody and Weiss, 2012).

But this is the minority opinion and response in the field to this particular research has found the data underlying the conclusions unconvincing and not statistically significant. Critics argue there are no trustworthy baseline data and many confounding variables are not taken into account. Critics worry that promotion of these findings "may not only be ineffective in increasing satisfaction, but, in fact, may be harmful if it creates idealized expectations and places undue stress (sexual performance anxiety) on individuals and couples. This socially constructed dysfunction/disease could, in turn, decrease satisfaction" (Charland *et al.*, 2012, p. 334).

Who Comes First

There is really very little research on who comes first and whether couples come together. A study by Darling *et al.* (1991) is based on observations of various forms of sexual stimulation among heterosexual couples. It found that women preferred it when they had their orgasm first—either through clitoral and vaginal stimulation before intercourse or through a combination of foreplay and intercourse. These researchers suggest that a woman may have increased frustration if her partner had an orgasm during intercourse and left her to climax on her own. This frustration could intensify for a woman whose partner is more affectionate and more active before he has an orgasm and is tired or in some way less actively engaged with her afterwards. Alternatively, a woman might feel pressure to have an orgasm quickly because her partner had already done so or perhaps because intercourse had not gone on long enough to be sexually and/or emotionally satisfying. Finally, when he comes first, a woman may feel that her partner has been selfish in not waiting for her.

But perhaps much of the reported dissatisfaction some women mention is not so much in the timing of orgasm but in the fact that many women have trouble reaching orgasm, period. When this is true, we believe that having to reach it on cue (whether to be quick after he's done or to attempt simultaneous climaxes) increases the chances that a woman will find it even more difficult to have a climax. This may encourage her to give up on a real one and fake it so as not to disappoint her partner's hopes for mutual bliss. (See Myth # 21 for more on faking orgasms.) The "you have to have an orgasm" script of lovemaking seems to pile on even more pressure if simultaneous orgasm is the goal.

The "Right Way to Have an Orgasm" Pitfall

There are a number of other myths that belong in the same basket as the simultaneous orgasm myth. Mostly, they center on the idea that there is a "right" way to have an orgasm. The modern version of this kind of sexual orthodoxy may have unintentionally begun with Masters and Johnson's research on sexual functioning which explained the four phases of the human sexual response cycle—excitement, plateau, orgasm, and refractory period (Masters and Johnson, 1966). Once this was enumerated in the literature and bought into by professionals it became a law of sorts. If a client didn't report a similar cycle to their sex therapist, the client, rather than the cycle, was presumed flawed (Ellison, 1984, p. 327). Today we know that individuals and couples vary in how they experience the stages of sexual response.

This pitfall is similar to the one women found themselves in when Freud declared vaginal orgasms to be the mature and proper way to climax. When this belief reigned supreme, women who couldn't climax through vaginal stimulation alone were considered damaged in some way. It took many years until Masters and Johnson showed in their laboratory setting that orgasms, however generated, rely on the same nerve system (though some people do say they experience them differently depending on how they are produced). The fact is that producing an orgasm during intercourse without direct clitoral stimulation is generally more difficult for most women—and for some women, it is just impossible. In fact, there is quite a bit of research indicating that the inner walls of the vagina are not very sensitive and therefore less likely to provide a quick route to orgasm (Kinsey, 1953, p. 582; Masters and Johnson, 1966).

The pressure to have simultaneous orgasms may in some way take us back to the days when women were supposed to climax through vaginal penetration alone. After all, it is the vaginal penetration that will likely produce a male orgasm. There are some positions in which a women can have vaginal penetration and direct clitoral stimulation either from her partner's fingers, her own fingers, or a sex toy. Even so, we believe that attempts at synchronization overemphasize pleasure from vaginal penetration.

Can Women Become Dependent on a Vibrator for Orgasm?

In truth, often one of the easiest ways for women to have an orgasm is to use a vibrator. The intense sensation that these devices can provide to the vulva and clitoris is extremely effective at bringing some women to climax (and some men love them too), but recently we've heard fears that vibrators can become addictive and that women who use them may never be able to orgasm in any other way. (Another version of the "right way to have an orgasm" pitfall.) We don't think you should worry, we've never heard of a woman leaving a note for her lover or spouse that said "I'm sorry dear, but I have fallen in love with my vibrator and the two of us are running away to Paris so that we can be continuously united forevermore."

Interestingly, vibrators were once thought of as a medical, not a sexual, device. In the late 1880s and at the turn of the century, middle and upper middle class ladies who had emotional or physical discomfort were taken to doctors who would lay them on a vibrating plank or apply a vibration machine to their genitals, causing a "quaking" or "hysterical paroxysm" that would allow sexual congestion to disappear and that was, oddly enough (yes, we are being snide here), ultimately very calming and pleasing to the delighted matron. Around the same time, an electric vibrator machine was patented in America and promoted as a device to cure womb problems that doctors (and patients) believed caused "nervous conditions" and "hysteria" (Maines, 2001). (The literal meaning of hysteria is emotional problems caused by the womb, and it is the origin of the word hysterectomy which is the surgery performed to remove a woman's uterus.) Using this machine was not thought of as masturbation, but as a "treatment" and, therefore, perfectly fine to do rather regularly in order to calm the nerves. Women did not become addicted to these "treatments" as far as we know, but they did like them quite a bit!

Today, vibrator use as a sexual device not a medical one is known to be quite common. A large study showed that nearly 50% of women of any age had used a vibrator (Northrup et al., 2013). The National Survey of Sexual Health and Behavior also found use among American women very common with 46.3% of women reporting they had used a vibrator for masturbation, 41% saying they had used a vibrator during a sexual session with a partner, and 37.3% saying they had used a vibrator during intercourse. Far from hurting women, vibrator use seems to be correlated with good sex and a positive attitude about it—users were more likely to have examined their own genitals, and reported higher levels of sexual arousal, desire, lubrication, and orgasm. Very few women reported any physical or emotional discomfort with the devices—3% of women reported some numbness, 3% reported pain, and 16% said they had some irritation. Almost all of these women, however, said these were temporary problems (Reece et al., 2009).

To be fair, it is true that people can get habituated to vibration. Any behavior that is physically or emotionally rewarding (and in this case, very efficient at producing orgasms) is likely to be repeated and certainly can become a habit. If we frequently have an orgasm in a certain way—no matter what that way may be—we will likely fall back on that pattern more often than not because we know it can be successful. In truth, we don't see a problem with that—if it works and everyone feels good, it can be a nice part of masturbation and partnered sex. But if you or your partner worries about one of you becoming too attached to the vibrator try to incorporate many different things into your lovemaking—a vibrator, a finger, a tongue, a penis, or all four—the sensations produced by each of these are different and can be used and combined inventively to make sure not all orgasms are produced the same way.

What's Important?

What we think is important is evolving a relationship that is sexually satisfying, trusting, and open. We think partners should be sensitive to each other's sexual needs and evolve a complementary style (or styles) of making love. Ideally, they would explore their sex life together, finding out what they do or don't like, what new things they'd like to try, what are their go-to ways of having pleasure. And, perhaps, trying out a vibrator (or vibrators) once in a while.

What we don't see is making anyone behave like a trained seal, having to juggle this or that, or to bend their own sexual response out of shape in order to please some abstract concept of how and when to come. Simultaneous orgasms are certainly a romantic notion but we think they take too much effort (such as having to be controlled when you want to feel absorbed with feeling, not thinking, and being unable to devote a lot of attention to what the other person needs since you are consumed by your own passion at the same time).

Our advice: sex and sexual pleasure are very specific to the individuals involved. Don't go out of your way to have sex in a way that is based on certain cultural directives—especially one that is mostly mythology.

References

Brody, S. (2007). Vaginal orgasm is associated with better psychological function. *Sexual and Relationship Therapy*, 22, 173–191.

Brody, S. and Costa, R.M. (2008). Vaginal orgasm is associated with less use of immature psychological defense mechanisms. *Journal of Sexual Medicine*, 5, 1167–1176.

Brody, S. and Weiss, P. (2010). Vaginal orgasm is associated with vaginal (not clitoral) sex education, focusing mental attention on vaginal sensations, intercourse duration, and a preference for a longer penis. *Journal of Sexual Medicine*, 7, 2774–2781.

Brody, S. and Weiss, P. (2012). Simultaneous penile-vaginal orgasm is associated with sexual satisfaction. *Journal of Sexual Medicine*, 9(9), 2476–2477.

Charland, L., Shrier, I., and Shor, E. (2012). Simultaneous penile-vaginal intercourse orgasm. *Journal of Sexual Medicine*, 9(1), 334.

Colson, M-H., Lemaire, A., Pinton, P., Hamidi, K., and Klein, P. (2006). Sexual behaviors and mental perception, satisfaction and expectations of sex life in men and women in France. *Journal of Sexual Medicine*, 3, 121–131.

Costa, R.M. and Brody, S. (2010). Immature defense mechanisms are associated with lesser vaginal orgasm consistency and greater alcohol consumption before sex. *Journal of Sexual Medicine*, 7, 775–786.

Darling, C.A., Davidson, J.K. Sr, and Cox, R.P. (1991). Female sexual response and the timing of partner orgasm. *Journal of Sex and Marital Therapy*, 17(1), 3–21.

Ellison, C.R. (1984). Harmful beliefs affecting the practice of sex therapy with women. *Psychotherapy: Theory, Research, Practice, Training*, 21(3), 327–334.

Kinsey, A.C, Pomeroy, W.B., Martin, C.E., and Gebhard, P.H. (1953). *Sexual Behavior in the Human Female*. W.B. Saunders, Philadelphia.

Maines, R. (2001). *The Technology of Orgasm, "Hysteria". The Vibrator and Women's Sexual Satisfaction*. Johns Hopkins University Press, Baltimore, MD.

Masters, W.H. and Johnson, V.E. (1966). *Human Sexual Response*. Little, Brown, Boston, MA.

Northrup, C., Schwartz, P., and Witte, J. (2013). *The Normal Bar: The Surprising Secrets of Happy Couples*. Harmony/Random House, New York, NY.

Reece, M., Herbenick, D., Sanders, S.A., Dodge, B., Ghassemi, A., and Fortenberry, J.D. (2009). Prevalence and characteristics of vibrator use by men in the United States. *Journal of Sexual Medicine*, 6, 1867–1874.

Van de Velde, T.H. (1932). *Ideal Marriage: Its Physiology and Technique*. William Heinemann (Medical Books) Ltd., London.

No Partner of Mine Has Ever Faked an Orgasm

The scene is unforgettable. *When Harry Met Sally* is a movie about a long-time friendship that over time turns into a love affair. (It's from 1988 but trust us, find it on Netflix or something, it's still good.) The two debate whether a friendship between a man and a woman can just be a friendship or whether some sexual attraction is involved. However, the good buddies don't acknowledge any attraction between them, and, as friends, hear about each other's unsuccessful romantic relationships. Indeed, the most memorable scene in the movie is one in a restaurant during which they are debating whether or not a man can tell when a woman fakes an orgasm. Harry says he knows that the women he's been with have never faked an orgasm. Sally is skeptical:

SALLY: Why? Most women at one time or another have faked it.
HARRY: Well they haven't faked it with me.
SALLY: How do you know?
HARRY: Because I know.
SALLY: Oh, right, that's right, I forgot, you're a man.
HARRY: What is that supposed to mean?
SALLY: Nothing. It's just that all men are sure it never happened to them and that most women at one time or another have done it so you do the math.
HARRY: You don't think that I could tell the difference?
SALLY: No.
HARRY: Get outta here.

Moments later, Sally launches into a full-scale set of moans, groans, facial expressions, and increasingly loud screams of ecstasy complete with the peak moment and the quiet, satisfied smile that comes afterwards. The extremely well-faked orgasm shocks and amuses all the other people in the dining room. The scene ends when a waiter approaches an older woman at a table next to them and she says: "I'll have what she's having."

Do many people fake orgasms? Sure they do. In a study at the University of Kansas, for example, 67% of the women and 28% of the men reported having faked orgasm. Most said they faked it during penile–vaginal intercourse, but some pretended during oral sex, manual stimulation, or phone sex (Muehlenhard and Shippee, 2010). An older study of 161 young adult women showed that over half of them said they had ever faked an orgasm. Analysis found that those women who had faked it were older, thought they were more attractive, had intercourse at a younger age, had more lifetime partners (including oral sex partners), and scored higher on measures of sexual self-esteem (Wiederman, 1997).

It's not that hard to fake an orgasm, especially if you've had real ones. You know how to make them look, sound, and possibly even feel authentic. The question for us is why would anyone want to fake an orgasm? And, much more secondarily, what *are* the signs of a real orgasm—could you tell if your partner was pretending?

Why Fake One?

Most women and men who fake orgasm want to please their partner, and they know their partner really wants to see them over the moon with pleasure. A woman may have a hard time having an orgasm, and it may get even harder if she thinks her partner will keep trying until she climaxes. She may know, for whatever reason, that it's not going to happen right now, and so—in order to get the whole thing over with (with her lover's feelings intact)—she gives a dramatic rendition of climaxing. Less research has been done on men faking orgasms but they might fake it for the same reason—to end sex without anyone feeling like a bad lover.

A 2014 study of 481 heterosexual female college students found four common reasons that women faked orgasms. The authors named the first "altruistic deceit" which they defined as faking orgasm out of concern for a partner's feelings. The second reason they found was "fear and insecurity" by which they meant women faking orgasm to avoid negative emotions associated with the sexual experience. Women also faked orgasm in an effort to achieve their own "elevated arousal." A little fake it until you make it—if you sound more turned on than you are maybe you will become that turned on for real. And, finally there was "sexual adjournment" which, as we said earlier, was simply faking an orgasm to end sex (Cooper *et al.*, 2014).

Another study hypothesized that women faked orgasm as a way to keep their boyfriends. Researchers surveyed 453 heterosexual women under 50 who had been in a relationship for at least 6 months. They found that those women who were more concerned that their partners might cheat on them were more likely to fake an orgasm. They also found that women who said they had faked orgasm were more likely to engage in other "mate retention" behaviors such as flirting with someone else in front of their partner or yelling at someone they perceived as flirting with their partner. Analysis suggested, however, that this correlation between faked orgasm and mate retention behaviors was diminished if they controlled for fear of infidelity. The authors believe that for women who fear that their partner might cheat, faking orgasm is part of a larger strategy to keep him around (Kaighobadi *et al.*, 2012). Other studies have also found that keeping a partner interested and preventing him from straying was a common reason for faking orgasm (Muehlenhard and Shippee, 2010).

Can You Tell?

Was Harry right, could he really tell that none of the women he had been with had ever faked an orgasm? Probably not. A good Oscar-worthy series of moans may fake some people, though others understand that orgasm isn't just about the noises. As excitement increases, not just breathing but heart rates increase dramatically, and near orgasm, a rash-like flush often appears across the person's body. When a woman has an orgasm, there is likely to be a sequence of involuntary uterine contractions and spasms, and the anal sphincter tightens. The uterus may have a strong afterwave of contraction for 10–20 seconds (Levin and Wagner, 1985). The vagina will also have engorged with blood and the tightening of the pelvic floor muscles and bulbospongiosus muscle will make the vagina feel tighter at the front and paradoxically looser at the back. The clitoris flattens near orgasm and turns a slightly different color (although that would be hard to see unless a lover is giving oral sex). Yet many of these things are likely felt by a partner, especially if he or she has a penis or finger inside the partner's vagina at the time of orgasm. The overall body changes are quite dramatic; it is not just a mounting volume of noises and hair tossing and writhing that marks an orgasm for a woman. Still, with some good moans and maybe a voluntary Keegle or two (an exercise that tightens the vagina muscles), many partners will likely be fooled.

Likewise, it is not just more noise, more thrusting, and ejaculation that marks an orgasm for a man. There is a systemic change in just about every part of the body. A man can also fake it—although it is harder since a woman might expect to feel some spasms and be wet with fluid. Still, if he's using a condom, she might not notice that he did not ejaculate and/or have an orgasm.

But Why Not Have A Real One Instead?

Let's face it. Difficulty having an orgasm is more common than the sex scenes we see on television and in the movies would have us believe. Most women, not just some women, are not orgasmic all the time. In a large random sample study, 71% of women and 25% of men said they did not always have an orgasm when they had sex with their partner (Laumann *et al.*, 1994).

In all fairness, sometimes fears of upsetting a partner with the fact that orgasms aren't happening can be justified. Some men or women will feel inadequate if their partner doesn't come. They may even act defensively by blaming their partner's inhibitions or background. Or they may become less attached to the relationship. The fear or intuition that a partner might react this way is certainly encouragement to fake it, but for people who are having consistent trouble achieving orgasm this is a short run answer to a long-term problem. Faking it actually makes it less likely that real orgasms will happen in the future, since no technique or revisions of lovemaking style or relationship context will have changed. Pretending might now become a way of life—and big secrets build up, sometimes over many years.

If either partner is never or rarely reaching orgasm, more communication (not less) is needed. Partners should talk about techniques that are or aren't working (maybe someone is rubbing or thrusting too hard), they should experiment with penetration angles to see if certain ones are more pleasurable than others. Likewise, if relationship issues are impeding orgasm, those relationship issues need to be dealt with in order to create the right emotional climate for a climax. Communication is the bedrock of sexual pleasure—the belief that talking is embarrassing or that honesty is risky means the relationship is not on stable footing. If the relationship is unable to take the weight of some honest discussion about how things are going or what feels good, what chance do the two people have of becoming more intimate—and therefore more effective at pleasing one another? Talking about sex can be more intimate than doing it, but it may also be more important.

Faking orgasm may be a card to play under some circumstances, but if it is played often, it changes the game from one of intimacy and openness to performance and dishonesty. That is a big change. So while there might be people who are so good at faking that you'd never know, what you want to work on is having a relationship that is so honest and open that it includes being honest and open about what is, and what is not, happening between the sheets.

References

Cooper, E.B., Fenigstein, A., and Fauber, R.L. (2014). The faking orgasm scale for women: Psychometric properties. *Archives of Sexual Behavior*, 43, 423–435.

Kaighobadi, F., Shackelford, T.K., and Weekes-Shackelford, V.A. (2012). Do women pretend orgasm to retain a mate? *Archives of Sexual Behavior*, 41(5), 1121–1125.

Laumann, E.O., Gagnon, J.H., Michael, R.T., and Michaels, S. (1994) *The Social Organization of Sexuality: Sexual Practices in the United States*. University of Chicago Press.

Levin, R.J. and Wagner, G. (1985). Orgasm in women in the laboratory: Quantitative studies on duration, intensity, latency, and vaginal blood flow. *Archives of Sexual Behavior*, 14, 439–449.

Muehlenhard, C.L. and Shippee, S.K. (2010) Men's and women's reports of pretending orgasm. *Journal of Sex Research*, 47, 552–567.

Wiederman, M.W. (1997). Pretending orgasm during sexual intercourse: Correlates in a sample of young adult women. *Journal of Sex and Marital Therapy*, 23(2), 131–139.

Myth #22   Women Want to Be Dominated in Bed, Rough Sex Is the Most Fun

Where do men get the idea that women like rough sex and where do women get the idea that they ought to like rough sex? Well, one place might be popular culture—although we think it goes much deeper than that.

Let's start with the movies and take one as an example. A number of years ago a movie with Al Pacino called *Sea of Love* told the story of a policeman searching for a woman who murdered men she met in the personal ads. In the movie, he meets a woman, played by Ellen Barkin, whom he suspects (but who turns out not to be the murderer). Nevertheless, there is a game of "cat and mouse" as he becomes tremendously attracted to her and tries to decide if she is guilty. When they finally do have sex, it's rough. They claw at each other and he pushes her with some force against a wall. It is clear that we are supposed to believe this is the height of passion.

But is this the way it goes in real life? Would women really like this? Or might it feel scary and unsexy?

Images of Gender and Rough Sex

This myth stems directly from gender roles that suggest that men should be sexually assertive and a man that isn't, well, he's not much of a man after all. Likewise, the companion piece for women is that their natural state is much more passive and they need to be aroused (Kiefer and Sanchez, 2007). The idea is that "consensual rough sex" where the woman is hesitant, then aroused, and then inflamed with passion, is all due to male sexual agency. Her sexual submission is what he is after and so whatever level of intensity he provides (up to and including violence or physical abuse) is okay. Unfortunately, it is not clear what would qualify as "abuse" and what is supposed to be mutual passion. And our culture, through sexual imagery, feeds this blurred line. Consider these common concepts from porn, mainstream movies, and books.

Hard, Fast Action   Male movements in sex scenes are often intense. They grab women roughly and hold women tightly by their arms, necks, and butts—tight enough that if it were real, the woman could get bruised. And then of course, there's the deep and hard thrusting that often goes on for quite some time. We believe that many real women would get tired of this or find it painful after just a few minutes.

Sexual Compliance   In much of our imagery, women are not just submissive, they are thrilled with that submission. Of course, its most popular and extreme presentation is in the wildly successful *50 Shades of Grey* trilogy in which a 21-year-old-virgin meets an extraordinarily handsome, smart, and successful man who likes dominance and bondage and whose sexual mode varies from slightly to greatly sadistic. The young woman's sexual pleasure is, in general, hugely enhanced by her helplessness and very rough sex, including heavy spanking, pain, and the inability to do anything but receive that kind of "pleasure." While she stops him when he becomes too violent, the kind of sex they enjoy together could certainly be described as dominating, male directed, and rough, to say the least. Obviously, at the level of fantasy many women found it arousing (at one point it seemed like everyone was reading it and the first movie is being made as we write this) and its success certainly fed into the idea that women are interested in rougher treatment.

The real life explanation, however, may be more disturbing—that is not that women are interested in rougher treatment, but they are compliant to it when they are worried about even more aggression from their lover or partner (Katz and Tirone, 2010). Women may also acquiesce because they want to be in the relationship and so they agree to what is asked of them, even though they don't like it (Katz and Tirone, 2009).

Token Resistance The overstatement of women's desire to have rough sex is also supported by the idea that their protests are just part of the dance of male initiation, female coyness, and ultimately women's aroused submission. A total misunderstanding of women's protests and clear statements of not wanting to have sex, or not wanting a certain kind of sex, can badly damage or even end a relationship. Moreover, the whole idea of "token resistance"— that men should press on with their sexual advances over and above what a woman says because she ultimately really wants to be pressed into sex—puts women at risk of being mauled or raped and men at risk of being jailed for sexual assault. Indeed, there is a correlation between having the belief that women say no but mean yes, and whether or not a man thinks that date rape has occurred. When shown scenarios of coercive sex, men who believed that saying no was just part of the dance were less likely to label the scenario rape if the woman only resisted verbally (Osman and Davis, 1999).

Consequences of Rough Sex

Some women who are having rough sex seem to be experiencing discomfort and even pain. In a large random sample study published in the *New England Journal of Medicine* (Laumann *et al.*, 1999) one of the most common complaints of women who had sexual issues was pain caused by intercourse. These women were not all having rough sex—some of the pain was caused by women who were in menopause or who, for other reasons, did not lubricate enough. But there were also reports of pain caused by abrasions to the cervix and vagina through too vigorous thrusting. Women and men should remember that some positions, such as "doggie style" or legs over the man's shoulders, foreshorten the vagina and make very deep penetration possible. This deep penetration can lead to battering of the cervix which can cause intense pain and even injury as well as making pre-existing issues such as very sensitive skin or pelvic floor problems much worse (Coady and Fish, 2011).

There are also dangers to having rough anal sex, especially without enough lubrication. The delicate skin around the anus can tear which can increase the risk for HIV infection and other STIs (if the sex is not protected by a condom). Even actions often seen in porn movies such as raking long nails across a man's back or holding a partner down tightly by the wrists can lead to unnecessary scrapes and bruises.

Creating a Mutually Pleasing, Safe Sexual Style

If rough sex is the assumed approach, it may very well hurt, bewilder, offend, or anger a partner (be they male or female). Many people would just be perplexed and wonder if they were being loved or used. Others might have strong emotional reactions, especially men or women who had been the victim of rape or other violence. Many people enjoy fantasizing about rough sex and some people (though we bet this number is smaller) enjoy having it in real life but there are others who want nothing whatsoever to do with any sex that is not gentle and loving.

We are not opposed to rough sex, it can be fun and spice up a sex life. However, it has to be something both partners agree to in advance. Don't assume that your partner (male or female) likes it rough—ask and then come up with a plan that you both like.

References

Coady, D. and Fish, N. (2011). *Healing Painful Sex*. Seal Press, New York.

Katz, J. and Tirone, V. (2009). Women's sexual compliance with male dating partners: Associations with investment in ideal womanhood and romantic well-being. *Sex Roles*, 60, 5–6.

Katz, J. and Tirone, V. (2010). Going along with it: Sexually coercive partner behavior predicts dating women's compliance with unwanted sex. *Violence Against Women*, 16(7), 730–742.

Keifer, A.K. and Sanchez, D.T. (2007). Scripting sexual passivity: A gender role perspective. *Personal Relationships*, 14(2), 269–290.

Laumann, E.O., Paik, A., and Rosen, R.C. (1999). Sexual dysfunction in the United States: Prevalence and predictors. *Journal of the American Medical Association*, 281(6), 537–544.

Osman, S.L. and Davis, C.M. (1999). Belief in token resistance and type of resistance as predictors of men's perceptions of date rape. *Journal of Sex Education and Therapy*, 24, 189–196.

Myth #23 Only People Who Aren't Getting Any Masturbate

Many people would be horrified and hurt if they caught their partner masturbating. We have somehow been taught to believe that masturbation is a lesser sexual activity; one that people only do if and when they don't have a partner or aren't satisfied by the partner that they do have. After all, no one brags about the great time they had all alone last night (though maybe they should).

The short answer is that masturbation is quite different from partner sex. It's like scratching an itch. It's a shortcut. It is like having having cereal for lunch because you like cereal and it's easy to prepare—it doesn't mean that you like cereal better than, say, steak, or that you don't like your partner's cooking. Sex expert Bernie Zilbergeld put it this way:

> You don't really need a reason for masturbating other than the fact that you want to do it. Sometimes you may be feeling sexy and also want to be alone (yes, *want* to be alone, not *have* to be alone). You may not want to deal with another person at the time, and there's no reason why you should have to. After all, dealing with a partner requires energy and consideration, and it is ludicrous to assume that you are going to want to expend such energy and give such consideration each time you feel sexy. Sometimes you just don't want to be concerned with someone else's needs and desires. And must you be? (Zilbergeld, 1978, pp. 168–169)

We All Do It (And It's Good For You)

Masturbation is so convenient that you might call it a national pastime. Surveys of American university students found that two-thirds of the women and almost all of the men reported frequent masturbation in the past 3 months (Pinkerton *et al.*, 2002). The National Survey of Sexual Health and Behavior found that solo masturbation was the most common sexual behavior for most age groups. For example, 94% of men and 83% of women aged 25–29 report having masturbated at some point in their lifetime (Herbenick *et al.*, 2010). And guess what? Other studies show us that those people who were the most sexually active masturbated more often, which tell us that masturbation is not a substitute for other sexual activity (Rye and Meaney, 2007, p. 32).

Far from being proof of a damaged partner or a troubled relationship, masturbation is part of healthy sexual development and drive (Bancroft *et al.*, 2002). It's a way to learn how your body works, what excites you, what your favorite sexual fantasies are, and how you achieve the best (or maybe easiest) orgasm (Atwood and Gagnon, 1987). Research on masturbation indicates it is linked to orgasmic capacity, healthy sexual functioning, and sexual satisfaction in relationships. Research has found that married women who masturbate to orgasm have greater marital and sexual satisfaction than women who do not masturbate (Hurlburt and Whittaker, 1991). In fact, masturbators tend to have more positive attitudes about sexuality in general and are more likely to be orgasmic (Kelly *et al.*, 1990).

Almost all research and commentary by legitimate sex experts focus on masturbation as a healthy practice and as a lifelong pleasure before and during a committed relationship (Laumann *et al.*, 1994; Coleman, 2002). Again, research shows that an exchange of masturbation (touching to orgasm) improves sexual satisfaction in partnered relationships. In fact, when things are problematic in a relationship, or for an individual, sex therapists often use masturbation as a treatment for sexual inhibition, inability to have an orgasm, and other issues (Heiman and LoPiccolo, 1988; Leiblum and Rosen, 1989; Zilbergeld, 1992; Robinson *et al.*, 1999; Coleman, 2002; Bridges and Morokoff, 2011).

Masturbation Gets a Bad Rap

There is reasons that one's own, or one's partner's masturbation scares a lot of people. Masturbation is probably the most stigmatized sexual behavior (other than truly antisocial or abusive acts such as child abuse or rape). Masturbation seems to be in a special class of discomfort for many people. Maybe myths about it causing blindness or hairiness or insanity are still floating around. Or perhaps, as Coleman (2002) argues, the intensity of our discomfort comes from religious and associated cultural beliefs that forbid masturbation, most often because it is only for pleasure and has no procreative value.

Coleman, head of a prestigious sex therapy program at the University of Minnesota, states: "This can lead to further problems in intra-personal and interpersonal functioning, sexual and mental disorders. Because of the stigma of masturbation promoted by many of the world's religions, this can contribute to spiritual alienation as well" (Coleman, 2002, p. 9). Naturally, this can also cause misunderstanding of the meaning of masturbation in interpersonal relationships (Hunt, 1974; Coleman, 2002).

So What if Catch Your Partner Masturbating?

We don't think you should worry about it if you catch your partner pleasuring him/herself. For the most part masturbation is harmless to both the person and the relationship. As Dekker and Schmidt (2003) put it "masturbation peacefully coexists with sex between partners and a loving relationship" (p. 36). College students seem to agree. One study of masturbation showed little difference in how often students had masturbated during the last 4 weeks between students who were in a satisfying sexual relationship and those who had no relationship. Three-quarters of the students stated that they felt masturbation was a form of sex in its own right and did not affect or interfere with partnered sex (Dekker and Schmidt, 2003, p. 36).

However, if your partner is avoiding you, or masturbating constantly, something more than just having a few extra orgasms may be going on. It may indicate a fixation or there may be an issue with the power dynamic. Some men may be asserting their right to masturbate, or, in an extreme situation, a man may be so angry at his partner that masturbation is seen as preferable to intercourse. Conflict in a relationship may increase masturbation especially when there is long-term dissatisfaction—but this means masturbation is a symptom of the couple's problems, not the cause (Betchen, 1991, p. 270).

In the absence of these issues, however, we believe that a sexual relationship can (and maybe should) include masturbation by either partner without any detriment to the relationship or their mutual sex life.

References

Atwood, J.D. and Gagnon, J. (1987). Masturbatory behavior in college youth. *Journal of Sex Education and Therapy*, 13, 35–42.

Bancroft, J., Herbenick, D., and Reynolds, M. (2002). Masturbation as a marker of sexual development. In Bancroft, J. (ed.) *Sexual Development*. Indiana University Press, Bloomington, IN.

Betchen, S.J. (1991). Male masturbation as a vehicle for the pursuer–distancer relationship in marriage. *Journal of Sex and Marital Therapy*, 17(4), 269–278.

Bridges, A.J. and Morokoff, P.J. (2011). Sexual media use and relational satisfaction in heterosexual couples. *Personal Relationships*, 18(4), 562–585.

Coleman, E. (2002). Masturbation as a means of achieving sexual health. *Journal of Psychology and Human Sexuality*, 14(2–3), 5–16.

Dekker, A. and Schmidt, G. (2003). Patterns of masturbatory behaviour. *Journal of Psychology and Human Sexuality*, 14(2–3), 35–38.

Heiman, J. and LoPiccolo, J. (1988). *Becoming Orgasmic: A Sexual and Personal Growth Program for Women*. Prentice Hall, Englewood Cliff, NJ.

Herbenick, D., Reece, M., Schick, V., Sanders, SA, Dodge, B., and Fortenberry J.D. (2010). Sexual behavior in the United States: Results from a national probability sample of men and women 14 to 95. *Journal of Sexual Medicine*, 7(Suppl 5), 255–265.

Hunt, M. (1974). *Sexual Behavior in the 1970s*. Playboy Press, Chicago.

Hurlburt, D. and Whittaker, K. (1991). The role of masturbation in marital and sexual satisfaction: A comparative study of female masturbators and nonmasturbators. *Journal of Sex Education and Therapy*, 17, 272–282.

Kelly, M.P., Strassberg, D.S., and Kircher, J.R. (1990). Attitudinal and experiential correlates of anogasmia. *Archives of Sexual Behavior*, 19(2), 165–167.

Laumann, E.O., Gagnon, J.H., Michael, R.T. and Michaels, S. (1994). *The Social Organization of Sexuality: Sexual Practices in the United States*. University of Chicago Press, Chicago.

Leiblum, S. and Rosen, R.C. (1989). *Principles and Practices of Sex Therapy*, 2nd edn. Guilford, New York.

Pinkerton, S.D., Bogart, L.M., Cecil, H., and Abramson, P.R. (2002). Factors associated with masturbation in a collegiate sample. *Journal of Psychology and Human Sexuality*, 14(2/3), 103–121.

Robinson, B.E., Manthei, R., Scheltema, K., Rich, R., and Koznar, J. (1999). Therapeutic uses of sexually explicit materials in the United States and the Czech and Slovak Republics: A qualitative study. *Journal of Sex and Marital Therapy*, 25, 103–119.

Rye, B.J. and Meaney, G.J. (2007). The pursuit of sexual pleasure. *Sexuality and Culture: An Interdisciplinary Quarterly*, 11(1), 28–51.

Zilbergeld, B. (1978). *Male Sexuality*. Bantam, New York.

Zilbergeld, B. (1992). *The New Male Sexuality*. Bantam, New York.

Myth #24

Not Horny? Horny Goat Weed Can Help

Aphrodisiacs are substances that increase sexual desire, pleasure, or ability (Sandroni, 2001; Shamloul, 2010). But here's a rule of thumb: most substances labeled as aphrodisiacs are not. The things on your pharmacy shelf or favorite website are not the fabled aphrodisiacs that will make a reluctant partner into a raging stud or nymphomaniac (Krychman *et al.*, 2007). Some have no effect. Some "work" simply because you believe they will (a placebo effect) and some work because you are hallucinating or disoriented (Sandroni, 2001; Melnyk and Marcone, 2011). Some have an effect, but only if you swallow a truck load (in which case the sheer amount would likely have adverse consequences). Some are dangerous in any amount. Some are dangerous to animals—the search for ground rhino horn is in danger of wiping out that species, all for a substance that does nothing.

The term aphrodisiac is derived from the Greek word *aphrodisia*, which means sexual pleasure, as well as the Greek goddess of love, Aphrodite (Krychman *et al.*, 2007). The search for aphrodisiacs is documented way back to antiquity (Shamloul, 2010). Ancient Greeks, Romans, Chinese, and Indo-African populations all prescribed a range of substances to increase male potency as well as interest and pleasure in both men and women. Early documents, even hieroglyphics, include different kinds of potions and various roots and weeds that supposedly increased desire. Among substances we would recognize today, yohimbine and gingseng are often mentioned. Both of these have modest effects, if any, but that doesn't seem to have discouraged users over the ages (Kotta *et al.*, 2013). Spices are also commonly mentioned, among them nutmeg, ginger, saffron, and cacao. There is validity in the effect of these spices as they promote blood flow—which helps erections and sexual arousal—but a cure for sexual disinterest does not lie in your next bowl of paella (Melnyk and Marcone, 2011, p. 841).

Alcohol and Other Aphrodisiacs

Stimulants of any kind can be classified as aphrodisiacs if they improve sexual response in any way. So, many foods, vitamins, and beverages have been put in this category. Most commonly, alcoholic drinks are thought of as aphrodisiacs because they act as disinhibitors and make sex more likely to happen. Also by relaxing people's inhibitions (such as how they feel about their body) participants may be more able to feel passion or achieve orgasm (Krychman *et al.*, 2007; Melnyk and Marcone, 2011). In fact, some studies have found that if one believes that alcohol increases desire, it will—again the placebo effect. One study found that students who thought they were drinking alcohol reported more desire even if they were actually given a non-alcoholic drink by the researchers (George *et al.*, 2000). Students were also likely to find their partner more attractive if they expected to be drunk or picked up cues from their partner that he or she had been drinking or was going to start (Friedman *et al.*, 2005, pp. 672–673). (See Myth # 40 for more about sex and alcohol.)

Of course, we have to remember that alcohol can also be seen as a barrier to good sex since imbibing frequent and large quantities of alcohol narrows the veins and makes erection and orgasm more difficult.

Other, less common substances have also been studied as possible aphrodisiacs.

Cantharides This substance, derived from blister beetles, is an ancient recipe for sexual inertia that affects blood flow and causes inflammation. For a while it was marketed as "Spanish Fly" and was said to be a real turn on. However, the buzz was dampened considerably when it turned out that not only did most people who used it feel unpleasant itching and burning, some people died. The toxic effects significantly outweighed the possibility of having more pleasure and ultimately it either went underground or disappeared from circulation entirely (Sandroni, 2001, p. 303).

Yohimbe Though this plant-based substance is often written about as a powerful aphrodisiac, there is no good evidence that yohimbe creates more sexual interest. Some animal experiments *in vitro* have shown stronger erections when test subjects take yohimbe and some studies with humans have found that respondents report more pleasure while on the drug. However, these studies are considered biased because the users knew they were taking the drug during the research (Melnyk and Marcone, 2011).

Panax Ginseng This is a plant-derivative used in traditional Chinese medicine that triggers nitric oxide synthesis in the vessels of many organs, including the corpora cavernosa (the spongy tissue found in the penis and the clitoris which fill with blood and become erect when a person is aroused). This nitric oxide reaction has been documented in both animal and human lab studies. Like the other substances mentioned, however, none of these have been double-blind studies which would be needed to test observational results (Melnyk and Marcone, 2011).

Bufo Toad Skin and Glands Toad doesn't sound very sexy, does it? But these animal parts do contain hallucinogenic properties. They are commonly used in potions in India and in China and can be very toxic (Sandroni, 2001, p. 303).

The truth is that, as much as we would all like to find that magic substance that would put us in the mood and make sex great every time, we haven't found one yet. There are a limited number of studies (many with methodological issues), the mechanisms by which these substances work is unclear, and we just don't know what the potential hazardous side effects of these substances may be (Kotta *et al.*, 2013).

Substances That Are Often Mistaken for Aphrodisiacs

Amphetamines, cocaine, caffeine, cannabis, and marijuana stimulate the central nervous system and some people find the heightened stimulation sexually arousing. Many people do report more pleasure and a more relaxed and sensual approach to lovemaking when using some of the substances, but again, it is not clear if much of this is a placebo effect. Plus, these substances, some of which are illegal in most states in the United States, have negative side effects. Amphetamines make some people very nervous and unable to concentrate, caffeine can have the same effect, and cocaine is addictive to many. Other substances that may be more dangerous are those derived from kola nut, betel nut, and guarana. These can also heighten sensation and speed up heart rates and are widely used in Africa, Asia, and parts of Latin America. The tannin in these plant products, however, has been linked to digestive problems and cancer (Sandroni, 2001, pp. 304–305; Fleshner *et al.*, 2005).

Though touted as aphrodisiacs, none of these substances has a specific sexual effect, rather there is a whole body feeling that may also increase sexual sensation. These effects are highly individualized. While these substances may help some people feel more turned on, some of them actually decrease potency for others (Sandroni, 2001).

Hydraulics Not Aphrodisiacs

The only substances that have actually been proven to increase erections are phosphodiesterase 5 (PDE5) inhibitors such as sildenafil (Viagra) and vardenafil (Levitra) (Sandroni, 2001, p. 305). As we talk about later (in Myth # 42), these drugs are only meant for men who cannot get an erection otherwise. They are not meant to be taken recreationally or to make normal erections harder, and they are not aphrodisiacs.

Even more dangerous are the herbal "equivalents," Libidfit, Satibo, and Viamax, which are often sold on the internet as plant-based alternatives to pharmaceuticals. These drugs are unregulated and can be dangerous (Shamloul, 2010, p. 39). Libidfit was actually sued and taken off the market because it was illegally distributed and potentially harmful (Venhuis *et al.*, 2008, p. e25). A recent investigation by the Food and Drug Administration (FDA) found that some supplements that were being sold as herbal or all natural actually contained drugs similar to those found in Viagra and Levitra. The supplement Weekend Warrior, for example, contained thiosildenafil which is very similar to the active ingredient in Viagra, even though this was not listed on the bottle (Zeltner, 2014). These substances can interact with other medications and some men should not take them at all because of their health history. It is, therefore, very dangerous for men to be ingesting these chemicals unknowingly.

There are some drugs in development for women as well. Though they are often referred to as the female Viagra, they work on the brain, not the genitals, and aim to increase sexual desire in women who have low or no libido. These drugs are not really aphrodisiacs in that a woman doesn't become horny instantly after taking one. They are taken continually in the hopes of increasing libido in the long term. Though at least one drug has been through clinical trials, none have yet to be approved by the FDA (Schiavocampo *et al.*, 2014).

So Why the Age-Old Quest for Aphrodisiacs?

It's obvious that many people feel inadequate sexually. Men feel their penises should be harder or bigger, or they should be able to have intercourse longer, or please their partner even more. If their partner is unexcited or having trouble reaching orgasm, they want a pill that would turn her into a vixen, completely enthralled by her lover's sexiness and prowess. Women who are never or rarely orgasmic or who find themselves unable to be aroused by their lover's attentions (even if they used to be) would like to end their frustration with a "magic pill" that would make them want their partner more or feel pleasure more intensely. We are a world that likes easy answers. But so far those easy answers do not exist.

As we have seen, not only do some of the compounds people use do nothing, some of them are dangerous or even deadly (Sandroni, 2001, p. 306). Most therapists whose patients come in looking for a cure for lack of sexual energy or interest will try to examine the nature of the relationship, whether either partner is depressed, and if either is experiencing extreme fatigue. They also look at the medications each partner is taking. Selective serotonin reuptake inhibitors (SSRIs), which include Prozac and Zoloft, are widely used to treat depression and anxiety and are widely known to affect sexual desire. Other medicines can have this effect as well. For men who really do have issues with erectile dysfunction there are a number of specific treatments (surgical and chemical) that work and are not life-threatening when deemed that are not life-threatening when deemed safe and appropriate by a doctor who has carefully examined the patient's general health. (Again, see Myth # 42.)

Mostly, though, there's no pill, powder, or vitamin that's going to do the trick. Sexual desire (our own or our partner's) may not come as easily or as quickly as we would have liked, but the only thing to do is try harder. The good news is that the effort itself can be fun.

References

Fleshner, M., Harvey, H., Adomat, C., Wood, A., Eberding, K., Hersey, E., *et al.* (2005). Evidence for contamination of herbal erectile dysfunction products with phosphodiesterase type 5 inhibitors. *Journal of Urology,* 174, 636–641 (discussion 641; quiz 801).

Friedman, R.S., McCarthy, D.M., Förster, J., and Denzler, M. (2005). Automatic effects of alcohol cues on sexual attraction. *Addiction,* 100(5), 672–681.

George, W.H., Stoner, S.A., Norris, J., Lopez, P.A., and Lehman, G.L. (2000). Alcohol expectancies and sexuality: A self-fulfilling prophecy analysis of dyadic perceptions and behavior. *Journal of Studies on Alcohol and Drugs,* 61(1), 168.

Kotta, S., Ansari, S.H., and Ali, J. (2013). Exploring scientifically proven herbal aphrodisiacs. *Pharmacognosy Reviews,* 7(13), 1–10.

Krychman, M.L., Gubili, J., Pereira, L., Holstein, L., and Cassileth, B. (2007). Female sexual enhancers and neutraceuticals. *Current Sexual Health Reports,* 4, 177–182.

Libidfit court case (2007). LJN: BA4929, No. 12/035253-04, Rechtbank Middelburg, The Netherlands, April 25, 2007. http://www.rechtspraak.nl (accessed July 23, 2014).

Melnyk, J.P. and Marcone, M.F. (2011). Aphrodisiacs from plant and animal sources:- A review of current scientific literature. *Food Research International,* 44(4), 840–850.

Sandroni, P. (2001). Aphrodisiacs past and present: a historical review. *Clinical Autonomic Research: Official Journal of the Clinical Autonomic Research Society,* 11(5), 303–307.

Schiavocampo, M., Jesko, J., and Effron, L .(2014). The fight of the 'little pink pill' raises sexism questions. *ABC News.* http://abcnews.go.com/Health/fight-pink-pill-boosting-womens-sex-drive-raises/story?id=23813586 (accessed July 22, 2014).

Shamloul, R. (2010). Natural aphrodisiacs. *Journal of Sexual Medicine,* 7(1), 39–49.

Venhuis, B.J., Blok-Tip, L., and de Kaste, D. (2008). Designer drugs in herbal aphrodisiacs. *Forensic Science International,* 177, 2–3.

Zeltner, B. (2014). FDA warns "Weekend Warrior" sexual enhancement supplement contains undeclared drug similar to Viagra, danger to heart patients. Cleveland Plain Dealer. http://www.cleveland.com/healthfit/index.ssf/2014/03/fda_warns_weekend_warrior_sexu.html (accessed July 22, 2014).

5 CONCEPTION AND CONTRACEPTION

Illusions and Delusions

She's Not Going to Get Pregnant if We Just Do It This Once

Let us start this one by saying that we've heard it all—from the pseudo-scientific to the clearly ridiculous. "She can't get pregnant the first time." "She can't get pregnant if we do it in a hot tub (the heat kills the sperm)." "She can't get pregnant if I drink a lot of Mountain Dew (it kills sperm)." "She can't get pregnant if she douches right afterwards." "She can't get pregnant if she douches with Mountain Dew right afterwards (it kills sperm)." "She can't get pregnant if we do it sideways while bouncing on one foot." You get the idea.

In truth, we're not sure these are myths because we would be surprised if a lot of people really believe them. We think of them more like excuses. They are things that people hear and then repeat in order to explain away what they did or are about to do, in order to justify having unprotected sex.

So our job here is pretty much to remind you that unless you are actively trying to conceive there is no excuse for unprotected sex, because no matter when, where, or how you do it there is a risk (sometimes large, sometimes small) of getting pregnant.

First, Biology

In order to understand the real risks involved in unprotected intercourse, you have to understand exactly how and when pregnancy happens. We hope you all learned this in high school or perhaps a human sexuality course in college

50 Great Myths of Human Sexuality, First Edition. Pepper Schwartz and Martha Kempner.
© 2015 John Wiley & Sons, Inc. Published 2015 by John Wiley & Sons, Inc.

but, just in case, here is our quick review of the biology of menstruation, ovulation, and conception.

Women are born with all of the ova (eggs) they are ever going to have (unlike men who begin producing sperm at puberty and continue to do so into old age). Somewhere between the age of 9 and 16 or so, young women begin to have a monthly menstrual cycle which is controlled by a number of hormones. Each month two important things happen. First, one of the eggs in the ovaries fully matures, pops out, and begins to travel down the fallopian tube toward the uterus. At the same time the uterus begins to build up a lining of blood and tissue to prepare a place for a fertilized egg to grow. If the egg is not fertilized during that month, this blood and tissue is shed as part of the woman's period (Kelly, 2010).

The first day of bleeding is actually considered day 1 of a woman's next period. Most women have cycles that last about 28 days and ovulate somewhere in the middle—around day 13 (Wilcox *et al.*, 2001). (Remember this for later because the risk of pregnancy is different on each day of a woman's cycle.)

Of course, in order for the egg to be fertilized and a pregnancy to occur, you need to add sperm. The typical amount of ejaculate contains several hundred million sperm. If released into the vagina, the sperm start swimming up through the uterus and into the fallopian tubes toward the waiting egg (if there is one). Some of the sperm will die from the acidity of the vagina, others will be attacked by white blood cells because they are foreign bodies, and some will get lost. But about 1000–2000 will make it to the egg (Goulet, 2009). Though technically only one sperm can fertilize an egg, that lucky guy needs a bunch of his friends to prepare the egg by creating a hole in the outermost layer of the egg (called the zona pellucida) for him to swim through. The hole then closes to keep out any other sperm because an egg fertilized by more than one sperm would not develop properly (Mader, 2002).

Then Comes the Math

Figuring out the risk of pregnancy does not just involve biology, it also involves some pretty basic math. Once released, an egg can last (meaning it can be fertilized) for only 12–24 hours. Sperm can live in the reproductive tract for about 3–5 days, but they use up some of that time swimming to the egg (it's a long journey if you're microscopic).

If we put these together, we find that there is about a 6-day window of fertility. It includes the 5 days before ovulation (because sperm could be waiting for the egg) and the day of ovulation (when the egg could be waiting for the sperm). The challenge, of course, is figuring out when those days are each month.

For women who have a regular cycle that ranges between 26 and 32 days, the fertility window is likely to fall between days 8 and 19. But some women have longer cycles, some have shorter cycles, and some have cycles that are different each month.

Some women use fertility awareness based (FAB) methods of family planning to prevent pregnancy which means they keep careful track of their menstrual cycles, calculate when their fertile window is, and either avoid sex during these days or use a second method like a condom during that time. FAB methods require women to have a 6- to 12-month history of their menstrual cycles so they can know their longest and shortest cycle and calculate correctly. Some FAB methods also suggest women collect other "data" to determine when they are ovulating, including figuring out how much cervical secretion they have each day (there is more during ovulation), noting the characteristics of the secretion (the mucus is stringier during ovulation), and taking their basal body temperature (it spikes at certain points in the month). FAB methods can work but they take a lot of effort and are only appropriate for women with really regular cycles (Jennings and Burke, 2011, p. 418).

And, Now the Statistics

For women who don't know when they are going to ovulate, researchers have done even more complicated math to try to determine the likelihood of getting pregnant from one random act of intercourse. Results have varied but the best guess is—knowing nothing else about how fertile a couple is or where a woman is in her cycle—one act of intercourse carries with it a 3.1% chance of pregnancy (Wilcox *et al.*, 2001).

In truth, though, this varies depending on the day of her cycle on which intercourse occurs: "the probability of conception is negligible during the first three days. By day 7, the likelihood of pregnancy with intercourse is nearly 2 percent. This rises to a peak of nearly 9 percent on day 13. This probability declines thereafter but remains around 1 percent as late as day 40 and beyond" (Wilcox *et al.*, 2001, p. 212).

These may seem like pretty low odds, but the researchers warn that they don't mean much for any individual woman. First, these rates don't apply well to adolescents, women who are approaching menopause, women who have less regular cycles, and women who have lower fertility rates. Moreover, they don't take into account other factors that impact fertility such as smoking, history of genital infections, and her partner's fertility. They conclude:

> For these reasons, the pregnancy probabilities shown here also provide poor estimates for any individual woman. For a given woman, it would be more useful to know the probability, on any particular day of her cycle, that she is within the 6 days of her fertile window. (Wilcox *et al.*, p. 214)

Plus, we have some other statistics we would like you to consider. First, we think you should know that about half of all pregnancies each year in the United States (adults and adolescents included) are unintended. This means the couples were not trying to get pregnant when they did. Think about that. If half of the couples who get pregnant weren't trying to, accidental pregnancies clearly happen a lot.

In fact, out of 100 couples who use no form of contraception, 85 of them will become pregnant within the course of the first year. Compare that with 18 out of 100 couples who use condoms; nine who use the pill, patch, or ring; six who use the shot; and less than one who use either the IUD or the implant (Trussell, 2011). These are all based on *typical* use rates which include couples who use the method incorrectly or forget to use it at all when they have sex which means that if they followed instructions better they would have even less chance of getting pregnant in the first year of use.

Finally, Some Common Sense

Now we want you to think back to high school. The thing that biology, math, and statistics have in common is that there are pretty much right answers and wrong answers. If you didn't study for those tests many (if not most of you) would have gotten wrong answers whether you took the test with pencil or pen and if you don't use contraception 85% of you will get pregnant the first year whether you do it in a bed, on the floor, or upside down on the ice. The chance of getting pregnant does not change whether it's the first time or the 500th. Yes, heat lowers sperm count over the long term but pregnancy can happen in hot water (Shefi *et al.*, 2007). Mountain Dew has no magic power over sperm (Pollock, 1999). Douching after sex would actually help sperm swim upstream, and we would be worried that douching with a highly sugary beverage might also lead to a yeast infection.

So let's stop with the excuses, they're all pretty silly and they're just not true. More importantly, right now there are so many methods of contraception on the market that everyone (and every couple) can find at least one that works for them. There is no reason that anyone should get pregnant unless that's what they're trying to do. (Reread this when you are trying to get pregnant, and you'll see some useful tips about the best times of the month to have sex.)

Also, let's not forget that unless you are in a relationship that you know to be mutually monogamous (as in no one is having sex with anyone else) and you and your partner are known to be free of any STIs (as in you have both been recently tested), you are at risk for STIs and should also consider using condoms for protection.

References

Goulet, T. (2009). Male fertility and the sperm saga. *Conceive Magazine*, July/August.
Jennings, V.H. and Burke, A.E. (2011). Fertility awareness-based methods. In Hatcher, R.A., Trussell, J., Nelson, A.L., Cates, W., Kowal D., and Policar, M. (eds) *Contraceptive Technology*, 20th edn. Ardent Media, New York, pp. 417–434.
Kelly, G.F. (2010). *Sexuality Today*, 10th edn. McGraw Hill, New York.
Mader, S. (2002). *Human Reproductive Biology*, 2nd edn. William C. Brown Publishers, New York.

Pollock, E.J. (1999). Why Mountain Dew is now the talk of the teen circuit. *The Wall Street Journal* (October 14), p. 1.

Shefi, S., Tarapore, P.E., Walsh, T.J., Croughan, M., and Turek, P.J. (2007). Wet heat exposure: A potentially reversible cause of low semen quality in infertile men. *International Brazilian Journal of Urology*, 33(1), 50–57.

Trussell, J. (2011). Contraceptive efficacy. In Hatcher, R.A., Trussell, J., Nelson, A.L., Cates, W., Kowal D., and Policar, M. (eds) *Contraceptive Technology*, 20th edn. Ardent Media, New York, pp. 779–863.

Wilcox, A.J., Dunson, D.B., Weinberg, C.R., Trussell, J., and Baird, D.D. (2001). Likelihood of conception with a single act of intercourse: providing benchmark rates for assessment of post-coital contraceptives. *Contraception*, 63(4), 211–215.

Myth 26 The Pill and Other Birth Control Methods Are Actually Dangerous to a Woman's Health

Men and women have been trying to prevent pregnancy since the dawn of time by using whatever device, potion, or magical charm was in favor at the time. Women in the sixth century were told to wear cat liver in a tube on their left foot while Islamic women in the thirteenth century favored peeing into the urine of a wolf to avoid pregnancy. Women also ingested recipes made from leaves of ivy and willow plants as well as other far more dangerous chemicals that were thought to prevent pregnancy. In the Middle Ages women ingested lead, arsenic, mercury, and strychnine, all of which were thought to act as birth control. Other women chose barrier methods instead and inserted all kinds of things into their vaginas to stop sperm—wool tampons soaked in wine, sponges, elephant dung, and gold balls were apparently popular in the time of Casanova (Connell, 1999).

In the modern age, we know better than to drink strychnine or stick excrement in our vaginas as a form of contraception and we would certainly think twice before using a douche containing Lysol®, a sperm-killing practice that was popular as recently as the 1950s (Connell, 1999). Despite our increase in knowledge and caution, many worry that even our modern methods of contraception are not safe. There are fears that the pill causes cancer, that implants will get stuck in a woman's arm requiring major surgery, and that IUDs will cause infertility. Though these fears are grounded in the inauspicious history of some of these methods, the truth is that today's versions of each of these contraceptives are thought to be safe for most women.

This entry reviews the history of the birth control pill, other hormonal methods, and IUDs in order to explain the origin of the safety concerns and the best science that we have today which, again, suggests these methods are safe for most women. As a caveat, we want to stress that by saying these methods are safe we are not attempting to say that they have no side effects or that they will be appropriate for every woman. We would always encourage women and their partners to talk to a health care provider about what method might be best for them.

The Birth Control Pill

In 1960, the first oral contraceptive pill was approved for sale in the United States after what many saw as a very short period from conception (pun completely intended) to market which took just 10 years. (In contrast, the implant that we talk about later began development in 1960 and wasn't on the market until 1990; Watkins, 2010). As the pill represented an entirely new way of preventing pregnancy—suppressing ovulation—there were many concerns about the health risks in both the long and short term. People wondered whether preventing ovulation for long periods of time would cause fertility problems when a woman decided to get pregnant and whether the hormones would increase risk of cancers.

Combination oral contraceptives (COCs) like the ones that were first available contain both estrogen and progestin, a synthetic version of the hormone progesterone. Early birth control pills contained significantly higher doses of both of these ingredients than those currently on the market. In fact, drug companies learned quickly that smaller amounts of the active ingredients were necessary to suppress ovulation. The first pill, Enovid-E, contained 150 µg estrogen and 9.85 mg progestin. When it was revised just 5 years later this was down to 100 µg estrogen and 2.5 mg progestin (Tyrer, 1999). Today, COCs contain as little as 20 µg estrogen (Nelson and Cwiak, 2011). There are also pills on the market today that only contain progestin— these are sometimes called the mini-pill. Most of the research we are talking about here, however, has been done on COCs, which contain both hormones.

The first generation pills did cause a lot of side effects. Women reported headaches, dizziness, and nausea. Within 2 years of the pill's release, there were also reports of serious adverse effects such as stroke, venous thromboembolism events (VTE), which is a blood clot in the veins, and myocardial infarction, which is the medical term for a heart attack. Though this was likely the result of the high doses of hormones in these early pills, it also reflected a lack of knowledge on the part of health care providers about who was not a good candidate to take birth control pills. Studies carried out since the introduction of the pill suggest that women with certain health conditions like high blood pressure, women who have had cardiovascular issues in the past, and heavy smokers are at increased risk of these side effects. For this reason, some health care providers suggest women with these histories avoid the pill and other hormonal methods (Tyrer, 1999).

While the pill has become safer over the years, its reputation for being dangerous continues and various myths and misperceptions have developed. *Contraceptive Technology*, one of the pre-eminent publications on the topic used frequently by health care providers, has a very good overview of the persistent myths surrounding the pill and we would like to share some of these with our readers. To prevent confusion for those readers who are merely skimming this chapter (not that anyone would do so), we present each topic with a positive, truthful statement rather than highlight the myth itself.

The Pill Does Not Cause Infertility. There is a persistent fear that the pill will permanently impact a woman's fertility. Research has shown this is not the case. A comprehensive review of all studies that were published between 1960 and 2007 found that fertility returns very quickly in women who stop using the pill in order to get pregnant. Most women who stop the pill will get their periods within 2 weeks. In fact, the study found that between 74% and 94% of women who discontinued the pill to conceive became pregnant within 1 year (Nelson and Cwiak, 2011).

The Pill Does Not Cause Breast Cancer. Those older pills that included higher doses of hormones were found to increase a woman's chance of getting breast cancer slightly. The newer, lower dose pills that were introduced after 1975, however, have not been found to do so. Numerous studies have been carried out on this topic with varying designs and varying results. A case-controlled study found no difference in pill use among women who had breast cancer and women who did not. A large study, conducted by the Royal College of General Practitioners (RCGP) in England, found no increase in the risk of breast cancer between those who had ever used the pill and those who never had. In fact, research has found that even women who carry the *BRCA1* and *BRCA2* genes (which are known to increase breast cancer risk) and women with a family history of breast cancer do not increase their risk by taking the pill (Nelson and Cwiak, 2011).

Interestingly, the pill actually provides a protective factor against ovarian cancer (cancer of the ovaries) and endometrial cancer (cancer of the lining of the uterus). Women who use COCs are significantly less likely to get ovarian cancer, which is considered the most lethal of gynecological cancers because it is often not caught until late stages. Research has shown that women who use certain types of the pill for at least 10 years can reduce their risk of developing ovarian cancer by 80%. A study by the RCGP that followed women for up to 39 years also found that those who had ever used the pill were 47% less likely to die from ovarian cancer than those who never had (Nelson and Cwiak, 2011).

Similar results have been found for endometrial cancer which occurs in over 40,000 women in the United States each year. Use of COCs for just 1 year reduces a woman's chance of getting this kind of cancer by 40% whereas use for 10 years can reduce the risk by 80% compared to a woman who has never used the pill. Moreover, the protective factor can stay with a woman for as long as 20 years after she stops taking the pill (Nelson and Cwiak, 2011).

The Pill Does Not Ruin Most Women's Libido. This is a tricky one because, as we know, everyone experiences side effects from medications differently and some women have reported a decrease in sexual desire when they are on the birth control pill. We do not want to dismiss these women's complaints or suggest that low libido is something they (or anyone for that matter) should just live with. Women who experience this side effect should talk to their health care provider. Sometimes a change in the brand or dose of pill can get rid of any side effects (be it loss of libido, moodiness, or breast pain).

We would like to reassure our readers that for most women this is not an issue. In fact, clinical trials have found that loss of libido is experienced by only 1–5% of users. A study of women taking a certain kind of pill (one containing drospirenone) found that they had significant improvements in sexual enjoyment, satisfaction, and frequency of orgasm but no change in libido (Nelson and Cwiak, 2011).

The Pill Does Not Cause Weight Gain in Most Women.   Some women have complained that they gain a lot of weight the minute they go on the pill. Clinical trials may appear to back this up but that is because any weight gain a woman does experience while in the trial is attributed to the pill (even if it's really just the freshman 15 or the result of an expired gym membership). Unlike clinical trials for efficacy, studies that look at noncontraceptive benefits of the pill can use a placebo design which allows for better study of some side effects. These studies have found that the percentage of women who gain an excessive amount of weight is similar in the pill group and the placebo group (Nelson and Cwiak, 2011).

We do want to underscore, however, that like all medications the pill does have side effects—some annoying and some serious. Even at today's lower doses, the pill does increase the risk of blood clots for women with certain risk factors including older age, obesity, heavy smoking, and genetic predispositions. The risk of blood clots is greatest in the first 3–12 months that a woman is on the pill. For this reason, health care providers suggest that new users (or those who have recently changed formulations of the pill) should watch out for certain symptoms including abdominal pain, chest pain, headaches, eye problems (like loss of vision), and severe leg pain. These symptoms are presented this way because if you put the first letters of each together it spells ACHES. Hopefully, this can help women remember what to look for.

Recent Research on Certain Hormonal Contraceptive Methods

Concerns about the pill have seen new life lately because of attention the media has paid to a number of studies and lawsuits involving the brand name pills Yaz and Yasmin, the contraceptive ring NuvaRing, and the contraceptive patch sold as Ortho Evra. These represent the three newest hormonal methods of contraception that have been released. Anecdotal stories have suggested that each of these methods puts women at much greater risk of blood clots than older versions of the pill. In addition, there have been several high profile cases of fatal blood clots in otherwise healthy young women and lawsuits have been filed against the manufacturers of these products, alleging they knew of the increased risk and should have warned women.

Much of what has been written about this has been quite sensational. In December 2013, *Vanity Fair* ran a headline online asking "Why is a potentially lethal contraceptive NuvaRing still on the market?" which linked to a full article by Marie Brenner called "Danger in the Ring." That same month, the *Huffington Post* ran an article called "Side effects may include death: The story of the biggest advance in birth control since the pill." Both articles hint at a conspiracy to cover up data from the original drug trials which suggested a higher risk of blood clots for ring users than pill users. Siddiqui also notes that Food and Drug Administration (FDA) officials were concerned that an otherwise healthy young woman in the initial clinical trial experienced a blood clot but that negotiations with the manufacturer ultimately result in no additional warnings being included on the label (Brenner, 2014; Siddiqui, 2013). We don't feel in a position to comment on the conspiracy theory and assume that more will be written as the lawsuits proceed. However, we do want to provide our readers with the latest research information on these methods.

Part of the problem is that research results have been mixed. Of eight studies completed by 2013 on DSRPs (formulations of the pill, like Yaz and Yasmin, that rely on drospirenone/ethinyl estradiol), five have shown an increased risk of VTE (remember from earlier that this is venous thromboembolic events or blood clots in the veins) compared with women on low dose COCs that have been on the market longer. Three of the eight studies showed no increased risk. As for the contraceptive patch, two out of five studies showed an increased risk of VTE but three did not. There has also been a recent study that found a slightly increased risk of VTE with the contraceptive ring (Sidney *et al.*, 2013).

In an effort to clear up the confusion, Sidney *et al.* looked at the medical records of over 573,000 new users of either low dose COCs or one of the newer hormonal methods between 2001 and 2007. They chose new users because most blood clots take place in the first 3–12 months of use. They found that women using the ring or the patch were at no higher risk of blood clots than women using low dose COCs. Women taking DSRPs, however, were at a significantly higher risk of blood clots than those on older types of pills. This study concluded that "initiation of new use of DRSP-containing CHCs was associated with a 77 percent increase in the risk of hospitalization for VTE relative to the use of a comparator group of four low-dose estrogen CHCs" (Sidney *et al.*, 2013).

Another study released in 2013 compared vaginal ring users with those who used COCs. It followed 33,295 users of the vaginal ring or COCs recruited by 1661 study centers in both the United States and Europe. The women were followed for 2–4 years. Researchers were particularly concerned with cardiovascular issues the women might have, specifically venous and arterial thromboembolism (VTE and ATE). They found similar rates in the two groups of participants and concluded that "vaginal ring use and combined OCP use were associated with a similar venous and arterial thromboembolic risk during routine clinical use" (Dinger *et al.*, 2013).

So, despite the headlines, the best evidence right now is that all hormonal birth control methods increase a woman's risk of blood clots slightly when compared with those women not on hormonal birth control. The newer DSR pills seem to increase this risk over women taking regular COCs. The patch and the ring, however, do not.

We want to acknowledge that research continues to be conducted and released and the current thinking might change. In the meantime women who have concerns about this should talk to their health care provider.

Though some would say that this is comparing apples with oranges, we also think it's worth noting that what puts women at the most risk of blood clots is pregnancy and childbirth. This is not to dismiss the risks of hormonal contraception but to remind readers that preventing unintended pregnancy is important for many reasons.

Contraceptive Implants

Implants are a form of hormonal contraception that are categorized as long-acting reversible contraceptives (LARCs). (IUDs are the other form of birth control referred to as a LARC.) They consist of one or more thin rods that are inserted under the skin on a woman's upper arm which continually release hormones for a number of years. They need to be inserted and removed by a health care provider.

The first implant released in the United States was Norplant which was approved by the FDA in 1990. Norplant was hailed as a breakthrough in contraception because once it was inserted a woman was protected from pregnancy for 5 years without having to do anything as potentially difficult as remembering to take a pill every day. For a few years, health care providers and women agreed that this was a great new option—in 1992 sales of Norplant reached $120.7 million (Watkins, 2010, p. 104).

The negative press around Norplant, however, started early and continued to grow as it focused on three separate issues—civil rights, cost, and side effects. It became clear early on that some states were looking at Norplant as a way to control birth rates in women on welfare and low-income women, who were also disproportionately women of color. In 1992, the Mississippi legislature, for example, introduced a bill that would require women with four or more children to get Norplant in order to receive public aid. In fact, that year 13 states considered bills that involved Norplant—some made it a condition for receiving welfare, others would have provided financial incentives for women to choose the method, and still others attempted to require the implant as a condition of parole or probation. None of these measures passed but the public debate over Norplant had begun in a bad light (Watkins, 2010, p. 93).

Congress then became involved in a different issue surrounding the new method—cost. Hearings asked why the same device that cost $23 overseas was being sold to American women for $365. Family planning clinics pointed out that it made more financial sense for them to provide birth control pills to many women than Norplant to just a few (Watkins, 2010).

What may have received the most attention, however, were the reports of side effects. Though researchers knew, and women were told, that the implant would likely disrupt their menstrual cycle and that this was normal, many users complained about it. For some women, Norplant completely stopped their periods while others found they bled or spotted for many days of the month. Many women found this more disruptive than they had anticipated. Other side effects included those that are common to all hormonal methods such as headaches, acne, and mood changes. One issue exclusive to Norplant, however, was the removal process. As women began to remove the implants—either because the 5 years were up or because they decided they didn't want to continue using it—there were reports that it was difficult to take out, that not enough providers were trained in removal techniques, and that what should be a 15-minute procedure was turning into a painful 2-hour operation (Watkins, 2010, p. 99). Not surprisingly, a number of lawsuits were filed against the manufacturer.

The negative press led to diminished demand but the final nail in Norplant's coffin turned out to be manufacturing issues. In 2000, the manufacturer announced that some of the implants it had made the previous year might have a shorter shelf-life than the promised 5 years. They stopped shipping new supplies out, suggested women who had received the implant in 1999 use back-up birth control, and told clinicians to stop inserting them. Two years later, the company announced that due to "limitations in product component supplies" it was going to stop manufacturing the implant altogether (Watkins, 2010, p. 104).

This complicated history is fascinating and may help explain why people are wary of the newer implants on the market. That said, today's implants have none of the problems of Norplant.

The FDA approved Implanon in 2006. This newer version consists of just one rod which makes it less obtrusive and ensures that insertion and removal are much easier. In trials in the United States and Europe, for example, the average insertion time for Implanon was 1 minute and removal time was 3 minutes. In contrast, Norplant required up to 10 minutes to insert and 1 hour to remove (Darney, 2006).

The company that made Implanon has since developed Nexplanon which is even easier to insert and remove. Nexplanon also contains barium which makes the rod detectable by X-ray in cases of deep insertion. Implanon remained safe and continued to be used in the United States until supplies ran out at which point it was replaced by Nexplanon. Implanon and Nexplanon last for 3 years (Mansour, 2010).

Implants are safe and, because they contain only progestin (no estrogen), they do not carry the same risks of blood clots, stroke, or heart attack that other combined contraceptive methods do. They do still change women's menstrual bleeding patterns—some women bleed much less and less frequently, while others have prolonged or frequent periods. There are no health implications for this but some women find it annoying.

The other question many people have about implants is whether they cause weight gain. In 11 clinical trials that included 942 women the median weight gain was less than 5.6 pounds over a period of up to 3 years. There is no way to know, however, if this weight gain was caused by the implant or would have occurred anyway (Raymond, 2011).

IUDs

The first intrauterine device (IUD) was made in 1909 out of the gut of a silkworm. More sophisticated versions were introduced in the 1920s and 1930s but they fell out of favor until modern, all plastic models came on the market in the 1960s (Connell, 1999). The IUD is an interesting method of birth control because with all the science and research we have on it there are still some questions about how exactly it works. One of its mechanisms for action is what's known as the "foreign body effect"—our bodies are naturally programmed to react to something foreign by releasing white blood cells. A foreign body in the uterus causes an inflammatory reaction that is toxic to both sperm and egg which prevents implantation. Modern IUDs, which are sometimes referred to as intrauterine contraceptives (IUCs), also contain chemicals—either copper which impairs sperm function or hormones similar to those in the some birth control pills which thicken cervical mucus—both of these mechanisms can help prevent fertilzation (Dean and Schwarz, 2011, p. 150). But before we get to today's generation of IUCs, we have to talk about the 1970s.

By that decade there were 17 models of IUDs on the market manufactured by 15 different companies. The fourth one to be released was the Dalkon Shield made by A.H. Robins. The Dalkon Shield looks a little like the shell of a horseshoe crab that you would find washed up on the beach except miniaturized, and instead of one large spike out of the top it has five short spikes off each side. These spikes were meant to keep the IUD in place. They turned out to be very irritating to the lining of the uterus and caused many users to develop pelvic inflammatory disease (PID) which in turn caused infertility. The Dalkon Shield also had a higher failure rate than other IUDs meaning some women became pregnant. Those who did were at risk of septic miscarriage, a miscarriage followed by a severe infection. Eighteen women who used the Dalkon Shield died from this (Couzin-Frankel, 2011).

In 1974, A.H. Robins took it off the market but stories of complications and negative press continued to roll in and more than 400,000 lawsuits were filed, which kept the story in the headlines. In 1986, a public service announcement that aired on television implored women to have their Dalkon Shields removed. A year earlier the manufacturer had gone bankrupt. Ultimately, a $3 billion fund was set up to compensate women who had had issues with the IUD. Though only the Dalkon Shield was implicated in these medical issues, the impact was felt by all IUDs. By 1986 there was only one IUD on the market and few women were using it (Couzin-Frankel, 2011).

Today, however, there is a new generation of IUDs that are very safe and effective. The first to be introduced was ParaGard, which is a small T-shaped device made of plastic wrapped in copper. The second was Mirena, which releases a continuous amount of the synthetic hormone levonorgestrel (LNg) which is found in some birth control pills. Originally, these methods were approved for use only in women who had already had children as people were still wary of what happened in the 1970s. But as research came out it became clear that these models were safe for women of all ages regardless of whether they'd been pregnant or given birth.

In 2011, the American College of Obstetricians and Gynecologists (ACOG) revised its official practice guidelines on LARCs, including implants and IUDs. After reviewing the latest available research, the guidelines concluded that, "Nulliparous women and adolescents can be offered LARC methods, including IUDs" (ACOG Practice Bulletin, 2011). These guidelines represent the best practices in obstetrics and gynecology and strongly influence what health care providers recommend to patients.

In fact, the manufacturer Bayer recently released a new version that is smaller and specifically designed to be inserted in young women and those who have not had children (such women tend to have smaller uteruses). The new version, Skyla, also releases LNg.

Despite the fact that these new IUDs are safe and effective, uptake has been slow. Many believe that this is because so many myths exist about IUDs. *Contraceptive Technology* does a good job of dispelling these myths. Again, we flipped them around so that the truth is highlighted rather than the misperception.

IUDs Do Not Cause Pelvic Inflammatory Disease. The IUD itself does not increase the risk of PID. There is a slight risk that during the insertion process bacteria could be introduced to the upper genital tract that might cause PID but this risk is so small that experts do not even suggest prophylactic antibiotics (Dean and Schwarz, 2011).

IUDs Do Not Cause Ectopic Pregnancy. An ectopic pregnancy is one that implants and starts to develop outside the uterus, most often in the fallopian tubes. An ectopic pregnancy cannot survive and can pose a danger to women if not caught early. By preventing conception, IUDs, like other birth control methods, actually reduce the risk of ectopic pregnancies. And IUDs are one of the most effective forms of contraception—a woman with an IUD has just a 0.1–0.5% chance of getting pregnant in the first year of use. A woman who does get pregnant while she has an IUD is at a higher risk of ectopic pregnancy (Dean and Schwarz, 2011).

IUDs Can Be Used by Teenagers. IUDs are safe for use in women of all ages regardless of whether they have had children. ACOG recommends IUDs as a first line choice for sexually active adolescent women. A concern with this age group is that IUDs raise the risk of STIs. While this is not true, it is important that all women who use IUDs understand that they do not provide any protection against STIs and that women and their partners should continue using condoms. Writing for the *Contraceptive Journal* of the Association for Reproductive Health Professionals (ARHP), experts Speidel *et al.* write:

> Unfortunately, outdated perceptions about appropriate patient candidates for LARC among health care providers continue to negatively impact their use. An emerging body of research has disproved a number of contraindications to IUC use. Specifically, women of any age or parity and those who are postpartum or post first or second trimester abortion are eligible for IUC. The benefits of IUC also outweigh the risks of a wide variety of medical conditions that might contraindicate the use of combined hormonal contraceptives. (Speidel *et al.*, 2008)

IUDs Do Not Cause Abortions. As we mentioned earlier, the exact method of action for IUDs is a bit of a mystery which has left room for speculation and discussion about whether IUDs could be considered an abortifacient— something that ends an established pregnancy. Experts say this is not the case. In *Contraceptive Technology*, Dean and Schwarz write simply, "IUC's prevent fertilization and thus are true contraceptives." A nurse practitioner friend of ours said it was helpful to think about an IUD like a goalie. Sperm are trying to get into and past the uterus to get to the egg while it's still in the fallopian tubes—through various methods discussed earlier, the IUD blocks that path.

Moving Beyond the Myths

Again, our goal with this entry is not to dismiss concerns over the safety of contraceptive methods. We think that women (and men, of course) should be informed consumers which means, in part, understanding the risks of any medicine or device they use as all do come with some risks. We also understand the desire for caution especially based on the history of some methods. Nevertheless, we are confident that, as of now, the best science suggests that modern methods of contraception are safe for most women.

References

ACOG Practice Bulletin (2011). ACOG Practice Bulletin No. 121: Long-acting reversible contraception: Implants and Intrauterine devices. *Obsetrics and Gynecology*, 118(1), 184–196.

Brenner, M. (2014). Danger in the ring. *Vanity Fair* (January 14). http://www.vanityfair.com/politics/2014/01/nuvaring-lethal-contraceptive-trial (accessed August 1, 2014).

Connell, E.B. (1999). Contraception in the prepill era. *Contraception*, 59(1), 7S–10S.

Couzin-Frankel, J. (2011). Contraceptive comeback: The maligned IUD gets a second chance. *Wired Magazine* (July 15). http://www.wired.com/2011/07/ff_iud/all/1 (accessed August 1, 2014).

Darney, P. (2006). Everything you need to know about the contraceptive implant. *Journal of Family Planning*, 18(9).

Dean, G. and Schwarz, E.B. (2011). Intrauterine contraceptives. In Hatcher, R., Trussell, J., Nelson, A.L., Cates, W., Kowal, D., and Policar, M. (eds) *Contraceptive Technology*, 20th edn. Ardent Media, New York, pp. 147–182.

Dinger, J., Möhner, S., and Heinemann, K. (2013). Cardiovascular risk associated with the use of an etonogestrel-containing vaginal ring. *Obstetrics and Gynecology*, 122(4), 800–808.

Mansour, D. (2010). Nexplanon: what Implanon did next. *Journal of Family Planning and Reproductive Health Care*, 36(4), 187–189.

Nelson, A.L. and Cwiak, C. (2011). Combined Oral Contraceptive (COCs). In Hatcher, R., Trussell, J, Nelson, A.L. Cates, W., Kowal, D., and Policar, M. (eds) *Contraceptive Technology*, 20th edn. Ardent Media, New York, pp. 249–320.

Raymond, E.G. (2011). Contraceptive implants. In Hatcher, R., Trussell, J., Nelson, A.L., Cates, W., Kowal, D., and Policar, M. (eds) *Contraceptive Technology*, 20th edn. Ardent Media, New York, pp. 193–204.

Siddiqui, S. (2013). Side effects may include death: The story of the biggest advance in birth control since the pill. *Huffington Post* (December 18). http://www.huffingtonpost.com/2013/12/18/nuvaring-blood-clots_n_4461429.html (accessed August 1, 2014).

Speidel, J.J., Harper, C.C., and Shields, W. (2008). The potential of long-acting reversible contraception to decrease unintended pregnancy. *Contraception*, 78(3), 197–200.

Sidney, S., Cheetham, T.C., Connell, F.A., Ouellet-Hellstrom, R., Graham, D.J., Davis, D., *et al.* (2013). Recent combined hormonal contraceptives (CHCs) and the risk of thrombo-embolism and other cardiovascular events in new users. *Contraception*, 87(1), 93–100.

Tyrer, L. (1999). Introduction of the pill and its impact. *Contraception*, 59(1), 11S–16S.

Watkins, E.S. (2010). From breakthrough to bust: the brief life of Norplant, the contraceptive implant. *Journal of Women's History*, 22(3), 88–111.

Myth 27 Withdrawal Is Just as Good as Any Other Contraceptive Method

We can all picture the moment at which a couple is on the brink of getting it on and realizes they don't have any contraception. She's not on the pill and neither one of them has a condom. What should they do? Fool around but stop short of intercourse? Pause for a quick pharmacy run? Throw caution to the wind and risk it? Many couples answer this particular conundrum by agreeing that the man will pull out before he ejaculates.

Withdrawal is the least complicated of all methods—other than not having sex—in terms of how it works to prevent pregnancy during penile–vaginal intercourse. The male partner simply takes his penis out of the vagina before he ejaculates thereby preventing sperm from having access to the vagina, the uterus, the fallopian tubes, and ultimately the egg. If sperm and egg are kept separated there can be no pregnancy.

Once upon a time, public health experts would have scoffed at this as the folly of youth or the poor decision making of being in the moment, but newer research suggests withdrawal has prevented countless pregnancies since the dawn of time and that it may be a decent option for some couples some of the time. A recent article in *New York Magazine* suggests that some younger women have decided to forgo other birth control methods like the pill or even condoms in favor of withdrawal. This sent the media abuzz with headlines about pulling out and statistics suggesting it's just as good as things you might buy in the drug store.

We'd like to weigh in. Our short answer is—there are better methods. While we would definitely say that pulling out is better than nothing for couples with no other options, we think most couples have other, better options. Let us explain.

How Good Is Withdrawal at Preventing Pregnancy?

Our apologies as we have gone over this before, but we think it is very important that everyone understands how contraceptive effectiveness rates are calculated since this is the math that people use to make their own decisions about which methods to use.

It is difficult to calculate exact contraceptive efficacy because every couple has a different risk of pregnancy based on how fertile they are and how often they have sex. Researchers estimate how well contraceptive methods work based on clinical trials and other tests of the methods as well as studies that ask couples to recount when they had sex, what methods they used, and whether they had ever experienced an unintended pregnancy. These numbers are plugged into complicated equations and then each contraceptive method is given two efficacy rates: the *perfect use rate* refers to how well the method will work if used consistently and correctly such as in a controlled clinical trial, while the *typical use rate* refers to how well the method will work when used by a normal couple under real-life conditions (Trussell, 2011, p. 779).

Rates are expressed by showing how many couples out of 100 who use the method will experience an unintended pregnancy in the first 12 months. The perfect use rate for condoms, for example, is 98% because when used consistently and correctly only 2 out of 100 couples will experience an unintended pregnancy in the first year. Put another way, under perfect conditions condoms only fail to prevent pregnancy 2% of the time. Other methods like IUDs have even higher perfect use rates—over 99% (Trussell, p. 784).

For most methods, typical use rates are lower because human error enters the picture. The typical use rate for condoms is 82% because 18 out of 100 typical couples who say they use condoms as their primary method of birth control will experience an unintended pregnancy during the first year of use. This includes couples who were not using condoms correctly when they became pregnant. It also includes couples who were not using condoms at all when they became pregnant (Trussell, p. 784). Methods like IUDs have typical use rates that are almost identical to perfect use rates because once they are properly inserted by a health care provider they work—without the user having to doing anything to ensure that they work and without the chance of the user doing anything to interfere with how they work.

When looking at the numbers, withdrawal compares favorably to other methods. There is some debate about the exact efficacy rates of withdrawal, but it is generally accepted that it can be 96% effective with perfect use. The 20th edition of *Contraceptive Technology* cites the typical use rates as 78% but other research says it is closer to 82% (Jones *et al.*, 2009).

We Need More Research

In a commentary titled, "Better than nothing or savvy risk-reduction practice? The importance of withdrawal," Jones *et al.* (2009) suggest that research consistently underestimates the number of couples who use withdrawal either as their primary method or as a back-up. Part of the problem is how the questions are usually asked and another part is what researchers then do with the answers.

In the National Survey of Family Growth, for example, which is the basis for many of the calculations on efficacy, participants are asked to choose from a list of over 20 methods and check all of the ones they used in a particular month. It is clear from qualitative research, however, that some people don't think of withdrawal as a method, meaning that they might not check that box even if they have used withdrawal that month. Moreover, for the purposes of analyzing the data, researchers prioritize the most effective of the methods checked. Someone who used the pill and withdrawal would therefore be categorized as a pill user. This can lead to an underestimate of how many people are using withdrawal and, because researchers don't know which method a couple was actually using (if any) the day they experienced an unintended pregnancy, may also have an impact on efficacy rates.

> We expect that results from some studies underestimate the use of withdrawal. It is unclear what impact, if any, the likely mis-measurement of withdrawal might have on estimates of typical-use failure rates for withdrawal and, perhaps, condoms. This depends in part on the frequency and type of measurement error—for example, whether it is more common to mis-measure use of withdrawal as a primary or as a "backup" method. (Jones *et al.*, 2009, p. 6)

Jones *et al.* believe that the way couples use birth control in real life is more complicated than research measures. They suggest that some couples may go back and forth between condoms and withdrawal in a month or may be more deliberate about using condoms during the times of a month when a woman is more fertile and then relying on withdrawal for the rest of her cycle. This could be seen as a modified rhythm method. They also note that lots of couples, even those on a more effective method such as the birth control pill, are likely to use withdrawal as extra protection at least once in a while. They suggest more research needs to be done to determine how withdrawal is really being used. They also believe that better communication is needed about the research so that couples know it can work: "Both couples and clinicians could be well served in approaching withdrawal as part of a larger risk reduction strategy in which couples intermittently employ a variety of pregnancy prevention techniques" (Jones *et al.*, 2009, p. 7).

In the Meantime, We Have Concerns

We agree that public health professionals should be better equipped to discuss withdrawal and that research needs to be expanded. That said, we have some concerns about suggesting any couple rely on pulling out as a method of birth control.

STIs. One of our strongest objections to withdrawal as a method of contraception is that it provides no protection against sexually transmitted diseases infections (STIs). Of course, this is true of most contraceptive methods. Condoms are the only birth control method that also provides protection against STIs. We believe that condoms are a vital protection method at least until individuals are sure that they are not at risk of STIs (meaning both partners have been tested and neither partner is having sex with anyone else).

Improving Efficacy. When using other methods of contraception there are easy ways to ensure that one's own efficacy is closer to the perfect rates than the typical rates. A woman who takes the pill, for example, can achieve perfect use rates by remembering to take it every day which might also involve remembering to go to the pharmacy at least a few days before she starts a new package and never letting her prescription run out. Similarly, there are some basic and easy steps that couples can take to improve the efficacy of condoms. Most condom errors are user errors, such as not putting it on until after intercourse has started, taking it off before ejaculation, or not using it at all. It is unfair to blame a condom for a pregnancy that happened while it was still in the night table drawer or after it had been thrown away, but the typical failure rates nonetheless include couples who say condoms were their primary method of contraception but weren't using a condom when they got pregnant. If couples who rely on condoms use one every time and make sure to use it correctly, they will get closer to perfect use rates which show condoms can be as much as 98% effective in preventing pregnancy.

It is less clear how couples could improve the efficacy of withdrawal. Part of the issue may be physiological and depend on a man knowing his body, sensations, and what it feels like when he's about to ejaculate so that he can learn exactly when he needs to pull out. Though some men may be able to learn this behavior, others may have more difficulty perfecting the timing.

Sperm in Pre-ejaculate. In addition, there is the issue of whether a man's pre-ejaculate includes sperm. Most men leak a little fluid before they ejaculate called pre-ejaculate or pre-cum. This can come out of the penis at any time during foreplay or sex. If pre-cum contains sperm it would be introduced to the vagina before ejaculation, meaning there is a risk of pregnancy even if the man later pulls out.

For many years it was a known "fact" that there was indeed sperm in pre-cum though the source of this fact was a mystery. It appears that this assertion was a bit of an educators' myth—information that is repeated even though it was never substantiated. The notion may have originated with Masters and Johnson, who wrote about it in their famous 1966 book *Human Sexual Response* but could never produce the scientific basis for it. Nonetheless, it was passed on for decades by scientists and educators, until the 1990s and early 2000s, when some researchers took on the subject with mixed results. For a while, the best information said there was no sperm in pre-cum, then new information said there might be. This went back and forth for some time (Killick *et al.*, 2011).

The best evidence currently available is from Killick *et al.* (2011). This research analyzed samples of pre-ejaculate and found that in 41% of men it contained sperm. Though some experts had theorized that sperm would only be in pre-ejaculate if the man had ejaculated recently leaving viable sperm in his urethra, this study refutes that theory as well. The men in this study had urinated numerous times (cleaning the urethra) before the pre-ejaculate was collected, and sperm was still found in their samples. The researchers concluded that some men leak sperm as part of pre-ejaculate, and some men don't. However, it is not possible for a man to know which category he falls into and therefore it is not possible for a couple to know their personal risk if they rely on withdrawal.

Performance Anxiety. Finally, we understand that contraceptive use is often a matter of trust between partners—men have been believing women for years that they are on the pill or have an IUD without proof. Trust is particularly important when using withdrawal—it is not just that a woman needs to trust that her partner intends to pull out, she needs to trust that he can follow through. Even men with the best intentions can fail to withdraw in time. We think that this can cause anxiety in both men and women. Worrying about whether you or your partner will be able to pull out in time can make sex a much less pleasurable experience.

Our Bottom Line

We know that some of our colleagues put more faith in withdrawal than we are comfortable with doing. We absolutely believe that couples should have the most recent information about withdrawal. And we agree that in some situations (when no other method is available), withdrawal may be a couple's best option for preventing pregnancy and there is no denying that it is "better than nothing."

Still, we think that with a little bit of planning and more widespread access, couples can and should turn to the many methods of contraception that provide potentially better efficacy and additional benefits.

References

Jones, R.K., Fennell, J., Higgins, J.A., and Blanchard, K. (2009). Better than nothing or savvy risk-reduction practice? The importance of withdrawal. *Contraception*, 79(6), 407–410.

Killick, S.R., Leary, C., Trussell, J., and Guthrie, K.A. (2011). Sperm content of pre-ejaculatory fluid. *Human Fertility*, 14(1), 48–52.

Trussell, J. (2011). Contraceptive efficacy. In Hatcher, R.A., Trussell, J., Nelson, A.L., Cates, W., Kowal D., and Policar, M. (eds) *Contraceptive Technology*, 20th edn. Ardent Media, New York, pp. 779–788.

Myth #28   Condoms Don't Work Very Well, Plus They Take All the Fun Out of Sex Anyway

Despite over 400 years of helping people prevent pregnancy and sexually transmitted diseases, the poor condom has been much maligned lately. We have read far too many articles that say it isn't a good method of birth control, question whether it really protects against sexually transmitted infections (STIs), suggest that it's hard to use, and argue that it saps all the joy and spontaneity out of the moment.

We know that there are forces out there that want to see an end to premarital sex and the use of birth control. We are never surprised, for example, when abstinence-only-until-marriage programs deride condoms and exaggerate their failure rates. (Angry that so many kids across the country get misinformation in school but not surprised.) We get even more upset, however, when those in the public health community get involved by suggesting either that condoms don't work, or that they are no fun to use.

A lot of attention has also been paid to the Gates Foundation's recent challenge which is asking entrepreneurs to design a "better" condom and offering money to help produce any winning designs (Lupkin, 2013). We are all for making even better condoms and we think the challenge is a great idea which will help foster even more great ideas. The problem is that the framing for the contest essentially suggests that the condoms we have now are no good and that's why we have to start over.

We have also seen companies and public health experts promote other birth control methods—such as IUDs or emergency contraception—by suggesting that condoms don't work very well. Many experts, for example, tell stories of couples who use emergency contraception (the only birth control method that works after unprotected sex) because the condom broke. We understand the instinct to take the blame off the couple, but, given the low rates of breakage and slippage of male condoms that are used correctly, we have a hard time believing that so many couples have had this experience.

Condoms are cheap, reliable, easy to access, and easy to use. But, most importantly, they are the only method of contraception that also protects against STIs. In fact, other than abstinence, they are the best protection that individuals have against STIs.

So, we are going to devote this entry to the humble little condom and explain why this method of birth control has such an important role in our sex lives and why we should all stop throwing it under the bus. Before we get started, we think our readers should know that both of us are founding members of the Trojan Sexual Health Advisory Council which helps the manufacturer of Trojan brand condoms examine and promote a broad definition of sexual health. For this reason, some of our discussion may use Trojan condoms as examples because we are more familiar with their products. That said, in this entry we are not talking about any one brand of condoms or suggesting which make or model you should buy. All condoms sold in this country have to meet certain standards and we have faith in all of them.

They Are Made Very Well

Condoms have been around forever. Seriously. One of the earliest representations of a condom was found in an ancient cave painting (at least 12,000 years old) at the Grotte des Combarelles in France. The painting depicts a man and woman having sex, and the man's penis is covered (Collier, 2007, p. 1). Ancient Egyptians also provide accounts, written between 1350 and 1200 BCE, of using a cover to protect the tip or glans of the penis. These were likely made of oiled animal intestines or bladders (which are still used today in some condoms). Other accounts suggest that Egyptian royalty used condoms made of paper to cover their penises during sex with some partners (Collier, 2007, p. 13).

Today, the materials and technology for making condoms are a little bit more advanced. We were thrilled to have been able to visit a condom factory based in the United States and see first-hand how condoms are made and tested.

Most condoms are made out of latex which is a very thin and flexible form of rubber that is used to make everything from tires to surgical gloves. (About 3% of the population has a latex allergy, these people may want to try condoms made out of polyurethane or polyisoprene. There are still condoms made out of lambskin and these protect against pregnancy but not STIs.) Latex actually starts as a liquid that contains suspended rubber particles. Glass molds are dipped in the latex and then run through water. The open end of the condom is then rolled slightly before the condom is taken off the mold and dried.

The next step was our favorite to watch but also one of the most important things to note for critics who claim that condoms have small holes in them (some abstinence-only curriculums take this so far they seem to suggest that on a microscopic level condoms resemble a soccer net). Each condom is placed on a metal rod called a mandrel. The rod is then passed over another metal rod that has an electric current running through it. An intact condom will block the electric current. If it doesn't, it means there is a hole in it and that condom will be discarded. Quite simply this means that every condom is tested for holes before being wrapped and shipped.

Testers then also pick a certain number of condoms from each lot at random for additional testing. The condoms are filled with water and then rolled around and squeezed, again to test for any holes. Another test fills a condom with air and sees how much pressure it can take before it bursts. This test ensures that the latex is strong enough to resist breaking. And, it shows us that condoms can be blown up to the size of a basketball without bursting.

They Protect Against Pregnancy

Condoms—if used consistently and correctly—are 98% effective in preventing pregnancy. Though we know we have gone over this in other myths (see Myth # 27 on Withdrawal for example), we feel that it's important to explain once again how efficacy rates are calculated for all birth control methods including condoms. (In case some people don't read it cover to cover.)

It is difficult to calculate exact contraceptive efficacy because every couple has a different risk of pregnancy based on how fertile they are and how often they have sex. Researchers estimate how well contraceptive methods work based on clinical trials and other tests of the methods as well as studies that ask couples to recount when they had sex, what methods they used, and whether they had ever experienced an unintended pregnancy. These numbers are plugged into complicated equations and then each contraceptive method is given two efficacy rates: the *perfect use rate* refers to how well the method will work if used consistently and correctly such as in a controlled clinical trial and the *typical use rate* refers to how well the method will work when used by a normal couple under real-life conditions (Trussell, 2011, p. 779).

Rates are expressed by showing how many couples out of 100 who use the method will experience an unintended pregnancy in the first 12 months. The perfect use rate for condoms, for example, is 98% because when used consistently and correctly only 2 out of 100 couples will experience an unintended pregnancy in the first year. Put another way, under perfect conditions condoms only fail 2% of the time (Trussell, p. 784).

For most methods, typical use rates are lower because human error enters the picture. The typical use rate for condoms is 82% because 18 out of 100 typical couples who say they use condoms as their primary method of birth control will experience an unintended pregnancy during the first year of use. This includes couples who were *not using condoms correctly* when they became pregnant. It also includes couples who were *not using condoms at all* when they became pregnant (Trussell, p. 784).

Contraceptive Technology describes use as an "elastic concept" in large part because studies rely on self-report: "So typical use of the condom could include actually using a condom only occasionally, and a woman could report that she is 'using' the pill even though her supplies ran out several months ago" (Trussell and Guthrie, 2011, p. 53).

That's right, the failure rate of condoms includes those people who said they were condom users but didn't use a condom that particular night (or afternoon or morning). We think we can all agree that the condom cannot be blamed for a pregnancy if it was left in his room, her purse, or on the drug store shelf.

They Protect Against STIs

We understand that some methods of birth control have higher efficacy rates than condoms, especially under typical use conditions. IUDs, for example, have typical use rates that are nearly identical to their perfect use rates because once they have been properly inserted by a medical provider they work for between 5 and 10 years without the user doing anything. We think these are great options for women as they can "set it and forget it." There is a giant caveat, however, which is that no birth control method other than condoms (and to a lesser extent female condoms) provide protection against STIs. Even if you or your partner has an IUD or is on the pill, unless you are positive that there are no other risk factors for STIs (which in our minds means that you have both been tested and are both remaining 100% faithful), you should be using condoms as they significantly reduce the risk of contracting an STI.

All STIs are transmitted differently. Some are genital secretion diseases—like chlamydia and gonorrhea which are transmitted through secretions from the urethra, vagina, and cervix. These diseases are very easy to transmit. Condoms have been shown to significantly reduce the risk of transmitting genital secretion diseases by acting as a barrier between these secretions and the uninfected partner. For example, Niccolai et al. (2005) analyzed the medical records of 1455 patients at a public STI clinic. Among patients who were known to have been exposed to chlamydia, consistent condoms users were less likely to be diagnosed with the infection. The analysis suggests that consistent condom use was associated with a 90% reduction in chlamydia infection.

Other STIs, like HIV, are transmitted through bodily fluids—specifically, blood, semen, vaginal fluids, and breast milk. The virus can be transmitted when these fluids come into contact with a sore, a cut, a wound, or mucous membranes in an uninfected person. HIV cannot be transmitted through unbroken skin such as that on a person's hand. This is why certain sexual activities are riskier than others—unprotected vaginal and anal intercourse are riskiest, for example, because the skin in the vagina, anus, and urethra are lined with mucous membranes. The skin around these areas is also more delicate and can tear more easily. But, the risk is not the same for both partners—the receptive partner is at increased risk because semen comes into contact with mucous membranes and any cuts and sores that may be present. Moreover, semen often stays in the vagina or anus for some time giving it more opportunity to enter the bloodstream. Condoms have been shown to significantly reduce this risk, again by providing a barrier that prevents these bodily fluids from coming into contact with an uninfected partner.

There have been lab studies that show that latex condoms provide an impermeable barrier to the HIV virus (CDC, 2013). The real life studies of HIV are also better than for many other STIs because there are couples—known as serodiscordant—in which one partner has HIV and the other does not. Studying the condom use habits of these couples allows researchers to get a very clear picture of how much protection condoms provide. (It would be unethical to do these kind of studies with STIs that are curable as the goal would be to cure the infected partner long before he/she could transmit the virus to anyone else. It would also be unethical to try to do a double blind study of this sort in which serodiscordant couples were randomly assigned to use or not use condoms. Instead, researchers observe the results of the safer sex choices these couples make on their own.) The results suggest consistent condom use reduces the risk of HIV transmission by between 80% and 94% (Weller and Davis, 2002).

The last category of STIs are those that are transmitted via skin-to-skin contact such as herpes, syphilis, and human papillomavirus (HPV). Whether or not a condom will protect against these diseases is mostly a function of where the infected skin (the sores or warts) is located. If it is located in an area that is covered by the condom, such as on the shaft of the penis or inside the vagina, condoms will again provide a barrier. But sores can be located outside of this area such as on a man's scrotum.

Still, research suggests that consistent use of condoms does provide protection against these diseases as well as the health issues they might cause. For example, a study of college women found that none of the women who reported using condoms all of the time (100%) had genital warts (which are caused by HPV) on their cervix. In contrast, 14 of the women who did not use condoms or used them inconsistently were found to have HPV on their cervix (Winer *et al.*, 2006).

They Can Be Fun, Too (Really They Can)

This is the hardest myth about condoms to debate because they've been getting a bad rap on this issue for years. Moreover, we can't really argue with anyone's personal perception of how it felt the first time or last time they used a condom. Still, we wonder how much of this myth is based on actual experience and how much of it is because if everyone thinks this, then clearly it must be true. We also wonder whether some of it is left over from previous generations of condoms which were thicker and had a stronger latex smell.

Today, there are some pretty cool condoms designed not just to protect pregnancy, but to make sex feel good. First of all they are really thin. One of the complaints about condom use is precisely about putting a barrier between your skin and hers or his because skin on skin feels good—it's part of what makes sex pleasurable. Using thinner condoms can help get that sensation back.

Another thing that can help is lubrication on the inside and the outside of the condom. In vaginal sex, the lubricant on the outside can help women enjoy sex by reducing friction. The lubrication on the inside is meant to feel like a vagina would naturally feel during sex—wet. This can increase the sensation for men as well.

And speaking about sensations, some of the lubricants have chemicals in them that can make skin warm or tingly. Some couples love these and others aren't crazy about them. You can't know until you try and the chances that you will have fun experimenting are pretty high.

While you are experimenting, look at the shelf and note that condoms come in different shapes and textures. Some condoms are expanded at the top so that the penis can move around inside the condom, which again provides more of the sensation of unprotected sex without the risk. (Don't worry, the bottom ring is still tight which prevents the condom from slipping off.) As for the textures, there are bumps and ridges which are designed to be felt by the woman. Some women say that the ribbing, for example, helps stimulate their clitoris during intercourse. Our opinion—it can't hurt to try.

Perhaps our favorite condom invention of late, however, is the vibrating ring which looks a little like a clear plastic bracelet. On one side, a small oval vibrates. These, too, come in different styles and speeds: some are more gentle, others more intense. The ring goes over the penis (once the condom is on) and the vibrating part can be positioned for clitoral contact during intercourse. We sometimes joke that it can turn your partner into your own personal sex toy. (Given that the point of this entry is to increase condom use, we probably shouldn't say this but you can use these rings without a condom as well—as long as you don't need STI protection.)

If at First You Don't Like It, Try, Try Again

We believe in condoms for many reasons. As we said earlier, they are cheap, easy to get, require almost no forethought, and work really well against pregnancy *and* STIs. And, we think that sex is best when it does not come with any fear of getting unintentionally pregnant or contracting an STI. We want all couples to be able to relax and enjoy it and we think the plethora of condom options out there today can help them do that.

Our suggestion is a field trip to a drug store. Most have taken condoms out from behind the counter and you can easily wander the aisle and find something that looks fun. If you like it, buy it again; if not try a different brand, a new texture, or one with a different kind of lube. Or, if you planning on a really long night, pick up a variety pack and start rating them as soon as you get home.

References

Centers for Disease Control and Pevention (CDC) (2013). Male latex condoms and sexually transmitted diseases: Condom fact sheet in brief. http://www.cdc.gov/condomeffectiveness/brief.html (accessed August 12, 2014).

Collier, A. (2007). *The Humble Little Condom: A History*. Prometheus Books.

Lupkin, S. (2013). Bill Gates offers grant for 'Next Generation Condom.' *ABC News* (March 25). http://abcnews.go.com/blogs/health/2013/03/25/bill-gates-offers-grant-for-next-generation-condom/ (accessed August 1, 2014).

Niccolai, L.M., Rowhani-Rahbar, A., Jenkins, H., Green, S., and Dunne, D.W. (2005). Condom effectiveness for prevention of *Chlamydia trachomatis* infection. *Sexually Transmitted Infections*, 81(4), 323–325.

Trussell, J. (2011). Contraceptive efficacy. In Hatcher, R.A., Trussell, J., Nelson, A.L., Cates, W., Kowal D., and Policar, M. (eds) *Contraceptive Technology*, 20th edn. Ardent Media, New York, pp. 779–788.

Trussell, J. and Guthrie, K.A. (2011). Choosing a contraceptive: Efficacy, safety, and personal considerations. In In Hatcher, R.A., Trussell, J., Nelson, A.L., Cates, W., Kowal D., and Policar, M. (eds) *Contraceptive Technology*, 20th edn. Ardent Media, New York, pp. 45–74.

Weller, S. and Davis, K. (2002). Condom effectiveness in reducing heterosexual HIV transmission. *Cochrane Database of Systematic Reviews*, 1, CD003255.

Winer, R.L., Hughes, J.P., Feng, Q., O'Reilly, S., Kiviat, N.B., Holmes, K.K., *et al.* (2006). Condom use and the risk of genital human papillomavirus infection in young women. *New England Journal of Medicine*, 354(25), 2645–2654.

Myth
#29

Abortion Causes Breast Cancer and a Host of Mental Health Issues

Abortion may be the most hotly debated issue in this country. Every day advocates who believe that a woman facing an unintended pregnancy has the right to choose abortion clash with those who believe that abortion is immoral and should be illegal. In 2012 alone, 43 provisions designed to restrict access to abortion were enacted in 19 states (Guttmacher Institute, 2012). Of course, many more were introduced and debated but did not pass. Abortion also continues to be a major political issue with candidates on both sides carefully crafting their views in an attempt to alienate the fewest number of voters possible.

We do not think that this book is the place to debate this issue broadly because most views on abortion are based on opinions or deeply held beliefs and not on myths or misperceptions. That said, we do think it is important for our readers to understand those myths about abortion that are being perpetuated. Specifically, there are some opponents of abortion rights who, in their attempts to limit access to this procedure, argue that there are physical and psychological risks involved. Over the years, the ideas that have gained the most traction are that abortion causes infertility, that women who have abortions are more likely to get breast cancer, and that women who have abortions are likely to experience mental health issues or post-abortion stress syndrome. Despite the overwhelming amount of evidence available that refutes these ideas, the arguments are still used in efforts to limit abortion access on a broad scale or to dissuade individual women from terminating a pregnancy.

In particular, these arguments are used by crisis pregnancy centers (CPCs), organizations that provide counseling to women from a distinctly anti-abortion point of view. These organizations often advertise in such a way that makes women think they offer abortions when, in fact, they exist to dissuade women from choosing that option. A report prepared for Representative Henry Waxman in 2006 found that 87% of the CPCs surveyed (this survey was limited to those CPCs that received funding from the federal government), disseminated inaccurate information (U.S. Committee on Government Reform, 2006). The most common misinformation touched on the three issues we are highlighting here—future fertility, breast cancer, and mental health.

Legal Abortions are Safe for Women and Their Future Fertility

Induced abortion is a very safe procedure. In fact, it is far safer than carrying a pregnancy to term and delivering a baby. The risk of dying from a legal abortion procedure is 1 in 100,000. In contrast, pregnancy-related deaths are twice as high for spontaneous abortions (also known as miscarriages) and 12 times as high for continuing pregnancy and childbirth. Writing for

Contraceptive Technology, Paul and Stein report that "in the largest study of legally induced first-trimester abortions reported to date, minor complications occurred in 8 per 1,000 cases and complications warranting hospitalization occurred in 0.7 per 1,000 cases" (2011, p. 722).

Most abortions are performed in the first trimester (defined as the first 12 weeks after a woman's last menstrual period), and research shows that abortions performed at this stage do not lead to future fertility issues. Paul and Stein also report that several well-designed cohort studies have found no association between aspiration abortions (the most common type of surgical abortion) and future fertility—the ability to get pregnant and carry the pregnancy to term. Similarly, women who chose medication abortion (in which they take a series of drugs designed to terminate the pregnancy) are also not at increased risk of ectopic pregnancy, preterm delivery, or low birth weight babies in the future (p. 726). (An ectopic pregnancy is one that begins to grow outside the uterus, most often in the fallopian tubes.)

It is important to note, however, that all of this research is based on legal first trimester abortions which have been available in the United States since the early 1970s when the United States Supreme Court ruled that laws banning abortion were unconstitutional. Before this time many women sought illegal abortions, some of which were done under unsafe and unsanitary conditions. In fact, since abortion was made legal in all parts of the United States, abortion-related deaths have dropped by 90%—most of this drop occurred in the 3 years after the Court's decision (p. 722).

Abortion Does Not Cause Breast Cancer

Despite being disproven many times, the myth that abortion causes breast cancer also remains pervasive. A quick Google search reveals the headline "abortion has caused 300 K breast cancer death since Roe vs. Wade" as well as a website for the Coalition on Abortion that claims eight medical institutions have acknowledged the link in recent years. Let these serve as another reminder that not everything found on the internet is accurate or unbiased (we would actually argue that little on the internet fits into both of those categories).

There is a great deal of scientific evidence that abortion does not increase a woman's risk of breast cancer. In fact, this issue has been rigorously studied for many years because of questions about how the hormones involved in early pregnancy and abortion or miscarriage would impact a woman's future health. A number of large prospective studies—in which researchers follow a group of individuals over many years to observe any health issues they may encounter—have found no association between induced abortion and later diagnosis of breast cancer (Paul and Stein, 2011, p. 727). One of these studies, published in the *New England Journal of Medicine*, involved 1.5 million women in Denmark born between 1935 and 1978. Included in this group of women were over 280,000 who had had abortions and over 10,000 who were diagnosed with breast cancer. Researchers found no relationship between the two events. They note, "No increase in risk were found in subgroups defined according to age at abortion, parity [whether the women had children at another time], time since abortion, or age at diagnosis of breast cancer." Ultimately, the authors conclude: "Induced abortion have no overall effect on the risk of breast cancer" (Melbye et al., 1997).

In February 2003, the National Cancer Institute (NCI) convened a meeting of over 100 experts to look at the existing data on the link between abortion and breast cancer. Panel members examined existing research including population-based studies, clinical studies, and studies done on animals to determine if there was any relationship between pregnancy and breast cancer risk, including relationships between breast cancer and induced abortions or miscarriages. They concluded that having a miscarriage or an abortion does not increase a woman's subsequent risk of developing breast cancer (National Cancer Institute, 2003). The NCI continues to examine research as it is published and has not changed its conclusions.

Abortion and Mental Health Issues

Opponents of abortion often argue that women who choose to terminate a pregnancy are likely to suffer from a host of psychological issues, from depression and anxiety, to guilt, numbness, and a need to avoid all pregnant women and children. In the early 1980s, they coined the phrase "post abortion stress syndrome" or just "post abortion syndrome" and argued that it was similar to the post-traumatic stress syndrome that is often experienced by soldiers coming back from war or victims of violent crimes.

In 1987, urged by those who wanted abortion made illegal, President Ronald Reagan asked Surgeon General C. Everett Koop to analyze the health effects of abortion and write a report. Dr. Koop had previously acknowledged his personal opposition to abortion but surprised everyone when, after reviewing the available scientific evidence on the subject, he announced that he was abandoning the report because the existing evidence found that abortion was physically safe and he could find no evidence to support the concept that abortion was damaging to mental health (Major et al., 2009, p. 863).

More recent reviews have reached the same conclusion. A review by Adler et al. (1990) found that "severe negative reactions after legal, nonrestrictive, first-trimester abortions are rare and can best be understood in the framework of coping with normal life stress" (Adler et al., 1990, p. 43). These findings also formed the basis of a task force opinion for the American Psychological Association in 1989. In 2008, the American Psychological Association convened a new task force to review any new research that had been published in the intervening decades. It came to a very similar conclusion and began by saying that "most women who terminate a pregnancy do not experience mental health problems." It went on to say that "The most rigorous studies indicated that within the United States, the relative risk of mental health problems among adult women who have a single, legal, first trimester abortion of an unwanted pregnancy is no greater than the risk among women who deliver an unwanted pregnancy" (Major *et al.*, 2009, p. 863).

The task force makes the important distinction of terminating an unwanted pregnancy versus needing to terminate a wanted pregnancy because of health issues for either the mother or the fetus. Obviously these two situations will produce very different feelings in women. In fact, a number of studies have found that the predominant feeling after an abortion is one of relief. Follow-up studies also show that women remain happy with their decision to terminate a pregnancy years after it happened (Paul and Stein, 2011, p. 726).

The task force also noted that abortions do not occur in a vacuum but within a complicated social context in which some woman are stigmatized for getting pregnant (such as teenagers) and women who seek abortions are also stigmatized. The task force writes "From a sociological perspective, social practices and message that stigmatize women who have abortions may directly contribute to negative psychological experiences postabortion" (Major *et al.*, 2009, p. 867). Another way to look at this, according to the task force, is that "A sociocultural context that encourages women to believe that they "should" or "will" feel a particular way after an abortion can create a self-fulfilling prophecy whereby societally induced expectancies can become confirmed" (p. 867).

The Need for Truth

The truth is that every woman who seeks an abortion does so under her own unique set of life circumstances and her feelings about the procedure will be similarly unique. It is not appropriate to tell women how they should feel and it is not accurate to tell them how they will feel. Most importantly, however, it is never appropriate to mislead women about the risk of abortion (or any other medical procedure) in the hopes of persuading them to make one choice over another. There are now many rigorous scientific studies that show that abortion does not cause future infertility, breast cancer, or inevitable mental health issues. Abortion opponents need to stop perpetuating these myths for political gain.

We believe that CPCs are particularly insidious because they prey on women in a vulnerable position (those facing an unintended pregnancy) by advertising services they do not provide. There are an estimated 2500–4000 CPCs in the United States and many are affiliated with national anti-abortion organizations and evangelical Christian networks and have as their mission preventing abortion (Rosen, 2012). Yet they often advertise as if they were any other nonpartial medical clinic offering free services. Women who go to CPCs are most often young, poor, and poorly educated, in part because this is the group that is most likely to experience unintended pregnancies but also in part because these are the women that are most attracted by free services (Rosen, 2012). Though CPCs have not been systematically studied on a national level, the report by Representative Henry Waxman mentioned earlier and some state-level reports provide a disturbing view of what happens once women come into the center. We know from these reports that CPCs regularly perpetuate the three myths we have discussed here.

As Rosen points out in her editorial on CPCs, these practices are contrary to the legal and ethical standards of informed consent to which medical providers are held. CPCs, however, are not held to the same high standards because they are often staffed by volunteers and because, despite their advertising, they are not actually heath care providers. Still, Rosen notes that their practices also run counter to the goals of public health:

> [W]hen these centers disseminate inaccurate information to women seeking reproductive health care services, and blur the line between prolife advocacy group and health care provider, their practices risk delaying or interfering with a woman's access to abortion and contraceptives, improperly influencing women's reproductive health decisions and potentially increasing the number of unintended births. Collectively the practices jeopardize the health of women and their children, and a public health response is warranted. (Rosen, 2012, p. 203)

Regardless of how any of us personally feel about abortion, we should remember that one out of every three women in the United States will have one in her lifetime (Guttmacher Institute, 2013). And, we should agree that it is never okay to lie to women in order to influence their decisions.

References

Adler, N.E., David, H.P., Major, B.N., Roth, S.H., Russo, N.F., and Wyatt, G.E. (1990). Psychological responses after abortion. *Science*, 248(4951), 41–44.
Guttmacher Institute (2012). Laws Affecting Reproductive Health and Rights: 2012 State Policy Review. http://www.guttmacher.org/statecenter/updates/2012/statetrends42012.html (accessed August 1, 2014).
Guttmacher Institute (2013). Facts on Induced Abortion in the United States. http://www.guttmacher.org/pubs/fb_induced_abortion.html (accessed August 1, 2014).
Major, B., Appelbaum, M., Beckman, L., Dutton, M.A., Russo, N.F., and West, C. (2009). Abortion and mental health: Evaluating the evidence. *American Psychologist*, 64(9), 863.
Melbye, M., Wohlfahrt, J., Olsen, J.H., Frisch, M., Westergaard, T., Helweg-Larsen, K., *et al.* (1997). Induced abortion and the risk of breast cancer. *New England Journal of Medicine*, 336(2), 81–85.
National Cancer Institute (2003). U.S. National Institutes of Health. *Summary Report: Early Reproductive Events and Breast Cancer Workshop*, March 25, 2003. http://www.cancer.gov/cancertopics/causes/ere/workshop-report (accessed August 1, 2014).
Paul, M. and Stein, T. (2011). Abortion. In Hatcher, R.A., Trussell, J., Nelson, A.L., Cates, W., Kowal D., and Policar, M. (eds) *Contraceptive Technology*, 20th edn. Ardent Media, New York, pp. 695–736.
Rosen, J.D. (2012). The public health risks of crisis pregnancy centers. *Perspectives on Sexual and Reproductive Health*, 44(3), 201–205.
United States House of Representatives Committee on Government Reform-Minority Staff Special Investigations Division (2006). *False and Misleading Health Information Provided by Federally Funded Pregnancy Resource Centers*.

6 STIs AND PROTECTION

The Risks of Romance

There's a Cure for HIV and AIDS

Recent news headlines have trumpeted a few individuals who were "cured" of HIV; there was an American man who underwent a bone marrow transplant in Germany using cells from a donor with a rare HIV resistance, there were two men in Boston who also had bone marrow transplants, and there was a 2-year-old in Mississippi who got a high dose of drug therapy immediately after she was born. There have also been some promising laboratory tests, including one that found a common cure for athlete's foot could kill the virus in a Petri dish.

Decades before these supposed cures were announced came the news that Magic Johnson, one of the first celebrities to use his HIV-positive status to help build awareness of the disease, was "cured." His doctors quickly pointed out that "cure" was the wrong word. The virus had become undetectable in his blood which meant he was reacting well to the drug regimen he was on but did not mean that the virus was gone (Tom, 1997).

Still, in the United States where antiretroviral drugs are readily available to many people with HIV, there seems to be a perception that HIV is no longer deadly—some people may believe it has been cured while others figure that at worst it is an easily manageable chronic disease. Don't get us wrong, the scientific and medical community has done a masterful job responding to the threat of HIV/AIDS and drug therapies have meant that people with HIV can live long, productive, and healthy lives. However, like all public health experts, we fear that the inaccurate perception of a cure is dangerous because it may stop individuals from taking the steps they need to prevent HIV transmission and, as of right now, prevention is the best defense we have for this disease which has caused a global pandemic and killed millions of people around the globe.

In order to understand the progress that has been made toward a cure and the hurdles that remain, we need to review some basic information about HIV and AIDS. As most of us know, HIV stands for the human immunodeficiency virus. It is a virus that is spread through bodily fluids (blood, semen, vaginal fluids, and breast milk). Once in the body, HIV affects specific cells, called CD4 cells or T cells, which are part of the body's immune system. The immune system is supposed to protect us from illness by fighting off germs, but over time HIV destroys so may CD4 cells that the body can't do that anymore and individuals become susceptible to infections and diseases often called "opportunistic infections." When this happens the individual is diagnosed with acquired immune deficiency syndrome (AIDS). Though medical treatment can help individuals fight many opportunistic infections, AIDS can be fatal (AIDS.gov, What Is HIV?).

In fact, at the beginning of the epidemic many people thought HIV itself was a death sentence because there was no way to fight the progression of the disease or to stop the virus from destroying the immune system. In 1987, however, just a few years after the official discovery of HIV/AIDS, scientists introduced the first drug that could slow the advancement of the virus. Called azidothymidine or AZT, the drug remains important and is now one of at least 30 medications used to fight HIV. These medications work in a few different ways to prevent the virus from attaching to CD4 cells and replicating itself. AZT, for example, is part of a class of drugs called NRTIs (nucleoside/nucleotide reverse transcriptase inhibitors) which block the ability of HIV to use a special type of enzyme (reverse transcriptase) that it needs to build new genetic material (DNA) and make copies of itself. Another type of drug used to fight HIV is a protease inhibitor which blocks a different enzyme, this time one that HIV needs to cut long strands of genetic material into shorter, usable strands. There are also drugs called entry/fusion inhibitors that target the receptors on CD4 cells so that HIV can no longer attach to them. Today, these drugs and others are used in combination often called a "cocktail" or referred to as antiretroviral therapy (ART) or highly active antiretroviral therapy (HAART). HIV-positive individuals stay on ART for most of their lives to keep the virus in check and their immune system functioning (AIDS.gov, Overview of Treatment Options).

In order to determine how HIV is progressing, doctors pay close attention to two different measures—the CD4 count and the viral load. The CD4 count measures how many healthy CD4 cells there are in the blood to fight infection—a normal CD4 count is between 500 and 1000 cells per cubic milliliter of blood (mm^3). At 350 cells per mm^3, the Centers for Disease Control and Prevention (CDC) recommends individuals begin drug therapies. A CD4 count of 200 cells per mm^3 or less is one of the markers used to diagnose AIDS (AIDS.gov, CD4 Count).

The other important measure is the viral load which notes how many particles of HIV (or copies of the virus) there are in someone's blood. Scientists haven't declared a "normal" range for the viral load but the objective is to have as few copies in the blood as possible. The ultimate goal is to have the virus be declared "undetectable" which usually means somewhere between 40 and 75 particles per blood sample (AIDS.gov, Viral Load).

Put in the simplest terms, to be healthiest an HIV-positive person wants a high CD4 count and a low viral load. People on ART can live for many years or decades with a functioning immune system and a low viral load. In fact, it is estimated that a 20-year-old starting ART today can live well into his/her sixties (Broder, 2010). This has led some to believe inaccurately that these individuals have been cured. They have not. Even when the viral load is low, HIV remains in the person's body. Scientists have discovered what they call "HIV reservoirs," cells that hold the genetic code of HIV but are dormant and invisible to the immune system and drug regimes. These cells hide in the brain, bone marrow, genital tract, and other places in the body. If individuals stop taking their drug cocktails, the reservoirs are likely to become active and HIV can start replicating itself again (AIDSresearch.org).

It is also important to note that HIV can mutate into forms that are drug resistant which may make certain medications ineffective in stopping its progression.

Cases of Cures

ART is credited with changing the perception of HIV from "inherently untreat-able" to a condition that can be successfully managed over long periods of time (Broder, 2010). Still, it is not a cure and a true cure for HIV/AIDS—one that actually eradicates the virus from the body and prevents it from returning (without reinfection)—has not yet been found. Over the years, however, doctors and scientists have made some discoveries that have been touted as cures. While each represents progress, using the word cure is likely premature.

The first case in which that word was used is that of Timothy Brown, an HIV-positive American who was living in Germany when he needed a bone-marrow transplant to treat leukemia (a cancer of the blood). The physician who was working on his case searched for a donor with a rare genetic muta-tion that is resistant to HIV. This mutation is present in about 1% of Caucasians and the theory was that by replacing Brown's own bone marrow with cells that had this mutation, his body could fight the return of HIV. Brown's transplant was in 2006 and as of 2010 when a peer-reviewed article about his case was published, he was considered virus-free without the help of medication (Castillo, 2013). Since then, doctors have found some traces of HIV in his blood and tissues but scientists disagree on what this means. It may be the result of a contamination in the testing process; he could have been re-infected; or it might mean that Brown was never actually "cured" of HIV. Interestingly, the HIV detected in his body were different strains than those he had in 2006. Again, scientists say this could be because Brown was re-infected or could show that the virus "evolved and persist(ed) over the last 5 years" (Fox News, 2013).

Two other men, known as the Boston patients, also received bone marrow transplants, this time as treatment for Hodgkin's lymphoma, a cancer of the lymph tissue. Physicians monitored the men for several years and were intrigued when HIV remained undetectable in their bodies. As an experiment the men agreed to stop taking their ART drugs so that researchers could determine whether it was the drug treatment or the bone marrow transplant that was keeping the virus in check. In July 2013, the researchers were excited to report that the men had been off their drugs for a period of time (one for 7 weeks and the other for 15 weeks) and HIV remained undetectable (McNeil, 2013). Unfortunately, their excitement was short lived. In August of that year, HIV became detectable in one of the men, who immediately went back on his medication. Researchers gave the other man the option of continuing to see if his HIV would return or going back on the medications. He opted to keep the experiment going, but by November of 2013 HIV was detectable in his blood as well (Castillo, 2013).

Even if they had seen longer term success, this type of treatment could not be considered a cure that could be replicated and used on everyone who has HIV. Bone marrow transplants are quite dangerous as they require strong chemotherapy to prepare the body for donor cells. Many patients are not strong enough to survive that. For now, such transplants are only considered appropriate for those HIV patients who are suffering from cancer that isn't responding to other treatment.

The researchers believe that their results point to just how deep HIV reservoirs are in the body. Dr. Timothy Heinrich, the lead researcher on the Boston study, told the *Boston Globe* that the latent cells throughout the body that carry the genetic code of HIV, are more persistent than we realized: "[W]e need to look deeper, or we need to be looking in other tissues ... the liver, gut, and brain. These are all potential sources, but it's very difficult to obtain tissue from these places so we don't do that routinely" (Lazar, 2013).

The other case that has been hailed as a cure is that of a young girl in Mississippi. Her mother had received no prenatal care during her pregnancy and therefore had not received the drug therapies that could have prevented mother-to-child transmission of HIV. When doctors realized this, they immediately started the baby on three antiretroviral drugs. She remained on this cocktail for about 18 months and then disappeared from the system when her mother stopped going to the clinic. When the baby returned at the age of 23 months, she had no detectable virus in her bloodstream, despite having been off of the medication for 5 months (Bloomberg News, 2013). Though many were hopeful that she had been "cured," this turned out not to be the case. In 2014, after 27 months without medication, routine blood tests revealed detectable levels of the virus in her blood (Harris, 2014).

In many ways, science has already solved the issue of mother-to-child transmission of HIV. Women who are known to be HIV-positive during pregnancy are given drug therapies that reduce the chance of infection in the infant from 30% to 1%. Most HIV-positive pregnant women in the United States receive this therapy, and only about 200 HIV-positive babies are born each year in the country. This case was a bit of an outlier, because the infant's mother did not receive any prenatal care (CDC, Pregnant Women and Children).

Worldwide, the numbers are different. In 2010, less than half of pregnant women (48%) living with HIV in low- and middle-income countries received effective antiretroviral regimens and it was estimated that more than 1000 babies were born with HIV every day (World Health Organization, 2011; UNICEF, 2010). While the Mississippi case still provides a testable hypothesis for treating HIV-positive infants, it's unclear whether this treatment—even if it worked in the long term—would make much of a difference on a global level. The same resource issues that are preventing mothers from taking drug therapy during pregnancy would prevent physicians from providing such therapies to infants as well.

The search for a cure goes on as scientists try to figure out how to get HIV out of the body completely. One of the more recent laboratory findings shows that a common antifungal drug is able to "kill" HIV cells, or more accurately make the cells kill themselves. The drug, ciclopirox, is a topical cream frequently prescribed by dermatologists and gynecologists to treat fungal infections. As the researchers explain, most cells have a natural tendency to destroy themselves when they become damaged or infected in order to protect healthy cells, but one of the things that makes HIV so persistent is that it blocks this altruistic instinct. In lab cultures, ciclopirox was able to reactivate the suicide pathway of infected cells without affecting healthy cells in any way. Even more promising, the HIV cells did not rebound after the treatment was stopped. No one yet knows, however, if or how this finding will translate to medical practice and there is a long way between positive news in the laboratory and success in the field (Hanauske-Abel et al., 2013).

Search for a Vaccine

Because HIV is so hard to eradicate from the body once it is there, some researchers are focusing on a vaccine that can prevent infection in the first place. In 1984, the US Secretary of the Health and Human Services announced that a vaccine for HIV would be available for testing within 2 years. Unfortunately, she was off by a few decades. Thirty years later, scientists have learned a lot about HIV from a number of vaccines that have been developed and tested but none have been declared successful. In fact, some trials have been stopped midstream when researchers realized that there was no hope of success. In April 2013, for example, an oversight committee pulled the plug on the clinical trial of a vaccine called HTVN-505 because it did not prevent those who received it from contracting the virus. In fact there were more cases of HIV among those who got the vaccine than among those who received the placebo (Knox, 2013). A 2007 trial, called the STEPS trial, was also halted midstream because of chances that the vaccine being tested increased the likelihood of transmission (Esparza, 2013; International AIDS Vaccine Initiative, 2012).

To date only one clinical trial of a vaccine has seen success. A 2009 study in Thailand found that a vaccine, RV 144, reduced the rate of infection by 31%. These results were considered too modest to warrant bringing that exact vaccine to market but many believe this success (combined with the other failures) have provided scientists with important information about where to focus further efforts to develop vaccines (Esparza, 2013; International AIDS Vaccine Initiative, 2012).

For Now: Prevention

While we are waiting for science to develop either a cure for HIV or a vaccine that will prevent it, the most important thing that individuals can do is to focus on prevention. Since the beginning of the epidemic, it has been clear that condoms are one of the best ways for sexually active individuals to prevent the spread of HIV. Both laboratory tests and real world studies have found that latex condoms provide an impermeable barrier to HIV and can significantly reduce the chances of transmission. Studies of serodiscordant couples, those in which one partner has HIV and the other does not, have found that consistent use of condoms reduces the risk of HIV transmission by between 80% and 94% (Weller and Davis, 2002).

Other prevention efforts have focused on abstinence (eliminating the risk of sexual transmission by not have sex) and reducing the number of sexual partners a person has—in particular the number of partners someone has at the same time, as concurrent partners pose the most risk of HIV transmission. Worldwide some efforts have also focused on male circumcision which has been shown to reduce the risk of transmission as well. (See Myth # 3 for more on male circumcision.)

In the United States, focus has also recently turned to pre-exposure prophylaxis (PrEP). In 2011, the FDA approved the use of an existing HIV medication, Truvada, as a once-daily pill designed to prevent infection. Studies have shown that it is effective. For example, a study among men who had sex with men found that those who were given PrEP were 44% less likely to contract HIV than those who weren't. Moreover, those who remembered to take their medication every day or almost every day saw a reduction in risk of 73% or even more (some up to 92%). Similar studies of HIV discordant, heterosexual couples found that PrEP reduced the risk of the uninfected partner becoming infected by 75% and as much as 90% for those who took the pill every day or almost every day (CDC, PrEP, 2014).

Despite this success, PrEP remains controversial in the United States. Many people argue that it is too expensive (Truvada costs about $1000 a month) especially when compared with condoms which can cost less than a dollar each. In addition, experts argue that it is hard to get people to adhere to any drug regimen that requires them to take medication daily, especially when they have no symptoms. Others are worried that people taking PrEP will stop using condoms which can put them at increased risk of HIV if they don't take their PrEP medication every day and increased risk of other STIs even if they do. A recent study, however, shows that this fear may be unfounded as people on PrEP were not more likely to engage in risky sexual behavior (Marcus *et al.*, 2013).

Still, as *The New York Times* reported in December 2013, this new prevention option is not nearly as popular as public health experts had expected. Many experts see this as yet another sign that people in this country mistakenly believe the risk of HIV/AIDS has passed. The big fear, of course, is that if people are no longer worried about HIV, they will no longer take preventative measures. There are some data to suggest that this is already happening especially among men who have sex with men. For example, the proportion of men who reported anal sex without a condom rose from 48% in 2005 to 57% in 2011 (Paz-Bailey *et al.*, 2013).

We also need to remember that the characteristics of the epidemic in resource-rich countries like the United States where ART therapy is readily available is not at all representative of how the disease plays out elsewhere. In the United States there are approximately 1.1 million people living with HIV; 50,000 new infections occur each year; and about 15,500 people died of the disease in 2010 (CDC, HIV basic statistics, 2014). Elsewhere this is very different. The World Health Organization estimates that in 2012 there were over 35 million people living with HIV around the world, approximately 2.5 million new infections, and 1.6 million deaths from the disease. And, although great progress has been made in bringing drug therapy to the developing world, WHO estimates that only 61% who need this therapy are receiving it (UNAIDS, no date).

In the history of medicine, HIV is a relatively young disease. It has been truly understood for just a few decades and in that time science has made enormous strides in preventing and treating this disease. Worldwide, new infections have dropped 33% since 2001, new infections in children have dropped 52% since 2001, and AIDS-related deaths have dropped 30% since they peaked in 2005 (UNAIDS, no date). Nonetheless, this is not the time to be complacent. There is still no cure for this disease and it can still be deadly.

References

Bloomberg News (2013). HIV and AIDS researchers analyze reports of cured baby. *Bloomberg News* (March 5). http://voxxi.com/2013/03/05/hiv-aids-researchers-cured-baby/ (accessed August 3, 2014).

Broder, S. (2010). The development of antiretroviral therapy and its impact on the HIV-1/AIDS pandemic. *Antiviral Research*, 85(1), 1–18.

Castillo, M. (2013). Two men "cured" of HIV no longer taking treatments. *CBS News* (July 3). http://www.cbsnews.com/news/two-men-cured-of-hiv-no-longer-taking-treatments/ (accessed August 3, 2014).

Centers for Disease Control and Prevention (CDC) (2014). HIV pregnant women and children. http://www.cdc.gov/hiv/risk/gender/pregnantwomen/index.html (accessed August 3, 2014).

Centers for Disease Control and Prevention (CDC) (2014). PrEP: How well does PrEP work? http://www.cdc.gov/hiv/basics/prep.html (accessed August 3, 2014).

Centers for Disease Control and Prevention (CDC) (2014). HIV basic statistics. http://www.cdc.gov/hiv/basics/statistics.html (accessed August 3, 2014).

Esparza, J. (2013). A brief history of the global effort to develop a preventive HIV vaccine. *Vaccine*, 31(35), 3502–3518.

Fox News (2012). HIV may have returned in man "cured" of virus. *Fox News* (June 13). http://www.foxnews.com/health/2012/06/13/hiv-may-have-returned-in-man-cured-virus/ (accessed August 3, 2014).

Hanauske-Abel, H.M., Saxena, D., Palumbo, P.E., Hanauske, A.R., Luchessi, A.D., Cambiaghi, T.D., *et al.* (2013). Drug-induced reactivation of apoptosis abrogates HIV-1 infection. *PloS One*, 8(9), e74414.

Harris, R. (2014). Mississippi child thought cured of HIV shows signs of infection. http://www.npr.org/blogs/health/2014/07/10/330538734/mississippi-child-thought-cured-of-hiv-shows-signs-of-infection (accessed August 12, 2014).

International AIDS Vaccine Initiative (2012). Progress on the path toward an AIDS vaccine. www.iavi.org (accessed August 12, 2014).

Knox, R. (2013). Failure of latest HIV vaccine test: A "huge disappointment." *NPR* (April 26). http://www.npr.org/blogs/health/2013/04/26/179231916/failure-of-latest-hiv-vac cine-test-a-huge-disappointment (accessed August 3, 2014).

Lazar, K. (2013). HIV virus returns after cure hope rose; 2 Boston patients had transplants of marrow, halted powerful drugs. *Boston Globe* (December 6). http://www.boston globe.com/lifestyle/health-wellness/2013/12/05/hiv-virus-returns-after-cure-hope-rose/ kSUyH1YkgJ27AP4aZwpUXJ/story.html (accessed August 3, 2014).

Marcus, J.L., Glidden, D.V., Mayer, K.H., Liu, A.Y., Buchbinder, S.P., Amico, K.R., *et al.* (2013). No evidence of sexual risk compensation in the iPrEx trial of daily oral HIV preexposure prophylaxis. *PloS One*, 8(12), e81997.

McNeil, D.G. (2013). After marrow transplants, 2 more patients appear HIV-free without drugs. *New York Times* (July 3). http://www.nytimes.com/2013/07/04/health/post-transplant-and-off-drugs-hiv-patients-are-apparently-virus-free. html?pagewanted=all&_r=1& (accessed August 3, 2014).

Paz-Bailey, G., *et al.*, for the Centers for Disease Control and Prevention (2013). HIV testing and risk behaviors among gay, bisexual, and other men who have sex with men— United States. *Morbidity and Mortality Weekly Report*, 62(47), 958–962.

Tom, D.A. (1997). Doctors: Magic's HIV is at undetectable levels, but he's not virus-free. *Associated Press* (April 4). http://lubbockonline.com/news/040597/doctors.htm (accessed August 3, 2014).

UNAIDS (no date). HIV/AIDS Fact Sheet. http://www.unaids.org/en/resources/campaigns/ globalreport2013/factsheet/ (accessed August 3, 2014).

UNICEF (2010). Children and AIDS Fifth Stocktaking Report, 2010. http://www.unicef. org/esaro/Stocktaking_Key_Facts.pdf (accessed August 3, 2014).

Weller, S. and Davis, K. (2002). Condom effectiveness in reducing heterosexual HIV trans-mission. *Cochrane Database of Systematic Reviews*, 1, CD003255.

World Health Organization (2011). Key facts on global HIV epidemic and progress in 2010. http://www.who.int/hiv/pub/progress_report2011/global_facts/en/index1.html (accessed August 3, 2014).

Myth #31 STIs Are No Big Deal as Long as You Take Your Medicine

It is not surprising that many people don't give much thought to sexually transmitted infections (STIs)—after all, none of us have seen blindness or madness brought on by syphilis and men and women who contract gonorrhea today will not have a metal rod heated to 111 degrees Fahrenheit inserted into their rectum in order to kill the bacteria (Simmons, 1937). In fact, by 1943, penicillin was being used to cure gonorrhea with a 96% success rate so it doesn't take too much of a leap of faith to think that with today's science nothing we pick up could be all that bad (Sternberg and Turner, 1944).

Modern medicine does mean that some of today's diseases are curable and others can be kept in check, but it would be a mistake to think that STIs are just no big deal. On an individual level they can cause a great deal of pain and lead to long-term health issues such as infertility and cancer, and on a societal level they represent a huge public health and economic burden.

Before we explain more, let us go on record as saying our goal here is not to scare you about all of the horrible diseases you will inevitably get that will ruin your lives or make body parts fall off. We've read all of the abstinence-only-until-marriage curricula and seen gory slide presentations that show oozing sores and cauliflower-sized warts, and we don't think that's the best way to educate anyone.

The goal of this entry is to remind our readers that STIs are an epidemic in this country that can cause problems for individuals and society and that we should not take them lightly. Everyone must take responsibility for their sexual health by getting tested and treated for STIs when necessary. More importantly, though, the goal of this entry is to remind us all that there are ways that each of us can significantly cut down on the likelihood of infection—like reducing the numbers of partners we have and using condoms regularly. Ultimately, the only way to stop the STI epidemic is to prevent infections in the first place.

There is plenty of good information available online and most human sexuality textbooks and courses spend a good deal of time discussing the different STIs that are out there so we don't want to go into too much detail about each disease. Still, it is helpful to know the names and understand the basics about how each disease is transmitted, how people know they have it, how many people get it, and whether they can get rid of it. Also important to combatting the myth of "no big deal" is looking at what can happen if these diseases—even the ones that can be cured—are not properly treated. What follows is by no means an exhaustive list but it does cover the most common STIs.

The Ones That Can Go Away

STIs are most often classified by what causes them, in part because that helps explain whether they can be cured. In general, STIs that are caused by bacteria or parasites can be cured with antibiotics. That does not mean, however, that they always go away without a trace.

Chlamydia

Chlamydia is the most common reportable STI in the United States. Reportable means that health care providers who diagnose a case of chlamydia must alert the Centers for Disease Control and Prevention (CDC). This allows the CDC to track STIs and be on the lookout for outbreaks in certain geographic areas or among certain populations. (Gonorrhea, syphilis, and HIV are the other reportable diseases.) There were over 1.4 million cases of chlamydia reported to the CDC in 2011 but many infections go undiagnosed and the CDC estimates that there are over 2.86 million cases each year (CDC, *Chlamydia*, 2013; CDC, *Incidence, Prevalence, and Cost*, 2013).

Chlamydia is caused by a bacterium, *Chlamydia trachomatis*, which can be found in semen, vaginal fluids, and cervical secretions. It is transmitted from an infected person to an uninfected person during any kind of sexual behavior in which individuals come in contact with these fluids (think oral, vaginal, or anal sex). Chlamydia can infect the male and female genitals, the anus, and the throat.

If caught early, chlamydia is easily curable with antibiotics though in order to be sure that the infection does not keep spreading all of a person's partners should be contacted and treated. The problem with chlamydia is that it often has no symptoms. Some women may have an unusual discharge or pain when they urinate and some men may have discharge or swelling in their testicles. For the most part, however, the only way to know you have chlamydia is to test for it. Testing can be as easy as peeing in a cup or a clinician can take a swab from the urethra or cervix to culture the secretions (CDC, *Chlamydia*, 2013).

If not treated, the infection can move up the reproductive tract into the uterus and fallopian tubes and lead to pelvic inflammatory disease (PID) but even PID often has no symptoms. Women with PID can also be treated using antibiotics but depending on how long they have the infection it can cause scar tissue to build up in a woman's uterus or fallopian tubes. Fallopian tubes are only the width of two human hairs which means that even a little bit of scar tissue can block the path of an egg to the uterus, which can make a woman unable to get pregnant (CDC, *STDs and Infertility*, 2013). Chlamydia can also cause infertility in men by mutating their sperm (Gallegos *et al.*, 2008).

Most young people are too busy thinking about not getting pregnant to worry about whether they will be able to do so someday and we completely understand and applaud these priorities. Everyone should assume they are very fertile and take steps to prevent pregnancy accordingly. Of course, someday down the line many young people want to start a family and taking care of your sexual health from the moment you become sexually active can help make that a more easily achievable goal. This is why we believe condoms to prevent chlamydia and regular screening to detect it are both very important (as is treatment of all partners when needed).

Gonorrhea

Gonorrhea is a bacterial STI that can infect the fluids in the cervix, vagina, and penis and is easily spread through many kinds of sexual activity. Though less common than chlamydia, the CDC estimates that 820,000 people will become infected each year and that's nothing to sneeze at (CDC, *Incidence, Prevalence, and Cost,* 2013). Gonorrhea also has the same general lack of symptoms as chlamydia (though many men and women will experience a discharge or burning on urination) and the same possible long-term health effects. It can lead to PID and infertility in women as well as infertility in men (CDC, *Gonorrhea,* 2013).

Here's the kind of scary thing about gonorrhea, though, it's really smart. The bacterium that causes this infection, *Neisseria gonorrhoeae,* has developed the ability to resist nearly all of the antibiotics that have been thrown in its path. Over the last half-century or so, it has steadily developed resistance to entire classes of antibiotics—as early as the 1940s it was resistant to sulfanilamides, by the 1980s penicillins and tetracyclines no longer worked, and in 2007 the CDC stopped recommending the use of fluoroquinolones. Today, the only class of antibiotics that remains effective are cephalosporins, but its susceptibility to these drugs is declining rapidly in the United States and other countries have already seen cephalosporin-resistant cases (Bolan *et al.,* 2012).

This means that while gonorrhea is still on the easy-to-cure list for now, that may change. The CDC recently released a report that called antibiotic-resistant gonorrhea an urgent threat (CDC, *Antibiotic Resistant Threats,* 2013). The part we find scariest is that as of this writing there are no antibiotics in development that will take the place of cephalosporins when those become useless. Public health experts are working on different combinations of existing drugs to combat resistant strains but they agree that what we really need is new drugs and few of those are even at the laboratory stage.

Again, this makes prevention really important because the best way to not get infected with a strain we can't cure, is not to get infected. Plus cutting down on the overall number of infections in the country will cut down on the bacteria's exposure to antibiotics and, therefore, its ability to morph and change. Interestingly, the CDC also notes that we can help prevent all antibiotic-resistant infections, not just gonorrhea, by relying less on antibiotics overall and by always finishing the whole course of treatment when these medications are prescribed to us (CDC, *Antibiotic Resistant Threats,* 2013).

Syphilis

Syphilis is the oldest STI, appearing in Europe in the late fifteenth century, and the very first one to have a cure (Quetel, 1990). It is caused by a bacterium and transmitted when an uninfected person comes in contact with a syphilis sore. The sores are usually firm, round, and painless, and most often first appear at the location where syphilis entered the body. The sores last 3–6 weeks whether a person is treated or not. If a person isn't treated, the infection progresses to the secondary stage which often presents as a rash on the palms of the hands or all over a person's body. (This rash is likely why syphilis was referred to as "the great pox" in the sixteenth century; Quetel, 1990.) People with secondary syphilis can feel sick in other ways such as fever, swollen glands, sore throats, and headaches (CDC, *Syphilis,* 2014).

If it continues to go untreated the symptoms will disappear but the syphilis will remain and essentially go into hiding in cells and organs. This stage, called the latent stage, can last as long as 10–30 years before symptoms of syphilis kick back in. People with late stage syphilis can have difficulty moving muscles, numbness, blindness, dementia, and brain damage, as well as damage to internal organs, nerves, eyes, heart, blood vessels, and joints. Late stage syphilis can result in death (CDC, *Syphilis*, 2014).

The truth is, very few people have died of syphilis in the United States in many years. In 2011, for example, only 45 people were estimated to have died from this disease (Hoyert and Xu, 2012). Most cases are caught and cured at the primary or secondary stage. At one point, the number of people who got syphilis at all in the United States was so low that the CDC believed it was close to being eradicated altogether. Unfortunately, the trend has gone in the opposite direction and primary and secondary syphilis is on the rise especially among men who have sex with men. The CDC estimates that there are 55,400 cases of syphilis each year. It also notes that 72% of cases occur in men who have sex with men which can increase their risk for other STIs, including HIV (CDC, *Incidence, Prevalence, and Cost*, 2013).

Trichomoniasis

Here's an STI that is really common and yet many people don't know anything about it. Dubbed "trich" for obvious pronunciation reasons, this is the most common curable STI in the United States, with an estimated 7–8 million people infected each year. This means that it infects more people than chlamydia, gonorrhea, and syphilis combined each year. (Trich is not reportable to the CDC which may be one reason it gets less attention than these other infections.)

Trich is actually caused by a parasite that can be passed from one person to another during most kinds of sexual activity. Again, most people who have trich, especially men, have no symptoms. Women who do experience symptoms may have itching, burning, redness, or soreness in their genitals; discomfort when they urinate; a thin discharge that can be clear, white, yellowish, or greenish and has an unusual smell; and pain or discomfort during sex. However, these symptoms mimic those of other STIs as well as simple vaginal infections, such as yeast infections, which means many women don't get tested (CDC, *Trichomoniasis*, 2014).

If left untreated trich can be dangerous, in part because the vaginal irritation it can cause leaves women more vulnerable to becoming infected with HIV. Moreover, it can be very risky to pregnant women; pregnant women infected with trich are more likely to give birth early and have low birthweight (less than 5.5 pounds) babies.

The good news is that trich can be easily diagnosed using a swab of cervical and vaginal fluid or a urine test. New tests can even look for trich, chlamydia, and gonorrhea using the same sample. Once diagnosed, trich is easy to cure with a single round of antibiotics. The most important thing is that women have to ask to be tested (CDC, *Trichomoniasis*, 2014).

The Ones That Stay

The other most common STIs are caused by viruses. As anyone who has had the flu or even a cold knows, there is no medicine you can take to cure a virus. If you go to the doctor with one of these, you will likely be told to go home, rest, and let it run its course. Sexually transmitted viruses also can't be cured. For the most part, they remain in person's body indefinitely. However, that does not mean the individual always has symptoms.

Herpes

Genital herpes is an extremely common viral infection, so widespread that the CDC estimates 16% of all adults—or about one in six people aged 14 to 49—has this STI and that each year an additional 776,000 people will become infected (CDC, *Herpes*, 2013). Those numbers are truly staggering, especially when you realize that once a person is infected with genital herpes he/she can have outbreaks over and over again.

Genital herpes is caused by one of two viruses—herpes simplex virus-1 (HSV-1) or herpes simplex virus-2 (HSV-2). It used to be thought that HSV-1 caused oral infections which most often present as cold sores or "fever blisters" on the lips and that genital infections were caused by HSV-2. Medical experts now understand that these viruses are interchangeable; either can infect the mouth or the genitals.

Genital infections show up as sores on the vulva, penis, testicles, or anus. These sores can be very painful especially if they are near the urethra and come in contact with urine, which is very acidic. A person can become infected with herpes through oral, vaginal, or anal sex. In fact, some experts attribute the rise in HSV-1 infections of the genitals to the growing practice of oral sex among young people. Some people who become infected will never know it and others may have one initial outbreak of sores and never have any other symptoms. For some, however, herpes outbreaks recur on a regular basis. There is no cure for herpes but people can take antiviral medications to reduce the number and severity of outbreaks (CDC, *Herpes*, 2013).

New research suggests that young people today may be more at risk for herpes than their counterparts who are just 10 years older. Researchers compared records of those who were 14–19 years old between 2005 and 2010, with those who were the same ages between 1999 and 2004. They found that fewer teens in the more recent group (30%) had antibodies to HSV-1, compared with the older group of teens (39%). Antibodies are part of the immune system's reaction to being exposed to a virus, once formed they can help the body fight that virus if it ever comes in contact with it again. Researchers think that in the past young people were exposed to HSV-1 as kids and built up antibodies that could protect them if they were exposed to it again once they became sexually active. In recent years, more hygienic living conditions have meant fewer exposures and fewer antibodies. The researchers believe that the lack of antibodies coupled with an increase in oral sex is a recipe for more genital herpes infections in the future (Bradley *et al.*, 2014).

We are by no means suggesting that you scale back on personal hygiene as a way to build up protections. We love showers. Like any other STI, the best way to protect against herpes is to avoid all sexual contact or to use condoms if you are going to be sexually active. Condoms can't protect against all herpes transmission because sores can be located in areas like the testicles that are not covered by the condom. Even so, condoms have been shown to provide good protection against the spread of herpes. For example, one study found that using condoms just 25% of the time reduces a person's risk of getting genital herpes by 92% (Wald *et al.*, 2001). Of course, we would say that you should use condoms 100% of the time, but you know that by now. Condoms can also be used when someone performs oral sex on a man—they come in flavors for just this reason. There is also a product on the market called a dental dam which is a rectangular piece of latex that can be stretched over the vulva during oral sex to prevent transmission of STIs like herpes.

Human Papillomavirus

Human papillomavirus (HPV) is a big one because so many people have it. In fact, we would probably not be wrong if we were to tell you without knowing anything else about you that most of your friends have it and you might too. The CDC estimates that 79 million people are infected with HPV and 14 million more become infected each year.

HPV is actually a group of about 150 related viruses that can infect various parts of the body. There are 40 strains of the virus that are known to infect the genitals. Most of the time, the body can clear these infections on its own within 1–2 years without the person ever having any visible signs that they have it. Many will never even know. Some strains of the virus, specifically strains 6 and 11, are known to cause genital warts—small raised bumps that may appear on the external genitals, the anus, or the cervix. Warts may go away on their own or can be removed by a health care provider.

Other strains have the potential to cause bigger health problems. Researchers have identified approximately 13 strains that can cause cancer. Two of these strains—16 and 18—are thought to cause 70% of all cervical cancers (National Cancer Institute, 2012). Approximately 12,000 women get cervical cancer each year and more than 15,000 additional men and women get cancers of the head, neck, throat, genitals, or anus caused by HPV (CDC, *HPV*, 2013).

The good news about cervical cancer is that it is very slow growing which means that health care providers can detect precancerous changes to the cervix using a Pap test and other tests that collect and examine cervical cells. If abnormal cells are detected, health care providers can treat the area before cancer develops. Widespread use of the Pap test in the United States began in the 1960s. Between 1975 and 2001, this test is credited with having cut incidence of cervical cancer by half as well as dramatically reducing deaths from the disease in this country (National Center for Health Statistics, 2005).

Sexually active women should talk to their health care providers about how often they should have a Pap test or new tests that look for HPV specifically. Unfortunately, there are no routine HPV screening tests for men but it is still important to talk to your health care provider about your sexual behavior.

The even better news is that both men and women can get a vaccine that prevents those strains of HPV most likely to cause cervical cancer. There are currently two vaccines on the market—Gardasil and Cervarix—both protect against cancer-causing strains 16 and 18. Gardasil also protects against two strains that cause most genital warts. A newer version of the vaccine that will protect against nine strains in total is in development. Anyone between the ages of 9 and 26 can get the vaccine but they must get all three doses, given over the course of 6 months, for it to be effective. The CDC recommends that girls and boys receive the vaccine at a younger age—11 and 12—to be sure that all three doses are completed before they become sexually active (CDC, *HPV Vaccine Information for Clinicians*, 2012). Still, anyone who is in the under-26 age group and has not been vaccinated should consider it.

As we talk about in Myth # 32, unfortunately the HPV vaccine has been controversial. While some of the controversy comes from an overall misunderstanding about the safety of vaccines (there is a lot of misinformation out there on this topic), much of it comes from a fear of even discussing sexuality with young people. Some people mistakenly believe that helping an 11-year-old protect her sexual health in the future will somehow make her more likely to have sex or likely to start having sex earlier. Research has shown that this is not the case (Bednarczyk *et al.*, 2012). The HPV vaccine is a huge medical breakthrough that deserves to be celebrated—this is the very first time that we have a vaccine that can prevent cancer.

Of course, sexually active individuals should continue to use condoms as there are strains of HPV that are not covered by the vaccine. Like with herpes, a condom provides protection against HPV when the infection is somewhere that it covers. Research confirms that condoms reduce not just the likelihood of getting HPV, but also the chance of getting related health problems such as cervical dysplasia, genital warts, and cervical cancer. One study, for example, found no cervical lesions in women who used condoms 100% of the time (Winer *et al.*, 2006).

The Bottom Lines

As we said, this is not an exhaustive list of STIs or their signs and symptoms. We did not, for example, talk about HIV at all because Myth 30 is devoted to clearing up misinformation about that topic. We also did not yet mention hepatitis B which is a sexually transmitted infection of the liver that affects about 19,000 people each year. There is a vaccine to prevent hepatitis B which is required of most college students. As always though, it is important to continue to use condoms to prevent this infection if you are choosing to be sexually active.

We do not expect you to learn each disease by name, rank, and symptoms. Instead, we provided all of this information to try to impress upon our readers that STIs are a real problem both for individuals and society. In fact, it is estimated that the diagnosis and treatment of STIs cost the government $16 billion dollars each year (CDC, *Incidence, Prevalence, and Cost*, 2013). Even the ones that are curable can cause health problems that cost time and money and alter futures.

Individuals can make a difference in this epidemic by focusing on prevention. Remember that the only sure way to avoid STIs is to remain abstinent from any sexual activity that involves contact with another person's genitals or genital secretions. People who choose instead to be sexually active should use a condom every time they have sex and should make sure they are using it correctly. It's not hard as most errors are user errors like putting the condom on after genital contact has been made or taking it off before sex has ended. (See Myth # 28 for more information about condoms.)

Other prevention efforts include reducing the number of partners you have—especially the number of partners you have during one period in time. Concurrent partners, as they are called in the public health world, significantly increase the risk of disease transmission. Sexually active individuals are also urged to get screened regularly for STIs. As we've said in this entry, most testing is as easy as rolling up your sleeve for a blood test or peeing in a cup for urinalysis. STI screening, however, is often not a routine part of annual checkups. If you want to be screened, you have to ask (and don't be shy, your health care provider will most likely be proud of you). Finally, if something feels off or looks off—your vulva itches, there's discharge from your penis, etc.—get it checked as soon as possible. There's no need to diagnose yourself, your health care provider will be able to figure out what's wrong and help you figure out what to do.

References

Bednarczyk, R.A., Davis, R., Ault, K., Orenstein, W., and Omer, S.B. (2012). Sexual activity-related outcomes after human papillomavirus vaccination of 11- to 12-year-olds. *Pediatrics*, 130(5), 798–805.

Bolan, G.A., Sparling, P.F., and Wasserheit, J.N. (2012). The emerging threat of untreatable gonococcal infection. *New England Journal of Medicine*, 366(6), 485–487.

Bradley, H., Markowitz, L.E., Gibson, T., and McQuillan, G.M. (2014). Seroprevalence of herpes simplex virus types 1 and 2: United States, 1999–2010. *Journal of Infectious Diseases*, 209(3), 325–333.

Centers for Disease Control and Prevention (CDC) (2013). *Antibiotic Resistance Threats.* Centers for Disease Control and Prevention, Atlanta, GA. http://www.cdc.gov/drugresistance/threat-report-2013/pdf/ar-threats-2013-508.pdf (accessed August 4, 2014).

Centers for Disease Control and Prevention (CDC) (updated February 2013). *Chlamydia: CDC Fact Sheet.* Centers for Disease Control and Prevention, Atlanta, GA. http://www.cdc.gov/std/chlamydia/STDFact-Chlamydia.htm (accessed August 4, 2014).

Centers for Disease Control and Prevention (CDC) (2013). *Incidence, Prevalence, and Cost of Sexually Transmitted Infections in the United States: CDC Fact Sheet.* Centers for Disease Control and Prevention, Atlanta, GA. http://www.cdc.gov/std/stats/STI-Estimates-Fact-Sheet-Feb-2013.pdf (accessed August 4, 2014)

Centers for Disease Control and Prevention (CDC) (updated February 2013). *Gonorrhea: CDC Fact Sheet.* Centers for Disease Control and Prevention, Atlanta, GA. http://www.cdc.gov/std/gonorrhea/STDFact-gonorrhea.htm (accessed August 4, 2014).

Centers for Disease Control and Prevention (CDC) (updated February 2013). *Herpes: CDC Fact Sheet.* Centers for Disease Control and Prevention, Atlanta, GA. http://www.cdc.gov/std/Herpes/STDFact-Herpes.htm (accessed August 4, 2014).

Centers for Disease Control and Prevention (CDC) (updated July 2013). *HPV: CDC Fact Sheet.* Centers for Disease Control and Prevention, Atlanta, GA. http://www.cdc.gov/std/HPV/STDFact-HPV.htm (accessed August 4, 2014).

Centers for Disease Control and Prevention (CDC) (updated 2012). *HPV Vaccine Information for Clinicians: CDC Fact Sheet.* Centers for Disease Control and Prevention, Atlanta, GA. http://www.cdc.gov/std/hpv/STDFact-HPV-vaccine-hcp.htm (accessed August 4, 2014).

Centers for Disease Control and Prevention (CDC) (updated 2014). *Syphilis: CDC Fact Sheet.* Centers for Disease Control and Prevention, Atlanta, GA. http://www.cdc.gov/std/syphilis/STDFact-Syphilis.htm (accessed August 4, 2014).

Centers for Disease Control and Prevention (CDC) (updated 2014). *Trichomoniasis: CDC Fact Sheet.* Centers for Disease Control and Prevention, Atlanta, GA. http://www.cdc.gov/std/trichomonas/STDFact-Trichomoniasis.htm (accessed August 4, 2014).

Centers for Disease Control and Prevention (CDC) (updated October 2013). *STDs and Infertility: CDC Fact Sheet.* Centers for Disease Control and Prevention, Atlanta, GA. http://www.cdc.gov/std/infertility/ (accessed August 12, 2014).

Gallegos, G., Ramos, B., Santiso, R., Goyanes, V., Gosálvez, J., and Fernández, J.L. (2008). Sperm DNA fragmentation in infertile men with genitourinary infection by *Chlamydia trachomatis* and *Mycoplasma. Fertility and Sterility*, 90(2), 328–334.

Hoyert, D.L. and Xu, J. (2012). Deaths: preliminary data for 2011. *National Vital Statistics Report*, 61(6), 1–65.

National Cancer Institute (2012). *HPV and Cancer.* National Cancer Institute, Bethesda, MD. http://www.cancer.gov/cancertopics/factsheet/Risk/HPV (accessed August 4, 2014).

National Center for Health Statistics (2005). *Health, United States 2005.* US Department of Health, Hyattsville, MD, p. 56. http://books.google.com/books?id=Y7IfxSyZWXkC&printsec=frontcover&source=gbs_ge_summary_r&cad=0#v=onepage&q&f=false (accessed August 4, 2014).

Quetel, C. (1990). *History of Syphilis*, trans. Judith Braddock and Brian Pike. Johns Hopkins University Press, Baltimore, MD.

Sternberg, T.H. and Turner, T.B. (1944). The treatment of sulfonamide resistant gonorrhea with penicillin sodium: Results in 1686 cases. *Journal of the American Medical Association*, 126, 157–163.

Simmons, E.E. (1937). Value of fever therapy in the arthritides. *American Journal of Medical Science*, 194, 170–178.

Wald, A., Langenberg, A.M., Link, K., Izu, A.E., Ashley, R., Warren, T., *et al.* (2001). Effect of condoms on reducing the transmission of herpes simplex virus type 2 from men to women. *Journal of the American Medical Association*, 285(24), 3100–3106.

Winer, R.L., Hughes, J.P., Feng, Q., O'Reilly, S., Kiviat, N.B., Holmes, K.K., *et al.* (2006). Condom use and the risk of genital human papillomavirus infection in young women. *New England Journal of Medicine*, 354(25), 2645–2654.

Myth #32 HPV Vaccines (and Other Prevention Methods) Turn Girls into Sluts

Human papillomavirus (HPV) is the most common sexually transmitted infection (STI) in the United States. It is estimated that 79 million Americans have HPV and that 14 million become infected each year (CDC, *HPV*, 2013). HPV is easily spread from infected skin to uninfected skin. Transmission can be prevented by condoms, but only if the infected skin is in an area covered by the condom. If it is on an area such as a man's scrotum condoms cannot help reduce transmission.

In truth, for many people HPV is not much of a problem. Most people who have HPV will have no symptoms or health problems and may never even know they have it. Some people will get genital warts, which may go away on their own or may need to be removed by a health care provider. However, certain strains of the virus, if left untreated, can lead to cervical cancer which is a potentially life-threatening disease.

So, when a new vaccine came out that could prevent infection with these strains—a vaccine that could essentially prevent cancer—everyone was clearly thrilled, right? Well, not so fast. Some people argued that giving girls a vaccine was like giving them a license to have sex and could, in fact, be dangerous. That's right, some people suggested not vaccinating young women against cancer because they might become sluts. We've heard similar logic to this many times before and we can assure you that it is a myth (and an offensive one at that).

The History

In 2006, the Food and Drug Administration (FDA) approved Gardasil, a vaccine that successfully protects women from four strains of HPV, including two that account for 70% of cervical cancer and two that account for 90% of genital warts. Cervarix, a second vaccine that also prevents against the two strains that cause most cervical cancers, was approved in 2009. The vaccines are given as a series of three shots, which are approved for young people (both male and female) between the ages of 9 and 26. In order to make sure that it works, all three shots must be given before a young person becomes sexually active which is why the Centers for Disease Control and Prevention (CDC) recommended that this become part of the routine vaccinations of girls at age 11 or 12 (CDC, 2013).

Cervical cancer can be prevented through early detection using Pap tests and other medical tests, but approximately 12,000 women in the United States get this disease each year and around 4000 die from it (CDC/National Cancer Institute, 2012). The global numbers are much scarier: half a million women in the world develop cervical cancer each year and as many as 250,000 die from the disease (World Health Organization, 2012).

For this reason, many public health experts regarded the HPV vaccines as huge medical breakthroughs capable of saving millions of lives. Because HPV is so easily spread through sexual contact, however, they explained that the only way to eliminate HPV forever would be to vaccinate everyone or nearly everyone.

Not everyone liked this idea. Some social conservatives and proponents of abstinence-only-until-marriage programs argued that vaccinating young girls against a sexually transmitted disease was morally questionable and dangerous.

They suggested that such a vaccine would give young women a false sense of security and lead to promiscuity. They also took issue with the young age at which the vaccine was recommended and complained that at the very least this would cause parents to have uncomfortable and age-inappropriate conversations with their daughters. For example, Bridget Maher of the Family Research Council told the British magazine, *The New Scientist,* in 2005 that: "giving the HPV vaccine to young women could be potentially harmful, because they may see it as a license to engage in premarital sex" (Gibbs, 2006).

The truth is that we've seen this argument made repeatedly—whether it's about giving young people access to contraception, making condoms available in schools, providing sex education, or letting emergency contraception (EC) be sold over the counter. The idea that access to protection will cause young women to run wild is deeply ingrained in our culture. Just recently, for example, conservative talk radio host Rush Limbaugh accused a law student of being a "slut" because she testified in front of Congress that she and her peers needed access to affordable birth control.

The Fear of Female Promiscuity

Though they likely began earlier (perhaps with the introduction of short skirts or bathing suits that showed some knee), the arguments about women's barely controlled promiscuity were prominent during the 1960s as the birth control pill became a medical and cultural phenomenon. In a 1966 article on birth control and morality, *US News and World Report* asked: "Is the Pill regarded as a license for promiscuity? Can its availability to all women of childbearing age lead to sexual anarchy?" Two years later, author Pearl Buck warned the audience of *Reader's Digest* that: "Everyone knows what The Pill is. It is a small object—yet its potential effect upon our society many be even more devastating than the nuclear bomb" (American Experience, 2001).

The introduction of the pill did coincide with a changing of social values and norms around sexuality and women's sexuality in particular. Some believe that by separating sex from procreation and giving young women control of their own fertility (thereby allowing them to pursue education and employment), the pill is, in fact, responsible for the sexual revolution. Others believe it was a convenient scapegoat for a societal change that was already in the works (Asbell, 1995). Four and a half decades later, we are still debating the impact of contraception on women's sexual behavior.

During his 2012 run for the Republican presidential nomination, Rick Santorum said that contraception was a problem: "It's *not* okay because it's a license to do things in the sexual realm that is counter to how things are supposed to be. They're supposed to be within marriage, they are supposed to be for purposes that are, yes, conjugal, but also [inaudible], but also procreative" (Amira, 2012). We heard this same idea back in 1998 when the FDA was first considering approval for EC and then over and over again as the agency decided whether EC should be available without a prescription.

During one of these debates, the Family Research Council (FRC), a conservative not-for-profit organization, said this: "one might expect the medical profession to speak out against promiscuity, if only to prevent the disease and destruction it causes. Instead, public health professionals have not only made peace with sexual license (against society's practical interests), but now virtually advocate it. The campaign for the morning after pill is just one case in point" (Stranton and Evans, 2005).

We've also heard it for decades when it comes to sexuality education; teaching kids about sex, the argument goes, will give them ideas, encourage experimentation, and undermine any message about abstinence they might have received (see Myth # 46). In a 1986 newspaper article, conservative activist Phyllis Schlafly derides a sexuality education textbook as far too liberal, saying: "It's no wonder that our country has a high rate of teenage promiscuity and the unhappy consequences it causes, including out-of-wedlock pregnancy, abortion and venereal diseases. Those things are the result of the sexual liberation that students are taught in required courses in 'health' and 'sex education' " (Schlafly, 1986).

Though sociologists may continue to argue the precise role of the pill in the sexual revolution for at least four more decades, we now have research that directly counters the notion that recent advances in women's sexual health have paved the way for a generation of tramps.

Stacks of Research

For every argument that says a new advance—be it EC or comprehensive sexuality education—is going to turn young women into whores, there is a stack of peer-reviewed research that proves otherwise.

Condom Availability Programs. The first major study of condom availability programs was carried out in 1997 by researchers who compared students at New York City public high schools that provided condoms to students at similar public high schools in Chicago that did not. The study found that condom availability does not increase rates of sexual activity but does increase the rate at which sexually active young people use condoms (Guttmacher *et al.*, 1997). A similar study carried out a few years later in Massachusetts found that sexually active students in schools that had a condom availability program were more likely to have used contraception at last intercourse than sexually active students in schools without one (Blake *et al.*, 2003).

Sexuality Education. Numerous evaluations of sexuality education programs have found the very same thing. These programs do not increase sexual behavior among teens, they do not cause teens to have sex at a younger age, they do not increase the number of partners young people have, and they do not increase the frequency with which young people have sex. In fact, they tend to do just the opposite. Young people who have gone through highly effective sex education and HIV-prevention programs tend to delay sex and have fewer partners. In addition, when these young people do become sexually active they are more likely to use condoms and other contraceptive methods (Kirby, 2007).

Emergency Contraception. In 2008, the Bixby Center for Global Reproductive Health at the University of California San Francisco conducted a review of 16 studies on the impact of providing EC to adult and adolescent women. The review found no evidence that access increased sexual risk taking. Specifically, it found that women did not abandon their regular method of contraception when they had access to EC; did not use EC repeatedly just because it was available; did not engage in increased sexual activity; and did not have increased incidences of STIs. In addition, it found that adolescent women were no more likely than adults to engage in sexual risk taking when they were given access to EC (Bixby Center, 2008).

HPV Vaccine Too

Most recently, research has found the same to be true of the HPV vaccine. A study followed almost 1400 girls in Atlanta for 3 years after they'd received their shots. They did not ask the girls if they'd had sex but instead looked for markers in their medical records, such as pregnancy tests, STI diagnoses, or contraceptive counseling, which would indicate sexual activity. They found no differences between girls who received the HPV vaccine and girls who received other vaccines but not HPV. In fact, there were only eight cases of either pregnancy or STI infection among the girls in the study and the researchers noted the rates of these issues were identical in the HPV vaccine and non-HPV vaccine group (Bednarczyk *et al.*, 2012).

An earlier study found that having received the HPV vaccine did not affect whether young women engaged in sexual activity. Researchers used data from the National Survey of Family Growth (NSFG) to look at the behavior of young women aged 15–24. They found that young women who were vaccinated against HPV were no more likely to be sexually active or to have more partners than unvaccinated girls (Liddon *et al.*, 2012).

And, there was more good news from the study as the research also found that young women who were vaccinated were more likely to use condoms than their unvaccinated peers. Specifically, sexually active young women who had received the vaccine were more likely to report *always* using a condom in the 4 weeks prior to the study than sexually active young women who had not received the vaccine. The researchers say that it's possible that those young women who received the vaccine are more likely to be concerned about STIs and safer sex in the first place or that receiving the vaccine and perhaps the education that goes with it can lead to safer sex. Either way, they concluded that "data do not suggest that receipt of HPV vaccine causes dis-inhibition or perceived lessened risk and thus more sexually risky behavior" (Liddon *et al.*, 2012).

Changing the Conversation

The unfortunate truth is that years of research showing that access to information about sex and to contraception (in whatever form) does not change women's sexual behavior for the worse has not been enough to stop some people from suggesting that each new advance will cause a generation of women to become sluts.

We think that at its heart any such argument suggests that women's sexual behavior is a problem to be controlled and that the only way to do this is to ensure negative consequences at every turn. It says that women can't be trusted to make good decisions unless they're scared to death of their bad ones.

We think this is a terrible message to give young women and young men. We think it is offensive, and we know it's a myth.

References

American Experience (2001). *People and Events: The Pill and the Sexual Revolution.* PBS, New York. http://www.pbs.org/wgbh/amex/pill/peopleevents/e_revolution.html (accessed August 4, 2014).

Amira, D. (2012). Rick Santorum fine with shaming women in certain situations. *New York Magazine* (February 15). http://nymag.com/daily/intel/2012/02/rick-santorum-contraception-birth-control-sex.html (accessed August 4, 2014).

Asbell, B. (1995). *The Pill: A Biography of the Drug that Changed the World.* Random House, New York.

Bednarczyk, R.A., Davis, R., Ault, K., Orenstein, W., and Omer, S.B. (2012). Sexual activity–related outcomes after human papillomavirus vaccination of 11- to 12-year-olds. *Pediatrics,* 130(5), 798–805.

Bixby Center for Global Reproductive Health (2008). *Does Emergency Contraception Promote Sexual Risk Taking?* Bixby Center for Global Reproductive Health, University of California San Francisco, CA. http://bixbycenter.ucsf.edu/publications/files/DoesECPromoteSexRiskTaking_2008.pdf (accessed August 4, 2014).

Blake, S., Ledsky, R., Goodenow, C., Sawyer, R., Lohrmann, D., and Windsor, R. (2003). Condom availability programs in Massachusetts high schools: Relationships with condom use and sexual behavior. *American Journal of Public Health,* 93(6), 955–961.

Centers for Disease Control and Prevention (CDC) (updated July 2013). *HPV: CDC Fact Sheet.* Centers for Disease Control and Prevention, Atlanta, GA. http://www.cdc.gov/std/HPV/STDFact-HPV.htm (accessed August 4, 2014).

Centers for Disease Control and Prevention, and National Cancer Institute (2012). *United States Cancer Statistics: 1999–2008 Incidence and Mortality Web-based Report.* US Cancer Statistics Working Group, Department of Health and Human Services, Centers for Disease Control and Prevention, and National Cancer Institute; Atlanta, GA. http://www.cdc.gov/uscs (accessed August 4, 2014).

Gibbs, N. (2006). Defusing the war over the "promiscuity" vaccine. *Time Magazine* (June 21). http://content.time.com/time/nation/article/0,8599,1206813,00.html (accessed August 12, 2014).

Guttmacher, S., Lieberman, L., Ward, D., Freudenberg, N., Radosh, A., and Des Jarlais, D. (1997). Condom availability in New York City public high schools: Relationships to condom use and sexual behavior. *American Journal of Public Health,* 87, 1427–1433.

Kirby, D. (2007). *Emerging Answers 2007.* National Campaign to Prevent Teen and Unplanned Pregnancy, Washington, DC.

Liddon, N., Leichliter, J.S., and Markowitz, L.E. (2012). Human papillomavirus vaccine and sexual behavior among adolescent and young women. *American Journal of Preventive Medicine*, 42(1), 44–52.

Schlafly, P. (1986). Teaching promiscuity. *Reading Eagle* (May 26). http://news.google.com/newspapers?nid=1955&dat=19860526&id=2FIiAAAAIBAJ&sjid=7aYFAAAAIBAJ&pg=5908,5510963 (accessed August 4, 2014).

Stranton, D. and Evans, E. (2005). Plan B: The facts behind the controversy. *US Pharmacist* 9, 41–46.

World Health Organization (2012). *Cancers of the Cervix*. World Health Organization, Geneva. http://www.who.int/reproductivehealth/topics/cancers/en/index.html (accessed August 4, 2014).

RELATIONSHIPS

Dating and Desire

Hooking Up Never Leads to a Relationship

As you can imagine, there has been a lot of interest in hook up culture recently. Casual sexual connections may have been common for young men in previous decades (or centuries) but it seemed like big news when women began readily participating in hook ups. Suddenly researchers everywhere began to worry about the impact of hooking up and whether it was deleterious for the people who engaged in it—especially women. And the media began writing stories about how kids today have neither the time nor inclination for real relationships so they hook up instead.

But is that true? Is hooking up pervasive? Are college students doing it instead of having long (or short) term relationships? Is it really a cultural shift? And, possibly most important to our readers, what happens after a hook up? Can a real relationship start this way?

The whole idea behind hooking up is that sex can be spontaneous, casual, and without expectations of a deeper relationship. But the facts seem to be that for some people, hooking up is the gateway to a real relationship.

What is Hooking Up and Who is Doing It?

Hooking up is a bit of an umbrella term for sexual behavior outside of a traditional romantic relationship. The definition varies pretty widely and there are other terms that fall within it including one night stands, friends with benefits, booty calls, or even fuck buddies. Again, each of these has its

50 Great Myths of Human Sexuality, First Edition. Pepper Schwartz and Martha Kempner.
© 2015 John Wiley & Sons, Inc. Published 2015 by John Wiley & Sons, Inc.

own connotation and for that reason some researchers prefer the term casual sexual experiences (Claxton and van Dulmen, 2013).

One of the first really large studies that investigated hook ups was the Online College Social Life Survey (OCSLS), which looked at thousands of college students at more than 20 universities and has continued to produce on-going research. The OCSLS found that hooking up was a very common experience—by senior year 72% of heterosexual students reported at least one hook up and most students had had an average of five casual partners (England *et al.*, 2008). This didn't mean they all had intercourse because "hooking up" covers anything sexual—from just hanging out and hoping, to kissing, touching, or full-fledged intercourse. The study found that one-third of students said they had intercourse during their last hook up, while another third said they had oral sex or some kind of genital touching. Another third said they only kissed or touched above the waist.

Though the media would have us believe that college students are hooking up with total strangers on a nightly basis, only 20% of students who had ever hooked up said they hooked up frequently (defined as 10 times or more), 40% of the students who had hooked up had done it between four and nine times, and another 40% said they'd done it three or fewer times. In addition, most hook up partners were not exactly strangers. In fact, only 12% of the males and 10% of the females said they didn't know the person they hooked up with at all beforehand. However, "knowing" is a relative word: 17% of the men and 23% of the women said their hook up was someone whom they knew "very well" compared to 29% of males and 20% of females who said they knew their hook up "a little bit" (England *et al.*, 2008).

Most hook ups, by the way, also included alcohol. Men on average consumed six drinks before the hook up and women drank four.

Is The Hook Up Culture New?

Though hooking up seems like a new phenomenon and many people are worried about what it means for our definitions of love and relationships, a new study suggested that the hook up culture represents a smaller cultural shift than has been suggested. For the study, researchers at the University of Portland compared a survey of sexual practices conducted between 1988 and 1996 with one conducted between 2004 and 2012. They found that respondents from the more recent survey did not report more sexual partners after age 18, more frequent sex, or more partners during the past year than respondents from the earlier survey. In addition, the new generation of college students did not seem to be having sex that was more casual than their predecessors. In the recent study, 78.2% of those surveyed reported that their sexual partner was either a spouse or a significant other, compared with 84.5% in the earlier survey. The researchers suggested that the difference could be explained by the fact that some students in the earlier study were likely married during college because the age of marriage was lower in the 1980s and 1990s (Monto and Carey, 2014).

Ultimately, they conclude: "These modest changes are consistent with cultural shifts in the 'scripts' and terminology surrounding sexuality. We find no evidence of substantial changes in sexual behavior that would indicate a new or pervasive pattern of non-relational sex among contemporary college students. We find no evidence of substantial changes in sexual behavior that would indicate a new or pervasive pattern of non-relational sex among contemporary college students" (Monto and Carey, 2014, p. 1). Later they note: "Overall, our results provide no evidence that there has been a sea change in the sexual behavior of college students or a general liberalization of attitudes toward sexuality" (Monto and Carey, 2014, p. 9).

Is the Hook Up Culture Damaging (Especially to Women)?

Many scholars have wondered if hook up culture creates emotional and social problems for both men and women. Some research has suggested that after casual sex individuals report feeling ashamed, used, guilty, and angry. They may also feel differently about their hook up partner: about a third of men and 23% of women in the England *et al.* study (2008) said they respected their partner less than they had before. The gender differences here are somewhat expected as women have historically been judged differently for their sexual behavior than men. (See Myth # 47 about the double standard.) It's not surprising, therefore, that men tend to experience more pleasure, less guilt, and less regret after a casual sexual relationship than women (Fisher *et al.*, 2012). Interestingly, a study of first semester college students found that men who did not engage in hook ups had higher psychological distress than those who did (Fielder and Carey, 2010).

Women, unfortunately, often do experience psychological distress after hook ups. That same study found that having had penetrative sex outside of a relationship led to increased psychological distress in women 2.5 months after the incident (Fielder and Carey, 2010).

This worries us and we believe it has to do with the fact that women get judged more harshly than men in these hook ups. While no specific number of hook ups labels a man as a "slut," there seems to be some unwritten number of hook ups that stigmatizes women. Men, for example, do not seem to be judged for having intercourse on a first hook up, but women generally do get a "reputation" (Hamilton and Armstrong, 2009). Hamilton and Armstrong's study found that, like men, many women students wanted to "party" and have casual sex but that a prevailing double standard punished these women way more than the men who were doing the same thing.

The good news is that other studies have found that there can be positive emotional reactions to hooking up for both men and women. These included feeling happy, desired, pleased, and excited. And, let's not forget sexually satisfied. Others felt a kind of public self-esteem boost when people found out about their hook-up. Moreover, many people say that they do not regret their casual sex experience. Some researchers have argued that casual sexual experiences are easier than relationships for college students as they are less time consuming and there is less to lose than in a serious relationship. Bisson and Levine (2009), for example, found that friends with benefits can include some of the upsides of a traditional romantic relationship, like close friendship, but without the pressure of commitment.

What Happens After the Hook Up?

While scholars may be wondering what hook ups mean for the sexual scripts in society, many young people want to know what a hook up means for them. Is it possible that casual sex will eventually lead to relationship? Research suggests it is. In the England *et al.* (2008) study, for example, about 70% of both men and women said they contacted their hook up partner again by email and 80% said they called or saw the partner again in person.

The research on whether hook ups lead to dates is confusing—on the one hand most hook ups do not lead to dates, but on the other hand most people who start dating someone (at least in the above study) say that the relationship began with some kind of hook up. Some studies have found that an equal proportion of men and women report hooking toward the purpose of getting into a romantic relationship. As for friends with benefits relationships, it does seem like women are more likely than men to want these to morph into romantic relationships (Garcia and Reiber, 2008; Lehmillier *et al.*, 2011).

We think the important thing here, though, is that both men and women seem to want romantic relationships at some point. The image of today's young adults as after only casual sex or having replaced the idea of a romantic relationship with one person with a slew of random hook ups is just inaccurate. Consider this: the England *et al.* (2008) study found that by senior year, 69% of those in their heterosexual sample had been dating someone for at least 6 months and 67% of those people said the relationship they were in started as a hook up!

References

Bisson, M.A. and Levine, T.R. (2009). Negotiating a friends with benefits relationship. *Archives of Sexual Behavior*, 38(1), 66–73.

Claxton, S.E. and van Dulmen, M.H. (2013). Casual sexual relationships and experiences in emerging adulthood. *Emerging Adulthood*, 1(2), 138–150.

England, P., Shafer, E.F., and Fogarty, A.C. (2008). Hooking up and forming romantic relationships on today's college campuses. *The Gendered Society Reader*, 3.

Fielder, R.L. and Carey, M.P. (2010). Predictors and consequences of sexual "hookups" among college students: A short-term prospective study. *Archives of Sexual Behavior*, 39(5), 1105–1119.

Fisher, M.L., Worth, K., Garcia, J.R., and Meredith, T. (2012). Feelings of regret following uncommitted sexual encounters in Canadian university students. *Culture, Health and Sexuality*, 14(1), 45–57.

Garcia, J.R. and Reiber, C. (2008). Hook-up behavior: A biopsychosocial perspective. *Journal of Social, Evolutionary, and Cultural Psychology*, 2(4), 192.

Hamilton, L. and Armstrong, E.A. (2009). Gendered sexuality in young adulthood double binds and flawed options. *Gender and Society*, 23(5), 589–616.

Lehmiller, J.J., VanderDrift, L.E., and Kelly, J.R. (2011). Sex differences in approaching friends with benefits relationships. *Journal of Sex Research*, 48(2–3), 275–284.

Monto, M.A. and Carey, A.G. (2014). A new standard of sexual behavior? Are claims associated with the "hookup culture" supported by general social survey data? *Journal of Sex Research*, 51, 605–615.

Myth #34   If You Feel Attracted to Someone Else, There Must Be Something Wrong With Your Relationship

Somewhere, sometime, somebody made the statement that once you're in a romantic relationship you should be "pure of mind and body" and everyone just bought it hook, line, and sinker. Swallowed it whole. But think about it: your mind is a wandering, untamable machine. Yes, you can usually control your actions. But your thoughts? When you are sleeping your mind is busy, concocting amazing and weird stories in dreams. When you are awake and you see a sexy person, it switches on automatically and codes the vision as pleasurable, even erotic. Is this a problem? A sin? A sign that something is terribly wrong with your relationship?

No—it is just the way the human mind works.

Our minds' proclivities for fantasy and lust are going to be working on auto-pilot whether or not we are in love, engaged, or married. Of course, there are different degrees for different people and there are some gender differences, but fantasies and attraction to individuals other than our partners is normal.

Outside Attraction Is Normal

Attraction takes many forms and while it is often not acted on, it becomes embedded in our fantasy world. When an anonymous questionnaire was administered to 349 heterosexual university students (young and old), 98% of the men and 80% of the women mentioned that they had had fantasies about someone who was not their current partner. The frequency of such fantasies increased with the length of the present intimate relationship for both men and women but was only correlated with having had a larger number of prior partners for women, likely because women were more likely to fantasize about a previous partner than men were (Hicks and Leitenberg, 2001).

It is easy to see why desire for someone else might increase with relationship duration and not even say much about how good the relationship is. There is a habituation effect and people start imagining a new kind of sex with a new kind of partner, even if they are in love and even if they have no intention of breaking any vows of monogamy they might have made. It is also possible that if people have more partners, they have been more sexually focused and miss the added stimulus that new partners have brought them over the years. The good news is that Hicks and Leitenberg (2001) found no evidence in the study that the fantasies about and attractions to others interfered with their present relationship.

A large, but non-random study by Northrup *et al.* (2013) found that there were all kinds of attractions and fantasies about other partners, even among very happy couples. In fact, 61% of the women and 90% of the men in the study said they fantasized sexually about people they met but there was no correlation between these kinds of fantasies and the happiness or unhappiness of the couple.

Most research does indicate that men have more outside fantasies and attractions than women do whether it's during masturbation or random thoughts throughout the day (Leitenberg and Henning, 1995). One study had college students keep diaries of their sexual thoughts. Men recorded 7.2 fantasies a day and women recalled 4.5. These covered a wide variety of images and could be about a partner, a specific act, or random people such as someone they had met or seen in a picture. Note that some of these fantasies may have been about their partner (Jones and Barlow, 1990).

Who Are They Fantasizing About?

As we mentioned earlier, women are somewhat more likely to fantasize about an ex-partner but if one isn't fantasizing about a current partner or an ex—who is getting them hot and bothered? The truth is that it can be anyone—a hot guy they saw on a subway, an attractive girl in class, an actor or actress, a porn star, or absolutely anyone the brain can recall or make up. In many cases, however, it's a friend or acquaintance.

Friends of the opposite gender, the subject of many romantic comedies, are also apparently the subject of many fantasies. One study found that three out of four people believed that they could have opposite sex friendships, eight out of ten people actually had them, but six out of ten people admitted that they felt some sexual attraction for this friend and more than half said they had told their friend about the attraction (Halatsis and Christakis, 2009). Most friendships survived this admission, but, in a few situations the two either changed the nature of their relationship or the friendship ended. In general, however, the authors decided that these attractions between friends were not "calamitous."

Northrup *et al.* also found that friends, and more interestingly a partner's friends, were common subjects of fantasies. In fact, 45% of men and 26% of women said they were attracted to their partner's friends. Their partners might find this surprising. When asked, 86% of men and 85% of women said they didn't think any of their friends were tempting fantasies for their partners. To give us more proof that fantasies and actions are not the same, however, only 17% of people who were sexually satisfied said they found these friends tempting in terms of real life actions.

Setting Boundaries

Just because we are saying that fantasizing about people other than your partner is normal and does not show a problem within the relationship doesn't mean your partner will agree. Partners have "rules" about how attraction is expressed and fantasy is not necessarily allowed. A *New York Times* poll (*New York Times Magazine*, 2000) tapped into the psyches of a random group of people and found that 48% of respondents did not think it was okay to fantasize about having sex with someone other than their partner even if they didn't act on it.

Acting on them is certainly another thing entirely (see Myth # 36 for more about cheating), but as for fantasies the truth is they are pretty private. If you think your fantasies about other people would hurt your partner's feelings, keep them to yourself. If your partner starts to tell you about someone he/she is fantasizing about and that upsets you, speak up and ask that in the future this kind of information not be shared. In the meantime know that fantasies are common even among the happiest of couples and try not to read too much into them.

References

Halatsis, P. and Christakis, N. (2009). The challenge of sexual attraction within heterosexuals' cross-sex friendship. *Journal of Social and Personal Relationships*, 26(6-7), 6–7.

Hicks, T.V. and Leitenberg, H. (2001). Sexual fantasies about one's partner versus someone else: Gender differences in incidence and frequency. *Sage Family Studies Abstracts*, 23(4), 411–568.

Jones, J.C. and Barlow, D.H. (1990). Self reported frequency of sexual urges, fantasies and masturbatory fantasies, in heterosexual males and females. *Archives of Sexual Behavior*, 19, 269–279.

Leitenberg, H. and Henning, K. (1995). Sexual fantasy. *Psychological Bulletin*, 117, 469–496.

New York Times Magazine (2000). The way we live now poll. *New York Times Magazine* (May 7), p. 76.

Northrup, C., Schwartz, P., and Witte, J. (2013). *The Normal Bar: the surprising secrets of happy couples and what they reveal about creating a new normal in your relationship.* Harmony/Random House Press, New York.

Myth #35 Most Female Fantasies Revolve Around a Love Story

Much of the vision of the inner life of women is surmised from the outer life of women because of assumptions made about women from their taste in written and visual media, particularly love stories. And there is no denying that the once extremely popular Harlequin romances, written for and by women, are pure fantasy material all about love, and romantic passion, as are the more modern romantic comedies (which often fall under the rubric of chick flicks). But understanding the fantasy life of women is not that simple. When the erotic and kinky trio of books *50 Shades of Grey* came out—and became a world-wide marketing phenomena—myths about female fantasy started to be questioned.

First Theories on Female Fantasy

Much of the early writing on the inner life of women came from the earliest of sex researchers in the mid-nineteenth century. In the beginning, the writing on fantasy was laid down in medical books from clinical observations by men who mistook their female patients' fantasies as betraying essential female psychology as opposed to just a reflection of the lives they had been socialized to lead. Victorian women were educated by mothers to be asexual, "proper," and subordinate to men, but the medical men who wrote about them at the time thought women's lack of intense sexual desire was biologically innate. Masoch, a nineteenth century doctor, gave his name to what he believed was a natural condition of women, "masochism"—sexual pleasure through subordination, even pain. Sigmund Freud, a man of the same generation, became even more famous as the father of the new field of psychoanalysis. Freud's writings guided generations of psychoanalysts. His conclusions about the fantasy world of women were also deeply influenced by mid-nineteenth century Victorian conceptions of women. Freud (1963) doubted that women were asexual, but he did believe in female passivity, and thought that fantasy was a form of blocking sexual energy ("repression") rather than exercising it. Later in his life Freud actually wrote that he really didn't understand women at all—but that was long after his writing had created an image of women as sexually passive, and sexually neurotic.

Students of Freud carried on the theme. Deutsch (1944) recorded his subjects' fantasies of rape and prostitution as part of sexual repression; a kind of a rehearsal for allowing themselves to be sexual in real life. A famous psychologist of the same period, Maslow (1942) played with themes of women's social conformity to submissive roles and argued that more "dominant" women (who were obviously out of step with their very nature) used sexual fantasies to help them "yield" and, by so doing, render themselves capable of enjoying sexual intercourse.

This kind of thinking remained relatively standard for decades through the 1970s even as the feminist movement started to question these older stereotypes. Hariton and Singer (1974) summarized the literature of the time and found that most commentary concluded that sexual fantasies reflected women's essentially masochistic nature as well as their sexual inhibition.

Later Writing on Female Fantasy

As social values and customs liberalized and women became more openly sexual, journalists and scientists started studying and questioning these sexual prescriptions and constraints. Some feminists and sexual adventurers defied current values that prescribed female sexual desire only in the context of marriage, or committed relationships, lest a woman's reputation suffer— and writing on all aspects of women's sexualities multiplied. Researchers began to accept that fantasizing was normal for women. Studies varied, but by the late 1970s the estimate in the research was that between 88% and 99% of both married and unmarried women had sexual fantasies in the past year (Brown and Hart, 1977; Crepault et al., 1977).

Scholars also began to hypothesize that modern women might have different sexual fantasies because they were having different sexual lives. Sure enough, women with more frequent and varied experiences reported having more varied sexual fantasies (Pelletier and Herold, 1988) and less sex guilt (Moreault and Follingstad, 1978). Harris et al. (1980) had compatible findings; they found that women who reported detailed sexual fantasies also indicated higher levels of arousal and greater ease of arousal.

As post-feminist movement writing continued, research on female fantasies looked not just at the existence of these fantasies (both awake and in dreams), but also at their impact. Hariton (1973) found that having sexual fantasies while engaging in marital sexual intercourse did not indicate marital maladjustment. In fact, Kelly (1978) found that fantasy enhanced sexual arousal in the marriages she studied. The frequency of sexual fantasy was positively related to arousal as well. Davidson and Hoffman (1986, p. 203) found that their most sexually satisfied subjects had sexual fantasies about their current sexual partner.

What Do Women Fantasize About?

The 1970s brought full bore fascination with female sexuality and some books, written by lay researchers rather than trained sexologists, caught the public imagination. Nancy Friday, a journalist, wrote an immensely popular book, *My Secret Garden* (1973), that listed page after page of verbatim quotes of women's fantasies that included sexual intercourse with a stranger, having sex in front of an audience, being a dominatrix, being raped, having sex as a prostitute, as well as having sex with a boy, an African-American man, a woman, an animal, and someone other than their husband. Later, another journalist did a study for a mass magazine and found that younger women were more likely to fantasize about their current sex partner or a famous person, whereas older women were more likely to fantasize about having sexual intercourse with an acquaintance, a stranger, or an animal (Wolfe, 1981, p. 372).

More scientific studies also emerged during this period. An extensive study of female orgasm found that "40 percent of the women who had sexual fantasies had fantasies that typically involved a sex partner other than the husband" (Fisher 1973, p. 213). Fisher reported that the most frequent (and usually the most preferred) fantasies were reliving a sexual experience from their past (other than the first sexual experience), visualizing different sexual positions, thinking about their current sexual partner, having sex in a room in their house other than the bedroom, having sex with a new sex partner, having an extramarital affair, having sex with someone who was more romantic or affectionate than their current partner, and having sex on a carpeted floor (where that one came from, who knows?!). The fantasy of being overpowered by an acquaintance and being forced to have sex was not as frequent but it was a favorite of the women who used it at all. If the categories of "new sex partner" and "extramarital affair" were combined, sex with someone other than one's partner would have been the most common of all the fantasies. So much for all female fantasies being about love.

It is interesting how common the desire for a "taboo" partner came up in later studies on sexual fantasies. Davison and Hoffman (1986) report studies that found that women and men were equally likely to fantasize about "forbidden fruit" and women were no more likely to feel guilty about these fantasies than men were.

How Are Women's Fantasies Different from Men's?

This doesn't mean women have no attachment in their fantasies or that men's and women's fantasies are entirely similar. Many scholars have found that female sexual fantasies are more likely than male fantasies to have emotion in them and to utilize a familiar partner, albeit in a more elaborately detailed setting (Barclay, 1973; Gagnon and Simon, 1973; Hass, 1979; Wilson and Lang, 1981; Wilson, 1987). Although a recent study found that the majority of heterosexual men's favorite fantasy was about their wife or partner doing various acts to them (Northrup et al., 2013), in general, women's sexual fantasies are reported to contain more affection and commitment between the partners (Kelley, 1983; Pryzbyla et al., 1983), and are more likely to express tenderness and deeper emotion (Hessellund, 1976). Female sexual fantasies also were found to imply sex rather abstractly whereas male sexual content had more explicit and detailed sexual scenes though often with much less context (Brickman, 1978). As might be expected from sexual patterns in real life, women were more likely to imagine themselves as being desired and receiving sexual attention while men were more likely to see themselves as the sexual aggressor taking charge of someone sexually desirable (Barclay, 1973; Iwawaki and Wilson, 1983; Knafo and Jaffe, 1984; Mednick, 1977; Wilson and Lang, 1981). A more vivid difference is reported by Davidson and Hoffman (1986, pp. 540–541); only 12% of men, but 43% of women said they never switch partners during the course of a sexual fantasy. Imagery of being forced or overpowered into a sexual act were common to both sexes, but more common among women (Sue, 1979; Knafo and Jaffe, 1984; Ellis and Symons, 1990, pp. 528–529).

Other interesting findings from the Ellis and Symons study indicate that women were more than twice as likely as men to focus on their own physical or emotional response in the fantasy and far more likely to report that touching was an important part of their visualization. Women were also more than twice as likely than men to focus on the personal or emotional characteristics of the partner in their fantasy, more likely to report that their imaginary partner was uniquely capable of arousing them, and twice as likely to have a fantasy about someone they had previously been involved with. Overall, women cared more about the mood and ambience of their fantasy, had more sequences of nongenital caressing, and more often had a slow build to sexual activity while men activated sexual activity almost immediately (pp. 541–542).

When Do Women Fantasize?

Though we may have an image of a lonely woman fantasizing because she doesn't have a partner or her partner is far away, the truth is women often fantasize during partnered sex. There is certainly a difference in the fantasies women have when alone from those employed when having sex with a partner. Fisher (1973) found the majority of women surveyed (75%) reported experiencing sexual fantasies during sexual intercourse. Similarly, Crepault found that 28% of the women in their study used sexual fantasies in order to expedite an orgasm and 53% reported using sexual fantasies during the "initial part of sexual intercourse" (as reported in Davidson and Hoffman, 1986, p. 2002). This means that sometimes when women are having intercourse, their body is present—but their psyche is far away.

Okay, So What About the Whole Female Submission Thing?

We started talking about this myth with the Victorian discussion of female sexual submission. Were they so far off? Actually, there is certainly a lot of evidence of submission fantasies. Pelletier and Herold (1988) found that 51% of their female sample reported fantasies of being forced to submit sexually, and Knafo and Jaffe (1984) noted that the fantasy reported most frequently during intercourse for women was "I imagine that I am being overpowered or forced to surrender." Talbot et al. (1980) also found that "being overpowered and forced to sexually surrender" was the second most often utilized sexual fantasy by their respondents during various sexual activities, including sexual intercourse.

A recent study on female rape fantasies sheds more light on these types of fantasies; 62% of a large sample (355) of college women indicated that they had either fantasized about having forced sex by a man, forced sex by a woman, or a number of forced sexual acts. About 20% of this group had this fantasy quite often—at least one or more times a week (Bivona et al., 2012, p. 1111).

This sounds like something that would make Masoch or Freud proud (they might feel it confirms their models of female sexuality)—but the data indicate that these submissive feelings are part of the range of imagination for sexually secure and "sex positive" women who are less likely to experience guilt and more likely to try a variety of sexual experiences (Strassberg and Lockerd, 1998; Pelletier and Herold, 1988). While some of these fantasies surely come from women with more difficult sexual histories, most have no basis in real experience. Many of the rape fantasies correlated mostly to openness to fantasy rather than any kind of pathology or real desire for such an experience. Moreover, the reported fantasies carried none of the actual violence that might occur in a real rape. These fantasies do not allow for unpleasantness, which would occur in a real rape and, importantly, all of the action is controlled by the woman herself—it is after all, her imagination (Bivona *et al.*, 2012, p. 1111; Bivona and Critelli, 2009; Kanin, 1982; Shanor, 1974).

In contrast, some women do have dominance fantasies. Unlike men's dominance fantasies, women's fantasies allow for romance as well as the partner's pleasure and emotion, and tend to involve more than just one partner. Men's dominance fantasies were more self-involved and objectified the target person more. Byers (1996) felt that women's focus on partner pleasure might occur because women tending to men is encouraged (even dictated) in their real world. Some researchers on women's fantasies hypothesize that since being sexually "free" in the real world has been impossible for women until lately (and then only in certain countries, certain classes, and certain religions) that "the realm of fantasy may be a private and safe sphere in which women can experience desire and pleasure free from danger" (Zurbriggen and Yost, 2004, p. 289).

Wait, What do Women Fantasize About?

In sum, female fantasies are complicated, explorative, and hardly only about love. We think it is important to remember that sexual fantasies are exactly that: the roaming of the psyche to explore erotic territory and mold it to the needs of the moment without ever testing it out in real life. A fantasy about being carried off by the Sheik of Arabia can be erotic because it doesn't have to take into account the smell of a man who lived in the desert on a camel, the language problems, the contempt such a man might have for a sexually free woman or a woman who was not his wife, the physical risk of such an encounter, or the fact that the person fantasizing this episode would never allow him/herself to be with such a person or in that desert. It can be just erotic fun—and not an exposé of deepest desires.

References

Barclay, A.M. (1973). Sexual fantasies in men and women. *Medical Aspects of Human Sexuality*, 7, 205–216.

Bivona, J.M. and Critelli, J.W. (2009). The nature of women's rape fantasies: An analysis of prevalence, frequency, and contents. *Journal of Sex Research*, 46, 33–45.

Bivona, J.M., Critelli, J.W., and Clark, M.J. (2012). Women's rape fantasies: An empirical evaluation of the major explanations. *Archives of Sexual Behavior*, 41(5), 1107–1119.

Brickman, J.R.R. (1978). Erotica: Sex differences in stimulus preferences and fantasy content. Doctoral dissertation, University of Manitoba.

Brown, J.J. and Hart, D.H. (1977). Correlates of females' sexual fantasies. *Perceptual and Motor Skills*, 45, 819–825.

Byers, E.S. (1996). How well does the traditional sexual script explain sexual coercion? Review of a program of research. *Journal of Psychology and Human Sexuality*, 8, 7–25.

Crepault, C., Abraham, G., Porto, R., and Couture, M. (1977). Erotic imagery in women. In Gemme, R. and Wheeler C. (eds) *Progress in Sexology*. Plenum, New York, pp. 267–283.

Davidson, J.K. Sr. and Hoffman, L.E. (1986). Sexual fantasies and sexual satisfaction: An empirical analysis of erotic thought. *Journal of Sex Research*, 22(2), 184–205.

Deutsch, H. (1944). *The Psychology of Women*. Greene and Stratton, New York.

Ellis, B.J. and Symons, D. (1990). Sex differences in sexual fantasy: An evolutionary psychological approach. *Journal of Sex Research*, 27(4), 527–555.

Fisher, S. (1973). *The Female Orgasm*. Basic Books, New York.

Freud, S. (1963). *The Relation of the Poet to Day-dreaming. Sigmund Freud: Character and Culture*. Collier, New York.

Friday, N. (1973). *My Secret Garden*. Simon and Schuster, New York.

Gagnon, J.H. and Simon, W. (1973). *Sexual Conduct*. Aldine, Chicago.

Hass, A. (1979). *Teenage Sexuality*. Macmillan, New York.

Hariton, E.B. (1973). Women's fantasies during sexual intercourse with their husbands: A normative study with tests of personality and theoretical modes. Dissertation Abstracts International, 33, 3917B. (University Microfilms No. 73-02,839)

Hariton, E.B. and Singer, J.L. (1974). Women's fantasies during sexual intercourse: Normative and theoretical implications. *Journal of Consulting and Clinical Psychology*, 42, 313–322.

Harris, R., Yulis, S., and Lacoste, D. (1980). Relationships among sexual arousability, imagery ability, and introversion-extraversion. *Journal of Sex Research*, 16, 72–87.

Hessellund, H. (1976). Masturbation and sexual fantasies in married couples. *Archives of Sexual Behavior*, 5, 133–147.

Iwawaki, S. and Wilson, G.D. (1983). Sex fantasies in Japan. *Personality and Individual Differences*, 4, 543–545.

Kanin, E.J. (1982). Female rape fantasies: A victimization study. *Victimology: An International Journal*, 7, 114–121.

Kelley, K. (1983). Sexual fantasy and attitudes as functions of sex of subject and content of erotica. *Imagination, Cognition, and Personality*, 4, 339–347.

Kelly, L.A.S. (1978). Imagining ability, marital adjustment, and erotic fantasy during sexual relations in married men and women. Dissertation Abstracts International, 39, 1457B–1458B. (University Microfilms No. 78-15,595)

Knafo, D. and Jaffe, Y. (1984). Sexual fantasizing in males and females. *Journal of Research in Personality*, 18, 451–462.

Maslow, A.H. (1942). Self-esteem and sexuality in women. *Journal of Social Psychology*, 16, 259–264.

Mednick, R.A. (1977). Gender specific variances in sexual fantasy. *Journal of Personality Assessment*, 41, 248–254.

Moreault, D. and Follingstad, D.R. (1978). Sexual fantasies of females as a function of sex guilt and experimental response cues. *Journal of Consulting and Clinical Psychology*, 46, 1385–1393.

Northrup, C., Schwartz, P., and Witte, J. (2013). *The Normal Bar: The surprising secrets of happy couples and what they reveal about creating a new normal in your relationship*. Harmony/Random House Press, New York.

Pelletier, L.A. and Herold, E.S. (1988). The relationship of age, sex guilt and sexual experience with female sexual fantasies. *Journal of Sex Research*, 24, 250–256.

Pryzbyla, D.P.J., Bryne, D., and Kelley, K. (1983). The role of imagery in sexual behavior. In Sheikh, A.A. (ed.) *Imagery: Current Theory, Research, and Application*. Wiley, New York, pp. 436–467.

Shanor, K.I.N. (1974). Social variables of women's sexual fantasies. Dissertation Abstracts International, 35, 532B. (University Microfilms No. 74-14,319)

Strassberg, D.S. and Lockerd, L.K. (1998). Force in women's sexual fantasies. *Archives of Sexual Behavior*, 27, 403–414.

Sue, D. (1979). Erotic fantasies of college students during coitus. *Journal of Sex Research*, 15, 299–305.

Talbot, R.M.R., Beech, H.R., and Vaughan, M. (1980). A normative appraisal of erotic fantasies in women. *British Journal of Social and Clinical Psychology*, 19(1), 81–83.

Wilson, G.D (1987). Male–female differences and sexual activity, enjoyment, and fantasies. *Personality and Individual Differences*, 8, 125–127.

Wilson, G.D. and Lang, R.J. (1981). Sex differences in sexual fantasy. *Personality and Individual Differences*, 2, 343–346.

Wolfe, L. (1981). *The Cosmo Report*. Arbor House, New York.

Zurbriggen, E.L. and Yost, M.R. (2004). Power, desire, and pleasure in sexual fantasies. *Journal of Sex Research*, 41(3), 288–300.

Myth #36

Men Cheat, Women Rarely Do

Where did this idea come from? Probably from the fact that historically, if a woman cheated, she was a dead woman. She could get stoned, buried alive, or shot—more or less with impunity. So, just in terms of survival instincts, a woman who suppressed her sexual desires in general, and outside of marriage in particular, might live a longer life.

Then of course there is the mythology that went along with terrorizing women into monogamy. Some religions have pathologized female sexual interest as abnormal. Think about how Eve was seen as the evil temptress who ruined Adam's purity (and their stay in the Garden of Eden) by encouraging the devil snake's offer of the apple of shame and guilt. Still, the Old Testament has some wonderful romantic scenes of both men and women wanting each other and loving each other. The New Testament, on the other hand, worships Mary, a woman who was a virgin and could stay a virgin even though she bore a child.

Theology has changed some over the centuries but the image of women as modest and sexually pure, having sex not because of lust but because of a desire to have children, seems to have remained, at least to some degree. Men have always been seen as much less sexually and emotionally dependable.

But the historical record as well as contemporary studies show us a different picture. While it is true that men quite commonly stray from the vows of monogamy (an almost universal part of the marriage ceremony, at least in the West), women are not always the aggrieved spouse. More often than we realize, they are the sexual adventurer.

We Disapprove of Infidelity

Though most cultures have come a long way from the days of stoning women for cheating on their husbands, this does not mean that most cultures approve of infidelity. Most studies report that 80% or more of men and women believe that it is "always" or "almost always" wrong for a married person to have sex with anyone besides their spouse (e.g., Smith, 1994).

In fact, though there are differences across cultures, it seems that no one is entirely okay with it. The World Values Survey Association (2000) ranked 47 countries on their feelings about nonmonogamy using a five-point scale in which one indicated it was unacceptable and five that it was acceptable. Few countries ranked a five. Even liberal countries like Holland scored closer to a two than a five, which was similar to the scores of those in Belgium, Canada, Germany, Japan, and Russia (Lammers *et al.,* 2011, p. 1195).

And Yet, We Cheat

For the most part we don't approve of cheating, and yet most studies show it is relatively common. One study of 506 men and 412 women who indicated they were in a monogamous relationship showed that quite a few of them had a strange definition of monogamy—23% of the men and 19% of the women admitted to cheating while in their current relationship (Mark *et al.,* 2011, p. 971). Other data over the years seem to support this finding. National studies using random samples on infidelity in heterosexual relationships indicate that around 20–33% of men and 10–25% of women engage in "outside" sexual relationships at least once in their lives (Kinsey *et al.,* 1948, 1953; Laumann *et al.,* 1994). Some scholars believe that these numbers are actually low because people are uncomfortable telling the truth about their extra-relationship activities. Remember, an overwhelming majority of men and women disapprove of cheating—that would certainly encourage underreporting.

The studies we have cited from the early and mid-1990s showed that men were far more likely to be unfaithful than women (Wiederman, 1997), but more recent research indicates the infidelity gender gap has narrowed (Barta and Kiene, 2005; Burdette *et al.,* 2007). In fact, when sexual behaviors other than intercourse are inquired about (kissing, fondling, and emotional affairs), the gap between men's and women's extracurricular sexuality totally disappears (Allen *et al.,* 2005; Treas and Giesen, 2000). It's hard to know if earlier studies were incorrect, if women's behavior has change substantially, or if their willingness to be honest about infidelity has changed, but it is clear that the data from research that is 15 or 20 years old shows more traditional sexual behavior than more recent studies.

What Causes Infidelity?

In the entry on faking orgasm (see Myth # 21) we quote the 1988 romantic comedy *When Harry Met Sally,* and since it remains one of our favorite movies some 25 years later, we are going to quote it again. Harry and his best friend Jess are at a football game discussing how Harry's wife just announced that she was leaving him for a man from her office. Jess is sympathetic but tries to be logical:

> JESS: Marriages don't break up on account of infidelity. It's just a symptom that something else is wrong.
>
> HARRY: Oh really? Well, that "symptom" is fucking my wife.

Unfortunately for Harry, his friend has a point—infidelity is often a sign that something else is going on, either within the relationship or with one of the partners.

Relationship Problems

Unhappiness in the relationship and conflicts in sexual attitudes and values are particularly powerful motivations for women. Research clearly shows that relationship quality affects women's sexual satisfaction more than it appears to affect men's, and women are more likely than men to have sex outside the relationship because of either relationship or sexual issues that stem from relationship incompatibilities (Mark *et al.*, 2011; Byers, 2001; Dennerstein *et al.*, 2005; McCabe and Cobain, 1998; Ellison, 2001; Nicholls, 2008).

Relationship status is another issue for women's behavior. It doesn't seem to matter for men whether or not they are cohabiting or married, but married women are less likely to say they have been unfaithful than cohabiting or dating women (Mark *et al.*, 2011). Perhaps women's level of infidelity is more linked to commitment, or relationship quality, and less linked to adventure (Preveti and Amato, 2004). There does seem to be some research that would validate that idea (Spanier and Margolis, 1983; Mattingly *et al.*, 2011) but, to be fair (albeit, confusing), other studies have not found that extramarital sex is necessarily related to marital happiness or even the quality of marital sex (Choi *et al.*, 1994).

Personality and Mood

Some research has given up gender altogether as a predictor of nonmonogamy and centered on personality types. A group of researchers have looked at the level of impulsive or uninhibited behavior in people and found it to be predictive for both men's and women's infidelity. It has been correlated with the tendency to have casual sex (Bancroft *et al.*, 2004; Carpenter *et al.*, 2008), and take sexual risks (Turchik and Garske, 2009). Even situations that affect mood may be predictive. Several studies have found that a significant minority of men and women experienced increased sexual interest or response when they were feeling "down" or, conversely, when they were feeling "invulnerable and powerful" (Bancroft *et al.*, 2003; Lykins *et al.*, 2006; Mark *et al.*, 2011).

Dominance and Power

The more powerful someone feels, the more likely they are to believe they can handle extramarital sexuality, and even to believe that they deserve this kind of additional pleasure. This seems to be true for women as well as men. These findings from a study of over 1500 professional men and women, for example, suggest that when power is culturally unbalanced between men and women, men will be more nonmonogamous than women. But in situations where women have the same amount of power in a relationship, and in a culture that allows them to act without more drastic consequences than men, then they will be just as nonmonogamous as men (Lammers *et al.*, 2011).

A powerful position or sense of personal power increases the likelihood that someone will approach an attractive target (Wilkey, 2011), and increases the person's optimism about their chances of being sexually and romantically successful with people they approach (Kunstman and Maner, 2011; Lerner, 2011; Gonzaga *et al.*, 2008). Such individuals, be they women or men, may actually increase their own attractiveness because of their posture of confidence, including direct eye contact and moving close to the person they are interested in (Friedman *et al.*, 1988; Lammers *et al.*, 2011). Or, to put it another way, if people believe they are likely to get what they want, they may be more encouraged to go out and get it—and be successful, which might encourage more sexual forays. Researchers who believe self-confidence and personal power predict infidelity fully expect women soon to exercise as much nonmonogamous choice as men do (Buller, 2005; Eagly and Wood, 1999; Smuts, 1992; Wood and Eagly, 2007; Lammers *et al.*, 2011).

Opportunity

There used to be jokes about female infidelity that ended with the idea that a homemaker's child might look a lot like the "milkman." That was in the days when milk was actually delivered to the door step of most homes—and also when the only man the homemaker was likely to meet was the milkman. Men had far more opportunities to cheat, such as on business trips—hence the old joke about stewardesses asking a traveling businessman if he'd like "coffee, tea or me." Opportunity certainly does play a part in extramarital affairs but it is very hard to measure just how much and research has come to a variety of conclusions.

Researchers have measured opportunity by looking at employment and income. Some (Atkins *et al.*, 2001) found a positive relationship between infidelity and opportunity when they did this, but others (Liu, 2000) found that this was only true for men. Research has shown that the workplace seems to provide the most opportunities for cheating—a study by Wiggins and Lederer (1984) found that among those who had cheated, half had done so with a coworker, and a study by Treas and Geison (2000) found that workplace opportunity increased the likelihood of infidelity (Blow and Hartnett, 2005).

Emotional Affairs

Emotions can be the impetus for infidelity even when no desire was initially present and the relationship in question started out as a friendship. There is no doubt that women are different from men in the sense that they are more likely to develop desire from emotional closeness without initial attraction, whereas for most men the initial attraction comes first (Glass and Staeheli, 2004; Neuman, 2009; Pittman, 1990; Spring and Spring, 1997).

In some cases, these relationships turn into what has become known as an emotional affair—a friendship that starts out gradually but becomes as intense as a sexual relationship even if there is no actual sex involved. Allen and Rhodes (2007) explain that emotional affairs most often do indicate issues in the main relationship as one partner is seeking something that the other is not providing. For example, in a study of 345 undergraduates and 115 people not in school who had had intense and emotional relationships outside of a a current relationship, most expressed disappointment with the level of intimacy in the primary relationship (p. 51).

Some studies have found that the internet provides a route for women in particular to engage in these kinds of emotional affairs. Studies looking at nonmonogamous behavior on the internet have seen gender differences: women tend to flirt more, and inject more emotion (Whitty, 2003, 2004).

There have been many debates about whether these kinds of affairs—ones that involve emotional connection, flirting, and possibly sexual behavior through the internet or phone but no in-person touching—really count as cheating. Most women, even the ones who were doing it, believe it does. And most said it affected their offline relationships (Whitty, 2005; Hertlein and Piercy, 2006). More proof that women think this kind of behavior is actually cheating—in one study about 40% reported being anxious about their behavior and over 50% removed the evidence of their behavior from their computer (Wysocki and Childers, 2011).

Same-Sex Infidelity

As with many of the topics we discuss in this book, we wish we could give you more information about same-sex couples. The truth is that we just don't know. Blow and Hartnett (2005) report in their literature review on infidelity, "limited research exists on same-sex couples, outside of the large Blumstein and Schwartz study (1983)." We have mentioned this study before as it was conducted by co-author Pepper Schwartz. That study found that nonmonogamous lesbians were less satisfied with their primary relationship and less committed to a future together which could be interpreted as a desire for monogamy among lesbian couples. A more recent qualitative study (Worth et al., 2002) found that although sex outside of the relationship appears to be more acceptable in some gay couples than it is in heterosexual ones, infidelity still causes pain and jealousy in these couples (Blow and Hartnett, 2005).

We would have hoped that more scholars had studied same-sex couples and asked the same questions of them that are asked of heterosexual couples but that has yet to happen. Perhaps as same-sex marriages become legal across the country and therefore more common, more scholars will choose to examine these relationships.

Consequences of Infidelity

In a study of 160 cultures, infidelity was the most common reason for divorce (Betzig, 1989). A large study of Western countries found that between a quarter and half of all divorces cited a spouse's infidelity as the primary reason for the end of the marriage (Kelly and Conley, 1987). Of course, this does not mean that most infidelity leads to divorce and we know from very public acts of infidelity (think of President Bill Clinton) that some couples choose to stay together and work out their differences.

Some researchers suggest that whether a marriage survives infidelity has a lot to do with what caused the situation in the first place. If couples were unhappy for other reasons, and the unhappiness ultimately led to one partner cheating, it is unlikely that the couple will remain together afterwards. Couples with more relationship satisfaction may be more likely to weather the storm (Charny and Parnass, 1995; Buunk, 1987). Whether the relationship will end also depends on the infidelity relationship itself and how deeply involved the cheating partner was with another person (Charny and Parnass, 1995).

Clearly, not all relationships that involve infidelity end. In a study by Schneider *et al.* (1998), 60% of participants threatened to leave their partners after learning of infidelity but less than 25% actually left. Of course, ending the relationship is just one consequence of cheating—research finds there are many others. One or both members of the couple often report feeling rage, loss of trust, decreased self-confidence, decreased sexual confidence, damaged self-esteem, and a fear of abandonment. Other emotional issues, in particular depression, may also follow infidelity (Blow and Hartnett, 2005). A study found that women whose husbands had cheated were more likely to experience major depressive episodes (Cano and O'Leary, 2000).

We don't tell you all this as a prelude to saying "So don't cheat on your spouse." Every individual and every couple has their own set of values around infidelity and how harmful it may be to a relationship. We think it is one of the many things that couples need to talk about as they are deciding to make a long-term commitment to each other whether in marriage or another partnership. Just know that violating whatever rules and guidelines you come up with within your own relationship can cause pain and even bring about the end of the relationship itself.

Also, to put on our public health hats for a second, couples often stop using condoms when they become monogamous because they believe their risk for STIs is over. Every time someone has sex outside of their primary relationship, the risk of STIs is brought back. It is unfair, dangerous, and deceitful to let your partner continue to think he/she is at no risk when that is no longer true.

References

Allen, E.S., Atkins, D.C., Baucom, D.H., Snyder, D.K., Gordon, K.C., and Glass, S.P. (2005). Intrapersonal, interpersonal, and contextual factors in engaging in and responding to extramarital involvement. *Clinical Psychology: Science and Practice*, 12, 101–130.

Allen, E.S. and Rhoades, G.K. (2007). Not all affairs are created equal: Emotional involvement with an extradyadic partner. *Journal of Sex and Marital Therapy*, 34(1), 51–65.

Atkins, D.C., Baucom, D.H., and Jacobson, N.S. (2001). Understanding infidelity: correlates in a national random sample. *Journal of Family Psychology*, 15(4), 735.

Bancroft, J., Janssen, E., Carnes, L., Strong, D.A., Goodrich, D., and Long, J.S. (2004). Sexual activity and risk taking in young heterosexual men: The relevance of personality factors. *Journal of Sex Research*, 41, 181–192.

Bancroft, J., Janssen, E., Strong, D., Vukadinovic, Z., and Long, J.S. (2003). The relation between mood and sexuality in heterosexual men. *Archives of Sexual Behavior*, 32, 217–230.

Barta, W.D. and Kiene, S.M. (2005). Motivations for infidelity in heterosexual dating couples: The roles of gender, personality differences, and sociosexual orientation. *Journal of Social and Personal Relationships*, 22, 339–360.

Betzig, L. (1989). Causes of conjugal dissolution: A cross-cultural study. *Current Anthropology*, 30, 654–676.

Blow, A.J. and Hartnett, K. (2005). Infidelity in committed relationships II: A substantive review. *Journal of Marital and Family Therapy*, 31(2), 217–233.

Blumstein, P. and Schwartz, P. (1983). *American Couples*. William Morrow, New York.

Buller, D.J. (2005). *Adapting Minds: Evolutionary Psychology and the Persistent Quest for Human Nature*. MIT Press, Cambridge, MA.

Burdette, A.M., Ellison, C.G., Sherkat, D.E., and Gore, K.A. (2007). Are there religious variations in marital infidelity? *Journal of Family Issues*, 28, 1553–1581.

Buunk, B. (1987). Conditions that promote breakups as a consequence of extradyadic involvements. *Journal of Social and Clinical Psychology*, 5, 271–284.

Byers, S.E. (2001). Evidence for the importance of relationship satisfaction for women's sexual functioning. *Women and Therapy*, 24, 23–26.

Cano, A. and O'Leary, D. (2000). Infidelity and separations precipitate major depressive episodes and symptoms of nonspecific depression and anxiety. *Journal of Consulting and Clinical Psychology*, 68, 774–781.

Carpenter, D., Janssen, E., Graham, C.A., Vorst, H., and Wicherts, J. (2008). Women's scores on the Sexual Inhibition/Sexual Excitation Scales (SIS/SES): Gender similarities and differences. *Journal of Sex Research*, 45, 36–48.

Charny, I.W. and Parnass, S. (1995). The impact of extramarital relationships on the continuation of marriages. *Journal of Sex and Marital Therapy*, 21, 100–115

Choi, K.H., Catania, J.A., and Dolcini, M.M. (1994). Extramarital sex and HIV risk behavior among US adults: Results from the National AIDS Behavioral Survey. *American Journal of Public Health*, 84, 2003–2007.

Dennerstein, L., Lehert, P., Burger, H., and Guthrie, J. (2005). Sexuality. *American Journal of Medicine*, 118, 59S–63S.

Eagly, A.H. and Wood, W. (1999). The origins of sex differences in human behavior: Evolved dispositions versus social roles. *American Psychologist*, 54, 408–423.

Ellison, C.R. (2001). A research inquiry into some American women's sexual concerns and problems. *Women and Therapy*, 24, 147–159.

Friedman, H.S., Riggio, R.E., and Casella, D.F. (1988). Nonverbal skill, personal charisma, and initial attraction. *Personality and Social Psychology Bulletin*, 14, 203–211.

Glass, S.P. and Staeheli, J.C. (2004). *Not "Just Friends": Rebuilding Trust and Recovering Your Sanity After Infidelity*. Free Press, La Jolla, CA.

Gonzaga, G., Keltner, D., and Ward, D. (2008). Power in mixed-sex stranger interactions. *Cognition and Emotion*, 22, 1555–1568.

Hertlein, K. and Piercy, F. (2006). Internet infidelity: A critical review of the literature. *Family Journal*, 14(4), 366–371.

Kelly, E.L. and Conley, J.J. (1987). Personality and compatibility: A prospective analysis on marital stability and marital satisfaction. *Journal of Personality and Social Psychology*, 52, 27–40.

Kinsey, A.C., Pomeroy, W.B., and Martin, C.E. (1948). *Sexual Behavior in the Human Male*. W.B. Saunders, Philadelphia.

Kinsey, A.C., Pomeroy, W.B., Martin, C.E., and Gebhard, P.H. (1953). *Sexual Behavior in the Human Female*. W.B. Saunders, Philadelphia.

Kunstman, J.W. and Maner, J.K. (2011). Sexual overperception: Power, mating motives, and biases in social judgment. *Journal of Personality and Social Psychology*, 100, 282–294.

Lammers, J., Stoker, J., Jordan, J., Pollmann, M., and Stapel, D. (2011). Power increases infidelity among men and women. *Psychological Science*, 22(9), 1191–1197.

Laumann, E.O., Gagnon, J.H., Michael, R.T., and Michaels, S. (1994). *The Social Organization of Sexuality: Sexual Practices in the United States*. University of Chicago Press, Chicago.

Lerner, B. (2011). Power, physical attractiveness, and sexual overperception. Poster presented at the annual meeting of the Society for Personality and Social Psychology, San Antonio, TX.

Liu, C. (2000). A theory of marital sexual life. *Journal of Marriage and Family*, 62(2), 363–374.

Lykins, A., Janssen, E., and Graham, C. (2006). The relationship between negative mood and sexuality in heterosexual college women and men. *Journal of Sex Research*, 43, 136–143.

Mark, K.P., Janssen, E., and Milhausen, R.R. (2011). Infidelity in heterosexual couples: Demographic, interpersonal, and personality-related predictors of extradyadic sex. *Archives of Sexual Behavior*, 40(5), 971–982.

Mattingly, B.A., Clark, E.M., Weidler, D.J., Bullock, M., Hackathorn, J., and Blankmeyer, K. (2011). Sociosexual orientation, commitment, and infidelity: A mediation analysis. *Journal of Social Psychology*, 151(3), 222–226.

McCabe, M.P. and Cobain, M.J. (1998). The impact of individual and relationship factors on sexual dysfunction among males and females. *Sexual and Marital Therapy*, 13, 131–143.

Neuman, M.G. (2009). *The Truth About Cheating: Why Men Stray and What You Can Do to Prevent It*. Wiley, New York.

Nicholls, L. (2008). Putting The New View classification scheme to an empirical test. *Feminism and Psychology*, 18, 515–526.

Pittman, F. (1990). *Private Lies: Infidelity and the Betrayal of Intimacy*. W.W. Norton & Co., New York.

Preveti, D. and Amato, P.R. (2004). Is infidelity a cause or consequence of poor marital quality? *Journal of Social and Personal Relationships*, 21, 217–230.

Schneider, J.P., Corley, M.D., and Irons, R.K. (1998). Surviving disclosure of infidelity: Results of an international survey of 164 recovering sex addicts and partners. *Sexual Addiction and Compulsivity: The Journal of Treatment and Prevention*, 5(3), 189–217.

Smith, T.W. (1994). Attitudes toward sexual permissiveness: Trends, correlates, and behavioral connections. In Rossi, A.S. (ed.) *Sexuality Across the Life Course*. University of Chicago Press, Chicago, pp. 63–97.

Smuts, B. (1992). Male aggression against women: An evolutionary perspective. *Human Nature*, 3, 1–44.

Spanier, G.B. and Margolis, R.L. (1983). Marital separation and extramarital sexual behavior. *Journal of Sex Research*, 19, 23–48.

Spring, J.A. and Spring, M. (1997). *After the Affair: Healing the Pain and Rebuilding Trust When a Partner Has Been Unfaithful*. Harper, New York.

Treas, J. and Giesen, D. (2000). Sexual infidelity among married and cohabiting Americans. *Journal of Marriage and Family*, 62, 48–60.

Turchik, J.A. and Garske, J.P. (2009). Measurement of sexual risk taking among college students. *Archives of Sexual Behavior*, 38, 936–948.

Whitty, M.T. (2003). Pushing the wrong buttons: Men's and women's attitudes toward online and offline infidelity. *CyberPsychology and Behavior*, 6, 569–579.

Whitty, M.T. (2004). Cyber-flirting: An examination of men's and women's flirting behaviour both offline and on the Internet. *Behaviour Change*, 21(2), 115–126.

Whitty, M.T. (2005). The realness of cybercheating: Men's and women's representations of unfaithful Internet relationships. *Social Science Computer Review*, 23(1), 57–67.

Wiederman, M.W. (1997). Extramarital sex: Prevalence and correlates in a national survey. *Journal of Sex Research*, 34, 167–174.

Wilkey, B. (2011). Power's effect on motivating romantic approach. Paper presented at the Close Relationships preconference at the annual meeting of the Society for Personality and Social Psychology, San Antonio, TX.

Wiggins, J.D. and Lederer, D.A. (1984). Differential antecedents of infidelity in marriage. *American Mental Health Counselors Association Journal*, 6, 152–161.

Wood, W. and Eagly, A.H. (2007). Social structural origins of sex differences in human mating. In Gangestad, S.W. and Simpson, J.A. (eds) *Evolution of the Mind: Fundamental Questions and Controversies*. Guilford Press, New York, NY, pp. 383–390.

World Values Survey Association (2000). World Values Survey official data file 2000, v.20090914. http://www.worldvaluessurvey.org/wvs/articles/folder_published/survey_2000 (accessed August 5, 2014).

Worth, H., Reid, A., and McMillan, K. (2002). Somewhere over the rainbow: Love, trust and monogamy in gay relationships. *Journal of Sociology*, 38(3), 237–253.

Wysocki, D.K. and Childers, C.D. (2011). "Let my fingers do the talking": Sexting and infidelity in cyberspace. *Sexuality and Culture*, 15(3), 217–239.

Most Couples have Matched Sexual Appetites

When you first fall in love (or lust) there is so much hormonal action going on that many couples just can't keep their hands off each other. It may seem like you are a matched sexual set. Most couples in their twenties start out having sex about three times a week (Herbenick *et al.*, 2010) and that is happily sustained the first year they are together, whether that first year is cohabitation or marriage (Call *et al.*, 1995). But once that "honeymoon" period is over, that automatic desire for sex every time one person sees the other usually wanes. Over time, as a more natural set of circumstances reasserts itself, individuals' sex drives modifies a little or a lot.

Waning Desire

The attenuation of desire for sex as a relationship moves on is attributed to a wide variety of issues including habituation, fatigue, depression, work, children, personal health, weight gain, and relationship issues. It may also be a slide toward each person's more natural desire level once the relationship is no longer novel (Call *et al.*, 1995).

Indeed, for some couples experts conclude that nothing is wrong and in fact maybe less sex happens because sexual techniques have become more satisfying or there is more emotional comfort and security in the relationship, which is tied to a less hungry libido. This latter theory posits that more comfort and less anxiety in a relationship may make people happier but not sexier. The thought is that much of the motor that drives people to reconnect sexually is insecurity; remove the insecurity and some of the sexual intensity will be removed as well (Liu, 2003; Perel, 2006; Schwartz, 1994).

Sex can, however, be seen as a barometer of how the relationship is going. Many partners lose interest in sex because they are disappointed in the relationship. A boring, conflict ridden, or distant relationship is rarely a turn on for either partner, but women's sexual interest seems to be even more affected by their feelings about the relationship than their male partner's might be (Hyde and Delamater, 2011).

Gender Differences

A lot of issues around desire and amount of sex focus on differences between men and women. The assumption is that men want a lot of sex and women not so much. Though levels of desire differ for all individuals and couples, there is some truth to this gender generalization.

Some researchers believe that gaps in desire are biologically based. One theory is that women have less intense desire because they have an evolutionary disposition to be more choosey about sex in order to avoid becoming pregnant by someone who would make an inferior long-term partner and father (Symonds, 1979, Buss, 1994). Another idea focuses on the hormones that are the driving force of sexual interest and argues that differences between testosterone and estrogen dictate differences in sexual arousal (Blum, 1997). (See Myth # 5 for more on testosterone.) On the other hand, there are feminists and other writers who believe that the lower sexual interest of many women comes not from biology or "issues" in the relationship, but from gender inequality, which corrodes the kind of desire that might otherwise surface (Hallway, 1993).

Others agree that that differences in desire can be based more on the gender roles we adopt rather than anything in our genetic make-up or relationship. According to Laurie Mintz, author of *A Tired Woman's Guide to Passionate Sex*, a full third of women lose some of their interest in sex over time (2009). There are many reasons that the flame is lower than it burned early on. Some may be the result of physiological changes. For example, it is well established that hormonal changes associated with childbirth and breastfeeding may complicate sexual desire which is already affected by the "wear and tear" of childbirth and taking care of infants and young children. Fewer men are primary child care providers but, whether a partner is a man or a woman, the person home with young kids is often exhausted and sex, even though generally desired, can be victim to fatigue.

Gagnon and Simon (2005) have written about the sexual "scripts" that men and women have, culturally approved ways of acting that guide how people treat each other. In this case, the cultural script for sexual interactions in most parts of America is that men initiate sex and women decide whether or not it will happen by saying yes or no.

Whatever the reason for these differences, research has shown that there are gender differences in the pattern of initiation of sex. For the most part men initiate sex and women either accept or refuse the offer. In one study, only about 16% of the women were the primary initiators of a desire for sexual activity. Given that initiation is not a woman's primary role or behavior in many households, lack of initiation may be seen as natural, and as evidence of a lower sexual need, even when it is actually a comment on where the relationship is at the moment. Only about a third of couples equally trade initiating sex and these couples who initiate about equally are generally more interested in sex and have more of it (Blumstein and Schwartz, 1983). Men are more likely to be the person who wants less sex when he has some kind of erectile dysfunction or an embarrassing sexual issue such as rapid ejaculation (Lewis et al., 2004; Bancroft et al., 2009; Hyde and DeLamater, 2011). The more common pattern, however, is one in which the complaining partner is the man in a heterosexual couple, with women less bothered by having less sex (Basson, 2006, Maurice, 2007).

The Blumstein and Schwartz study is particularly interesting here because it compared four kinds of couples: married, living together, gay males, and lesbians, and found that lesbians initiated less, overall, than other kinds of couples. Sexual initiation, at least in the early 1980s when this study was carried out, may not be a role that women, be they heterosexual or homosexual, adopt as much as men do. However, the authors thought that the lack of female initiation might be less an outcome of lower sexual interest than a consequence of having higher standards for the emotional context needed to pave the way for having sex (Blumstein and Schwartz, 1983).

Desire Gap

Dwindling desire for sex is not a problem in and of itself. Some couples settle into a rhythm where sex is less frequent but both members are satisfied with its quality and quantity. Problems start when one partner becomes less interested in sex than the other.

This can become a real issue in the relationship especially if there is no communication about it. For example, if a couple gets into a pattern in which they usually have sex at a specific time (say Sunday morning or Saturday night) and then one partner doesn't initiate, or does and the other partner refuses, this may have more symbolic meaning to each of them than one missed sex act might seem to connote. And, once one partner wants less sex than the other one, desire may be even further affected by unwanted approaches (Rutter and Schwartz, 2012). According to McCarthy and McCarthy, authors of *Rekindling Desire*, "If every touch is a demand for intercourse, the pressure is up and the pleasure is down" (2003, p. 160). Thus, what may have started as a difference in sexual appetite becomes a relationship issue, which in turn makes sex less desirable (for one or both parties) and less likely to happen often.

If refusal, or lack of initiation, becomes the norm, avoidance mechanisms can reduce the amount of sex in the relationship and increase one or both person's unhappiness with the situation and perhaps the relationship. The old joke "not tonight honey I have a headache" comes from real excuses (as well as realities) that stop sex from happening (Rutter and Schwartz, 2012).

Sex therapists often write that the most common presenting problem they get is a large difference in sexual desire (Resnik, 2012; McCarthy and McCarthy, 2003). David Schnarch, a well-respected sex therapist, talks about people having different "stimulus thresholds" caused by genetics, personal history, and relationship histories (Schnarch, 1991). This "threshold" is essentially what it takes for him/her to get aroused and that may change over a lifetime due to aging, psychological differences, and other circumstances. Gender role differences in how men and women are expected to behave may also affect the threshold. Schnarch believes, however, that therapy can change desire patterns and bring partners' sexual energy to a place that will not starve the higher interest person, nor objectify or harass the lower interest partner (Schnarch, 1997, 2001).

Couples for whom sex has become so infrequent as to be catastrophic to the relationship may have a more serious problem. Sex researchers and clinicians have coined a word to describe someone who doesn't want to have sex at all or wants it so rarely that it hardly counts—hypoactive sexual desire (Basson, 2006). And they differentiate between people who have never liked sex and those who have "acquired hypoactive sexual desire disorder" which may have occurred because of abuse, a bad relationship, or other emotional and perhaps behavioral circumstances (Leiblum, 2007). Of course, this is quite different than just having a discrepancy of desire, but a big desire gap between lovers or spouses can sometimes get diagnosed as a hypoactive condition (Zilbergeld and Ellison, 1980).

Whatever the etiology, sexual desire is hardly predictable in longer relationships. Perhaps more forecasting about desire is possible if people do not make long-term commitments while they are still "in heat" as part of the infatuation phase of love. Waiting longer may help couples determine if their sexual appetites in their normal state are well matched. Once the commitment has been made, it is important to understand that desire will probably lessen for one or both partners over time. If it is no longer matched, both partners—both the person who wants more and the person who wants less—will have to find a way to come to a fair and loving compromise about how often they'll have sex.

References

Bancroft, J., Graham, C., Jannsen, E., and Saunders, S. (2009). The dual control model: Current status and future directions. *Journal of Sex Research*, 46, 221–241.
Basson, R. (2006). Sexual desire and arousal disorders in women. *New England Journal of Medicine*, 354, 1497–1506.
Blum, D. (1997). *Sex on the Brain*. Penguin, New York, NY.

Blumstein, P. and Schwartz, P. (1983). *American Couples: Money, Work and Sex*. William Morrow, New York, NY.

Buss, D. (1994). *The Evolution of Desire: Strategies of Human Mating*. Basic Books, New York, NY.

Call, V., Sprecher, S., and Schwartz, P. (1995). The incidence and frequency of sex in a national sample. *Journal of Marriage and the Family*, 57, 639–652.

Gagnon, J.H. and Simon, W. (2005). *Sexual Conduct: The Social Sources of Human Sexuality*. Transaction Publishers.

Hallway, W. (1993) Heterosexual sex: power and desire for the other. In Fox, B. (ed.) *Family Patterns in Gender Relations*. Oxford University Press, Oxford.

Herbenick, D., Reece, M., Schick, V., Sanders, S.A., Dodge, B., and Fortenberry, J.D. (2010). Sexual behavior in the United States: Results from a national probability sample of men and women ages 14–94. *Journal of Sexual Medicine*, 7(s5), 255–265.

Hyde, J. and DeLamater, J. (2011). *Understanding Human Sexuality*. McGraw Hill, New York, NY.

Leiblum, S. (ed.) (2007). *Principles and Practices of Sex Therapy*, 4th edn. Guildford, New York, NY.

Lewis, R.W., Fugl-Meyer, K.S., Bosch, R., Fugl-Meyer, A.R., Laumann, E.O., Lizza, E., *et al.* (2004). Epidemiology/risk factors of sexual dysfunction. *Journal of Sexual Medicine*, 1(1), 35–39.

Liu, C. (2003). Does quality of marital sex decline with duration? *Archives of Sexual Behavior*, 32, 55–60.

Maurice, W. (2007). Sexual desire disorders in men. In Leiblum, S. (ed.) *Principles and Practice of Sex Therapy*, 4th edn. Guildford Press, New York, NY, pp. 181–211.

McCarthy, B. and McCarthy, E. (2003). *Rekindling Desire*. Brunner-Routledge.

Mintz, L. (2009). *The Tired Women's Guide to Passionate Sex*. Adams Media, Avon, MA.

Perel, E. (2006). *Mating in Captivity*. Harper Collins, New York, NY.

Resnick, S. (2012). *The Heart of Desire*. John Wiley, Hoboken, NJ.

Rutter, V. and Schwartz, P. (2012). *The Gender of Sexuality*. Rowland and Littlefield, Lanham, MD.

Schnarch, D. (1991). *Constructing the Sexual Crucible*. Norton, New York, NY.

Schnarch, D. (1997). *Passionate Marriage*. Norton, New York, NY.

Schnarch, D. (2001). *Resurrecting Sex*. Harper Collins, New York, NY.

Schwartz, P. (1994). *Love Between Equals*. Free Press, New York, NY.

Symonds, D. (1979). *The Evolution of Human Sexuality*. Oxford University Press, New York, NY.

Zilbergeld, B. and Ellison, C. (1980). Desire discrepancies and sexual arousal problems in sex therapy. In Leiblum, S. and Pervin, L.A. (eds) *Principles and Practices of Sex Therapy*. Guilford, New York, NY, pp. 65–104.

8 WHEN SEX IS UNHEALTHY

Sex and Trouble

Jealousy Is Romantic

Sexual jealousy, called "mate guarding" by the sociobiologists, happens when someone we love shows attention to another potential suitor or mate. It can make us feel angry and insecure with reactions like "Get away from my girl" or "If she's interested in him, I can't compete" (Daly *et al.*, 1982). For some people, jealousy only comes out in certain situations or with certain people (your girlfriend's cute co-worker or your boyfriend's ex). And some researchers believe that a certain amount of jealousy over other suitors may be reasonable and useful in not taking a relationship for granted (Barelds and Barelds-Dijkstra, 2007). Unfortunately, for others there is an almost constant and unreasonable state of jealousy. Even when there is no clear and present threat, the idea of such a threat and insecurity about preventing it lurks (Buss, 2000).

Jealous people have many ways of protecting someone they love or lust for from competitors or "poachers," some of which can be destructive to the relationship or to their partner's dignity, privacy, and safety. They can monopolize their partner's time, they can try to elicit sympathy by acting hurt, or they can threaten either their mate, a suitor, or both.

Some women and men are flattered at these reactions. At least at first. But they shouldn't be. These behaviors come from a dark place of insecurity and anger, and they can result in violence.

50 Great Myths of Human Sexuality, First Edition. Pepper Schwartz and Martha Kempner.
© 2015 John Wiley & Sons, Inc. Published 2015 by John Wiley & Sons, Inc.

Origins of Sexual Jealousy

Socio-biologists think of jealousy as one of the most powerful emotions humans can feel and argue that the sexes will have different reactions to the threat of infidelity or abandonment based on different "reproductive strategies" (Holden *et al.*, 2014). Female sexual infidelity is dangerous from a man's evolutionary point of view because it can cast doubt as to whether offspring are really his own. Men, therefore, get most threatened and most jealous at the thought of women having sex with someone else. On the flip side, a woman never doubts that a biological child is hers but may doubt that its father will stick around and take care of both her and the child. This means that for women, a mate's one night stand may be less threatening than a deep but sexless friendship with another woman (Buss, 2000).

A famous study by socio-biologists presented a large group of undergraduates with two scenarios: one where their partner had sex with someone else and one where their partner became emotionally involved with someone else. True to the theory, 83% of the women found the emotional infidelity more upsetting than the sexual infidelity. In contrast, 60% of the men felt more threatened by sexual infidelity (Buss *et al.*, 1992). Additional research has also suggested that men and women react differently to varying kinds of betrayal.

That said, not all researchers believe that the roots of jealousy are evolutionary or biological. Some believe it's about the culture in which we are raised and what we have come to expect in relationships. Though the researchers in the above study were trying to prove a biological root of this reaction, it could well be the case that women have been taught to treasure emotional intimacy.

In an attempt to tease out the aspects of nature and nurture, anthropologists and other researchers have looked at different societies. For the most part they have found similar gendered responses at least in Western countries: Brazil (de Souza *et al.*, 2006); England (de Souza *et al.*, 2006); Norway (Kennair *et al.*, 2011); Germany, the Netherlands, Korea, and Japan (Buunk *et al.*, 1996). It is interesting, however, that in a Dutch study looking at how men and women reacted to scenarios of on and offline infidelity, women were more jealous than men about infidelity that only took place online, but both men and women in gay and lesbian relationships showed less intense jealousy than heterosexuals displayed (Dijkstra *et al.*, 2013, p. 328).

Individual Origins of Jealousy

Regardless of the origins of jealousy for the species, it seems clear that on an individual level intense jealousy comes from a place of low self-esteem and insecurity (Buunk 1982; DeSteno *et al.*, 2006; White, 1981; Murray *et al.*, 2003; Mullen and Martin, 1994, p. 35). For example, a study found that women who were always comparing their looks to other women's looks were more likely not only to be jealous, but also to be more aggressive toward their partners (Arnocky *et al.*, 2012, p. 290). Another study found that a woman who felt her partner was better looking than she was tended to be more anxious and jealous and more likely to suspect infidelity (Swami *et al.*, 2012, p. 798).

It is also not surprising that a person who does not have a job, does not have many friends, or perceives that he/she has few alternatives is more likely to be jealous (Berscheid and Fei, 1977; Buunk 1982). In fact, the more dependent a person feels, the more likely he/she is to be intensely jealous (White, 1981). In contrast, people who have a secure sense of self are more likely to use their partner as a source of strength rather than as a source of vulnerability and are therefore less likely to display jealousy (Simpson *et al.*, 1992; Skowron and Dendy, 2004; Karakurt, 2012).

Bottom Line: It Can Be Dangerous

Jealousy is a form of protecting your emotional investment in another person. When jealousy gets out of control, however, it has the potential for extreme consequences. There are many studies on spousal violence, for example, that trace everything from beatings to homicide back to intense jealousy (Buss and Duntley, 2011). Unhappily, some women are at great risk when they awaken a partner's jealousy either by actually cheating on him, being perceived as having cheated on him, or trying to end the relationship. The injury to an already weak ego is more than some men can bear (Holden *et al.*, 2014). Though women have a lower propensity for violence in general, this can happen with them as well if they get intensely jealous.

People who become paranoid may try to isolate their partner from his/her friends, family, or anyone they think might not be "on their side." Both male and female partners might become obsessive detectives, going through their partner's pockets, cell phones, and computers or even following their partner in an attempt to prove that he/she is not cheating (or possibly is). This kind of surveillance has a high chance of ruining the relationship unless the anxious partner can be reassured and cease spying on the other person (Elphinston *et al.*, 2013).

We believe that everyone should be on the lookout for warning signs of jealousy that may become extreme. While it may be cute that your girlfriend wants to spend all of her time with you in the beginning of a relationship, it becomes less cute when outside friendships fade. A boyfriend who wants to know exactly where you are every minute may seem caring at first but there may be something else going on. These forms of jealousy can become extreme and lead to controlling behavior and ultimately violence. Don't take these behaviors as a form of flattery or a sign of love—talk about them as soon as they happen, try to assess what's really going on, and set your own boundaries for jealousy. A partner who can't respect those boundaries and can't help but be jealous all the time might not be the right partner.

References

Arnocky, S., Sunderani, S., Miller, J.L., and Vaillancourt, T. (2012). Jealousy mediates the relationship between attractiveness comparison and females' indirect aggression. *Personal Relationships*, 19, 290–303.

Barelds, D.P.H. and Barelds-Dijkstra, P. (2007). Relations between different types of jealousy and self and partner perceptions of relationship quality. *Clinical Psychology and Psychotherapy*, 14, 3.

Berscheid, E. and Fei, J. (1977). Romantic love and sexual jealousy. In Clanton, G. and Smith, L. (eds) *Jealousy*. Prentice Hall, Englewood Cliff, NJ, pp. 101–109.

Buss, D.M. (2000). *The Dangerous Passion: Why Jealousy is as Necessary as Love and Sex*. Simon & Schuster, New York, NY.

Buss, D.M., Larsen, R.J., Westen, D., and Semmelroth, J. (1992). Sex differences in jealousy: Evolution, physiology, and psychology. *Psychological Science*, 3(4), 251–255.

Buss, D.M. and Duntley, J.D. (2011). The evolution of intimate partner violence. *Aggression and Violent Behavior*, 16, 411–419.

Buunk, B. (1982). Strategies of jealousy: Styles of coping with extramarital involvement of the spouse. *Family Relations*, 31, 13–18.

Buunk, A.P., Angleitner, A., Oubaid, V., and Buss, D.M. (1996). Sex differences in jealousy in evolutionary and cultural perspective: Tests from the Netherlands, Germany, and the United States. *Psychological Science*, 7, 359–363.

Daly, M., Wilson, M., and Weghorst, S.J. (1982). Male sexual jealousy. *Ethology and Sociobiology*, 3, 11–27.

de Souza, A.A., Verderane, M.P., Taira, J.T., and Otta, E. (2006). Emotional and sexual jealousy as a function of sex and sexual orientation in a Brazilian sample. *Psychological Reports*, 98, 529–535.

DeSteno, D., Valdesolo, P., and Bartlett, M. (2006). Jealousy and the threatened self: Getting to the heart of the green-eyed monster. *Journal of Personality and Social Psychology*, 91, 626–641.

Dijkstra, P., Barelds, D.P., and Groothof, H.A. (January 01, 2013). Jealousy in response to online and offline infidelity: the role of sex and sexual orientation. *Scandinavian Journal of Psychology*, 54(4), 328–336.

Elphinston, R.A., Feeney, J.A., Noller, P., Connor, J.P., and Fitzgerald, J. (2013). Romantic jealousy and relationship satisfaction: The costs of rumination. *Western Journal of Communication*, 77(3), 293–304.

Holden, C.J., Shackelford, T., Ziegler-Hill, V., Miner, E.J., Kaighobadi, F., Starratt, V.G., *et al.* (2014). Husband's esteem predicts his mate retention tactics. *Evolutionary Psychology*, 12(3), 655–672.

Karakurt, G. (2012). The interplay between self esteem, feeling of inadequacy, dependency, and romantic jealousy as a function of attachment processes among Turkish college students. *Contemporary Family Therapy*, 34(3), 334–345.

Kennair, L.E.O., Nordeide, J., Andreassen, S., Strønen, J., and Pallesen, S. (2011). Sex differences in jealousy: A study from Norway. *Nordic Psychology*, 63, 20.

Mullen, P.E. and Martin, J. (1994). Jealousy: a community study. *British Journal of Psychiatry*, 164(1), 35–43.

Murray, S., Griffin, D., Rose, P., and Bellavia, G. (2003). Calibrating the sociometer: The relational contingencies of self-esteem. *Journal of Personality and Social Psychology*, 85, 63–84.

Simpson, J., Rholes, W., and Nelligan, J. (1992). Support seeking and support giving within couples in an anxiety-provoking situation: The role of attachment styles. *Journal of Personality and Social Psychology*, 62, 434–446.

Skowron, E.A. and Dendy, A.K. (2004). Differentiation of self and attachment in adulthood: Relational correlates of effortful control. *Contemporary Family Therapy*, 26, 337–357.

Swami, V., Inamdar, S., Stieger, S., Nader, I.W., Pietschnig, J., Tran, U.S., and Voracek, M. (2012). A dark side of positive illusions? Associations between the love-is-blind bias and the experience of jealousy. *Personality and Individual Differences*, 53(6), 796–800.

White, G.L. (1981). A model of romantic jealousy. *Motivation and Emotion*, 5(4), 295–310.

Myth #39

Alcohol Makes Sex Better

Alcohol is clearly thought of as an aphrodisiac or at least as a social lubricant that makes sex more likely—we challenge you to find a scene of adults dating in a movie or on television that doesn't include a glass of wine or bottle of beer. But does alcohol really make sex better? On the one hand alcohol is a drug that affects our central nervous system which will then affect our sexual functioning (and not necessarily positively). At the same time, however, alcohol has long had a social role in our interactions, and our own thoughts about it may also change how we act and even how we function sexually. When it comes to booze, it is difficult if not impossible to separate the physical from the psychological and the carnal from the cultural.

This entry looks at some of the science on how alcohol affects sexual response and behavior from both a pharmacological and a psychological perspective and then explores the very real problem of alcohol and sexual assault.

Alcohol Is a Drug

We tend not to think of alcohol as a drug because it is so readily available, but in terms of what it does to our bodies it can absolutely be described that way. Alcohol depresses the central nervous system which slows brain function, circulation, and respiration. Specifically, it increases the levels of a neurotransmitter (the chemicals in the brain that carry messages) known as gamma-aminobutyric acid (GABA) which is responsible for the regulation of muscle tone. GABA inhibits the transmission of impulses so as GABA levels rise the flow of information from the brain to the spinal cord decreases and we get slower (Peugh and Belenko, 2001). In theory, this slowdown should have an impact on sexual function—on both the ability to get aroused and to achieve orgasm. Research on this, however, has been mixed and results are different for men and women.

Most research suggests that in small doses alcohol has pretty much no effect on men. Peugh and Belenko's review points to a number of laboratory studies in which some men were given a small amount of alcohol and some were given no alcohol. The men then watched erotic movies and their arousal was measured both by asking them how turned on they were and by measuring their erections. The studies found no decrease in arousal and possibly a slight increase among the men who drank alcohol (Peugh and Belenko, 2001; Rubin and Henson, 1976). When men consumed large amounts of alcohol, however, they experienced "substantial reductions in arousal and impaired ability to ejaculate" (Peugh and Belenko, 2001). Another review of the available research on alcohol and sexual functioning by George and Stoner (2000) explained the results of "five seminal experiments" by saying this: "The findings revealed that, except at very low dosages, alcohol suppressed penile tumescence and increased male orgasm latency." To put that in more everyday language—drinking alcohol meant that men got less hard and took longer to climax.

The research on women is a little different. Women in research studies who were given alcohol said they were more aroused when compared with those in control groups who didn't drink. However, when their arousal was measured with a tampon-shaped probe that is inserted into the vagina to gauge blood flow, the results showed that the women who were given alcohol were actually less physically aroused than those who didn't drink (Peugh and Belenko, 2001). These results prove just how hard it is to separate the physical from the psychological for either alcohol or sexual arousal and certainly for both. Peugh and Belenko offer the following possibilities for this discrepancy between what women say and what the tools detect. First, the tools could be inaccurate, it is more difficult to measure arousal in woman than men. The other possibilities that they suggest are that women are interpreting "general alcohol-induced body changes as sexual arousal," that their answers are the "results of learned behavior response," or that answers show "the influence of expectancies of the effects of alcohol" (2001, p. 9).

Still, George and Stoner (2009) explain that by the end of the 1970s and certainly the 1980s it was generally accepted that alcohol suppressed genital arousal and most researchers had stopped pursuing this topic and turned their attention to the discrepancies between subjective reports from men and women and the objective observations of scientists in an attempt to untangle the psychological and social aspects of the impact that alcohol has on how we behave sexually. The emerging AIDS epidemic in the 1980s also meant increased concern and attention to risky sexually behavior.

Alcohol as a Social Lubricant: The Theories

There are a number of theories about how the physical and social play off each other to change our behavior and why this one drug affects different individuals in such different ways. We probably all know some people who become effusive when drunk, telling their friends how much they love them, others who become weepy and maudlin, and maybe even some who become belligerent and more likely to start a fight.

Alcohol Myopia Theory (AMT) suggests that what all this has in common is a sense of nearsightedness that comes with being drunk. Alcohol affects a person's cognitive ability to process information and read social cues. In their groundbreaking article on the topic, Steele and Josephs (1990) explain alcohol myopia this way: "a state of shortsightedness in which superficially understood, immediate aspects of experience have a disproportionate influence on behavior and emotion, a state in which we can see the tree, albeit more dimly, but miss the forest altogether" (p. 923). You could say that these researchers turned beer goggles into a legitimate academic theory.

When faced with a decision about taking a risk (maybe a social one—to go talk to that cute girl—or a sexual one—to have intercourse without a condom), an individual needs to process two kinds of cues. Impelling cues are ones that appeal to a person's most immediate desires—the girl is cute and the sex will feel really good. Inhibiting cues are basically the voice in the back of our heads that makes us think about the next steps—"She's in my sociology class and if she says no I will still have to see her twice a week" or "I could get an STD or pregnant." These are the cues that help us measure our impulses and keep us in line with the social customs and values of our communities. These are also the cues that are harder to see when drunk.

AMT relies on the idea that there are often conflicts between these two sets of cues—impelling cues telling you to do something that inhibiting cues suggest is a bad idea. If there's no conflict a person would likely act the same way drunk as they do sober. But if there is conflict, the myopia caused by alcohol may kick in, block the inhibiting cues, and allow for a person to act in a way they normally would not. Their behavior may be seen as more extreme by either their sober selves or their friends simply because it's not like them (Griffin et al., 2010).

Steele and Josephs note another aspect of myopia; a heightened or elevated view of oneself. As they put it: "Alcohol is a reliable means of self-inflation; during intoxication one gets closer to the self of one's dreams" (1990, p. 932). This is most applicable to people who have conflict about themselves and their self-worth. In these people, "intoxication apparently leaves enough capacity to experience the need for self-regard but not enough to access the reasons for humility" (Steele and Josephs, 1990, p. 932).

A number of studies have tested AMT and have found that it was able to predict the behavior of individuals as they became intoxicated. For example, Monahan and Lannutti (2000) recruited 50 college women and evaluated their self-esteem. They then had a man flirt with each woman as she consumed alcohol. They predicted that women with low self-esteem would be more inhibited under normal conditions and, therefore, more affected by alcohol and AMT. Their results confirmed these suspicions. Women with lower self-esteem were less anxious and more likely to disclose personal information (an important part of flirting) when they were drunk than when they were sober. In contrast, women with high self-esteem were not particularly affected by alcohol. Similarly, when women in another study were given stories about an encounter with a man, the women who consumed alcohol (or thought they had because they had been given a placebo drink and told it contained alcohol) were more likely to rate the male in the story positively, more likely to perceive a positive outcome to the story, and more likely to say they would act on sexually aggressive suggestions than those who were not drinking (Testa et al., 2000).

Another prevailing theory of how alcohol consumption changes our behavior—including sexual behavior—focuses less on what alcohol actually does to our bodies and brains and more on what we expect alcohol to do to our bodies and brains. Alcohol Expectancy Theory suggests that we have been socialized to believe that drunk people behave in particular ways and as a result we act in those ways when we get drunk. Our behavior when drunk is as much a self-fulfilling prophecy as anything else. When it comes to sex, television and movies have certainly told us that people (women especially) are less inhibited when they're drunk, more likely to flirt, and more likely to follow through.

Laboratory studies have supported this theory. One study, for example, found that men who were strong believers in the idea that alcohol stimulates sex reported more sexual arousal after consuming a placebo drink than men who were also given the placebo but didn't really believe that alcohol stimulates sex (George *et al.*, 2000). There is less information available about women and, according to George and Stoner (2001), the few reported studies have produced confusing results. Part of the problem, as mentioned earlier, is that women tend to say they are more aroused if they are intoxicated but their vaginal response indicates otherwise.

Alcohol Expectancy Theory also suggests that some people may be falling back on alcohol after-the-fact as an excuse for behavior that goes against social norms. This idea of "deviance-disavowal"—that people who believe alcohol is an acceptable excuse for unacceptable behaviors may behave in unacceptable ways while drunk—has also been supported by experimental studies with men (George and Stoner, 2001). In real life, this idea is supported every time we hear someone say "I can't believe I did that but I was so wasted." And, we've heard that more times than we care to recall.

Alcohol and Sex in Real Life

A number of studies have gone on to look at how these two theories play out in real life. Not surprisingly, researchers often focus their efforts on college students—a group that has been known to drink and have sex. Walk across any college quad on a weekend night and it is pretty clear that alcohol and sex go together though it is hard to find statistics on just how frequently. We do know from the Youth Risk Behavior Surveillance (YRBS) that 22% of sexually active high school students used alcohol or drugs before the last time they had sex (Eaton *et al.*, 2012). The numbers are likely similar if not higher once these teens reach college where alcohol is often more readily available.

One of the most salient questions for educators and researchers is whether young people who are having sex under the influence are putting themselves at increased risk of sexually transmitted infections and pregnancy. The results are mixed. In their review of studies based on AMT, Griffin *et al.* (2010, p. 528) note that "On the whole, studies have identified weak causal links between alcohol use and reduction of protective sexual behaviors; in many cases no association was found." Some studies have found that people who use condoms when they are sober also use them when they aren't. Other studies have found that there are differences based on partner type. A study of women, for example, found that drinking more increased the likelihood of sex occurring with either a long-term or a casual partner but only made unprotected sex more likely with a casual partner. In fact, there was a negative association between drinking and unprotected sex with a steady partner (Kiene *et al.*, 2009).

A more recent study actually found that drinking in and of itself did not affect condom use. When researchers looked only at the relationship between alcohol and condoms, they found that events involving alcohol were more likely to involve condoms. Condoms were used in 70% of events involving drinking compared with 59% of events that did not involve alcohol. The researchers noted: "Even in situations involving heavy drinking (four or more drinks), during which we might expect disinhibition to lead to decreases in safe-sex behavior, we found no evidence of decreased condom use across this sample of women" (Walsh *et al.*, 2013, p. 10). This does not mean, however, that the tipsier a girl gets the more likely she is to reach for a rubber. The researchers explain that the condoms were more likely in casual relationships (which makes sense as people in committed relationships often switch to other methods like the pill) and alcohol was also more likely in casual relationships. Overall, the researchers concluded that partner type was more likely to influence condom use than alcohol.

The other issue that impacts condoms use seems to be expectations. Women who believed alcohol would increase sexual risk taking behaved that way when drunk. Though only 13% of women in Walsh *et al.*'s (2013) sample strongly believed that alcohol would increase sexual risk taking, the ones who did were less likely to use condoms at events involving alcohol.

Clearly, we need to address the assumption that drunk people will take risks because the assumption itself is a large part of the problem. One of the activities we sometimes do with our students attempts to challenge the conventions by presenting the following scenario: "Last weekend, I was at this party and met this really cute guy/girl. We started talking and one thing led to another and..." Half the students are told that they're drunk at the time and the other half are told they were sober, they have to finish their story accordingly. Not surprisingly, people are more likely to say the night ended with sex if they thought they were drunk. Of course, we like to throw in at least one story that ends in mind-blowing sober sex just to mix it up a little bit.

It's not clear which aspect of expectancy is most influential—that drunk behavior is a self-fulfilling prophecy or that alcohol has become the best excuse for cutting loose and experimenting. We are not suggesting that college students shouldn't drink. We are not saying that college students shouldn't have sex. We are not even saying that college students shouldn't do both at the same time (or perhaps one after the other to prevent spilling beer all over the sheets; it will smell awful later). Instead, what we're hoping for is that college students would feel comfortable enough with their sexuality that they don't need to rely on alcohol to facilitate sex. That they could cut loose and experiment (safely of course) while sober.

We also worry that this is a much bigger issue for young women who get so many conflicting messages about sex from our society. They are supposed to be sexy but not want sex. Look willing but not really be willing. If they don't have sex they are prudes (which is bad) but if they have too much sex (measured on some arbitrary, unknown, and constantly changing scale) they are sluts, which is even worse. It does not surprise us, therefore, that women fall back on alcohol as both a social lubricant and an after-the-fact excuse. We are by no means blaming young women for this, but we do wish for the day when girls are given societal permission to want as much sex as any man and enjoy it as much as well. We can't help but wonder if that day comes, alcohol may become less necessary and less appealing.

References

Eaton, D.K., Kann, L., Kinchen, S., Shanklin, S., Flint, K.H., Hawkins, J., *et al.* (2012). Youth risk behavior surveillance: United States, 2011. *Morbidity and Mortality Weekly Report Surveillance Summaries*, 61(4), 1–162.

George, W.H. and Stoner, S.A. (2000). Understanding acute alcohol effects on sexual behavior. *Annual Review of Sex Research*, 11(1), 92–124.

George, W.H., Stoner, S.A., Norris, J., Lopez, P.A., and Lehman, G.L. (2000). Alcohol expectancies and sexuality: A self-fulfilling prophecy analysis of dyadic perceptions and behavior. *Journal of Studies on Alcohol and Drugs*, 61(1), 168.

Griffin, J.A., Umstattd, M.R., and Usdan, S.L. (2010). Alcohol use and high-risk sexual behavior among collegiate women: A review of research on alcohol myopia theory. *Journal of American College Health*, 58(6), 523–532.

Kiene, S.M., Barta, W.D., Tennen, H., and Armeli, S. (2009). Alcohol, helping young adults to have unprotected sex with casual partners: Findings from a daily diary study of alcohol use and sexual behavior. *Journal of Adolescent Health*, 44(1), 73–80.

Monahan, J.L. and Lannutti, P.J. (2000). Alcohol as social lubricant. *Human Communication Research*, 26(2), 175–202.

Peugh, J. and Belenko, S. (2001). Alcohol, drugs and sexual function: a review. *Journal of Psychoactive Drugs*, 33(3), 223–232.

Rubin, H.B. and Henson, D.E. (1976). Effects of alcohol on male sexual responding. *Psychopharmacology*, 47(2), 123–134.

Steele, C.M. and Josephs, R.A. (1990). Alcohol myopia: Its prized and dangerous effects. *American Psychologist*, 45(8), 921.

Testa, M., Livingston, J.A., and Collins, R.L. (2000). The role of women's alcohol consumption in evaluation of vulnerability to sexual aggression. *Experimental and Clinical Psychopharmacology*, 8(2), 185.

Walsh, J.L., Fielder, R.L., Carey, K.B., and Carey, M.P. (2013). Changes in women's condom use over the first year of college. *Journal of Sex Research*, 50(2), 128–138.

Myth #40 Alcohol and Sex Are a Harmless Combination

Whereas research may be inconclusive when it comes to alcohol and other sexual risks like unprotected sex, there are very few doubts about the role alcohol has in facilitating sexual assault. In 50% of reported date or acquaintance rape cases, the victim and/or the perpetrator said they had consumed alcohol. A study found that roughly 2% of all college students or 97,000 young people were victims of alcohol-related sexual assault in 2001 alone (Hingson *et al.*, 2009, p. 12). And, it is estimated that each year 100,000 young people aged 18–24 "report being too intoxicated to know if they consented to having sex" (NIAA, 2013).

In their review of the literature on alcohol and sex, George *et al.* (2000) note that alcohol has been found to impact behavior around sexual assault in a number of ways. Consistent with Alcohol Myopia Theory, alcohol focuses attention on impelling cues like a desire to have sex and away from inhibiting cues like the lack of consent from one's partner. Studies have found that men who had consumed alcohol or believed they had were slower to recognize rape in stories and to suggest the perpetrator should stop than men who were sober and knew they were sober. Alcohol also had noteworthy effects on victims of assault. Women who are drinking are more likely to be in risky situations but less likely to perceive the risk. Moreover, intoxicated women are less likely to use direct resistance to fend off assault than women who are sober.

The presence of alcohol also sways how individuals perceive rape and sexual assault. Studies have shown that when stories suggest that the rapist was drunk respondents see him as less blameworthy but the opposite is true of the victim. Respondents feel less sympathy for victims who were drunk at the time they were assaulted (George *et al.*, 2000). This may be a result of yet another common perception—that a woman who is drinking is looking for sex. Experiments conducted over the years have found that respondents believe characters in vignettes who are drinking are more sexually available, more willing to engage in sex, and more likely to initiate sex than characters who are behaving similarly but are not drinking (George *et al.*, 2003).

We have seen this play out a number of times recently in the media. In Steubenville, Ohio, two football players raped an intoxicated young woman while friends cheered them on and videotaped the incident. The victim apparently did not remember what had happened until she saw it on social media. Disappointingly, the town—adults and young people alike—rallied around the football players and blamed the victim. (Recently four adults in the community were actually indicted for trying to cover up evidence and protect the boys; Kempner, 2013a.) The general sentiment of the case was summed up by CNN reporter, Poppy Harlow, who showed a great deal of sympathy for the perpetrators on the day they were found guilty of rape. "These two young men who had such promising futures—star football players, very good students—literally watched as they believed their lives fell apart," she said. She did not express similar sympathy for the rape survivor in the case (Kempner, 2013b).

More recently, we learned of the case of Daisy Coleman, a 14-year-old girl in Maryville, Missouri, who snuck out of her house one day in January 2013 to go to a party with an out-of-town friend and a popular senior football player. The two girls were given alcohol by the boy and his friends and both were raped. Daisy's rape was caught on iPhone video. The football player then drove Daisy and her friend home and left Daisy passed out on her front porch in 30-degree weather. In the days following the incident, law enforcement officials and community members seemed to believe and support the girls and charges were filed against the boys. But public opinion quickly shifted, Daisy and her family became a target. Nasty comments were made on the internet and in person. Her mother was abruptly fired from her job in the town. When this all got to be too much, they moved away. But before they were able to sell their house in Maryville, it burnt to the ground for unknown reasons. Most notably, all of the charges against the boys were dropped (Kempner, 2013b).

That these young boys thought it was okay to have sex with girls who were undeniably intoxicated and incapable of giving consent is incredibly disturbing. That their friends did not just watch but documented the incidents as if they were something to be proud of is equally if not more upsetting. And the fact that the adults in these young people's lives were willing to shrug off this behavior as "boys will be boys" and wag fingers at the young victims for drinking is abhorrent.

We need to make sure that everyone understands the issue of consent. It is never acceptable to have sex with another person without their consent. The fact that one or both people were drinking alcohol does not change this basic tenet of sexual behavior nor can it be used as an excuse (legally or morally) after-the-fact. Here are some other non-negotiables about sex and alcohol: A girl is not "asking for sex" just because she comes to a party where there is alcohol and gets drunk. A girl who has passed out, even if it's in your bed and she got into that bed willingly, cannot give consent. If she's too drunk to carry on an intelligent conversation, she's too drunk to have sex.

It should be as simple as that but we understand that in real life things can seem trickier. So we give you this scenario. A cute girl has been flirting with you all night while downing beers and shots. Now she's pretty wasted but she's happy and falling all over you and asking to go back to your room. Our suggestion: get her cell number, help her get home, maybe tuck her in (on her stomach with a bucket next to her for vomit), and call her tomorrow. Not only will you be a better person, but the sex the two of you may eventually have will be better. Sex with a totally intoxicated partner is often not not very much fun. (In college, one of us, and we won't tell you which one, actually had a drunk boy fall asleep on top of her in the middle of intercourse. Not at all fun.)

Now for the bystanders. In each of these highly public rape cases, the assault took place in front of witnesses who did nothing to protect the victim. In fact, they further victimized these women by cheering on the perpetrators, taking pictures, and publicizing the event. We need to challenge the assumption that women who are drunk are "asking for it" and the way to do that is for individuals (like our readers) to start standing up and stepping in when they see something that looks off. Don't cheer, interfere.

There has been real controversy lately, however, about what we say to young women themselves. In a piece for the online news site Slate, Emily Yoffe suggested that one way to break the cycle of alcohol-fueled sexual assault is to tell college-age girls to stop getting wasted. She wrote:

> Let's be totally clear: Perpetrators are the ones responsible for committing their crimes, and they should be brought to justice. But we are failing to let women know that when they render themselves defenseless, terrible things can be done

to them. Young women are getting a distorted message that their right to match men drink for drink is a feminist issue. The real feminist message should be that when you lose the ability to be responsible for yourself, you drastically increase the chances that you will attract the kinds of people who, shall we say, don't have your best interest at heart. That's not blaming the victim; that's trying to prevent more victims. (Yoffe, 2013)

As Yoffe probably expected, reaction to her article was swift and negative, with people saying that, despite her cries to the contrary, she was blaming the victims, that she was acting as if rape just happened to them, and that she was absolving the perpetrators of their responsibility.

We understand that victim-blaming has been going on for years in this country and we do not want to do anything to perpetuate that, but we do believe that there needs to be a balanced approach to preventing sexual assault and that warning young women about the potential dangers of over-consumption of alcohol has a role. Most men are not rapists, even when drunk they will not assault a woman. Unfortunately, statistics prove that we can't say that about all men. Moreover, many young men are never taught how to recognize when a woman wants him to stop. Our society is replete with images of women saying no at first and then caving because of his steely blue eyes or passionate kiss. Not to mention the warped view we give young men when towns like Steubenville and Maryville rally around rapists and shun victims. Helping young men recognize consent and helping young women learn how to protect themselves can and should go hand-in-hand. And, like it or not, one of the ways that women can protect themselves is to stay somewhat sober.

Alcohol and Sexual Assault

As we said in the last entry, we are not suggesting that college students stop drinking altogether nor are we suggesting that drinking and sex can never come together in a positive experience. We just want all of our readers to keep in mind that for both physical and psychological reasons, alcohol may change your behavior and your sexual experience. It may be for the better but more likely it won't. Keeping this in mind may help you avoid the possible dangers of sex under the influence.

References

George, W.H. and Stoner, S.A. (2000). Understanding acute alcohol effects on sexual behavior. *Annual Review of Sex Research*, 11(1), 92–124.

George, W.H., Stoner, S.A., Norris, J., Lopez, P.A., and Lehman, G.L. (2000). Alcohol expectancies and sexuality: A self-fulfilling prophecy analysis of dyadic perceptions and behavior. *Journal of Studies on Alcohol and Drugs*, 61(1), 168.

Hingson, R.W., Zha, W., and Weitzman, E.R. (2009). Magnitude of and trends in alcohol-related mortality and morbidity among US college students ages 18–24, 1998–2005. *Journal of Studies on Alcohol and Drugs*, Suppl. 16, 12.

Kempner, M. (2013a). Could new Steubenville indictments send a message to communities about dealing with rape? *RH Reality Check* (November 25). http://rhrealitycheck.org/article/2013/11/25/could-new-steubenville-indictments-send-a-message-to-communities-about-dealing-with-rape/ (accessed August 6, 2014).

Kempner, M. (2013b). We have a rape problem. First step: We have to admit it. *RH Reality Check* (October 17). http://rhrealitycheck.org/article/2013/10/17/we-have-a-rape-problem-first-step-we-have-to-admit-it/ (accessed August 6, 2014).

National Institutes of Health, National Institute of Alcohol Abuse and Alcoholism (NIAA) (2013). College drinking. http://pubs.niaaa.nih.gov/publications/CollegeFactSheet/CollegeFactSheet.pdf (accessed August 6, 2014).

Yoffe, E. (2013). College women: Stop getting drunk. *Slate* (October 15). http://www.slate.com/articles/double_x/doublex/2013/10/sexual_assault_and_drinking_teach_women_the_connection.html (accessed August 7, 2014).

Myth #41   For Girls, Sometimes Sex Just Hurts

Sometimes sex is mind-blowingly fantastic and other times it is just alright but it's never supposed to feel bad. Unfortunately, that is not true for everyone, especially women. In fact, some estimates suggest that as many as three out of four women have experienced pain during sex. For many of these women it happens sporadically or just once, but for some it becomes a regular part of sex and even a part of their daily lives (ACOG, 2011). Pain during sex can be both physically and psychologically disturbing, affecting a woman's relationships and self-esteem. Yet many women think it's just a normal part of doing it.

We want our readers to understand that this just isn't so. Sex should not hurt. If it does there is something wrong (we're not talking about a character flaw or a moral failing, but something physically or, more rarely, psychologically wrong), and you should seek help.

This entry talks about some of the things that can get out of whack and result in sex that feels the opposite of how it should. We also look at chronic pain conditions—notably vulvodynia and vestibulodynia—that can interrupt some women's sex lives for months or even years.

A word of caution; we are providing this information so that you have a quick idea of what can cause problems but we are not trying to diagnose any issues you might have (neither of us is a medical doctor) nor are we suggesting that anyone should try to diagnose their own issues—that's your health care provider's job. The basic rule of thumb is that if your vulva hurts (before, during, or after sex), you should get it looked at by a medical professional. No one should just live with it.

The Easy Fixes

If something doesn't feel right, don't panic. In most instances there is an easy explanation and an easy solution.

We're Not Saying You're Doing It Wrong, But...

So the first problem with sex may be that you or your partner are doing it wrong. We're kind of kidding when we say that because there is no "right" way to have sex, but there is a grain of truth in our joke. Every vulva and clitoris is different and the kind of touch that works to give one woman an orgasm may make another feel like she's being rubbed raw. Women should know where they like to be touched, how hard, and in what way (big circles, rubbing back and forth, a little squeeze, perhaps). We think it's easiest if a woman figures it out herself through masturbation and then shares this information with her partner or partners through a fun tutorial (with charts and graphs, of course) or gentle suggestions in the moment (a little to the left, oh good, just a little lighter, yes, like that). If masturbation doesn't work for you, then try the same kind of exploration with a partner, you can learn together.

Everything's Better Down Where It's Wetter

This is probably not what the good folks at Walt Disney had in mind when the crab in *The Little Mermaid* sang, but it's what Sebastian's number always makes us think about. In order to enjoy intercourse and even some forms of foreplay, women need to be lubricated. Lubrication is the natural byproduct of the vasocongestion of the vagina—as the blood rushes to the vagina when a woman gets turned on, the vagina itself become wetter. This lubrication helps guard against chaffing and irritation when a woman is touched or penetrated. Sometimes women don't produce enough natural lubrication, possibly because they are not turned on enough (more foreplay anyone?) or for a variety of other reasons (Blonna and Levitan, 2005, p. 216).

The good news is that there are plenty of options for those who need a little more moisture. Most drug stores offer a wide array of personal lubricants made from oil, water, or silicone. Couples can also hit a local or online sex shop and choose from hundreds of formulations. In a pinch, you can also use things you find around the house like baby oil or olive oil. Just remember that if you are using a barrier method like a condom or a diaphragm, you need to avoid oil-based lubes because they can break down the latex. If you're using your lube with a sex toy, you want to stick to water-based ones. And, if you're hitting the kitchen cabinet to find your lube, avoid things that are very sugary—like honey and jam—as they can increase the likelihood of a yeast infection. The artificially flavored lubricants that you buy on store shelves are also not particularly vagina friendly (Herbenick and Schick, 2011, p. 95).

Herpes, Chlamydia, or Trich, Oh My

When we talk about sexually transmitted infections (STIs), we often emphasize the fact that they can be asymptomatic for many women, meaning that a woman feels no physical indications that there is anything wrong. When STIs do have symptoms, however, these often include itching, burning, or sores. And these can hurt, especially if rubbed during sex. So if there are any sores or spots that hurt or an overall sensation of itching, it's a good idea to get checked for the gamut of STIs.

When left untreated, bacterial STIs, such as chlamydia, trich, and gonorrhea, can lead to pelvic inflammatory disease (PID), an infection of the uterine lining, fallopian tubes, or ovaries. PID can also cause pain during sex, in particular during deep penetration (ACOG, 2011). The good news is that these STIs and PID itself can be cured with antibiotics. Herpes, however, which can also cause pain during intercourse, is a virus, and cannot be cured. There are treatments that reduce the frequency and intensity of herpes outbreaks and, when no sores are present, herpes should not cause pain during intercourse or otherwise.

Yeast, It's Not Just for Bread Anymore

Few women will make it through their reproductive years without having a yeast infection or two (or many) and with the itching and irritation, yeast infections can definitely cause sexual activity to be less fun. Yeast infections are most often caused by on overabundance of the fungus *Candida albicans* in the vagina. Though the fungus lives in the vagina without causing problems most of the time, when there is too much of it, it can cause redness, swelling, and most notably itching. Many women also get a thick, white, vaginal discharge when they have a yeast infection (Stewart and Spencer, 2002, Chapter 10).

Yeast infections can be brought on by many things. Some antibiotics, for example, are known to cause them. Certain soaps can cause them for some women. For others, it can be brought on by oral sex. Some believe that tight-fitting clothes, especially those made of synthetic fabric that doesn't "breathe," can cause them but this hasn't been proven. Though these infections are not sexually transmitted they can be related to sex in that intercourse can introduce yeast cells into the vagina, semen can promote yeast growth, and the onset of frequent intercourse is often associated with an increase in yeast infections (Stewart and Spencer, 2002, Chapter 10).

Yeast infections can be cured with antifungal creams or pills. Creams are available over-the-counter but Stewart and Spencer warn that it's not a good idea to run out and treat yourself every time you start to itch. It's wiser to have a health care provider confirm your personal diagnosis because itching and discharge can be signs of many things.

Vaginitis (but not Bacterial Vaginosis)

Vaginitis is actually a catch-all phrase for anything that causes an inflammation of the vagina and the annoying itching, irritation, and discharge (and pain during sex) that may go with it. Yeast infections cause vaginitis. So does trich. The other causes of vaginitis can be the loss of estrogen (such as what happens during menopause), strep infections of the vagina, or an overabundance of *mobiluncus* (another naturally occurring vaginal bacteria) (Stewart and Spencer, 2002, Chapter 11). These can all cause vulva pain.

Stewart and Spencer point out that one of the most common causes of vaginitis is bacterial vaginosis (BV), which occurs when the vagina becomes less acidic. Without the acid to keep them in check, the bacteria that are always present in the vagina in normal proportions can go crazy and overgrow. This can cause itching and irritation though some women have no symptoms. They note, however, that BV is rarely if ever the cause of pain during sex (Stewart and Spencer, 2002, Chapter 11).

The Chronic Culprits

Though most vaginal discomfort—whether during sex or not—is easily curable, for some women the pain becomes chronic. There are two conditions in particular that can cause women to have constant feelings of itching, burning, rawness, and irritation on their vulvas. Some women have this only when they attempt to penetrate the vagina with a partner's penis, a sex toy, a finger, or even a tampon. Others are sensitive to even the lightest touch on all or part of their vulva. And still others have pain all the time to the point that every day activities—such as wearing jeans—become uncomfortable.

In 1983, researchers gave this cluster of unexplained symptoms a name—vulvodynia. This is not so much a diagnosis as a description because basically the word means painful vulva. Some experts make a distinction between vulvodynia, which is generalized, constant pain in the vulva even when unprovoked by touch, and vestibulodynia, which is more localized pain caused by touch. In the latter, the pain is often confined to the vulva vestibule, which is the area between the labia majora where the vulva and vagina meet. This is a very sensitive spot which includes the Bartholin's glands (which makes vaginal lubrication) as well as other smaller vestibule glands and the urethra which is where urine comes out (Stewart and Spencer, 2002, Chapter 17).

It is not clear how many women suffer from vulvodynia as many women with these symptoms never hear the word. One study designed to estimate the number of women who have vulvodynia symptoms concluded that over the course of 1 year, approximately one in 20 women will experience new-onset genital pain (Sutton *et al.*, 2008). Other studies have suggested that about 9–16% of the population of US females will have this cluster of symptoms at some point in their lives (Arnold, 2007; Goetsch, 1991).

Nobody knows for sure what causes these symptoms to come on and to hang around for so long. Most theories seem to hinge on the body's reaction to pain. Stewart and Spencer consider vestibulodynia to be an inflammatory disorder in which the body gets confused:

> The irritation causes the release of various chemicals that affect the C fibers; prostaglandin, histamines, and others. If the irritation continues, prolonged firing of the nerve fibers alters nerves in the spinal cord. These fibers then mix up signals from light touch nerve fibers in the vulva (those A fibers) and tell the central nervous system that usually pleasurable light touch is painful. (Stewart and Spencer, 2002, Chapter 17)

The theory on vulvodynia is also one of a confused signals which may start with an injury to the pudendal nerve which runs from the base of the spine through the pelvis. The idea here is that some event (possibly one that is never given a second thought like a slip or a fall) causes an injury to the pudendal nerve, which responds by shooting pain signals to the vulva. The nerve injury heals but the nerve continues to send the pain signal (Stewart and Spencer, 2002, Chapter 17).

There is another loop that is involved with both of these syndromes. Women who have experienced pain on touch or had painful intercourse tend to be hypervigilant to pain. This means both that they are more tuned into anything that feels uncomfortable and that they may tense to the touch which makes many things—especially penetration—more likely to be painful. Researchers who interviewed women with vestibulodynia noted that they are likely to have "heightened awareness of pain and a distraction away from sexual stimuli resulting in an impaired sexual arousal, which itself may potentially exacerbate the pain experience" (Payne et al., 2005, p. 434). The reaction to the pain causes more pain.

Pain from either of these conditions can also wreak havoc havoc with women's self-esteem and relationships, which can cause anxiety and depression. Researchers in Sweden interviewed young women with chronic vulva pain and found that "coital pain becomes associated with their self-image as individuals, and the feeling of guilt becomes obvious; the ideal woman does not have sexual problems." The desire to be this ideal woman, who does not have pain on intercourse and can please her partner, led many of the women in this study to continue having sex even though it hurt (Elmerstig et al., 2008).

Another big problem for women with vulvodynia is finding a physician who knows enough about these issues to be able to help. Most women with these conditions are misdiagnosed at least at first and many find themselves shunted back and forth between unhelpful specialists. Part of the problem is that though the woman feels symptoms, there is no visible problem that can be seen by a health care provider. A colleague of ours who suffered from vulvodynia in her twenties was told by her gynecologist that this was a problem for a urologist, the urologist sent her to a different gynecologist, who sent her to a different urologist, who told her it would be best if she saw a psychologist because there was nothing physically wrong with her and clearly it was all in her head. She saw at least six doctors before hearing the word vulvodynia and another three before finding someone who knew how to treat it.

There are treatments for vulvodynia and vestibulodynia. Some women find relief with certain kinds of antidepressants—not because the symptoms are all in their heads but because these drugs can interrupt the pain loop that their bodies have gotten into. Antiseizure medications can also break the pain loop. Interestingly, one of the treatments for vulvodynia is physical therapy and biofeedback. The theory here is that the constant pain can cause the pelvic floor muscles to tense up and hold on to the pain. Physical therapy helps women release this tension so the muscles can go back to normal. Biofeedback uses a machine attached to a tampon-sized probe that is inserted into the vagina. It can gauge how tight the muscles in the vagina are and help women know when they are squeezing hard and when they are actually letting go (Stewart and Spencer, 2002, Chapter 17).

Sex Shouldn't Hurt

Sex shouldn't hurt. If it does there is something wrong and you need to find someone (a health care provider) who can help figure out what that is and fix it. This may be as easy as a round of antifungal medication to end a yeast infection or as complex as medication and physical therapy to end vulvodynia. We urge all our readers to find help and not just resign themselves to thinking that a little bit of pain or discomfort is okay. If the health care provider you first see suggests you're just being too sensitive, find another one. Organizations like the National Vulvodynia Association (www.nva.org) offer lists of physicians who specialize in vulva pain. Women who have experienced pain for a long time may also want to consider seeing a counselor or therapist who can help them work through issues of anxiety, anger, and depression.

References

American College of Obstetricians and Gynecologists (ACOG) (2011). Frequently asked questions: When sex is painful. http://www.acog.org/~/media/For%20Patients/faq020. pdf?dmc=1&ts=20140123T1520169504 (accessed August 6, 2014).

Arnold, L.D., Bachmann, G.A., Rosen, R., and Rhoads, G.G. (2007). Assessment of vulvodynia symptoms in a sample of US women: a prevalence survey with a nested case control study. *American Journal of Obstetrics and Gynecology*, 196(2), 128-e1.

Blonna, R. and Levitan, J. (2005). *Healthy Sexuality*. Brooks/Cole Publishing, MI.

Elmerstig, E., Wijma, B., and Berterö, C. (2008). Why do young women continue to have sexual intercourse despite pain? *Journal of Adolescent Health*, 43(4), 357–363.

Goetsch, M.F. (1991). Vulvar vestibulitis: prevalence and historic features in a general gynecologic practice population. *American Journal of Obstetrics and Gynecology*, 164(6), 1609–1616.

Herbenick, D.L. and Schick, V. (2011). *Read My Lips: A Complete Guide to the Vagina and Vulva*. Rowman & Littlefield, MD.

Payne, K.A., Binik, Y.M., Amsel, R., and Khalifé, S. (2005). When sex hurts, anxiety and fear orient attention towards pain. *European Journal of Pain*, 9(4), 427–436.

Stewart, E.G. and Spencer, P. (2002). *The V Book*. Bantam Books, New York, NY. Accessed as a kindle e-book.

Sutton, J.T., Bachmann, G.A., Arnold, L.D., Rhoads, G.G., and Rosen, R.C. (2008). Assessment of vulvodynia symptoms in a sample of US women: a follow-up national incidence survey. *Journal of Women's Health*, 17(8), 1285–1292.

Myth #42   Men Under 40 Rarely Have Trouble With Erections

Today's television watchers, at least those who don't use a DVR to skip commercials, might be surprised to know that there was a time not that long ago when the phrase "for erections lasting longer than 4 hours seek immediate medical attention" was not part of our cultural zeitgeist. When sitcoms hadn't yet learned how to milk the 4-hour erection for laughs and comedians hadn't yet asked "What about an erection that lasts 3 hours and 59 minutes, is that okay?" In fact, there was a time when no one knew the letters ED were supposed to stand for erectile dysfunction and we had never seen images of older couples sitting in separate bathtubs in a field of wild flowers or on a bluff overlooking the ocean. But it's true, there was a time when men couldn't get it up but nobody talked about it.

The introduction of Viagra in 1998 changed all of that. There is an ongoing debate as to whether Viagra and other widely publicized ED drugs have been good for our understanding of men's sexual health or have led to a model of sexuality that relies too much on the biological and the medical without taking into account the psychological, relational, societal, and behavioral factors that all have a role in sexual functioning (Tiefer, 2006). Regardless of which side one comes down on, it is hard to deny that the introduction of these drugs and, possibly more importantly, the advertising campaigns around them have started innumerable conversations about sexual dysfunction that we would not have otherwise had.

Watch these ads, however, and you will notice (with a few exceptions, of course), that the men are all silver-haired or slightly weathered with age. Many even discuss how sex "isn't what it used to be." It is true that as men age it can be more difficult to get or maintain an erection and the penis may never get as hard as it once did. In its attempts to normalize this experience for older men, much of the advertising around ED drugs has held on to the stereotype that this is a problem for the senior citizen-set and no one else. Unfortunately, that's simply not the case. Many young men experience difficulties with erections—either once in a while or all of the time.

What's ED exactly?

Erectile dysfunction (ED) is defined as the inability to attain and maintain an erection sufficient to permit satisfactory sexual performance. In order to qualify as ED, the issue must affect a man's physical and psychosocial health and have significant impact on the quality of life of sufferers and their partners and families (Lue *et al.*, 2004). It is estimated that 20–30% of men suffer from ED at some point in their lives, with 5–20% of men reporting moderate to severe ED (Hatzimouratidis *et al.*, 2010).

Though the prevalence is higher as men age, the problem is not limited to older men. A study, for example, looked at a large sample of men aged 25–50 in an effort to determine the prevalence of ED in men of these ages. The men completed a questionnaire called the Sexual Human Inventory for Males (SHIM). The SHIM scores suggested that at least one out of three men (26.9%) suffered from ED, with 19% suffering from mild ED, 7% from moderate, and 1% from severe ED. The authors note that ED was prevalent among the under-40 set as well (Heruti *et al.*, 2004).

ED can have its roots in physical issues and/or psychological ones and the solutions often lie in both realms. As erections require increased blood flow to the penis, it should not be surprising that cardiovascular problems often contribute to ED. Men suffering from heart disease, clogged blood vessels, high blood pressure, high cholesterol, diabetes, and obesity are at higher risk of ED, as are heavy smokers. Other health issues such as Parkinson's disease and multiple sclerosis can also increase its likelihood. Some prescription medications are known to limit sexual desire and functioning as can some illicit drugs and even alcohol when used in excess. Other issues more closely associated with sexual function also increase the risk of ED such as Peyronie's disease (a condition in which the penis is bent which sometimes causes scar tissue), prostate cancer and treatments for prostate cancer, low testosterone levels, and injuries to or surgeries on the pelvic area or spinal cord (Zilbergeld, 1999).

While some men may discover that one or more of these physical ailments is the cause of their ED and that treating the underlying issue "cures" their ED, many will not. For some men the roots of the problem are psychological while for others it is reflective of a larger problem in their relationship. Depression, stress, and anxiety can get in the way of sexual functioning as can any number of issues within a relationship.

In his book, *The New Male Sexuality*, sex therapist Bernie Zilbergeld points out that men have been told that a very hard penis is always necessary for sex and this puts them under a lot of pressure. He writes: "A woman can participate in intercourse or any other sexual act without being aroused or even interested....A man is in a more difficult situation. Because of the incorrect belief that sex demands a rigid penis, he feels that nothing can rescue him. His 'failure' is obvious, dangling in full view" (1992, p. 303). This stress alone can cause a one-time problem to become a repeat issue. (We would be remiss if we didn't take this opportunity to remind all our readers that regardless of whether couples have same-sex or opposite-sex partners there are plenty of things to do with mouths, fingers, and genitals that do not require a penis at all, let alone an erect one. Perhaps that knowledge alone can relieve some of the stress.)

Zilbergeld suggests a number of questions men can ask themselves in order to begin to determine the cause of their erectile issues. The starting point may be the chemicals—whether prescription drugs, other drugs, or too much alcohol—that you are putting in your body. Prescription drugs used to treat everything from depression to epilepsy to heartburn can affect erections. If you are on any of these, the first step is to talk to the doctor who prescribed them. Other drugs such as alcohol, marijuana, heroin, methamphetamines, Ecstasy, and more can also prevent erections. Consider eliminating the use of these drugs.

If chemicals are not the issue, it can be important to pinpoint the problem by keeping track of when it happens—does it happen all the time, with all partners, or just some of the time, with some people? Do you have erection problems when you are alone and want to masturbate? Do you ever wake up with an erection? Is the issue getting hard or staying hard? The answers to these questions can help you, with the help of your health care provider, figure out the problem which in turn will inform the solution.

The Little Blue Pill and Other Treatments

Before we talk about Viagra and the other drugs that have burst onto the scene in the last couple of decades, we want to take a minute to discuss the nonmedical options for men with erectile issues. Namely, psychotherapy and sex therapy. Though it may seem easier to pop a pill, we think it is important to consider these treatment possibilities because pills have side effects but also because therapy can help people become more sexually healthy in ways that medication cannot. As Zilbergeld puts it "These [pills] will not help you talk to or listen to your partner or be more sensitive, will not make you a better lover, will not improve sensation or give you a better orgasm, will not resolve relationship tension, and most certainly will not save a failing relationship" (1992, p. 311). A skilled therapist, however, can help resolve more than just the erectile issue because in many cases there is much more going on.

In some men, ED can be attributed to low testosterone levels which can be treated with prescription medication. Testosterone replacement comes in the form of patches, gels, injections, and implants. Though this can help some men with ED, there are side effects to consider. Testosterone therapy can lead to an enlarged prostate and cause prostate cancer to grow faster. It has also been linked to sleep apnea and heart problems. In fact, the Food and Drug Administration (FDA) recently announced that it is reassessing the safety of testosterone treatments after two studies found increased risk of heart attacks (Krans, 2014). While the FDA investigates, it is urging medical providers to be cautious about prescribing such therapies. (See Myth # 5 for more on the role of testosterone in sex.)

Now back to that little blue pill that has gotten so much attention. Sildenafil, marketed under the name Viagra, was introduced in 1998. It is the first in a class of medications called PDE5 inhibitors. By blocking the PDE5 enzyme, the medications help the smooth muscles in the penis relax and increase blood flow to the penis. Other PDE5 inhibitors have been introduced since then including tadalfil, sold as Cialis, and vardenfil, sold as Levitra. The differences between these drugs are mainly in how long they take before they begin to work and how long they last in the body before they stop working. Remember though, these pills are not meant to cause spontaneous erections, they are designed to make erections more possible when men get sexually excited (Hatzimouratidis *et al.*, 2010). These drugs are now considered first line treatment for most ED.

As with any medication there are side effects to PDE5 inhibitors. Common side effects include headaches (10–16%), flushing (5–12%), indigestion (4–12%), nasal congestion (1–10%), and dizziness (4–12%). When Viagra first came out, reports of men seeing blue got a lot of attention. And, in fact, about 2% of patients do experience vision issues that include seeing a blue haze, temporary increased brightness, and even sudden vision loss or partial vision loss (*New York Times Health Guides*, 2013). Most studies have found no long-term health risks that come with using these drugs and the drugs do seem to continue to be effective even if used for a long time (McMurray *et al.*, 2007). A recent study in the *Journal of the American Medical Association*, however, has found a link between PDE5 inhibitors and melanoma, one of the most serious forms of skin cancer. The study did not prove that PDE5 inhibitors cause skin cancer but did show the mechanism by which the drugs could increase the risk (Li *et al.*, 2014).

Possibly the most famous long- or short-term problem side effect of these drugs, however, is that 4-hour erection that we mentioned in the introduction. The condition is actually caused priapism and before anyone starts joking that it sounds like a good time—it hurts. What might be more painful though is the treatment for priapism which almost always includes sticking a large needle into the penis either to inject medication or to remove the old blood, and sometimes includes needles for both of those purposes (American Urologists Association, 2003). Though it is a rare condition on its own and is even a rare side effect for men who use PDE5 inhibitors, there is one group of men who are at higher risk for priapism—young men who have normal erectile functioning but use Viagra or other ED drugs for fun (*New York Times Health Guides*, 2013).

Recreational Use of ED Drugs

Which brings us to the recreational use of these drugs. A few years after Viagra was introduced, the news was flooded with stories of young men using these drugs to have a good time. Many of these reports included young men, often men who had sex with men, taking Viagra along with other drugs such as alcohol, cocaine, amyl nitrate, marijuana, or Ecstasy (Diaz, 2001). It is hard to tell from the media reports how widespread recreational use of the drugs really is and there have only been a few academic studies looking at this issue. One of these studies recruited a sample of almost 2000 college students from 497 colleges in the United States. Participants answered questions about their ability to get and maintain erections as well as whether they had ever used Viagra, Cialis, or Levitra. The results show that 4% of respondents had used these drugs recreationally at some point and almost 2% (1.9%) were currently using them for fun. The most common motive was curiosity (75% of users) but almost a quarter of users (24%) said their motive for current use was to increase erectile rigidity (Harte and Meston, 2011). Again, we remind our readers that a rock-hard penis is not a prerequisite for sex and a normal, unaided erection is definitely good enough.

A large portion of users (30%) also said they took the ED medication to counteract substances that decreased erectile functioning. This is important because 44% of the men who used ED medication combined it with illicit drugs and/or alcohol. Specifically, 61% combined it with marijuana, 46% with alcohol, 42% with Ecstasy, 36% with methamphetamines, and 30% with cocaine (Harte and Meston, 2011). Some of these combinations can be dangerous. One case report published in the *Journal of Clinical Cardiology* discusses a 41-year-old man who was healthy and had no risk factors for cardiac disease. Twelve hours after taking Viagra recreationally at the same time that he smoked marijuana, the man suffered a myocardial infarction which is more commonly known as a heart attack. The authors of the case study suggest that interaction between Viagra and marijuana was to blame (McLeod *et al.*, 2002).

Recreational use of ED drugs was also correlated with other increased risk behavior including number of partners in the last month, lifetime number of partners, and lifetime number of one-night stands. It was also correlated with unprotected anal or vaginal sex with a partner of serodiscordant or unknown HIV status. Finally, the findings show that men who had sex with men, whether they identified as gay or bisexual men, were more likely to use ED drugs recreationally than heterosexual men (Harte and Meston, 2011).

Most of the men who took these drugs recreationally said they did not know where the pill originally came from or what dose they had taken. Though there is some disagreement about exactly how widespread the problem is, it has been suggested that up to 77% of Viagra sold online is counterfeit (Haiken, 2013). These counterfeit pills have been found to have only 30–50% of the amount of active ingredient found in the real ones. More disturbing than what's missing, however, is what has been found in these pills: blue printer ink, amphetamines, the antibiotic metronidazole (which, by the way, causes vomiting when mixed with alcohol), and drywall or plaster (Haiken, 2013).

We can't stress enough how dangerous it is to use prescription drugs that were not specifically prescribed to you by a medical professional, how dangerous it is to use any drug whose origin you don't know, and how dangerous it is to mix prescription drugs with illicit drugs. All of these things can cause life-changing health problems.

We understand curiosity, but men who do not have problems getting erect or staying erect have no reason to turn to ED drugs and simply should not use them.

Young Men With ED Are Not Alone

That said, one of the interesting findings of the study of college students we just discussed is that some of the users of the drugs really did need them. In fact, a total of 5% of respondents had ever used ED drugs and though most of this use was recreational, 1% had actually been prescribed them by a doctor. Even more interesting, the researchers found, based on their questions about erections, that 13% of their sample of college-aged students did, in fact, meet the definition of ED and that 27% of those who admitted to using ED drugs recreationally actually had ED even though they had not been diagnosed (Harte and Meston, 2011).

We think these findings are significant because they show, first, that young men do have difficulties with erections and, second, that a significant portion of them are self-medicating. We would much prefer that any man—young or old—who has problems getting or maintaining an erection seek medical help either from a physician (often a urologist) or a therapist or both. ED drugs may be the solution to the problem for some young men but they need to be used under the watchful eye of a health care provider and should never be ordered online without a prescription or "borrowed" from a friend who has a prescription. Other young men may do better with a therapist or sex therapist who can help them understand and work through the psychological or relationship issues that are getting in the way of good erections. Either way, we want young men to know that it does actually happen to everyone at some point in their lives and for those for whom it happens too frequently, there are solutions.

References

American Urologists Association (2003). *Guidelines for the Treatment of Priapism.* https://www.auanet.org/education/guidelines/priapism.cfm (accessed August 6, 2014).

Diaz, J. (2001). Viagra's growing recreational use prompts health warnings. *Miami Herald* (March 4).

Haiken, M. (2013). Up to 77 percent of Viagra bought online may be fake, and possibly dangerous, research shows. *Forbes* (September 12). http://www.forbes.com/sites/melaniehaiken/2013/09/12/buying-viagra-online-its-very-likely-fake-and-possibly-dangerous-new-data-say/ (accessed August 6, 2014).

Harte, C.B. and Meston, C.M. (2011). Recreational use of erectile dysfunction medications in undergraduate men in the United States: Characteristics and associated risk factors. *Archives of Sexual Behavior,* 40(3), 597–606.

Hatzimouratidis, K., Amar, E., Eardley, I., Giuliano, F., Hatzichristou, D., Montorsi, F., *et al.* (2010). Guidelines on male sexual dysfunction: Erectile dysfunction and premature ejaculation. *European Urology,* 57(5), 804–814.

Heruti, R., Shochat, T., Tekes-Manova, D., Ashkenazi, I., and Justo, D. (2004). Prevalence of erectile dysfunction among young adults: Results of a large-scale survey. *Journal of Sexual Medicine,* 1(3), 284–291.

Krans, B. (2014). FDA Investigates the safety of testosterone drugs for 'low T'. *Healthline News* (February 4). http://www.healthline.com/health-news/men-hearts-could-be-at-risk-with-testosterone-therapy-020414 (accessed August 6, 2014).

Li, W., Qureshi, A.A., Robinson, K.C., & Han, J. (2014). Sildenafil use and increased risk of incident melanoma in US men: A prospective cohort study. *JAMA Internal Medicine,* 174(6), 964–970.

Lue, T.F., Giuliano, F., Montorsi, F., Rosen, R.C., Andersson, K.E., Althof, S., *et al.* (2004). Original Research: Summary of the recommendations on sexual dysfunctions in men. *Journal of Sexual Medicine,* 1(1), 6–23.

McLeod, A.L., McKenna, C.J., and Northridge, D.B. (2002). Myocardial infarction following the combined recreational use of Viagra® and cannabis. *Clinical Cardiology,* 25(3), 133–134.

McMurray, J.G., Feldman, R.A., Auerbach, S.M., DeRiesthal, H., Wilson, N.; Multicenter Study Group (2007). Long-term safety and effectiveness of sildenafil citrate in men with erectile dysfunction. *Therapeutics and Clinical Risk Management,* 3(6), 975.

New York Times Health Guide (2013). Erection problems (September 17). Accessed April 15, 2014, http://www.nytimes.com/health/guides/symptoms/erection-problems/oral-medications-(pde5-inhibitors).html (accessed August 6, 2014).

Tiefer, L. (2006). The Viagra phenomenon. *Sexualities,* 9(3), 273–294.

Zilbergeld, B. (1999). *The New Male Sexuality.* Random House.

Myth #43

People Can Get Addicted to Sex, Just Like They're Addicted to Alcohol or Drugs

Sex addiction is a fascinating concept and it is not surprising that the media and popular culture are littered with stories about people who are out of control or used to be out of control until they got help. The 2013 movie, *Thanks for Sharing*, which starred Mark Ruffalo and Gwyneth Paltrow, was about a recovering sex addict and his new love interest whose last boyfriend was also a sex addict. Other characters in the film include men from Ruffalo's 12-step recovery program. The FX original series *Legit* also includes scenes that take place in a group therapy program for sex addiction. And recently, television star Tori Spelling and her husband discussed his alleged sex addiction on their new reality show. We also can't forget the Tiger Woods scandal. When the golf superstar ruined his squeaky clean reputation by cheating on his gorgeous wife with what turned out to be many, many women, he tried to redeem his image by seeking help for a clear case of sex addiction.

But is there such a thing as a clear case of sex addiction? Is sex like alcohol, cocaine, or heroin? Does it affect the brain in such a way that addicts need more and more to achieve the same high? Are individuals who are acting out sexually truly unable to control their behavior? Will they suffer withdrawal if they do stop?

We are not convinced. While there is plenty of science to show us, without a doubt, what alcohol and drugs do to the body and brain, similar studies do not exist for sex. Moreover, many of the definitions of sex addiction rely on relatively arbitrary assessments of how much sex is too much sex and treatment asks people to significantly limit, if not completely abstain, from sexual activity. As sexual health experts, who believe that sex is natural, healthy, and life affirming, we worry about the messages this sends to self-described addicts, their partners, and everyone else.

This is not to say that sexual behaviors are never problematic for some people or that there are not people who need help understanding and changing their sexual patterns. In this entry we discuss the rise of sex addiction as a concept, the problems with this idea, as well as other frameworks that have been proposed for looking at impulsive, compulsive, or otherwise troublesome sexual behavior.

Rise of the Sex Addiction Model

The idea that some people have too much sex or at least think about it too much has been around for centuries—of course, the definition of what is too much and what is unacceptable even in small doses has changed drastically as time marched by. In the 1780s, Swiss physician Samuel Tissot suggested that masturbation at any level was a problem because it depleted the body of vital fluids and could result in memory loss, headaches, gout, or rheumatism (Ley, 2012, p. 10). American physician Benjamin Rush (who signed the Declaration of

Independence) added that masturbation could cause blindness and epilepsy and suggested leeches and bloodletting for treatment of too much masturbation (no, we don't know where he wanted to put the leeches). David Ley notes that Rush's work is still pointed to by sex addiction advocates. But it is Dr. Richard von Krafft-Ebing who named the problem of too much sex, calling it nymphomania in women and satyriasis in men. He argued it was dangerous because men with this condition were a constant threat to commit rape or pedophilia (Ley, 2012).

The modern image of sex addiction can be credited to Patrick J. Carnes (1983), a psychologist who wrote the book *Out of the Shadows* to describe what he had seen clients go through because of excessive sexual thoughts and behavior. Carnes based his theory of what these clients were experiencing on that of alcoholism and modeled his treatment on the 12-step program that had been made popular by Alcoholics Anonymous. Carnes' initial diagnosis of sexual addiction revolved around the SAFE formula suggesting that the potential for addiction and danger exists when sex is secretive, abusive, used to tamp down feelings, and empty (which he defined as outside a caring or committed relationship) (Ley, p. 12). Carnes argues that like other addictive disorders such as gambling or substance use, sex addiction involves a loss of control of compulsivity, continuation despite adverse consequences, and an obsession or preoccupation with the subject. He suggests that there are eight specific behaviors that are likely to become addictive: voyeuristic sex, exhibitionistic sex, paying for sex, trading sex, intrusive sex, anonymous sex, pain-exchange sex, and exploitative sex (Carnes, 2003, pp. 5–6).

While some of these behaviors are always a problem (like sex that exploits someone else), others only raise concerns under certain conditions. Carnes suggests they become problematic when they represent a pattern of behavior and particularly when they are used to cover up one's feelings. According to Ley (2012, p. 17), others have focused not on the addict but the partners and declared that the real problem is that addicts always see others as objects rather than people. Still others explain that the problem begins when the behavior becomes compulsive and the person cannot stop.

This is where the analogy to alcohol or substance abuse is often expanded. The group Sexaholics Anonymous (SA), for example, suggests that for its members, lust is the problem and sexual sobriety is the goal. It explains:

> The sexaholic has taken himself or herself out of the whole context of what is right or wrong. He or she has lost control, no longer has the power of choice, and is not free to stop. Lust has become an addiction. Our situation is like that of the alcoholic who can no longer tolerate alcohol and must stop drinking altogether but is hooked and cannot stop. So it is with the sexaholic, or sex drunk, who can no longer tolerate lust but cannot stop. (Sexaholics Anonymous, 2001)

The treatment, according to SA, is to enter into a 12-step program borrowed from Alcoholics Anonymous in which the first step is to admit you are powerless over lust. SA also suggests that the sex addict abstain from any sex with oneself or any partner other than one's spouse because such activities are driven by lust.

Why the "Sex Addiction Is Like Substance Abuse" Argument Is Lacking

The first problem that many experts have with using a substance abuse model to define sexual addiction is that it is far too subjective and open to far too many judgment calls. Sexologist Marty Klein, author of *America's War on Sex: The Continuing Attack on Law, Lust, and Liberty*, argues that the model is based on a number of troubling assumptions including that there is one *best* way to express sexuality, that sex that enhances intimacy is the *best* sex, that people need to be told what kinds of sex are wrong and bad, and that if you feel out of control you are (Klein, 2003). Some behaviors that the sex addiction model would label as signs of addiction could be something else entirely. Wanting nonmonogamous sex could simply be a sign of being adventurous, cruising bathrooms despite being married could be a sign of torment over one's true sexual orientation, and fetish behavior could actually be a sign of being highly self-aware about what you desire. And some of the behaviors labeled as dangerous might not be at all, like masturbating daily or enjoying submissive sex (Klein, 2003). In addition, Carnes' original definition that focused on whether sex was empty seemed to argue that all sex outside a committed or loving relationship is inherently empty. Many sexual health experts, including ourselves, would have to disagree. Casual sex, even one-night stands, can be a fun and healthy experience.

The other problem is the lack of science to support the assertion that sex and heroin, for example, do similar things to one's brain, body, or life. Sexual behavior definitely impacts brain chemistry, but unlike drug use it does not introduce foreign chemicals into the brain. Ley (2012, p. 29) argues that during sexual activity "the neurochemical and biological processes are working the way they are supposed to" because sex is a natural part of life. Heroin use is not. He also notes that the science to support sex as an addiction isn't there. For example, one aspect of an addiction diagnosis is "tolerance" which means your body becomes so accustomed to the substance you are abusing—be it alcohol or prescription drugs—that it no longer causes the same good feelings it used to and the addict has to continually increase their intake. While there is anecdotal evidence of escalating sexual behavior—a man who says he used to get off looking at mere photos of naked women but now only videos will do—there are few data to confirm this problem. In fact, this may be a natural process of life; adolescent boys can orgasm in 3 minutes by just thinking about a hot girl (or guy) they met but adult men probably need more stimuli and more time. Still, no one suggests that orgasms are less good at 30 than they were at 15 just because you've had more of them by then or it takes you longer to have one.

A diagnosis of addiction also suggests that a person will suffer withdrawal symptoms upon quitting. We've all seen movies in which characters with the heroin shakes are begging for a fix. This is based on chemicals in the brain and is a serious health problem with real risks. Not having sex might be upsetting or anxiety-producing but it is not physically harmful (Ley, p. 32). Coleman adds that categorizing sex as a behavioral addiction, say akin to compulsive gambling, is inaccurate because "it assumes that it has commonalities in clinical expression, etiology, comorbidity, physiology and treatment with substance use disorders (2011, p. 379)."

The scientific studies that have been done to support the sex addiction model have primarily been done on people who have described themselves as, or at least sought help because they fear they might be, sex addicts. Self-diagnosis in this case is rife with complications because of how Americans view sex. Klein argues, "Given the ways in which our culture is sex-negative the diagnostic criteria for sex addiction are in harmony with people's fundamental sexual assumption and experiences" (2003, p. 10). Society sends mixed messages at best which leaves a lot of people wondering whether they are "normal." Studying someone who is finding his/her sexual behavior troubling enough to seek treatment will give researchers limited insight, and likely only into people who are in similar situations. While this may be helpful to clinicians who will ultimately treat people with these concerns, it does not help us verify whether sex addiction is a real problem within the general public. Klein adds, "The sex addiction movement exploits people's fear of their sexuality. This fear is one of the major public health problems facing America today" (2003, p. 10).

Finally, the treatment of sex addiction is worrisome for a number of reasons. The first of the 12 steps of recovery is declaring yourself powerless over sex. This is exactly the opposite of what sexologists and sex educators hope people will learn about their sexuality. We agree that sexual behaviors can be unhealthy but worry that starting from this view of sex as an uncontrollable force is not the way to help people manage these behaviors. Some, including Carnes (2003), have argued that treating sex addiction is more akin to treating eating disorders than substance abuse because eating is also a natural process that can get out of control. But some eating disorders specialists disagree, noting that unlike addiction in which the sufferers feel out of control, eating disorders are used as a way to control one's world. Those with eating disorders cannot control what is going on outside of their body but they can strictly control what is going into it or how much time they will spend exercising. Asking them to surrender that control as a prerequisite to treatment could be dangerous, especially since abstinence from food is unhealthy (Ley, p. 41).

It's also worth noting that the treatment for sex addiction is a very lucrative field as patients may pay upwards of $500 a day to be in a residential treatment program. Profit motive alone is not enough of a reason to discount the diagnosis, but the fact that these programs continue to make so much money without a clear and agreed upon diagnosis is troublesome. Ley argues that some experts are using this demand for treatment as proof of the need for a recognized and standardized diagnosis of sex addiction but that this seems like putting the cart before the horse.

Other Models

The shortcomings of the sex addiction model and the lack of agreement on how to diagnose it have led researchers and clinicians to look for other ways to identify what is happening when sexual behavior becomes compulsive or causes distress and harm. Most recently, there has been a push to get the Diagnostic and Statistical Manual of Mental Disorders (DSM), which is the American Psychiatric Association's compilation of possible diagnoses, to recognize something called "Hypersexual Disorder." Martin Kafka has proposed that the following diagnostic measures be used. For a period of at least 6 months a person needs to have recurrent and intense sexual fantasies, urges, or behaviors that meet three of these five criteria:

A1 Time consumed by sexual fantasies, urges or behaviors repetitively interferes with other important (non-sexual) goals, activities, and obligations.
A2 Repetitively engaging in sexual fantasies, urges or behaviors in response to dysphoric mood states (e.g. anxiety, depression, boredom, irritability).
A3 Repetitively engaging in sexual fantasies, urges or behaviors in response to stressful life events.
A4 Repetitive but unsuccessful efforts to control or significantly reduce these sexual fantasies, urges or behaviors.
A5 Repetitively engaging in sexual behaviors while disregarding the risk for physical or emotional harm to self or other.

In addition to meeting three of these criteria, there needs to be "clinically significant personal distress or impairment in social, occupational, or other important areas of functioning associated with the frequency and intensity of these sexual fantasies, urges, or behaviors" (Kafka, 2010, p. 379). He notes that this last part is important because "excessive, repetitive or hypersexual behavior without significant personal distress, possible volitional impairment or significant adverse consequence do not designate a clinical pathological concern" (Kafka, p. 380).

This clarification does help take some of the judgment about behaviors themselves out of the diagnostic process. It's not just that the clinician disapproves of the fact that a person is seeking sex outside his relationship or frequently engaging in one-night stands, it is that this behavior is causing the person himself significant grief.

In his commentary on Kafka's proposal, Charles Moser, an outspoken critic of the sex addiction model says this caveat is not enough. He writes:

> There is no doubt that individuals with all levels of sexual interest exist and individuals can attribute their distress or impairment to their level of sexual interest. Nevertheless, just because the individual (or the psychiatrist) believes the level of sexual interest is problematic does not make it so. (Moser, 2011, p. 227)

He also points out that not all distress is indicative of a mental disorder. The man whose wife says she will divorce him if he doesn't stop looking at pornography is undoubtedly distressed but not necessarily in a way that indicates psychological issues.

He also argues that criteria A1–A5 remain too subjective and too broad. For example, A2 and A3 suggest that using sex as a mood enhancer is a sign of a mental disorder but Moser argues that many people use sex to relieve boredom, release stress, or get themselves or their partner out of a bad mood. Criterion A5 speaks to repeating behaviors despite the risk of harm but we do something similar every day, says Moser, when we drive on the freeway or swim in the ocean (Moser, 2011, p. 228). Ley adds that the criteria still hinge on a certain amount of sex being too much sex. Kafka has suggested, for example, that more than seven orgasms a week from masturbation is indicative of a problem. He gleaned this number from some of the scarce data on "typical" sexual behavior. Yet Ley notes that some research has found 10–23% of men masturbate daily. Research has also concluded that under Kafka's criteria levels as many as 40% of men and 21% of women would be labeled hypersexual (Kafka, 2010, p. 24).

We, too, know many men and women who masturbate to orgasm every day often as a way to relax before bed. The idea that one more orgasm by one's self during the week, perhaps as the result of a really boring Sunday afternoon or a really sexy movie, would put someone over a clinical threshold is disturbing to us. We also worry that the caveat of causing distress is not enough to temper the idea that there is such a thing as too much masturbation because so many people were raised to believe that masturbation was bad or shameful. When we talk to young people (and adults) we basically say there is no such thing as too much unless it is interfering with your everyday functioning. While that is in the proposed diagnostic criteria, we think it may get buried under other people's opinions of how much is too much.

Moser also makes an important point about the danger of focusing on sexual behaviors themselves. He uses the analogy of a person with an obsessive-compulsive disorder (OCD) who is compelled to wash her hands numerous times in a row. We would not say that this person has a hand-washing disorder: "Similarly, individuals who experience distress or impairment related to their sexual activities may have a psychiatric disorder, but not necessarily a sexual disorder" (Moser, 2011, p. 228).

Our colleague Eli Coleman, the past president of the World Association of Health, has done work in this area for several decades. He writes that he prefers the term Impulsive/Compulsive Sexual Behavior (ICSB) because it is descriptive and "leaves open the possibilities of multiple pathological pathways and treatments." By his definition ICSB is a clinical syndrome "characterized by the experience of sexual urges, sexually arousing fantasies, and sexual behaviors that are recurrent, intense, and a distressful interference in one's daily life" (Coleman, 2011, p. 379). He and his colleagues name some specific behaviors that are more likely to become impulsive or compulsive such cruising or multiple partners, fixation on unattainable partners, autoeroticism, use of erotica, use of the internet, multiple love relationships, and expression of sexuality in a relationship.

Within the definition of each of these categories, Coleman and colleagues add identifiers of what makes the behavior potentially problematic. For example, compulsive autoeroticism (which is a fancy word for masturbation) can be identified not just by the number of orgasms a person has but by the following criteria, among others: (i) when orgasms are followed by intense loneliness, and (ii) when masturbation is only stopped as a result of exhaustion, injury, or extreme social pressure as opposed to self-satisfaction. Similarly, compulsive sexuality in a relationship can be identified, in part, when it is demanded through manipulation, coercion, or violence or when the relationships are characterized by intense possessiveness, jealousy, and anger (Coleman, 2011, table 2).

Coleman recognizes and cautions against the very real possibility of over-pathologizing sexual behavior by failing to recognize the wide range of normal human expression both in terms of variety and frequency. The danger is even more real because so many clinicians lack any training in sexuality. In the absence of training, personal opinions of what's "normal" can get in the way: "There is an inherent danger in diagnosing ICSB simply because someone's behavior does not fit the values of the individual, group, or society" (Coleman, 2011, p. 386).

Finding Common Ground

We echo these fears when looking at the way sexual addiction has been treated both by those who specialize in it and by the popular media. It is simultaneously presented as a danger we need to be scared of and a punch line we need to laugh at. Quantifying sex and suggesting that people need to be within certain parameters (neither too much nor too little) fails to recognize how different we all are in terms of desires and libidos. Qualifying sexual behaviors as either within or outside "normal" boundaries fails to recognize how different we all are in terms of our likes and dislikes. Putting labels on the frequency or type of sexual behavior people choose is inherently judgmental and can be used for discriminatory purposes (remember it wasn't so long ago that homosexuality was considered a mental illness). And, focusing on sexual behaviors as a problem in-and-of-themselves may prevent clinicians from seeing it as a potential symptom of other underlying psychological disorders such as OCD, anxiety, or depression.

We understand that there are people who engage in destructive sexual behaviors that cause significant harm to themselves and, perhaps, others. We do want these people to get the help they need and we want clinicians to be able to treat them without any other agenda. We worry though that the popularity of the term sex addiction and the ubiquity of self-help websites and books designed to tell people how to cope with this self-diagnosed affliction will do little to actually help them and may, in fact, do harm.

References

Carnes, P. (1983). *Out of the Shadows: Understanding Sexual Addiction*. CompCare Publishers, Minneapolis, MN.

Carnes. P. (2003). Understanding sexual addiction. *SIECUS Report*, 31(4), 5–7.

Coleman, E. (2011). Impulsive/compulsive sexual behavior: Assessment and Treatment. In Grant, J.E. and Potenza, M.N. (eds) *Oxford Handbook of Impulse Control Disorders*. Oxford University Press, New York, pp. 375–388.

Kafka, M.P. (2010). Hypersexual disorder: A proposed diagnosis for DSM-V. *Archives of Sexual Behavior*, 39(2), 377–400.

Klein, M. (2003). Sex addiction: A dangerous concept. *SIECUS Report*, 31(4), 8–11.

Ley, D.J. (2012). *The Myth of Sex Addiction*. Rowman & Littlefield, New York, NY.

Moser, C. (2011). Hypersexual disorder: Just more muddled thinking. *Archives of Sexual Behavior*, 40(2), 227–229.

Sexaholics Anonymous (2001). What is SA? www.sa.org (accessed August 6, 2014).

Myth #44 She Was Asking For It, and Other Common Myths About Sexual Assault

In August 2012, Representative Todd Akin, a Republican from Missouri who was running for a seat in the Senate, explained why he was opposed to abortion even in cases of rape by saying:

> "It seems to me, from what I understand from doctors, that's really rare," Mr. Akin said of pregnancies from rape. "If it's a legitimate rape, the female body has ways to try to shut that whole thing down. But let's assume that maybe that didn't work or something: I think there should be some punishment, but the punishment ought to be of the rapist, and not attacking the child." (Eligon and Schwirtz, 2012)

Though his comments show a disturbing lack of understanding about human reproduction, they drew the most ire for the phrase "legitimate rape" which by its very nature suggests that some rapes are not, in fact, legitimate. Unfortunately, this view that rape is only "really rape" under certain circumstances—like when a stranger jumps out of the bushes wielding a weapon—is not uncommon. Many people in our society continue to believe that rape victims (who are most often, though by no means always, women) are complicit in the crime based on the clothes they were wearing, the area they were in, or the sexual messages they were sending. Others feel that rape can't occur in a couple that has already had consensual sex, especially one that is married.

These views are deeply ingrained in our society and stem from beliefs about sex, gender roles, and marriage that stretch back many hundreds of years (some would even say back to Biblical times). They are also the reason that so many rapes go unreported and so many perpetrators unpunished. Since the 1970s researchers have examined the prevalence of rape myths such as these, especially among students. A 2001 study, for example, used open-ended questions and found that 66% of college students believed in some combination of these myths (Buddie and Miller, 2001). Possibly more disturbing, studies have found that these myths exist among prosecutors and clergy members as well (Edwards *et al.*, 2011).

This entry explores some of the myths around rape in an attempt to underscore the basic premise that circumstances do not matter—sex without consent is never morally acceptable.

"She Was Asking For It"

This may be the most insipid of all of the myths about sexual assault because it essentially puts every aspect of a woman's behavior leading up to her attack under a microscope in order to somehow shift the blame from the perpetrator to the victim. People analyze what she was wearing, where she was walking, and how she was acting. One of the interesting things about this myth is that it often is indirect in nature. If you ask a college student, for example, if a particular woman was to blame for her attack he/she would most likely say "Of course not." But if you drill down into the woman's behavior and ask if certain actions—such as drinking or dressing sexily—may have contributed to her attack, students will likely say yes. One study found that though they would not blame her directly, 53% of college students agreed that the victim's actions led to her assault (McMahon, 2010).

Such attitudes have their roots in our culture and our religions. Edwards *et al.* remind us of the Biblical story of Dinah who goes out to meet a friend in town and is abducted and raped by a local prince on the way. The interpretation of this story by some theologians suggests that Dinah was responsible for what happened not just because she was alone but because by being alone she clearly wanted to be seen by local men. In an historical review of rape cases in Britain, Stevenson (2000) argues that Victorian stereotypes and expectations of how women should behave continue to have "profound implications for the ways in which modern women are regarded in the trial process." At that time:

> Women alleging rape were expected to act and portray themselves as unequivocal victims if their allegations were to have any credibility. Any woman who conducted herself in a manner suggestive of an "independent mind" risk meeting with skepticism—she was less likely to be believed and her attitude could evoke sympathy for the defendant. (Stephenson, 2000, p. 345)

Thus, it was not just what a women did on the day or night of her attack that was used to judge how much of what happened was her fault, it was also her general character and previous sexual behavior that was up for debate. Noting the unfairness of this kind of character valuation, feminists and advocates in the 1970s and 1980s pushed for laws excluding a victim's past sexual behavior from coming into play in court. The goal of rape shield laws was not only to protect victims from accusations and humiliation at trial, but also to increase the number of rape cases that were reported by making the trial experience less traumatic. The rape shield laws in many states, however, include pretty wide exceptions under which evidence of prior sexual behavior can be admissible. Some actually leave it up to the judge (Haddad, 2005). Moreover, rape shield laws only apply to a victim's past behavior, her behavior at the time of her attack—such as whether she was drinking or flirting with men—can and is often used.

In our entry on alcohol and sexual assault (see Myth # 40), for example, we note the case of Daisy Coleman, a 14-year-old who was raped at a party while clearly intoxicated and then left on her front porch in sub-freezing temperatures. Despite the fact that she was clearly too drunk to consent to sex, the town rallied around the alleged perpetrators and argued that Daisy was a troubled young woman who snuck out of her house. Though she claims that her attacker and his friends plied her with liquor, the fact that she had drunk some alcohol before leaving her house was used against her. She and her family were targeted, her mother lost her job, and their house burned down under suspicious circumstances (Arnett, 2013). This experience of rape and subsequent ostracizing of the victim remains way too common.

"She's Lying About It"

One of the problems with many rape cases is that there are rarely any witnesses. (Though it is interesting to us that in cases like Daisy Coleman or Steubenville, Ohio, the fact that there are witnesses does not seem to help the victim win public support.) It often comes down to a situation of he said/she said. The alleged perpetrator most frequently admits to having had sex with the woman but says that it was consensual while the woman argues it was rape. In these cases, women who report rapes are not just considered complicit in the incident (because they were drinking or agreed to go back to his room), they are frequently accused of outright lying.

One of the more high profile cases of this phenomenon occurred in 2003 when NBA star Kobe Bryant was indicted on charges of sexually assaulting a 19-year-old hotel employee in Colorado. Before the case made it anywhere near a court room, the woman was subject to intense scrutiny and massive violations of her privacy. Though her name wasn't officially released and a judge ordered that her personal information be kept private, within days her name, yearbook photo, phone number, home address, and email address were all available on the internet. Talk radio hosts called her nasty things and "friends" went on morning shows to tell stories about her past boyfriend, alleged drug overdose, and even a failed audition for *American Idol* (Haddad, 2005). People insisted she made her allegations in an attempt to get her 15 minutes of fame or extort money from Bryant. She received death threats. Not surprisingly, she refused to cooperate with the prosecution and the case was dropped because of her unwillingness to move forward.

As a result we will never truly know what happened in that hotel room but we do know, all too well, what happens to women who "cry rape."

Edwards *et al.* review the discrepancies between perception and reality. They note that reviews of rape allegations have found that very few of them are false. One international review of studies and law enforcement estimates, for example, found that only 2–8% of reported sexual assaults are false. Popular opinion, however, suggests far more. A 2007 sample of college students believed that 19% of all rape accusations were false. In a 2010 study of college men, 22% agreed that "women lie about rape to get back at men" and 13% agreed that "a lot of women lead men on and then cry rape." This represents some progress from 1980 when 50% of men and women said they believed this but clearly the attitude still exists (Edwards *et al.*, 2011).

Interestingly, this belief can be traced all the way back to the 1700s (and likely before). In 1736, Sir Mathew Hale, a judge, issued what would come to be known as the "Hale Warning" when he wrote that rape: "is an accusation easily to be made, hard to be proved, and harder to be defended by the party accused, tho' never so innocent." It's hard to believe but this statement was read in court to cast doubt on women's stories as recently as the late twentieth century (Edwards *et al.*, 2011, p. 768).

These beliefs seem to be particularly problematic on college campuses where the "he said/she said" scenario plays out time and time again. Boy and girl meet at a party where they are drinking, they go back to his room or hers, possibly fool around, and they have sex. Was it consensual or was it rape? No one outside of that room will ever know exactly what happened but everyone seems to have an opinion. If these cases are ever made public (which is a big if as many are never reported), opinions are often colored by the pervasive belief that women make up rape to get back at men or to explain away sexual behavior they subsequently regret.

"She Was Married to Him"

Another age-old misconception is that rape and sexual assault don't or even can't take place within a committed relationship and certainly not within marriage. A telephone survey in 2002 found that only 15% of the sample believed boyfriends and husbands could rape their partners. College students had somewhat similar responses with 31% of men and 19% of women in a study saying that having sex with one's wife without consent did not count as rape. In fact, 9% of men and 5% of women in that sample thought that even if a man used physical force to have sex with his wife, it did not constitute rape. A study in 2008 also found that even if respondents correctly identified an incident as marital rape they still viewed it as different from other attacks, "they were reluctant to believe that the act was a violation of the wife's right or that she will be psychologically damaged from the experience because the perpetrator is someone with whom she has had consensual sex in the past" (Ferro *et al.*, 2008, p. 774).

This myth is so deeply entrenched in our history and our view of marriage and women's rights that until recently it was barely challenged. Once again, we can thank Sir Matthew Hale for some of this thinking as he wrote in 1736 "the husband cannot be guilty of rape commitment by himself upon his lawful wife, for by the mutual matrimonial consent and contract the wife hath give herself in this kind unto her husband, which she cannot retract." Essentially, he's saying that on her wedding day the wife consented to any and all sex that her husband wanted until death did they part. For a long time, it was not legally possible for a wife to accuse her husband of rape because she was for all intents and purposes his property and could only be considered injured if he agreed she had been. Therefore she would need his consent to accuse him of sex without consent. English judge William Blackstone put it this way in 1765, "Husband and wife are legally one person. The legal existence of the wife is suspended during the marriage, incorporated into that of the husband...If a wife is injured she cannot take action without her husband's concurrence" (Edwards *et al.*, 2011, p. 764).

It might not be alarming that this was the attitude of the 1760s when women had very few rights, but it is disheartening that similar views of marital rape lasted for more than 200 years past that. In 1975, South Dakota became the first state to make marital rape a crime and in 1978 John Rideout became the first person ever charged with this crime. Though all states now have laws forbidding marital rape (as of 1993), 31 states have wide exemptions to their rules such as those that dictate marital rape is only a crime if physical force is used (Hasday, 2000).

To a lesser extent, the attitude that rape in marriage isn't a crime carries over to rape in dating and other relationships. Studies have found that the perceived seriousness of the crime decreases as the relationship between the victim and perpetrator increases. The true signifier here seems to be whether the couple has ever had sexual intercourse in the past. A study with college students, for example, asked them to respond to various vignettes about rape. It found that once couples had ever had sex, sympathy for and belief in the story of rape diminished. Moreover, there were no differences in the responses of participants to vignettes in which the couple had been in a sexual relationship when compared with those in which the couple was married. The researchers write, "these results suggest that once a female consents to sexual intercourse in a relationship and this is known, people's perceptions of the seriousness of the rape decreases as the victim's culpability increases" (Monson *et al.*, 2000).

So Complicated, and Yet so Simple

Rape myths pervade our culture and this crime is going to continue unabated until we change our thinking on many levels. A recent report by the White House Council on Women and Girls summarizes this well when it says:

> Sexual assault is pervasive because our culture still allows it to persist. According to the experts, violence prevention can't just focus on the perpetrators and the

survivors. It has to involve everyone. And in order to put an end to this violence, we as a nation must see it for what it is: a crime. Not a misunderstanding, not a private matter, not anyone's right or any woman's fault. And bystanders must be taught and emboldened to step in to stop it. We can only stem the tide of violence if we all do our part. (2014, p. 5)

On an individual level, however, these complicated societal issues boil down to some pretty simple rules of behavior. No one ever has a right to have sex with another person without their consent. Ever. Nothing that the other person wears, says, or does changes this fact nor does any prior sexual relationship between the two. Sex is only acceptable when both parties say it is.

Putting this into practice, unfortunately, remains far more complicated than it should be.

References

Arnett, D. (2013). Nightmare in Maryville: Teens' sexual encounter ignites a firestorm against family. *The Kansas City Star* (October 24). http://www.kansascity.com/news/special-reports/maryville/article329412/Nightmare-in-Maryville-Teens%E2%80%99-sexual-encounter-ignites-a-firestorm-against-family.htm (accessed August 13, 2014).

Buddie, A.M. and Miller, A.G. (2001). Beyond rape myths: A more complex view of perceptions of rape victims. *Sex Roles*, 45(3–4), 139–160.

Edwards, K.M., Turchik, J.A., Dardis, C.M., Reynolds, N., and Gidycz, C.A. (2011). Rape myths: History, individual and institutional-level presence, and implications for change. *Sex Roles*, 65(11–12), 761–773.

Eligon, J. and Schwirtz, M. (2012). Senate candidate provokes ire with "legitimate rape" comment. *New York Times* (August 19). http://www.nytimes.com/2012/08/20/us/politics/todd-akin-provokes-ire-with-legitimate-rape-comment.html?_r=0 (accessed August 6, 2014).

Ferro, C., Cermele, J., and Saltzman, A. (2008). Current perceptions of marital rape: Some good and not-so-good news. *Journal of Interpersonal Violence*, 23(6), 764–779.

Haddad, R.I. (2005). Shield or sieve? *People v. Bryant* and the rape shield law in high-profile cases. *Columbia Journal of Law and Social Problems*, 39(2), 185–221.

Hasday, J.E. (2000). Contest and consent: A legal history of marital rape. *California Law Review*, 88(5), 1373–1505.

McMahon, S. (2010). Rape myth beliefs and bystander attitudes among incoming college students. *Journal of American College Health*, 59(1), 3–11.

Monson, C.M., Langhinrichsen-Rohling, J., and Binderup, T. (2000). Does "no" really mean "no" after you say "yes"? Attributions about date and marital rape. *Journal of Interpersonal Violence*, 15(11), 1156–1174.

Stevenson, K. (2000). Unequivocal victims: The historical roots of the mystification of the female complainant in rape cases. *Feminist Legal Studies*, 8(3), 343–366.

White House Council on Women and Girls (2014). *Rape and Sexual Assault: A Renewed Call to Action*.

Myth #45 Pornography Is Dangerous

To hear some people tell it there is a bogeyman lurking inside your computer that is going to steal your daughter's innocence, turn your son into an unfeeling masturbation machine, and convince your husband to cheat on you daily with women he will never actually meet. But wait, that's not all, if left unchecked this digital beast will devastate the very fabric of our society by increasing sexual violence, ruining romantic relationships, and causing the downfall of the traditional, two-parent, married family. What is it you ask? Why pornography, of course.

The fear of porn isn't new. Anthony Comstock certainly had it when he helped pass the law that banned sending "obscene" materials through the United States' Postal Service in 1873. Remember, in 1873 there were few ways to access porn other than through the US Postal Service and the most you might get in your mailbox, were you or the sender willing to risk the penalty of imprisonment and hard labor, would be a picture of some naked girls perhaps posing together in suggestive ways.

What a difference 140 years can make. Today's pornography is usually in the form of a moving picture that has images and sound and maybe even a semi-believable plot. We are so spoiled that we can tailor it to our personal preferences or mood, choosing the basic set up (first times), the players (two redheads and a brunette), and the genre (amateur home porn or at least something that looks like it's homegrown). More importantly, we can find it now on any number of the internet-enabled devices we keep in our homes or our pockets.

Comstock is no doubt rolling over in his grave and his ideological descendants are, to put it mildly, totally freaking out. In November 2004, the Senate Commerce Committee's Science, Technology and Space Subcommittee held a hearing on the danger of pornography in which many so-called experts argued that porn was a scourge on society that had to be controlled lest all of our young women and men be permanently ruined. Some of the speakers used science-sounding words and warned of addiction and lasting changes to the teenage brain caused by "erotoxins." Psychiatrist Jeffrey Satinover testified that, "Pornography really does, unlike other addictions, biologically cause direct release of the most perfect addictive substance. That is, it causes masturbation, which causes release of the naturally occurring opioids. It does what heroin can't do, in effect." And Judith Reisman argued that the effect of "erotoxins" (a made-up word that seems to mean chemicals released when watching erotic images) is so bad that pornography should not be protected under the First Amendment's freedom of speech. It's unclear exactly why this hearing was called as no legislation on the subject was up for debate but then-Senator Sam Brownback (Republican, Kansas), the subcommittee's chairman, called the hearing the most disturbing one he'd ever seen in the Senate (Singel, 2004).

If these allegations (including that this is the worst thing a member of the US Senate had ever heard on the job) sound a little alarmist to you, know that we think so too. We are also concerned that the speakers were overwhelmingly conservative and religious. Satinover, for example, served on the advisory board of National Association for Research and Therapy of Homosexuality, a group that believes homosexuality can be cured. (See Myth # 10 for a discussion of so-called reparative therapy.) Reisman has spent much of her career trying to discredit the work of pioneering sexologist Alfred Kinsey and has argued that homosexuals are dangerous to society and the Jews are behind the availability of abortion (Blumenthal, 2004; Ley, 2012, p. 34). Brownback himself is a conservative Christian who is currently the Governor of Kansas and believes that young people should be taught to save sex for marriage (Brownback, 2008).

We mention the background of these speakers because we think it's important to recognize that the antiporn movement is part of a much larger conservative social agenda that would also like to do away with abortion, birth control, and, in many cases, gay rights. Further, we think understanding this agenda is particularly essential because most of the claims as to why pornography is dangerous have never been proven scientifically. Without unbiased research to back up what they say, the inherent biases of the people saying it become crucial.

We should add that porn may be one of the areas where people labeled "far right" and "far left" agree. While many feminists have no problem with pornography or even believe it can be a positive addition to our understanding of sexuality, others argue against it because they feel it reduces women to sex objects, presents a warped view of female sexuality, and glamorizes violence against women to the point where it can promote or even cause such violence. (See MacKinnon, 1989 or Wolf, 2003 for more on these theories and those who disagree with them.)

With that we should probably note our inherent biases. As sexual health experts we believe that, for the most part, viewing pornography, either alone or with a partner, is a healthy form of sexual behavior. Unlike Satinover, we like pornography in part because it does lead to masturbation and we think that masturbation is not just a pleasurable sexual activity in-and-of-itself but a way that people can learn about what makes them feel good which they can in turn share with their partner(s). We also believe that pornography can expand some people's view of sex and help them be more comfortable with experimenting or trying something new. In fact, research has shown that pornography has mostly positive effects (more on that later).

Of course, we have our limits. We are not comfortable with pornography that depicts children as sexual participants or objects even if the actors are technically not underage. We are also uncomfortable with the misogynistic nature of some porn. Moreover, though it is often hard to know what went on behind the scenes, we do not condone any pornography that was made without the explicit, informed consent of all of the players (meaning everyone knew what was going to happen in the scene and agreed to it before the cameras started rolling). Finally, we have to add that we have concerns about the health and welfare of those in the adult film industry as there have been recent outbreaks of STIs, including HIV, within the industry and we worry that performers are under too much pressure to have unprotected sex.

With those biases and caveats in mind, let us try to dispel some of the stubborn myths about pornography.

Porn Is Neither a Newfound Phenomenon Nor an Epidemic

First, let us start by dispelling the myth that the majority of pages on the internet are devoted to pornography. Though we wholeheartedly believe that any search term you could come up with has the possibility of sending you to a porn site, it turns out that a very small part of the World Wide Web is actually devoted to triple-X content. A new book, *A Billion Wicked Thoughts*, suggests that only 4% of web pages have pornographic content and only 14% of searches are seeking it (Rife, 2014). (We're pretty sure the rest is dedicated to cute pictures of cats.)

Here's something else that we find pretty interesting, although the internet has made accessing porn easier, the rates of porn usages haven't really changed in the last four decades. It surged in the early 1970s when the VCR allowed people to view pornography in the privacy of their own home. This was a huge change from having to go to XXX movie theaters in sketchy parts of town. (Here's something even funnier: In the early 1970s two different types of in-home movie players were introduced. Sony introduced the Betamax and JVC introduced its Video Home System (VHS). Sony refused to let pornographers use Betamax's technology but JVC allowed porn on VHS tapes. This has been credited with why VHS format ultimately won out in the market and Beta never took off; Van Scoy, 2000.)

So it was the VCR not the Web that introduced the era of home-viewing and changed porn forever. The most significant contributions of the Web, therefore, might be the immediacy of delivery and the sheer volume of content that a porn viewer can choose from. While a teenager in 1978 may have been stuck watching and re-watching *Debbie Does Dallas* time and time again, his 2014 counterpart can see something new whenever he wants to and can choose from a much wider variety. We agree that this newfound variety may make porn viewing more exciting and compelling than it once was.

Porn Does Not Increase Rape and Sexual Violence

Much has been made of an interview conducted in 1989 by James Dobson, founder of the conservative group Focus on the Family, with convicted mass murderer Ted Bundy in which Bundy traced his problems back to pornography he found in the neighbor's trash. He explained that he got addicted to it and began to need more explicit and more graphic porn in order to be satisfied. He called looking at violent acts in porn the jumping off point to actually committing violence and said that every violent man he knew had a problem with porn (Ley, 2012, p. 34).

Many were rightfully alarmed by this assertion, but we have to remember not just that this is the self-diagnosis of a serial criminal but that it cannot be offered as evidence of cause and effect. Even if he is correct that all the violent men he knows have a problem with porn, it does not logically follow that all men who watch porn (or even all men who have a problem with porn) are violent. It is more likely that men with a tendency toward violence are drawn to violent porn because of the other psychological and personality issues they are facing. To put the most reductionist logic on this point—most men view porn and most men do not rape or murder.

Some who argue against the idea that porn causes rape have noted that in the years since the internet has made porn far more accessible, rates of rape have gone down. A study looked at access to the internet across the country, noting that some states were faster to hop on the web wagon than others. This study found that a 10% increase in internet access in a state yields a 7.3% decrease in reported rapes, and that states that adopted the internet quickly saw the biggest declines. The authors say this effect remains even after controlling for other characteristics of states and their residents such as alcohol consumption, police presence, poverty and unemployment rates, or population density (as cited in Landsberg, 2006). This research is likely not enough to conclude that the internet with all of its porn reduces rape (there could still be another explanation for the correlation) but it certainly casts a doubt on those who say it is likely to increase sexual violence.

A review conducted before the internet became a household word looked at the theory that access to more pornography, and in particular more violent pornography, would lead to rape by examining four countries during a period in which porn was becoming much more widely available. A researcher looked at the United States, Denmark, Sweden, and West Germany between 1964 and 1984. (For those who don't remember, Germany was divided into two countries—the communist East Germany aligned with the Soviet Union and the capitalist West Germany aligned with European governments—after World War II and stayed that way until its reunification in 1990.) The researcher found "clear and undisputed evidence" that access to all forms of pornography went from "extreme scarcity to relative abundance during that time." The author then looked at the rates of rape and nonviolent crimes during that time period, noting that all crimes went up. According to the author: "The results showed that in none of the countries did rape increase more than nonsexual violent crimes. This finding in itself would seem sufficient to discard the hypothesis that pornography causes rape" (Kutchinsky, 1991).

A more disturbing link between rape and porn was suggested recently by Mary Anne Layden, a psychiatrist who was also among those who testified in front of the Senate in 2004. Layden believes that viewing pornography makes women more likely to be raped. In the *Washington Times*, Layden was quoted as saying: "The more pornography women use, the more likely they are to be victims of non-consensual sex" (Duke, 2010). She does not provide statistics to back this up or sufficiently elaborate on her theory to explain why this might be true. In an article for *Psychology Today*, David Ley writes: "The only way this has any kernel of truth is that highly sexual women are more likely to report use of pornography. Highly sexual women are also likely to report greater numbers of partners, and somewhat higher risk of an incident of sexual abuse or rape, possibly as a result of situations of date rape (Ley, 2010)." Even by this stretch of logic, there is no way that the fact that the woman watched pornography was in any way responsible for the crime someone committed against her. This screams of yet another way to blame the victims of sexual assault for their fate—she was dress like a slut, she was drinking, she was walking in a bad part of town, she watches porn.

Porn Is Not Addictive (and Won't Stop You from Bonding With a Real Person)

In Myth # 43 we talked about how we are skeptical of the sex addiction model which suggests that some people react to sexual behavior in the same way they would to alcohol, heroin, or cocaine. Ultimately, they can't stop despite the harm that it is doing to their careers and relationships. Though we acknowledged that for some people sexual behavior can feel out of control and become impulsive or compulsive, we don't believe that addiction is the proper term to describe what they are going through nor do we think that a 12-step program akin to Alcoholics Anonymous is the correct way to go about treatment.

The idea of an addiction akin to alcoholism or drug abuse is even more prevalent when it comes to pornography use, and internet porn in particular. The basic story is this— a young boy watches porn and likes it, he watches more porn and likes it, he keeps watching more porn, his porn habits escalate as he starts to look for more graphic and explicit porn (stuff that would have made him uncomfortable to start with), he becomes desensitized to the porn and desperate to get the same thrill he used to get, he searches for more and kinkier porn—he is a porn addict. The story has two endings—in one he starts acting out sexually (and violently) in real life, and in the other he can't act sexually because the boring sex he is offered in real life cannot compare to the exciting stuff he has seen on the internet (McConnell and Campbell, 1996).

Those who believe that pornography is addictive toss around many different ideas about what might be going on inside the user's brain. Some blame it on dopamine, a chemical in the brain that apparently "seeks novelty" (your brain on porn), others believe the neurochemical DeltaFosB (which is most often written as ΔFosB) is responsible, and still other blame oxytocin, the hormone released during orgasm and breastfeeding that is responsible for bonding. (See yourbrainondrugs.com for examples of these arguments.) We do not have the space or the degree in neurobiology necessary to refute each claim one by one. Instead, we fall back on the fact that none of these claims has ever been proven. In a recent critique of a study on porn addiction, Reid *et al.* write:

> [the authors] offer some interesting neuroscience perspectives on their conceptualization of pornography problems as an *addictive* disorder. They highlight several parallels between dysregulated pornography consumption and other maladaptive behaviors, some of which are viewed as addictions. Although we believe these parallels are worthy of scientific inquiry, [the authors] offered little, if any, convincing evidence to support their perspectives. Instead, excessive liberties and misleading interpretations of neuroscience research are used to assert that excessive pornography consumption causes brain damage. (Reid *et al.*, 2011)

Like the sex addiction model, the idea of an addiction to porn is based more on personal stories, theories, and conjecture than proven (or disproven) scientific study. We also think it is based on antiporn biases and until we see some high-quality studies proving that desensitization to porn is a biological process akin to needing higher doses of prescription painkillers rather than just the evolution of sexual curiosity, we remain skeptical.

Moreover, treating porn like drugs or alcohol once again opens the door to arbitrary assessments of how much is too much and how kinky is too kinky. As Eli Coleman, past president of the World Association of Sexual Health explains "What we know about alcohol and drug addictions cannot be simply transferred to other behavioral excesses." Calling it an addiction, he notes: "implies an underlying mechanism that is akin to alcohol and/or drug addiction and suggests a treatment approach which oftentimes recommends abstinence and reliance on a 12 step approach to behavioral control. We do not treat eating disorders as an addiction so why should we treat excessive pornography use in this way? This does not make sense" (American Sexual Health Association, 2014).

Marty Klein, author of *America's Sex Wars*, adds that often when he is presented with a "porn addict" seeking treatment it is because a spouse has declared the amount of porn the patient watches to be too much (Klein, 2010). Porn addiction has become a clever term for partnered men (and women) to hide behind rather than admit that they just really like watching sex on screen. This isn't a psychological problem but it may indicate a problem in the relationship.

Of course, both Coleman and Klein (and all the other authors we cite who cast doubt on porn as an addiction) acknowledge that some people have trouble regulating their intake of porn which can cause both personal distress and relationship issues. Coleman says that for some people sex, or in this case watching porn, can become "dysregulated or out of balance for a variety of reasons. For some it is a problem of impulse control, for others it is more like an obsession, and for others it is like a compulsion. And for others, it is a part of personality structure and has nothing to do with impulse control, obsessions or compulsions" (American Sexual Health Association, 2010).

As we said in our discussion of sex addiction, we want these people to get help. We are worried though that sites like yourbrainondrugs.com, which pops up first in a search on pornography addiction, will lead people down a self-help path that starts with the premise that all porn is bad.

Porn Is Not Real (Which Can Be Good and Bad)

We want to end by saying we think that the availability of porn on the internet brings with it a responsibility for adults to educate young people about how to be smart consumers. Preventing young people from ever watching porn would be an impossible (and inadvisable) task in this day and age. Working to ensure that they don't see it too soon (or don't see too much too soon) is an important part of parenting. All of the internet safety rules and advice apply. Keep the computer in a public place and monitor their online activities either by using software to limit the places they can go or by reviewing their history.

More importantly, though, we have to talk to our kids about porn. As the first sex education many young people will get it certainly will make an impression. Unfortunately, much of that impression will be wrong. Sex in real life doesn't look like that for a plethora of reasons. Porn may make things look easier or more seamless than they really are, it may give the wrong idea about what is likely to turn a partner on, promote unrealistic expectations of how long lovemaking lasts and how many orgasms one can expect, and it may undermine our efforts to teach about the importance of consent. Women in porn often do say no when they mean yes or appear to enjoy being forcibly taken which can easily give the wrong idea about consent.

Discussions about porn should also help young people understand and set their own personal limits. As we said before, we have absolute limits of what we find unacceptable. We each also have our own limits as to what we find enjoyable. Helping young people understand the need to decide on personal boundaries before they have consumed a vast amount of pornography can help them understand what they see.

Finally, all porn viewers should know that enjoying something on-screen does not have to mean that you would enjoy it in real life. Many heterosexual women prefer viewing lesbian porn despite having no real life intention of having sex with a women. Porn can be a safe place to explore a different kind of sex.

References

American Sexual Health Association (2014). Is pornography addictive? (January 20). http://www.ashasexualhealth.org/cgblog/100/Is-Pornography-Addictive.html (accessed August 6, 2014).

Blumenthal, M. (2004). Her Kinsey obsession. *Alternet* (December 14). http://www.alter net.org/story/20744/her_kinsey_obsession (accessed August 6, 2014).

Brownback, S. (2008). Press Release: Brownback testifies before house committee on importance of funding for abstinence education (April 23). http://votesmart.org/pub lic-statement/335937/brownback-testifies-before-house-committee-on-importance-of-funding-for-abstinence-education#.Uw9w9PldWmQ (accessed August 6, 2104).

Duke, R.B. (2010). More women lured to pornography addiction: Survey finds 1 in 6 caught up in steamy Web. *Washington Times* (July 11). http://www.washingtontimes.com/news/2010/jul/11/more-women-lured-to-pornography-addiction/ (accessed August 6, 2014).

Klein, M. (2010). Porn addict or selfish bastard? Life is more complicated than that. *Psychology Today Online* (May 6). http://www.psychologytoday.com/blog/sexual-intelligence/201105/porn-addict-or-selfish-bastard-life-is-more-complicated (accessed August 6, 2014).

Kutchinsky, B. (1991). Pornography and rape: Theory and practice?: Evidence from crime data in four countries where pornography is easily available. *International Journal of Law and Psychiatry*, 14(1), 47–64.

Landsburg, S.E. (2006). How the web prevents rape: All that internet porn reduces sex crimes. Really. *Salon* (October 30). http://www.slate.com/articles/arts/everyday_eco nomics/2006/10/how_the_web_prevents_rape.html (accessed August 6, 2014).

Ley, D. (2010). Watch out women, Porno will steal your soul! *Psychology Today Online* (July 18). http://www.psychologytoday.com/blog/women-who-stray/201007/watch-out-women-porno-will-steal-your-soul (accessed August 6, 2014).

Ley, D.J. (2012). *The Myth of Sex Addiction*. Rowman & Littlefield, New York, NY.

MacKinnon, C.A. (1989). Sexuality, pornography, and method: Pleasure under Patriarchy. *Ethics*, 99(2), 314–346.

McConnell, G. and Campbell, K. (1996). The stages of pornography addiction. *Focus on the Family*. http://www.focusonthefamily.com/marriage/divorce_and_infidelity/pornography_and_virtual_infidelity/stages_of_porn_addiction.aspx (accessed August 6, 2014).

Reid R.C., Carpenter B.N., and Fong T.W. (2011). Neuroscience research fails to support claims that excessive pornography consumption causes brain damage. *Surgical Neurology International*, 2, 64.

Rife, K. (2014). Porn MD's Live Search lets you see inside the minds of horny strangers. *The AV Club* (February 25). http://www.avclub.com/article/pornmds-live-search-lets-you-see-inside-the-minds--201494 (accessed August 6, 2104).

Singel, R. (2004). Internet porn: Worse than crack? *Wired* (November 19). http://archive.wired.com/science/discoveries/news/2004/11/65772 (accessed August 13, 2014).

Van Scoy, K. (2000). Sex sells, so learn a thing or two from it. *PC Computing*, 13(1), 64.

Wolf, N. (2003). The porn myth. *New York Magazine*, 20.

9 THE NOT-SO-PRIVATE SIDE OF SEX

Sex, Society, and the Law

Myth #46

Sex Education Makes Kids More Sexually Active

The question of whether to teach sexuality education in schools and how to approach it has been debated for well over 100 years. In fact, the National Education Association (NEA) discussed the role of sexuality education in the school curriculum at its annual meeting in 1892. A number of years later, in 1914, the NEA passed a resolution suggesting that "institutions preparing teachers give attention to such subjects as would qualify for instruction in the general fields of morals as well as in the specific fields of sex hygiene" (Carrera, 1971, p. 99). In 1920, the federal government weighed in with its manual, *Sex Education in High School*, which as the name suggests gave advice on how to teach older students about sexuality education (Yarber, 1994).

From the beginning, however, there were some who thought that sexuality education had no place in public schools. These opponents used many arguments to persuade parents that sex education was a bad idea. They argued that sex was a moral and religious issue not a health issue; that schools were usurping parental authority; that the topic was too risqué; and that teaching kids about sex would spoil their innocence, provide scintillating instruction in sexual technique, and give teens ideas that they would inevitably try. In later years (in particular after the start of the AIDS epidemic), they acknowledged that sex education could and should be addressed in schools, but suggested that the most appropriate message was one of abstinence. Teens need direction, they suggested, giving them information on safer sex—or worse, giving them condoms—was akin to giving them license to have sex. Instead, young people needed to understand sex outside of marriage is *inevitably*

50 Great Myths of Human Sexuality, First Edition. Pepper Schwartz and Martha Kempner.
© 2015 John Wiley & Sons, Inc. Published 2015 by John Wiley & Sons, Inc.

harmful and simply told not to do it. This would keep them safe from STIs and teen pregnancy.

Given that these debates have been unfolding over more than a century, it is not surprising to us that a lot of misunderstandings and misinformation about sexuality education continues to float around. In fact, if someone had asked us to write a book called 50 Great Myths of Sexuality Education, we are pretty sure we could have filled all the pages. Since we don't have that much room, we focus on a few of the most common and pervasive myths around sexuality education in the hopes of setting the 100-plus-year-old record straight.

"Teaching Kids about Sex Encourages Them to Do It"

Adults seem to have always worried that teaching young people about sexuality makes it more likely that they will go out and try it. A few rationales are given for this mistaken belief; some say that sex education is titillating and merely piques young people's curiosity, while others say that teaching about the topic carries the implicit message that having sex is okay.

The truth is that young people are naturally curious about sexual behavior (maybe it's the rivers of hormones that start flowing through their bodies around the time of puberty). Though we can't speak for what it was like in the 1890s when these debates began, today information about and images of sexuality are everywhere. Young people are bound to see a couple kissing or rolling around in bed any time they flip channels on basic cable, see models in skimpy underwear or bikinis on the cover of many mainstream magazines, and have access to vast quantities of full-on pornography at the click of a mouse. Sex education class may be the least titillating thing they do all day but it is the only one of these things that can help them think critically about what they are inevitably seeing, reading, and feeling.

And the research shows that giving them honest information about both abstinence and contraception does not make them have sex sooner, does not make them have sex more often, and does not make them have sex with more partners. In fact, just the opposite is true—young people who go through this kind of sexuality education are more likely to delay sex, have fewer partners, and use condoms and other contraceptive methods when they become sexually active (Kirby, 1997, 2001).

"Okay, but it Teaches Them How to Do It"

The fear that sex education makes kids have sex earlier may be rooted in a misunderstanding about what actually happens in the classroom. In many controversies, parents refer to sex education as "how to" instruction and argue that it's inappropriate for school. In fact, a *Time Magazine* (1969) article looked at some of the controversies around sex education that were raging at the time and concluded: "At the lowest level, the attacks consist of nothing more than innuendoes that the teachers involved are degenerates eager to seduce youngsters into a life of blatant immorality."

The idea of sex education as a tutoring session in making love reminds us of the famous Monty Python sketch set in a stodgy English boarding school. After a really detailed and boring description of foreplay which includes the phrase "vaginal juices," John Cleese's strict teacher flips the blackboard around to reveal a bed and proceeds to have really boring sex with his wife.

While some of what he tells his classroom full of uninterested boys in school uniforms are things we hope real sex education teachers could say—like the words clitoris or lubrication—no sex educators we know would provide in-person tutorials, even if it were allowed. It is totally inappropriate—very amusing—but totally inappropriate. And it is entirely a work of fiction—in real life a teacher recently got in trouble for using the word "vagina" in a sophomore lesson on reproduction (McGuiness, 2013). (We can't figure out how you could do a sophomore lesson on reproduction without mentioning the vagina—which plays numerous roles in the process—but we digress.)

Sexuality education does not teach young people how to have sex. The goal of the class is to give students the information they need to make responsible decisions. As such, comprehensive sexuality education provides them with information and opportunities to think critically about human development, reproduction, contraception, sexual health, relationships, and decision-making.

Interestingly, controversies about sexuality education as advanced training in bedroom sciences seem to heat up whenever teachers mention sexual behavior other than vaginal sex (Kempner, 2003). Many teachers have found themselves in trouble for even alluding to oral and anal sex, which takes us back to the myth of sex education giving teens ideas they didn't already have. While some adults might like to think teens don't already know about these behaviors, we can assure you they do. In fact, they are having it. One study found 11% of females and 10% of males aged 15–19 report engaging in anal sex with an opposite-sex partner and 1% of males that age report doing so with a partner of the same sex. That same study found that oral sex is quite common—27% of 15-year-old boys and 23% of 15-year-old girls have ever had oral sex with an opposite-sex partner and, by ages 18 and 19, these numbers jump to 70% for boys and 63% for girls. In addition, 7% of females and 2% of males aged 15–19 report oral sex with a same-sex partner (Chandra *et al.*, 2011).

By talking about these behaviors in class, teachers not only have the chance to explain the risk factors (both can spread STIs for example), they also give students the opportunity to think about what they are or are not comfortable doing with a partner.

"Still, It's Better to Be Directive—Tell Them to Say No"

Though many arguments around sexuality education focused on whether any kind of education about this topic belonged in schools, in the early 1980s a number of Christian conservatives began to push for a certain kind of sex education instead. They argued that young people needed to be taught the importance of chastity and self-discipline.

These proponents of what would come to be known as an abstinence-only-until-marriage approach got some support from the federal government under President Ronald Reagan, when the Adolescent and Family Life Act (AFLA) was created to prevent teen pregnancy through "chastity" programs. Over the next decade, the abstinence-only movement grew slowly as proponents convinced local school boards to adopt this new approach, organizations formed to sell their homegrown curricula, and religious institutions held chastity rallies. The push for these programs was part of a larger movement pushing conservative social values in public institutions. These programs got a huge boost in 1996 when the federal government began the Title V Abstinence-Only-Until-Marriage program and another one in 2001 with the passing of the Community-Based Abstinence Education Program. Hundreds of millions of dollars were given to organizations across the country each year to promote the concept of abstinence until marriage (Kempner, 2003).

Though they claimed to be designed to prevent teen pregnancy, these programs truly aimed to prevent any sexual activity outside of marriage. The authors of the definition guiding these federal programs explained that the funding "was intended to align Congress with the social tradition…that sex should be confined to married couples" (Haskins and Bevan, 1997). While some religions and individuals agree with this, it is far from a universally held value. Surveys consistently find that a majority of high school students have had sex by their senior year and few individuals are virgins when they marry. Indeed, this may have never been the standard as a full third of pilgrim brides were pregnant at their weddings (D'Emilio and Freedman, 1988).

Still, proponents of these programs sold them as teen pregnancy prevention and promised that they would work to prevent teen sexual activity. Research suggests otherwise, however. For example, a study commissioned by the US Department of Health and Human Services in 2007 looked at four of over 700 federally funded abstinence-only-until-marriage programs. These programs were not randomly selected but handpicked as the best. The study compared students in the programs with a control group of peers in the same communities who did not attend the programs. Researchers surveyed both groups of teens about their knowledge, attitudes, and behaviors related to sex before the program, immediately after the program, and again 4–6 years after the program ended. They found very few differences between those who had been exposed to the abstinence-only message and those who had not. Specifically, they found no evidence that abstinence-only-until-marriage programs increased rates of sexual abstinence—students in the abstinence-only-until-marriage programs had a similar age of first sex and similar numbers of sexual partners as their peers who were not in the programs (Trenholm *et al.*, 2007).

That same year, the *British Journal of Medicine* published a meta-review of 13 evaluations of abstinence-only programs. Combined, the studies included almost 16,000 students. The analysis found that abstinence-only-until-marriage programs were ineffective in changing any behaviors including the rate of vaginal sex, number of sexual partners, and condom use. The rates of pregnancy and sexually transmitted infections (STIs) among participants in abstinence-only-until-marriage programs were also not impacted by these programs (Underhill *et al.*, 2007).

Well, at Least They'll Get a Healthy Dose of Fear

Many of the abstinence-only-until-marriage programs that received federal funding were based on fear. They presented sex, or more accurately sex outside of marriage, as inevitably harmful and dangerous and frequently exaggerated the risk of STIs and pregnancy. One of the early abstinence-only curricula, *Sex Respect*, told students:

> These are simply natural consequences. For example, if you eat spoiled food, you will get sick. If you jump from a tall building, you will be hurt or killed. If you spend more money than you make, your enslavement to debt affects you and those whom you love. If you have sex outside of marriage, there are consequences for you, your partner and society. (Mast, 1997, p. 11)

A popular abstinence-only speaker, Pam Stenzel, offered a presentation entitled *The Price Tag of Sex*, in which she said: "I came here to tell you that if you have sex outside of a monogamous—and by monogamous I don't mean one at a time—relationship you will pay the price" (as cited by Kempner, 2007). Other programs showed larger-than-life slides of STIs in their advanced stages which did little to educate teens about what to look for (a genital wart caused by human papillomavirus will start out as a small raised bump not a giant cauliflower-shaped growth) (Kempner, 2001).

Any good sexuality educator—ourselves included—will tell you that they want teens to have a healthy understanding about the real risks involved with sexual behavior including the possibility of pregnancy or STIs. Presenting these risks as inevitable outside of marriage (and on the flip side, impossible inside of it)—is simply inaccurate, and thinking this will somehow prevent teens from having sex is foolish. Remember, teens tend to think they are invincible.

Teens need to know the risks of sexual activity but they also need to know how to reduce these risks such as by using condoms along with another method of contraception, reducing the numbers of partners they have, and seeking regular STI testing.

Moreover, it is never appropriate to give teens inaccurate or exaggerated information. Just like we don't teach kids to eat healthfully by telling them chocolate has worms in it—we can't teach them to behave responsibly by telling them sex is always bad and dangerous. They will try it anyhow, they will be unprepared when they do, and they will find out we were lying to them.

"So, Make Them Promise to Wait"

One of the strategies employed by abstinence-until-marriage supporters is virginity pledges. Many of the curricula would end by asking young people to sign a pledge promising that they would remain virgins until they got married. In addition, organizations such as True Love Waits (which has ties to the Southern Baptist Convention) and the Silver Ring Thing ran large-scale events across the country where young people were asked to pledge not to have sex until their wedding nights. These proceedings, which were often, though not always, religious in nature, sometimes looked like wedding ceremonies in which rings were exchanged between a father and his daughter. In some rituals, the ring would then be removed by the father during his daughter's actual wedding ceremony as proof that she had waited (Kempner, 2003).

Virginity pledges remained popular even after research found that they were ineffective. In two separate studies of data on young people, Bearman and Brückner found that virginity pledges did not work. Though under certain conditions, some kids who took pledges did delay sex for up to 18 months, the clear majority of young people who took such a pledge (88%) became sexually active before marriage. Even more troublesome, however, was the finding that young people who had taken pledges were less likely to use contraception when they did become sexually active than their peers who had not pledged and they were ultimately just as likely to contract an STI as their non-pledging peers (Bearman and Brückner, 2001; Brückner and Bearman, 2005).

Though the research didn't ask why teens did not keep their pledges and why they didn't use contraception when they did have sex, it makes sense to us on a number of levels. First, asking young people to make a binding decision at 15 that will last in some cases until they are older than 25 (the median age of first marriage is over 28 for men and over 26 for women) is simply unrealistic—people grow and change a great deal in any 10-year period, but this particular decade marks the transition from a child living with his/her parents to an independent adult (US Census, 2010). As for the decision not to use condoms, this seems like an unfortunate bit of human nature: carrying a condom and even using one might be seen as proof that you were planning to break your promise. Young people likely think it is somehow better that it "just sort of happened."

Again, these are just our gut instincts about why virginity pledges don't work but the fact that they don't work has been proven.

"Whatever You Do, Don't Give Them Condoms"

Supporters of more comprehensive sexuality education programs are often accused of peddling condoms and once again giving young people license to have sex. The argument suggests that if you make condoms available to kids any messages they have heard about waiting to have sex will be rendered moot and they will start boffing like bunnies. The good news is that it is pretty easy to test this theory and it has been proven untrue.

In the late 1990s, researchers compared students in New York City high schools with condom availability programs with those in similar Chicago high schools that did not provide condoms. They found that sexual activity among high school students in both cities was similar (59.7% in New York City compared with 60.1% in Chicago) but sexually active students in the New York City schools with condom availability programs were more likely (60.8%) to report using a condom at last intercourse than were those in Chicago (55.5%) where condoms are not available in school (Guttmacher *et al.*, 1997).

A similar study looked at over 4000 high school students in Massachusetts, some of whom were in schools with condom availability programs and some were in schools without such programs. They found that adolescents in schools where condoms were available were more likely to learn about condoms and condom use. Moreover, they were less likely to report ever having sexual intercourse or having sexual intercourse recently. Among those adolescents who were sexually active, those in schools with condom availability programs were twice as likely to have used condoms during their most recent sexual encounter than peers in schools without such a programs, though they were less likely to use other methods of contraception (Blake *et al.*, 2003). A review of literature by the World Health Organization also found that access to contraceptive services did not increase sexual behavior (Baldo *et al.*, 1993).

This argument—that access to sexual health services—will increase sexual behavior among young people—has been used to attempt to block teens (and women) from getting everything from condoms and birth control pills to emergency contraception and the HPV vaccine. No matter what the specific topic, the argument—that young people and women will become promiscuous if we let them protect themselves—is ridiculous. And it has been proven to be wrong time and time again. One of our favorite retorts to it came from a young man we met who said that it was like not giving us fire extinguishers to be sure we don't set any fires (see Myth # 32 for more on these arguments).

Sexuality education has been debated for over a century and we doubt that this is going to end anytime soon. Still, we find this very unfortunate as research has repeatedly shown that the arguments used against sex education in schools are specious at best.

References

Baldo, M., Aggleton, P., and Slutkin, G. (1993). Poster presentation to the Ninth International Conference on AIDS, Berlin, June 6–10. World Health Organization, Geneva, Switzerland.

Bearman, P.S. and Brückner, H. (2001). Promising the future: Virginity pledges and first intercourse. *American Journal of Sociology*, 106(4), 859–912.

Brückner, H. and Bearman, P. (2005). After the promise: the STD consequences of adolescent virginity pledges. *Journal of Adolescent Health*, 36(4), 271–278.

Blake, S.M., Ledsky, R., Goodenow, C., Sawyer, R., Lohrmann, D., and Windsor, R. (2003). Condom availability programs in Massachusetts high schools: Relationships with condom use and sexual behavior. *American Journal of Public Health*, 93(6), 955–962.

Carrera, M. (1971). Preparation of a sex educator: A historical overview. *The Family Coordinator*, 20(2). 99–108.

Chandra, A., Mosher, W.D., Copen, C., and Sionean, C. (2011). Sexual behavior, sexual attraction, and sexual identity in the United States: Data from the 2006–2008 National Survey of Family Growth. *National Health Statistics Reports*, 36. http://www.cdc.gov/nchs/data/nhsr/nhsr036.pdf (accessed August 7, 2104).

D'Emilio, J. and Freedman, E.B. (1988). *Intimate Matters: A History of Sexuality in America*. Harper and Row.

Guttmacher, S., Lieberman, L., Ward, D., Freudenberg, N., Radosh, A., and Des Jarlais, D. (1997). Condom availability in New York City public high schools: Relationships to condom use and sexual behavior. *American Journal of Public Health*, 87(9), 1427–1433.

Haskins, R. and Bevan, C.S. (1997). Abstinence education under welfare reform. *Children and Youth Services Review*, 19(5–6), 465–484.

Kempner, M. (2001). *Toward a Sexually Healthy America: Abstinence-only-until-marriage Programs that Try to Keep Our Youth "Scared Chaste."* Sexuality Information and Education Council of the United States (SIECUS).

Kempner, M. (2003). A controversial decade: 10 years of tracking debates around sexuality education. *SIECUS Report*, 31(6), 33–48.

Kempner, M. (2007). The rise of the abstinence-only-until-marriage movement. In Herdt, G. and Howe, C. (eds) *21st Century Sexualities: Contemporary Issue in Health, Education, and Rights*. Routledge, New York, pp. 124–129.

Kirby, D. (1997). *No Easy Answers: Research and Findings on Programs to Reduce Teen Pregnancy*. National Campaign to Prevent Teen Pregnancy.

Kirby, D. (2001). *Emerging Answers: Research Findings on Programs to Reduce Teen Pregnancy*. National Campaign To Prevent Teen Pregnancy.

McGuiness, W. (2013). Tim McDaniel, Idaho teacher, explained "vagina" in sex ed class, so he's being investigated. *Huffington Post* (March 31). http://www.huffingtonpost.com/2013/03/28/tim-mcdaniel-vagina-sex-education_n_2971710.html (accessed August 7, 2014).

Time Magazine (1969). Sex in the classroom. *Time Magazine* (July 25).

Trenholm, C., Devaney, B., Fortson, K., Quay, L., Wheeler, J., and Clark, M. (2007). *Impacts of Four Title V, Section 510 Abstinence Education Programs*. Mathematica Policy Research, Inc.

Underhill, K., Montgomery, P., and Operario, D. (2007). Sexual abstinence only programmes to prevent HIV infection in high income countries: Systematic review. *British Medical Journal*, 335(7613), 248.

US Decennial Census (2010). American Community Survey. http://www.census.gov/hhes/socdemo/marriage/data/acs/ElliottetalPAA2012figs.pdf (accessed August 7, 2014).

Yarber, W. (1994) Past, present and future perspectives on sexuality education. In Drolet, J.C. and Clark, K. (eds) *The Sexuality Education Challenge, Promoting Healthy Sexuality in Young People*. ETR Associates, Santa Cruz, CA, pp. 3–28.

Men Who Have a Lot of Sex Are Studs, Women Are Sluts

There is a double standard in our society when it comes to sex that few people even try to deny. It is "understood" at some subconscious societal level that men want more sex and have more sex than women and they are applauded for it. Women, on the other hand, are forced to walk a fine line between being a prude and being a slut. There are rules imposed on female sexuality—often unwritten or at least not expressed until after the fact—that say how much is too much and punish women for crossing that line. On the flip side there are expectations that men want sex at all moments from all (or almost all) women they see and if they don't there must be something wrong with them.

Few people deny this double standard exists and many even acknowledge just how unfair it really is. In fact, we were almost not going to include it in the book because it feels so obvious—like our readers would look at it and say, "Yeah, we know, that's bad, and we get it." We believe that many people, our readers included, are familiar with this myth and consider it a problem, and yet, it persists. It is so ingrained in our world view and our day-to-day dealings with people of our own and the opposite gender that despite having been acknowledged for decades, it continues. In conversations with college students, we are particularly surprised by how hard it is for young women to let go of the concept of sluts. This concept that puts some women down based on their perceived sexual excesses hurts all women and yet young women are often the ones who insist on labeling their peers. So we decided that we had to take this one on, despite the fact—or maybe because of the fact—that it didn't feel fresh.

In this entry we examine the sexual double standard, question where it came from and how it formed, and suggest just how dangerous it can be to the image and behavior of both genders. Though conversations like these have been going on for at least half a century (one of the articles we cite was written in 1959 and was by no means the first on the topic), we figure that the only way this myth will ever get completely defeated is if we keep talking about it.

In the Beginning

The sexual double standard that we continue to hold on to was deeply rooted in England for centuries and in many ways grew out of the overall gender inequality. As one politician said in 1923: "Chastity in women is a star that has guided human nature since the world began....We bow in humble reverence to that high star of chastity, and celebrate it in song and poetry. But I do not think any mere man would thank us for enshrining him in such a halo" (*Parliamentary Debates Commons*, as cited in Thomas, 1959, p. 195).

We have to remember that until very recently in human history, women had few rights—they could not vote, could not own property, and were actually considered the property of either their fathers or their husbands. A woman's virtue was therefore considered a commodity and destroying that through sex outside of marriage was in essence destroying another man's property.

In fact, some scholars believe that the prescription against extramarital sex for women was born out of a fear of property rights. Women are the ones who might bear children through a premarital or extramarital affair which could make the lines of inheritance difficult to determine. One expert who wrote in the 1930s explained why women could not commit adultery but men could be forgiven for such crime:

> [C]onfusion of the progeny constitute the essence of the crime; and therefore, a woman who breaks her marriage vows is much more criminal than a man who does it. A man, to be sure, is a criminal in the sight of God; but he does not do to his wife a very material injury, if he does not insult her; if, for instance, from mere wantonness of appetite, he steals privately to her chambermaid...Wise married women don't trouble themselves about infidelity in their husbands...The man imposes no bastards upon his wife. (Thomas, 1959, p. 209)

This thinking permeated the rules of those days. While men could be granted a divorce on the grounds of their spouse's adultery, women could not. Thomas (1959) talks of a case in 1832 in which a wife asked for a divorce because her husband started sleeping with other women on their wedding night and continued to have sex with all of their servants, one of whom got pregnant. The court rejected her petition and said she should forgive him (though acknowledged that a husband could not be asked to forgive the same behavior in a wife).

In noting the role property played in the sexual double standard, Thomas explains that the upper classes, those who held more property and titles and had more to lose, held on to these rules of behavior much more closely. In the middle class there was a more equal view of infidelity as harmful in both men and women (Thomas, 1959).

Only Bad Girls Do That

One of the more interesting aspects of the focus on female chastity in the 1800s and early 1900s is the widely acknowledged role of prostitutes. In 1841, the Chief of Police in London estimated that there were 3325 brothels in Metropolitan London alone. Though prostitutes were looked down upon with disdain, they were nonetheless thought of as doing a public service because men could not stay faithful or chaste. After referring to prostitutes as "that unhappy being whose very name is a shame to speak," Lecky (1913) writes: "Herself the supreme type of vice, she is ultimately the most efficient guardian of virtue. But for her, the unchallenged purity of countless happy homes would be polluted." The same vision was espoused by St. Augustine who wrote: "Remove prostitutes from human affairs and you would pollute the world with lust" (Thomas, 1959, p. 197).

What struck us as fascinating about this is how similar it is to today's dichotomy of good girls who don't versus bad girls who do. We think that in many ways the prostitute has been replaced by the "slut." In her book, *Fast Girls; Teenage Tribes and the Myth of the Slut*, Emily White (2002) writes about how high school students seem to have created a somewhat universal archetype of a slut: "While the girls in the stories had different names and nicknames, and while the rumors often varied in their specifics, the myth of the promiscuous female remained constant....It was a story with a specific cadence, identifiable themes, and a clear moral: Don't end up here. Don't end up in the basement like she did" (p. 13). Moreover, White explains that once labeled, the "slut" is part of a continuum in the world of teenage popularity and sexuality:

> Bring her up among people who know one another well, and instantly everyone finds themselves on common ground....The word's provocative power and the continued vitality of the myth behind the word imply that the slut is not a monster but a sign: she is a window to the unconscious, a way of deciphering how the culture dreams of women, even if we've learned civilized people shouldn't have such dreams. (White, 2002, p. 13)

Today's high school slut serves a similar purpose that prostitutes did in 1830s London; they keep others from crossing the line of unacceptable social behavior. Of course, in interviewing individuals who had themselves been labeled sluts in high school, White learned that the moniker was often given based on false information, innuendo, and rumors. Many of the women who were labeled sluts were outcasts for other reasons—because they were from the wrong side of town or were one of the only students in the school from a certain racial or ethnic group. Some of them got labeled simply because they were among the first of their peers to go through puberty and had more womanly bodies long before the other girls.

What is even more disturbing, however, is that once the label was given it often became true. Like a self-fulfilling prophecy these women began to behave in the ways that their peers said they had, and their self-esteem often suffered. After interviewing numerous girls who had been their school's slut, White notes: "In a culture that annihilates oversexed women, girls who have been ordained the high school slut often want to destroy themselves" (p. 73). Many of the women she spoke to talked about suicide attempts or stays in psychiatric hospitals. And the effect of their high school label had stayed with many of them well into adulthood.

The Double Standard Impacts Everyone

The myth of the slut does not just affect those who are saddled with such labels. In fact, it doesn't even just affect women. First, we have to acknowledge that the double standard is based in large part on a biological falsehood. The idea behind it is that men are full of raging hormones and simply cannot help themselves—they want sex. Women, on the other hand, have no natural desire for sex. They do it to keep their men happy, to get pregnant, and to experience love but their wants are not physical in nature. Consider this explanation by the Royal Commission in 1871 of why prostitutes should be punished but not the men who visited them: "With the one sex the offence is committed as a matter of gain; with the other it is an irregular indulgence of a natural impulse" (Thomas, 1959, p. 198). There's also this explanation from a modern abstinence-only-until-marriage program: "A young man's natural desire for sex is already strong due to testosterone, the powerful male growth hormone. Females are becoming culturally conditioned to fantasize about sex as well" (Mast, 2001, p. 11).

Though this is simply not true—women have innate desires for sex too—by perpetuating this theory for so long, we have turned women into the sexual gatekeepers. Boys will be boys and can't be expected to stop themselves, thus it is up to young women to take on that task. The same abstinence-only-until-marriage curriculum says this: "Yet, because they generally become physically aroused less easily, girls are still in a good position to slow down the young man and help him learn balance in a relationship" (Mast, 2001, p. 12).

The implications of this role are far reaching. It certainly is part of the rape culture that we have discussed in other myths (see Myths # 40 and 44 for more on rape culture). A woman who is dressed a certain way, drinking too much, or flirting too much is seen to have abdicated her role as gatekeeper and is therefore "asking for it."

Disregarding women's natural desire for sex also puts them in an awkward position in which they must walk a fine line between being not-at-all sexual and far too sexual. In essence we have told them that they don't want sex on their own but they do need to be sexy for men. As Tolman (2009) explains it in her book, *Dilemmas of Desire; Teenage Girls Talk About Sexuality*, "Acknowledgement of their sexual longings as an anticipated part of adolescence in virtually nonexistent. We have essentially desexualized girls' sexuality, substituting desire for a relationship and emotional connections for sexual feelings in their bodies."

Of course, young women do want sex and many do have it. Tolman (2009) says that the narrative of "it just kind of happened" has been universally invented as a way to cover up young women's desires. She writes: "Having sex 'just happen' is one of the few acceptable ways available to adolescent girls for making sense of and describing their sexual experiences….In a world where 'good,' nice, normal girls don't have sexual feelings of their own, this is one of the few decent stories that a girl can tell."

Sex that just kind of happens, however, is more often than not unprotected sex because the story won't ring true if you were prepared, say, by having a condom in your purse. As we discussed in Myth # 46, research on young people who take virginity pledges—promises to remain a virgin until you get married—shows that these young people are ultimately just as likely to have sex before marriage as their non-pledging peers (88% of them do have sex before marriage), but less likely to use condoms or contraception when they become sexuality active than non-pledging peers (Bearman and Brückner, 2001). The research couldn't determine why this was the case but it always felt kind of obvious to us. If you had promised not to have sex and then you got carried away and it just kind of happened, you could at least convince yourself or those around you that you hadn't meant to break your promise. Once the action is proven premeditated by the use of contraception, that ruse is also broken. The same holds true for young women who have been inculcated with the "good girls don't" message.

The message is not doing men any favors either. The image of them as wanting, if not needing sex, from any and all women is a relatively unflattering one that can change young men's behavior for the worse. Studies show that whereas young woman are labeled sluts for having too many partners, young men become more popular as their number of sexual partners increases. Not surprisingly, under this rubric, boys who don't have enough sexual partners are punished. In one study, researchers measured popularity by noting how many of an individual's peers considered that person a friend. They found that girls who had more than eight sexual partners had fewer friends but this was different for boys: "we find that sexually inexperienced boys have significantly less peer nominations than boys with one or more sexual partners, and more partners are associated with greater numbers of peer nominations" (Kreager and Staff, 2009, p. 155).

While this may seem like a good thing for young men, it puts pressure on them. Tolman (2009) points out that "In many circles, if a boy reaches mid-adolescence without having shown any perceptible interest in girls, those around him may become concerned about his masculinity and his sexual orientation." While girls are called sluts for having too much sex, boys are often labeled "fags" for not having enough. White (2002) says: "One of the most persistent forms of ostracism, outside the slut story, is to label someone a fag. Boys who are deemed fags or sissies undergo a relentless taunting that is similar to what the slut endures; like the girls I interviewed, boys who are deemed the fag find themselves at the receiving end of unpredictable violence and amazingly detailed rumors facilitated from a weird collective of sexual ignorance" (p. 116).

This label has even broader implications. Men have to prove their masculinity so as to avoid being labeled gay because, under this framework, being gay is clearly bad. The sexual double standard assumes that everyone is heterosexual and has negative implications for those who are not because it also perpetuates the idea that everyone *should be* heterosexual.

Time for Change

We wish that we could say that times are changing, that the playing field is leveling out, that women are not being penalized for having too much sex, and men are not ostracized for having too little, but this is just not true. In 2012, during a debate over whether health insurance plans should be required to offer contraception free of charge, this issue made national headlines thanks to conservative, syndicated radio host Rush Limbaugh. When the Republican-led House of Representative called a hearing on this issue that included no women, Democrats decided to hold their own version. Among the invited guests was law student Sandra Fluke who explained why her school's religious refusal to provide birth control (she attended Georgetown University Law School which is Jesuit) was a problem for her and her peers. Limbaugh promptly called her a slut: "What does that make her? It makes her a slut, right? It makes her a prostitute. She wants to be paid to have sex," Limbaugh continued. "She's having so much sex she can't afford the contraception" (Fard, 2012).

Aside from showing complete ignorance about how birth control works (prescription contraceptive methods like the pill or IUD do not cost more the more sex you have), it showed complete disrespect for Fluke and all women. Moreover, it completely absolved men of their role in pregnancy. Doesn't Limbaugh realize that women only need birth control if they are having sex with men? Why are these men, who will benefit from free contraceptive methods, not considered sluts as well?

There has been some suggestion that at least among young people, and college students in particular, the gender roles within sexual relationships are relaxing. Some say that the new "hook up" culture, in which sex either replaces or precedes romantic relationships, is equalizing sexual relationships between men and women, by letting women claim sexual desire and agency—giving them the right to want or enjoy casual sex. Yet research reveals that some vestiges of the double standard remain even in hook up relationships.

Reid *et al.*, (2011) enlisted 273 undergraduates and read them a story of a heterosexual hook up. The story essentially explained that a guy and a girl met at a party, left together, and had a night of wild sex. A few days later one of them calls the other and they go out on a date. At the end of the date, they kiss good bye but don't have sex. The vignette was told in two different ways, one of which made the woman the aggressor, the other, the man. The authors explain that "students generally accorded women sexual agency and desire in the hookup and validated men's post-hookups relationship interest." The motivations that students attributed to the sexless date, however, revealed that the concept of the slut is alive and well. Both men and women suggested that the woman wouldn't have sex on the date because she was embarrassed or ashamed of the hook up and wanted to avoid being thought of as easy or a "whore" (Reid *et al.*, 2011, p. 558). Hook ups were safe and carried no risks to the reputation only if they were a one-time, almost anonymous event.

Once the hook up partner made contact in "real life," the old rule kicked back in for women. In contrast, not having sex with the girl he had hooked up with was simply proof that the man did not want a relationship with her—respondents surmised that he had only accepted the date out of pity, and did not want the girl to get the wrong idea (Reid *et al.*, 2011).

Maybe we haven't come as far from the nineteenth century London full of brothels as we had hoped. So as not to end on that distressing thought, however, we leave you with the same thought with which we started. This myth is not new and it has gotten a great deal of attention in the past few decades. At the very least, it is widely recognized and even widely recognized as a problem. Hopefully, with more attention and more discussion, we can ensure that new generations of young people are being raised not to buy into it and that eventually it will sound as silly as women not having the right to vote or own property.

References

Bearman, P.S. and Brückner, H. (2001). Promising the future: Virginity pledges and first intercourse. *American Journal of Sociology*, 106(4), 859–912.

Fard, M.F. (2012). Sandra Fluke, Georgetown student called a "slut" by Rush Limbaugh, speaks out. *Washington Post* (March 2).

Kreager, D.A. and Staff, J. (2009). The sexual double standard and adolescent peer acceptance. *Social Psychology Quarterly*, 72(2), 143–164.

Mast, C.K. (2001). *Sex Respect: The Option of True Sexual Freedom*, 4th edn. Respect, Inc.

Reid, J.A., Elliott, S., and Webber, G.R. (2011). Casual hookups to formal dates refining the boundaries of the sexual double standard. *Gender and Society*, 25(5), 545–568.

Thomas, K. (1959). The double standard. *Journal of the History of Ideas*, 20(2), 195–216.

Tolman, D.L. (2009). *Dilemmas of Desire: Teenage Girls Talk About Sexuality*, 2nd edn. Harvard University Press.

White, E. (2002). *Fast Girls: Teenage Tribes and the Myth of the Slut*. Simon and Schuster.

Myth #48 Sexting is a Dangerous Epidemic Among Teens

Adults are always panicked by the newest fad in teen sexual behavior and tend to blow it way out of proportion—both in terms of how prevalent it is and how risky it might be. Sometimes we have to laugh because the truth is what kids today are doing—like having oral sex—is not really new. Perhaps more young people are engaging than did, say 30 years ago, or maybe (and we think this is often the case) society is just more willing to talk about it than we have been in the past. Sexting, however, is definitely new because the technology simply didn't exist until recently. Twenty years ago racy exchanges would have to be notes passed in class or at worst messages left on an answering machine. As for nude pictures, the best you could do there would be a Polaroid (otherwise you had to involve the techs at Fotomat). So this fad is actually new and adults are scrambling to figure out whether it is an epidemic or even a problem.

Clearly, there is some call to be concerned as we have seen sexting bring down the career of at least one United States Congressman. Anthony Weiner served seven rather unremarkable terms as a Representative for New York's 9th Congressional District. Then, in 2011, Weiner sent a picture of his erect penis to a college student in Seattle. Though he initially denied it, other women stepped forward to say they too had received sexts from the married congressman. Later that month, as the scandal continued to grow, Weiner resigned (*Fox News*, 2011). In 2013, Weiner attempted a run for remove Mayor of New York City and, at least initially, polls showed that New Yorkers were willing to forgive him and possibly even vote for him. That is until they learned about Carlos Danger, an alias Weiner used in sext exchanges with a 22-year-old woman long after he had sworn to the media that he had given up his sexting-ways (Kempner, 2013). Weiner did not pull out of the race but finished fifth in the Democratic Primary with just under 5% of the vote (*New York Times*, 2013).

Most young people are not—and will likely never be—under the same level of scrutiny as our elected officials but a behavior that can destroy a political career deserves at least a second look before being dismissed as harmless young fun. That is exactly what we do in this entry, take a second look at who sexts and whether any harm—be it psychological or legal—comes to them as a result. Be warned, we don't think we will solve the riddle of whether sexting is harmless fun or dangerous waters because that really depends on each person's individual situation and relationships. Our goal with this entry is simply to make our readers think before they ever hit send.

Sexting Statistics

As with other sexual behaviors, before deciding whether they are risky on an individual or population basis, researchers have to determine just how many people are doing it. Though the media would have us believe that sexting is sweeping the nation, research suggests that it's far more limited.

A survey by the Pew Research Center in 2009 asked questions of a nationally representative sample of teens 12–17. It found that 4% of teenagers who owned cell phones had sent a nude or nearly nude picture to someone else and that 15% of teenagers who owned cell phones had received such a picture. It also found that older teens (those aged 15–17) were more likely to have both sent and received a picture—8% of older teens had sent a picture and 30% had received one (Lenhart, 2009). A more recent survey polled a nationally representative sample of those aged 10–17 and found relatively similar results. In this survey 2.5% of respondents said they had been in or sent a nude or nearly nude picture or video and 7% said they had received one (Mitchell *et al.*, 2012).

These nationally representative results suggest that sexting among high school students is not widespread and that parents of teens can take a deep breath and relax just a little bit. That said, smaller studies have found higher percentages of sexters. For example, a study in 2012 surveyed 948 teens in public school (most of whom were 15 and 16) and found that 28% reported having sent a naked picture of themselves through text or e-mail, 31% had asked someone to send them a sext, and 57% had been asked to send a sext. There was no difference in the percentage of boys and girls who had sent sexts (27.8% boys and 27.5% girls) but girls were more likely to have been asked for a sext (68% versus 42%) and boys were significantly more likely to have done the asking (46% versus 21%) (Temple *et al.*, 2012).

The numbers found in that study are similar to those found on college campuses. Researchers at the University of Michigan surveyed 3447 young men and women aged 18–24 and found that over half (57%) were *not* sexters. Still, that leaves 43% who had either sent or received a sext, much higher than surveys found among high school students. Specifically, these researchers found that among those who had sexted, 28.2% were two-way sexters, 12.6% were receivers, and 2% were senders (Gordon-Messer *et al.*, 2012).

Are Sexters Having More Sex?

Every few months the headlines scream about how teens who sext are more likely to have sex. The take away message seems to be that sexting *causes* teens to have sex—perhaps by leading them down a path of ever-increasing debauchery—but the research actually tells a different story. The fact that young people sext may be a sign that they are otherwise sexually active but it is not the reason.

For one study, researchers attached a secondary questionnaire to the Youth Risk Behavior Surveillance Survey (YRBS) that was given to high school students in the Los Angeles Unified School District. The YRBS is a project of the Centers for Disease Control and Prevention (CDC), and surveys high school students across the country every 2 years to get a picture of all risky behaviors from unprotected sex to not wearing a bicycle helmet to using guns. The secondary survey asked about sexual behaviors and sexting. It found that 75% of respondents reported owning a cell phone and using it every day. More than 15% of respondents with cell phones reported ever sending a "sexually explicit message or photo." In addition, 41% of respondents with cell phones had ever had oral, vaginal, or anal sex, and 64% of these used a condom the last time they had sex (Rice *et al.*, 2012). The researchers noted that respondents who had sent a sext were statistically significantly more likely to have ever engaged in sexual intercourse. They concluded that their data: "reveal that sexting is associated with physical sexual risk taking. Unlike work that has suggested that sexting is a low risk or healthy alternative to sexual risk taking, we find that there is a clustering of sexual risk behaviors which includes sexting" (Rice *et al.*, 2012, p. 671).

A newer study, conducted with middle schools students, came to the same conclusion. This study may not be generalizable to the whole middle school population because it looked at students who had already been identified by school official as being "at risk." It found that those students who had sent sexts (this study included pictures and sexually explicit text messages) were between 4 and 7 times more likely to report sexual behaviors of all types, including oral and vaginal sex, touching genitals, and having a friend-with-benefits. Specifically, students who had sexted were five times more likely to have engaged in vaginal sex than their peers who had not. Moreover, students who had sent sexual photos of themselves were even more likely to engage in all of these sexual behaviors (except genital touching) than those who had just sent messages (Houck *et al.*, 2014).

Obviously, these results are of some concern because these students are quite young for sexual activity (the average age that young people start having sex is about 17) and they are exposing themselves to sexual risks such as pregnancy and sexually transmitted diseases. We know, for example, that adolescents who have sex before the age of 14 are more likely not to use protection their first time (Guttmacher Institute, 2013). So we should by no means dismiss the study's finding.

Still, we have to remember that like the study with high school students, these findings do not suggest that sexting caused these students to become sexually active or even that it was a gateway activity to things with greater risk. The authors simply conclude that sexting "appears to co-occur with sexual behaviors and may represent an indicator of sexual risk." They suggest that parents, educators, and physicians ask young people about their sexting behavior (or in the case of parents, directly monitor it) as a way to gauge the other risks young people may be taking (Houck *et al.*, 2014).

In the end, the association between sexting and sex seems to be a relatively obvious one to us. Though it may be new, sexting is ultimately a sexual behavior. It's a way to flirt with a partner, signal that you're interested or available, and possibly to turn them on or get them in the mood. It does not surprise us, therefore, that it is more common among people who have sexual partners and are already engaging in other sexual behaviors.

As for whether sexters have "riskier" sex, results are mixed. The study of high school students in Los Angeles did find that sexters "exhibited a trend toward unprotected sex during their last sexual encounter" (Rice *et al.*, 2012, p. 671). On the other hand, the study of college students in Michigan provides some reassuring results. Among participants who were sexually active in the past 30 days, the study found no differences "across sexting groups in the number of sexual partners or the number of unprotected sex partners in the past 30 days" (Gordon-Messer *et al.*, 2012).

The Risks of Sexting

The question that remains as we analyze this highly hyped new "threat" to sexual health is whether sexting is actually risky. When we talk about sexual behavior, the risks are usually obvious—one can get pregnant or contract an STI. Since neither of these can happen through a cell phone—and we've already established that sexting doesn't cause kids to hop into bed with each other—the tangible risks from sexting are not so straightforward. As with any sexual behavior, we have to worry about whether there is a psychological component.

The Michigan study suggests that there is no difference between those who sexted and those who did not on measures of psychological well-being. Specifically, sexters did not report increased anxiety, depression, or low self-esteem as has been suggested in media stories. Another study with high school students in Texas attempted to determine if teens who sext are more likely to be impulsive, use alcohol and drugs, or exhibit symptoms of depression and anxiety. The results were mixed. Sexting was correlated with impulsivity and drug and alcohol use but not with mental health. The researchers concluded: "for the time being, tween-focused and teen-focused health care providers may consider sexting as a risk marker for other risky behaviors, but not necessarily as an indicator of poor psychological health" (Temple *et al.*, 2014).

In her study of over 600 18-year-olds, Englander (2012) brings up another important question about sexting and mental health; how often are sexters coerced to send their messages? She separated subjects into three groups: those who had never sexted (74% of females, 67% of males); those who sexted under pressure (17% of females, 8% of males); and those who sexted without feeling any pressure to do so (16% of females, 17% of males). She then asked respondents to choose on a scale of 1 to 10 how "upsetting" the experience was. She found a clear difference between pressured sexters and voluntary sexters. "Among those who had sexted voluntarily, 79% selected the "least upset" rating (a 1 or 2 out of 10). However, only 17% of those who had been pressured to sext selected that rating. Taken together, these data suggest that sexting tends to be negatively impactful when it is coerced" (Englander, 2012).

Though it should go without saying, coercing a partner to send a naked picture of him/herself is just as wrong as coercing them into engaging in any other sexual behavior. And as difficult as it can be to do, we urge young people to stand up to coercion of any kind. If your gut tells you not to hit send, but your girlfriend is saying please, or your friends are goading you (Englander found some of the pressure was from friends), let us be the voice telling you to trust your gut.

It Always Ends Up on the Internet

The risks that people may be most worried about are not those that involve one's psyche but instead the risk to one's reputation. While few of us will ever share a spotlight like Anthony Weiner's, we can all imagine the situation in which a young girl sends a nude picture to a boyfriend, the relationship gets rocky, and suddenly the picture is being shared with everyone he has ever met and everyone they've ever met via social media, the internet at large, or a string of text messages.

The best research we have right now is that this situation is rare. In her study of sexting, Englander (2012) found that the majority of images (74%) were never shared with anyone other than the intended recipient. Mitchell *et al.* (2011), who looked at a national representative sample of 10- to 17-years-olds, also reported that very few images were ever forwarded or posted. Nonetheless, we know from highly publicized cases of cyberbullying that the worst case scenario can happen. In fact, there are now websites dedicated to revenge porn on which people are encouraged to post naked pictures of exes. Some have included identifying information and even addresses.

The most basic rule here is that once a picture leaves your phone for cyberspace, you are no longer in control of it. Current statistics suggest that it is unlikely to wind up anywhere other than on your boyfriend's or girlfriend's phone but you can't be sure that someday down the line you (or your future spouse, or the guy who just interviewed you for the job you really want, or even your kid) won't stumble across that very same picture online through one series of events or another. That is simply the risk you take every time you hit send.

The Legal Issues

There is another, potentially serious, risk that you take by hitting send (or being on the receiving end of that text) if the person in the picture is under age. Sexting actually violates a number of federal and state laws designed to curb child pornography. It is a felony under both federal and state laws to possess or distribute images showing, among other things, "lascivious exhibition of the genitals or pubic area of persons under the age of eighteen." Receiving just one picture can carry a mandatory minimum sentence of 5 years. Moreover, there is a federal law that says that anyone who does produce sexually explicit images that include "lascivious exhibition of the genitals or pubic area" is required to maintain certain detailed records and to keep his or her home available for FBI inspections. Failure to comply is also a felony. In his review of the law, Humbach points out that "Since it is unlikely that very many teens are keeping the required records, this law alone means that millions of American teenagers are felony sex offenders" (2010, p. 437).

These laws were designed to protect young people from predatory adults, they were not meant to apply to cases in which the "child pornography" is produced and distributed by the "child" in question. It does not make sense when teens become the perpetrator and the victim of the same crime. Nonetheless, many teens have found themselves in trouble with the law. Humbach points to a case in Florida in which teens sent over 100 nude pictures to each other. They were arrested under a state law that makes producing and distributing child pornography a second degree felony. The girl in the case pleaded no contest to felony delinquency. Humbach points out the irony of the ruling in which an appeals court upheld the judgment against the girl. The court said the situation was serious because if the pictures got out "future damage may be done to these minors' personal lives or career." The court did not, however, note the damage that could be done to their lives or careers by a felony child pornography charge (2010, p. 433).

These young people are not alone. Teens in other states have been prosecuted or faced with the threat of prosecution under child pornography statutes as the law attempts to catch up with technology. In fact, a national survey of over 2000 law enforcement agencies estimated that there were 3477 cases of youth-produced sexual images during 2008 and 2009. An arrest occurred in 36% of the cases that involved only youth and 62% of the cases in which an adult was also involved. Interestingly, most of the images (63%) were distributed by cell phone only and did not reach the internet (Wolak *et al.*, 2012). This shows that it doesn't always end up on the internet but that doesn't mean no damage was done.

Some states have changed their laws. Vermont and Utah, for example, passed laws in 2009 that reduced the nature of the crime when minors and first-time offenders were involved (Lenhart, 2009). While other states are working to do the same, some have taken a different approach. In 2013, West Virginia passed a law banning teen sexting. Specifically, the law bars juveniles from making, having, or distributing photos, videos, or other media that portray a minor in an inappropriate sexual manner. Minors found with such material would be guilty of juvenile delinquency. The law also directs the state supreme court to develop an education program that would show offenders the consequences of sexting, including the long-term harm it can do to relationships, school success, and future job opportunities. Minors who are caught sexting can choose to take this course as an alternative to juvenile charges (Associated Press, 2013).

We would argue that educating teens first (and not waiting until they break a law to do so) would make more sense. We would also hope that states would follow the lead of Vermont and Utah and rework laws so that the punishment better fits the "crime." In the meantime, we need to remind our readers that even if a nude picture is taken and sent with everyone's consent, criminal prosecution is not entirely out of the question.

Think Before You Send

The good news is that a review of the available data suggests that adults don't have to be panicked about sexting. Rather than an out-of-control fad among otherwise innocent teenagers, it is another (mostly consensual) sexual behavior in which a small (or perhaps, medium) proportion of teens and young adults may choose to engage. And rather than an inevitably dangerous behavior, the truth suggests that most sexts are harmless. Nonetheless, there is a dark side of sexting that has caused some teens humiliation and others felony convictions. As more time passes and more research is done, we may be able to paint a clearer picture of how risky sexting really is. In the meantime, we urge everyone to think carefully before they send.

References

Associated Press (2013). State adopts anti-sexting law for juveniles. *West Virginia Gazette* (May 16). http://www.wvgazette.com/News/201305060115 (accessed August 7, 2014).

Englander, E. (2012). Low risk associated with most teenage sexting: A study of 617 18-year-olds. Aggression Reduction Center, Bridgewater State University, Bridgewater, MA. http://webhost.bridgew.edu/marc/SEXTING%20AND%20COERCION% 20report.pdf (accessed August 7, 2014).

Fox News (2011). Timeline of Weiner sexting scandal. *FoxNews.com* (June 16). http:// www.foxnews.com/politics/2011/06/16/timeline-weiner-sexting-scandal/ (accessed August 7, 2014).

Gordon-Messer, D., Bauermeister, J.A., Grodzinski, A., and Zimmerman, M. (2012). Sexting among young adults. *Journal of Adolescent Health*, 52(3), 301–306.

Guttmacher Institute (2013). *Facts on American Teens' Sexual and Reproductive Health*. http://www.guttmacher.org/pubs/FB-ATSRH.html (accessed August 7, 2014).

Houck, C.D., Barker, D., Rizzo, C., Hancock, E., Norton, A., and Brown, L.K. (2014). Sexting and sexual behavior in at-risk adolescents. *Pediatrics*, 133(2), e276–282.

Humbach, J.A. (2010). "Sexting" and the First Amendment. *Hastings Constitutional Law Quarterly*, 37, 433.

Kempner, M. (2013). Political men behaving badly: Weiner and Filner won't quit even as more info emerges. *RH Reality Check* (August 1). http://rhrealitycheck.org/article/ 2013/08/01/political-men-behaving-badly-weiner-and-filner-wont-quit-even-as-more-info-emerges/ (accessed August 7, 2014).

Lenhart, A. (2009). *Teens and Sexting: How and why minor teens are sending sexually suggestive nude or nearly nude images via text messaging*. Pew Internet and American Life Project.

Mitchell, K.J., Finkelhor, D., Jones, L.M., and Wolak, J. (2012). Prevalence and characteristics of youth sexting: a national study. *Pediatrics*, 129(1), 13–20.

New York Times (2013). The Mayoral Primaries. *New York Times* (September 16). http:// www.nytimes.com/projects/elections/2013/nyc-primary/mayor/map.html (accessed August 7, 2014).

Rice, E., Rhoades, H., Winetrobe, H., Sanchez, M., Montoya, J., Plant, A., *et al.* (2012). Sexually explicit cell phone messaging associated with sexual risk among adolescents. *Pediatrics*, 130(4), 667–673.

Temple, J.R., Le, V.D., van den Berg, P., Ling, Y., Paul, J.A., and Temple, B.W. (2014). Brief report: Teen sexting and psychosocial health. *Journal of Adolescence*, 37(1), 33–36.

Temple, J.R., Paul, J.A., van den Berg, P., Le, V.D., McElhany, A., and Temple, B.W. (2012). Teen sexting and its association with sexual behaviors teen sexting and sexual behaviors. *Archives of Pediatrics and Adolescent Medicine*, 166(9), 828–833.

Wolak, J., Finkelhor, D., and Mitchell, K.J. (2012). How often are teens arrested for sexting? Data from a national sample of police cases. *Pediatrics*, 129(1), 4–12.

Myth #49   If Sex Is Consensual, It Can Never Be Illegal

In December 2013, the Utah Supreme Court heard arguments in a case that should make us wonder, yet again, if the age of consent laws in the United States are out of step with reality. The case stemmed from an incident in 2003 in which an unnamed 13-year-old girl had "consensual" sex with her then 12-year-old boyfriend. The state learned of this relationship when she became pregnant and it filed delinquency petitions against both teens for having committing sexual abuse of a child. The young woman, who is now 23, asked the court to overturn the finding of delinquency. She and her attorney argued that she can't be both the victim and the perpetrator of the exact same crime. Moreover, they said that she was not being treated fairly under the law because older teens are not prosecuted for having sex with someone of a similar age. The state, however, did not back down, arguing that it has an interest in protecting children even if it is from other children (Kempner, 2013).

Age of consent laws in this country vary by state and can be quite complicated. The specifics of each state's law can result in some cases in which seemingly consensual relationships between teenagers (say a 15-year-old sophomore and her 18-year-old senior boyfriend) become criminal cases. Though the government has an interest in protecting teenagers from sexual exploitation, such cases must make us question whether criminalizing teen sex is the way to go especially because the laws are unevenly enforced often at the whim of an angry parent or overzealous prosecutor.

Should we really treat teenagers who have sex with other teenagers as criminals? Should our legal system play any part in regulating "consensual" teen sexual behavior? Why are these laws so sporadically enforced? Is there a way to protect teens from exploitation without making them vulnerable to unnecessary prosecution? And what does all of this say about how society views teen sexual behavior?

History and Purpose of Statutory Rape Laws

Statutory rape laws (which are also called by a plethora of other names) refer to those laws that "criminalize voluntary sexual acts involving a minor that would be legal if not for the age of one or more of the participants" (Robertson, no date). The premise behind these laws is that until a certain age young people are incapable of giving their consent for sexual behavior, but the intent behind the laws has morphed over the 700 years or so since they were first codified. The first known law, passed in Westminster, England in 1275, made it illegal to "ravish" a "maiden" under the age of 12 (the age at which a girl could legally marry) without her consent. Later laws reduced this age to 10 or 11 (Cocca, 2004). The result was that an underage girl did not have to show that she had struggled in order to prove rape. Age of consent laws, therefore, made it easier to prosecute a man who sexually assaulted an underage girl. The acknowledged purpose of these laws, at least initially, was to protect the young girl's "chastity," possibly so as not to ruin her future chances for marriage (Robertson, no date).

Though they remained largely unchanged for several centuries, the laws began to morph in the late 1800s and early 1900s as other aspects of societies and the role of women changed. At that time "social purity reformers" were very concerned about the inability of men to control their sexual desires and the possibility that a young woman would fall into a moral disgrace that would ruin her for life. They were horrified to learn that the age of consent to sexual relations was 10: "This sanctioning of male access to the young female body came to embody the danger that unconstrained male sexuality posed to female virtue" (Ehrlich, 2006, p. 156). They were also concerned about the rise in teenage prostitution. These reformers campaigned to raise the age of consent as a means of protecting women. By the turn of the century almost all states in the United States had raised the age of consent to 16 or 18. Ehrlich suggests that:

> By insisting the state had a role to play in safeguarding the virtue of young women, the age-of-consent campaign transformed what had been largely a private concern—female sexual behavior—into a matter of public policy. Although the resulting laws clearly served an important protective function, they also pave the way for a greater acceptance of state control over the female body. (Ehrlich, 2006, pp. 157–158)

However, not everyone agreed with the older ages. Some argued that teenage women "were sufficiently developed not to need legal protection," and, moreover, that "by late adolescence girls possessed sufficient understanding about how to use the law to blackmail unwary men" (Robertson, no date). Robertson notes that the term "jailbait" gained popularity in the 1930s because people recognized "teenage girls as sexually attractive, even sexually active, but legally unavailable."

Still, even if people acknowledged young women as sexual, the general consensus was that the laws were necessary to protect them from exploitation: "in making it a crime for girls to decide to have sexual intercourse outside marriage, the law protected them from themselves and from the immature understanding that led them to behaviors reformers considered immoral" (Robertson, no date).

Feminists of the 1970s agreed that it was important to protect young people from exploitation but worked to ensure that these laws did not "unduly restrict the sexual autonomy of young women." They spearheaded efforts to make the laws gender-neutral and ensure an understanding of the rationale behind them: "Aiming to challenge stereotypes of female passivity and growing concern about male victimization, they made it clearer that the laws concerned all youth—male and female—and that the laws protected them from exploitation rather than ensuring their virginity" (Robertson, no date). The push for gender-neutral laws was part of an overall move by feminist to codify equality under the law. They felt that the statutory rape laws as written were a threat to the concept of female agency, and hoped that over time people would begin to "see statutory rape in terms of vulnerable teens rather than in terms of vulnerable females"(Cocca, 2004, p. 90).

During the debates over welfare reform in the mid-1990s—the same debates that brought us the federal government's increasing investment in abstinence-only-until-marriage programs—a new rationale for these laws was thrown about. Armed with the statistic that half of the children born to adolescent women are fathered by adult men and that many of these children end up on welfare, some lawmakers began to argue that stricter enforcement of statutory rape laws would deter older men from having sex with teenage girls and would therefore solve the teen pregnancy problem. In fact, as part of the Personal Responsibility and Work Opportunity Reconciliation Act of 1996 (PRWORA) the Senate urged states and local jurisdictions to aggressively enforce statutory rape laws (Sutherland, 2003). California invested millions of dollars into increasing the prosecution of such cases; Delaware passed the Sexual Predator Act of 1996 and began "stationing state police in high schools to identify students who have become involved with adult men;" and Florida passed a law that declared "impregnation of a minor younger than age 16 by a male aged 21 or older" to be a reportable form of child abuse (Robertson, no date). While some law enforcement officials thought this was the right approach, many advocates for adolescent health were skeptical at best, arguing that laws rarely serve as a deterrent to sexual behavior.

The argument about using age of consent laws to prevent teen pregnancy seems to have lost some of its momentum in recent years and the general consensus has returned to the idea that these laws remain important to protect young people (primarily young women) from exploitation. The question remains, however, how do these laws distinguish between exploitative relationships and consensual relationships between young people?

Today's Laws

The truth is that laws cannot make such distinctions but lawmakers seem to have attempted to account for variations in relationships. Each state has its own law and decides a number of factors for itself, including age of consent, minimum age of "victim," age differential, and minimum age of "perpetrator" in order to prosecute.

- *Age of consent.* This is the age at which an individual *can* legally consent to sexual intercourse under any circumstances.
- *Minimum age of victim.* This is the age below which an individual *cannot* legally consent to sexual intercourse under any circumstance.
- *Age differential.* If the victim is above the minimum age but below the age of consent, the age differential is the maximum age difference between the victim and the perpetrator where an individual *can* legally consent to sexual intercourse.
- *Minimum age of defendant in order to prosecute.* This is the age below which an individual *cannot* be prosecuted for engaging in sexual activities with minors.

According to a 2003 report prepared for the US Department of Health and Human Services[1], only 12 states have a single age of consent below which an

---

[1]The examples of state laws provided in this entry are pulled from this review prepared in 2003. It is possible that some state laws have changed since then but we are not aware of a more recent comprehensive review of the laws in all states.

individual cannot consent to sexual intercourse. In Massachusetts, for example, the age of consent is simply 16. That leaves 39 other states where the laws are more complicated. In most states, the law takes into account both the age of the victim and the difference in age between the victim and the perpetrator. In New Jersey, for example, the age of consent is 16 but "individuals who are at least 13 years of age can legally engage in sexual activities if the defendant is less than 4 years older than the victim" (Glosser et al., 2004).

Some states focus on that age difference between the two individuals. The District of Columbia, for example, says that it's illegal to engage in sexual intercourse with someone who is under the age of 16 if the perpetrator is 4 or more years older than the victim. But other states like to make it even more complicated by taking into account the age of both parties. Washington state's laws say that sexual intercourse with someone who is at least 14 but less than 16 is illegal if the defendant is 4 or more years older but changes the age gap for victims under 14 "in cases where the victim is less than 14 years of age (three years), further decreasing if the victim is less than 12 years of age (two years)." This would mean that in both of these states the case of a 15-year-old girl with an 18-year-old boyfriend would not be illegal. These exemptions for teenagers who are close in age are sometimes called "Romeo and Juliet laws" (Glosser et al., 2004).

Other states focus on the age of the perpetrator, either on its own or along with the age of the victim. Both Nevada and Ohio say that perpetrators cannot be prosecuted if they are under 18, thus two 16-year-olds are safe from prosecution but the 15-year-old's 18-year-old boyfriend is not.

It gets even more complicated than that because many states make a distinction between sexual contact and sexual intercourse. This means there are instances in which activities that under different circumstances we might refer to as foreplay, sexplay, fooling around, or "outercourse" can be illegal depending on the age of the participants. In Connecticut, for example, engaging in *sexual intercourse* with someone who is less than 16 is legal under certain circumstances but *sexual contact* with someone who is less than 15 is illegal regardless of the age of the perpetrator.

So are we supposed to give our teens law books or maybe decoder rings as they head out on a weekend date? Don't we think teens already have enough to worry about when it comes to choosing which sexual behaviors they are going to engage in with a partner?

Is There a Victim?

Most often when statutory rape cases between teens are prosecuted it is at the behest not of either of the young people involved but of their parents or law enforcement officials who have gotten involved in the young person's life for some reason. This means that the laws are most often used on young people who are already troubled in some way.

An article in the *Daily Beast* (2012) focuses on the case of Ken Thornsberry and Emily Thorton who met in 2004 when he was an 18-year-old senior and she was a 14-year-old freshman. The two went to different high schools but became fast friends after they met at a record store and eventually became sexually active. Emily's father did not approve of the relationship. One morning when Ken showed up at her house, he and Emily's father had a heated argument and he punched her father who then called the police. Ken admitted to the police that he and Emily had had sex but said it was consensual. Emily concurred but it did not matter—in the state of Michigan the legal age of consent is 16; their relationship was illegal. Ken was sentenced to a year in jail and 3 years of probation and was forbidden from seeing Emily. A few months after he was released, however, she contacted him and they started seeing each other again which violated his probation. When her father found out he contacted authorities and Ken was sent back to jail. He spent the beginning of his twenties behind bars and was released at 26 but forced to wear a monitoring bracelet and add his name to the sex offender registry alongside those of serial rapists and child abusers (Pesta, 2012).

Granted, Ken made a lot of mistakes including assaulting Emily's father and violating a judge's order but rape was not one of them. At a hearing to have his name removed from the sex offender registry, Emily testified on his behalf. She told the *Daily Beast* that the term victim makes her mad: "I'm not his victim. I'm not a minor. He didn't rape me" (Pesta, 2012).

Most "victims" of statutory rape agree. Sutherland (2003) reviews the case of 18-year-old Kevin Gilson who was prosecuted in Wisconsin when his 15-year-old fiancé became pregnant. As part of his sentence, he was not allowed to see her for 2 years. She told the court: "Thanks to the court system, I have lost the love of my life and the father of my unborn baby" (p. 316).

Even more disturbing, these "victims" can be prosecuted for consenting to sexual behavior based on the idea that they were "aiding and abetting the offender" or they could be forced to testify against their former partner. This happened to 16-year-old Amanda Winkler who refused to testify against her 21-year-old husband Jamie. Jamie had been arrested for having sex with Amanda 4 days before her sixteenth birthday (4 days before she would be legally able to consent). Her grandparents later gave their consent for her to marry him but neither the fact that she was so close to the age of consent or that the two had subsequently married stopped prosecutors from moving forward. Moreover, when Amanda refused to testify at Jamie's trial she was put in jail for 7 hours (Sutherland, 2003, p. 317).

The distressing irony of the situation is that so few cases of actual rape ever reach prosecution. Sutherland points this out when she notes the case of Brian and Jennifer. He was 19 and she was 15 when he attended a party at her house. She got drunk and though she remembers him helping her into bed, she doesn't remember what happened next. The fact that she ended up pregnant, however, seems to prove that they had intercourse at a time when she was too drunk to give consent. But he was not prosecuted for either rape or statutory rape. "On a strict liability standard, this ought to have been a clear-cut case given Jennifer's age and the solid evidence of the act of intercourse provided by the baby. However, prosecutors decide the case would be too difficult to win given the fact that Jennifer had been drunk" (Sutherland, 2003, p. 318).

Discriminatory Enforcement

The truth is that these laws are prosecuted sporadically at best. Most teens are sexually active by the time they graduate from high school. According to the Youth Risk Behavior Surveillance data from the Centers for Disease Control and Prevention, for example, 63% of high school seniors have had sexual intercourse (Eaton *et al.*, 2012). So why is it that most teens never run afoul of the law? Obviously, some of this can be attributed to the fact that the law in some states allows for consensual sex among similarly aged teenagers but a look at those cases that are prosecuted show us that there's another reason. These laws are only triggered when the state becomes aware of the relationship and that generally only happens in cases of irate parents, curious welfare officials, already involved law enforcement officers, or pregnant girls.

Sutherland puts it this way:

> The selective enforcement of age of consent laws leaves considerable space for teenage sex, provided that it does not transgress boundaries based on age, sex, class, and race. Heterosexual sex between white, middle-class peers is unlikely to generate state interventions. This is "normal" teenage sexuality. Sex between a white middle-class girl and a working-class boy or a black boy, or an older man is likely to generate parental outrage that will trigger state intervention. Sex between a poor or working class girl of color and a teenage boy or even an older man is unlikely to generate state intervention unless the welfare rolls are threatened by a resulting pregnancy. (Sutherland, 2003, p. 333)

In an opinion piece for the *American Bar Association Journal*, Richard Delgado argues that statutory rape cases should not be prosecuted in large part because they are discriminatory:

> Unable to prosecute the whole country, law enforcement officials apply the law principally against two groups; men, frequently older, who have sex with girls from "good homes;" and minority men, who are punished if they commit the crime of having sex with white women or impregnate women of color under circumstances that add to the welfare rolls. (Oberman, 1996, p. 87)

Racial Bias

The fact that these laws are racially biased can be seen simply by noting who is prosecuted. Sutherland (2003) points to the "most-wanted list" for the California Alliance of Statutory Rape Enforcement. In 2003, the list included 35 names; 32 were men, and all of the men were black or Latino. To underscore the role that Welfare plays in decisions of whether to prosecute, she points to Orange County, California. Over a 2-year period in the first half of the 1990s, social workers persuaded 15 pregnant teenagers to marry the men who got them pregnant in order to prevent either themselves or their partners from getting into legal trouble for their under-age sexual activity. The women were as young as 13 and the men as old as 30. The marriages were approved by a judge. "These girls, deemed too young to choose sex, were nevertheless judged mature enough to choose marriage" (Sutherland, 2003, p. 323). It is worth noting that all but one of these girls were Latina.

It is also interesting to note that an inherent racism is found in the very roots of these laws. Colonial America adopted statutory rape laws from England and as a result of our system of slavery, the laws naturally did not apply to black women whose bodies were to be commodified rather than protected. In the 1800s, the laws were meant to save white women from ruining their status as marriageable but Native American and black women were again not part of the concern. Social reformers of the 1900s were worried about immigrant women who had moved to newly industrialized cities to find work and were deemed unable to control themselves. The fear was that these sexually precocious young women would threaten social norms and family structure. Aiming statutory rape laws at these women was not necessarily to protect them but to protect the norms (Ehrlich, 2006). Finally, the focus on teenage pregnancy in the 1990s also had an underpinning of race and class as it is black and Latina teens who disproportionately give birth and, moreover, need assistance from the state. As Cocca (2004) argues: "Rather than consider the structural problems, institutional failures, or ideological contradictions, blamed for societal ills is placed on individuals—in this case, teens and their sex partners, especially those of low income" (p. 28).

Gender Biases

The selective prosecution also clearly favors going after older men who have sex with younger women. This reflects the roots of the laws which, as discussed earlier, were designed to protect the virtue of women. However, it also reflects a view of male sexuality that sees almost all sexual activity as wanted. There have been some highly publicized cases of older women arrested for having relationships with younger men. Many of us remember the media frenzy over the Mary Kay Letourneau case in which a 35-year-old teacher had sex with a 13-year-old former student and became pregnant. After serving 6 months of her 7.5 year sentence, she was caught having sex with him again and became pregnant again. She went back to jail and served the rest of her term but when she was finally released, the two married.

Since then there have been a number of cases of women, most often high school teachers in their twenties, having sex with 16 and 17-year-olds. The reaction of the media and the public is mixed; the women in these cases are often looked down upon as oversexualized tramps, but the men are rarely seen as victims. Many people believe the boys "got lucky." As Sutherland suggests, "This attitude can be read as according greater respect to autonomy and rational decision-making powers of boys than to those of girls. On the other hand, it may represent an adherence to sexual stereotypes about male desire that ultimately deny boys protection against non-consensual hetero-sexual encounters" (p. 321).

Bias Against Gay Men

Finally, these laws are more likely to be enforced in cases of same-sex behavior among a teen and a slightly older partner, particularly if the couple in question is male. Some of this can be explained by the overreaction of parents who are upset to learn of their child's sexual orientation and blame the older partner for "making my son gay." The laws themselves, however, also favor heterosexual couples. The case of Matthew Limon is often used to illustrate how age of consent laws are unfair to gay couples.

Limon had just turned 18 when he had oral sex with a boy who was about to turn 15. The two were both residents at a school for developmentally disabled youth. Limon was convicted of a felony and sentenced to 17 years in prison and 5 years of probation after release and was ordered to register as a sex offender. The school was in Kansas which has a Romeo and Juliet law that allows for leniency in cases in which the age gap between the two participants is small, but the provision only applies to heterosexual couples. Had Limon been caught with a girl who was just short of her fourteenth birthday he would have received a maximum sentence of 15 months and he would not have had to register as a sex offender (Higdon, 2008; Sutherland, 2003).

Higdon (2008) argues that Romeo and Juliet provisions that are worded specifically to exclude lesbian and gay teens are so discriminatory as to be unconstitutional.

Society's View of Teen Sexual Behavior

We wholeheartedly agree that young people need protection from exploitation by adults. We also agree they need protection from relationships where there are natural power imbalances (such as any relationship between a teacher and a student, regardless of age). Still, we think the laws in their current state do not provide this protection and have the potential to be harmful, especially if they continue to be discriminatory in their enforcement.

Instead of spending our time working on laws that can end up punishing teens for consensual relationships, we should be teaching teens how to look critically at a situation and assess whether it's a good idea to engage in any given sexual behavior. We should also be teaching teens about the importance of consent as rape and sexual assault are huge issues in this country (see Myths # 40 and 44 for more on rape and sexual assault). Given the skills to think critically about all of these aspects of sexual relationships many young people would themselves weed out the relationships that we as adults are most concerned about—whether it's a 15-year-old girl admitting that having sex with her 19-year-old boyfriend was really an attempt to prove she was mature enough to be with him or a 20-year-old boy questioning the wisdom of dating someone who is still in high school.

We believe concentrating on education and critical thinking can truly help protect young people.

References

Cocca, C. (2004). *Jailbait: The Politics of Statutory Rape Laws in the United States.* State University of New York Press.

Eaton, D.K., Kann, L., Kinchen, S., Shanklin, S., Flint, K.H., Hawkins, J., *et al.* (2012). Youth risk behavior surveillance: United States, 2011. *Morbidity and Mortality Weekly Report Surveillance Summaries,* 61(4), 1–162.

Ehrlich, J.S. (2006). From age of consent laws to the "Silver Ring Thing": The regulation of adolescent female sexuality. *Health Matrix,* 16, 151–181.

Glosser, A., Gardiner, K.N., and Fishman, M. (2004). *Statutory Rape: A Guide to State Laws and Reporting Requirements.* Department of Health and Human Services.

Higdon, M.J. (2008). Queer teens and legislative bullies: The cruel and invidious discrimination behind heterosexist statutory rape laws. *UC Davis Law Review,* 42, 195.

Kempner, M. (2013). Should a 13-year-old and her 12-year-old partner really be considered sex offenders? *RH Reality Check* (October 1). http://rhrealitycheck.org/article/2013/10/01/should-a-13-year-old-and-her-12-year-old-partner-really-be-considered-sex-offenders/ (accessed August 8, 2014).

Oberman, M. (1996). Statutory rape laws: Does it make sense to enforce them in an increasingly permissive society. *ABA Journal,* 82, 86–87.

Pesta, A. (2012). Laws gone wild: As teen sweethearts go to prison for sex, mothers rebel. *Daily Beast* (January 25). http://www.thedailybeast.com/articles/2012/01/25/should-teens-be-jailed-for-sex-offenses-a-growing-parental-rebellion-says-no.html (accessed August 8, 2014).

Robertson, S. (no date). Age of consent laws. In *Children and Youth in History,* Item #230. http://chnm.gmu.edu/cyh/teaching-modules/230 (accessed August 8, 2014).

Sutherland, K. (2003). From jailbird to jailbait: age of consent laws and the construction of teenage sexualities. *William and Mary Journal of Women and the Law,* 9, 313–349.

Myth #50 The Struggle for Gay Rights Is Over

In the summer of 2013, the United States Supreme Court struck down a 17-year-old law known as the Defense of Marriage Act (DOMA). The law defined marriage as between a man and a woman and was designed to prevent same-sex couples who got married in those few states that allowed it at the time from receiving the same federal benefits awarded to heterosexual married couples.

When the law was passed, same-sex marriage was a hot-button political issue that was being used to divide "red states" and "blue states." The Republican Party included defending traditional marriage as part of its platform saying, "We reject the distortion of [anti-discrimination] laws to cover sexual preference, and we endorse the Defense of Marriage Act to prevent states from being forced to recognize same-sex unions" (Republican Party

Platform, 1996). Conservative political groups declared same sex-marriage as a threat to the foundation of our society. Then-President Bill Clinton, a relatively liberal Democrat, said he thought the act was unnecessary and divisive but noted: "I remain opposed to same-sex marriage. I believe marriage is an institution for the union of a man and a woman. This has been my long-standing position, and it is not being reviewed or reconsidered" (Moss, 1996). And he signed DOMA into law.

In the late 1990s and early 2000s, states also got involved in efforts to prevent same-sex marriage with some passing referendums and others attempting to amend the state constitution in order to ensure the privilege of marriage was reserved for heterosexual couples. Conservative politicians continued to use this as a political issue and even liberals shied away from supporting marriage for same-sex couples, with some arguing that "civil unions" could be used to give these couples similar benefits as other married couples without threatening the institution of marriage. In 2004, for example, then-President George W. Bush said he supported a constitutional amendment banning same-sex marriage, but backed away from this in 2005 because he believed DOMA was sufficient (Hoffecker, 2005).

Less than a decade later, DOMA was declared unconstitutional. Struggles for civil rights usually move very slowly and the struggle for gay rights and same-sex marriage is no exception (the courts in Minnesota ruled that not allowing two men to marry did not violate the constitution as early as 1970), yet in recent years it certainly seems as if the pendulum swung in the opposite direction very quickly (Coyle, 2010). More states passed laws allowing same-sex couples to marry, public opinion polls suggested increasing support for the practice and decreasing passion among those who opposed it, and liberal politicians began to change their tune.

The case brought to the Supreme Court, *United States v. Windsor*, involved a widow who had to pay estate taxes when her wife passed away. She argued that had they been a heterosexual married couple, the money would have automatically transferred to the surviving spouse without the tax bill. In an opinion written by Justice Anthony Kennedy, the court wrote: "No legitimate purpose overcomes the purpose and effect to disparage and to injure those whom the State, by its marriage laws, sought to protect in personhood and dignity. By seeking to displace this protection and treating those persons as living in marriages less respected than others, the federal statute is in violation of the Fifth Amendment" (Wolf and Heath, 2013).

The court's opinion only applied to those marriages that took place in states that recognize same-sex marriage. It does not suggest that all states must do so. However, in his dissent, Justice Antonin Scalia suggested that "By formally declaring anyone opposed to same-sex marriage an enemy of human decency, the majority arms well every challenger to a state law restricting marriage to its traditional definition" (Wolf and Heath, 2013).

Indeed, in the months since the decision was handed down, there seems to be an onslaught of decisions in which state legislatures have passed laws allowing same-sex marriage and lower court judges have overturned bans on the practice. As of this writing, 17 states allow same-sex marriage and it seems likely that by the time anyone reads this entry more will have voted to do so (National Conference of State Legislatures, 2014).

With the seemingly rapid success in the fight for same-sex marriage, it would be easy to fall into a false sense that the battle has been won and the struggle for gay right is over. Unfortunately, that is just not the case. While there has been enormous progress, a look at recent attempts by lawmakers around the country (and around the world) shows that there is still a long way to go.

In this entry we look at some efforts here in the United States to pass or enforce laws that discriminate against gay and lesbian individuals. We also briefly turn our focus internationally and look at countries that continue to discriminate against gay and lesbian individuals and even punish them for their sexual orientation.

Anti-Sodomy Laws

In 1998, police responded to the home of John Lawrence on what turned out to be a false report of weapons use on the property. They found Lawrence and his partner, Tyron Garner, having sex and arrested them under a Texas law that made it a crime for two people of the same sex to engage in oral or anal intercourse. (These acts were legal in the state if done by a man and a woman.) Lawrence, Garner, and their attorneys challenged the law on the grounds that it violated the men's rights to both equal protection under the law and due process. Ultimately, the Supreme Court struck down the law for due process reasons. Many legal scholars have since argued that while the result of Lawrence is good, the decision is not, because the court never did take on the equal protection arguments which would have provided more precedent for treating same-sex couples the same as heterosexual couples. Nonetheless, the decision invalidated sodomy laws across the country (*Lawrence v. Texas*; Mackinnon, 2004).

Sodomy laws remain on the books in 13 states and recent events have suggested that some people would like to see them revived. When Virginia Attorney General Ken Cuccinelli, for example, was running for governor of his state in 2013, he launched a website in support of his efforts to reinstate the Commonwealth's "crimes against nature" law. Though the law, which was found unconstitutional, bans oral and anal sex between consenting adults, Cuccinelli argued that he needed it to protect children from sexual predators.

Like many states, Virginia kept its law on the books despite the *Lawrence* ruling and in fact the state continued to prosecute adults under some provisions of the crimes against nature law until March 2013, when a three-member panel of the United States Court of Appeals for the Fourth Circuit struck down the law as unconstitutional.

Cuccinelli continued to argue that his goal in reinstating the sodomy law was to protect children, but his open opposition to same-sex relationships does make us wonder about his true motives. In 2009, Cuccinelli told a newspaper, "My view is that homosexual acts, not homosexuality, but homosexual acts are wrong. They're intrinsically wrong. And I think in a natural law based country it's appropriate to have policies that reflect that ... They don't comport with natural law" (Israel, 2013). It's also worth noting that Virginia's law outlawed oral and anal sex regardless of the biological sex of the participants. Were it to come back, fellatio and cunnilingus would be illegal in the Commonwealth. (Cuccinelli not only lost the battle to have the law reinstated, he lost his bid for Governor.)

Virginia may not be the only place making an effort to revive sodomy laws. In Baton Rouge, Louisiana, 12 men have been arrested since 2011 as part of a sting operation set up by the local sheriff's office. In July 2013, a 65-year-old man unknowingly began a conversation with an undercover police officer who was staking out Manchac Park. According to court documents, the police officer (who had denied being a cop) asked the man whether he had any condoms and if he wanted to come back to his place for "some drinks and fun." The older man followed the officer back to a nearby apartment complex where he was promptly arrested, despite having broken no law—there was no suggestion that money would change hands and the men did not make plans to have sex in a public place.

The arrest was based on Louisiana's "crimes against nature" law, which has been on the books since 1805 and prohibits "the unnatural carnal copulation by a human being with another of the same sex or opposite sex." This aspect of the law, however, is unconstitutional based on the Lawrence decision. Moreover, when the Lawrence decision came down, then-State Attorney General Richard Ieyoub issued a statement saying the state's anti-sodomy law would be unenforceable except for provisions banning sodomy for compensation and sex with animals.

But, for whatever reason, this hasn't stopped the Baton Rouge sheriff's office from disrupting these men's lives with the sting operation. As a result of the publicity around the story, the sheriff's office issued an apology "to anyone that was unintentionally harmed or offended by the actions of our investigation" (Kempner, 2013a).

Kenneth Upton, senior staff attorney at Lambda Legal, sees an upside to the publicity the Louisiana sting operation received. He told *Time*, "The country is learning that leaving something on the books isn't harmless. Just because laws are not enforced, and are not prosecuted, doesn't mean that people can't be harassed." Unfortunately, similar laws also remain on the books in Alabama, Florida, Idaho, Kansas, Michigan, Mississippi, North Carolina, Oklahoma, South Carolina, Virginia, Texas, and Utah, and there does not seem to be a lot of support for repealing them (Gregory, 2013).

"No Homo Promo"

Another set of laws that seem to discriminate against gays and lesbians are often glibly referred to as "no homo promo" laws. These are laws on the books in a number of states that prevent teachers from discussing sexual orientation with students on the grounds that doing so is akin to promoting an alternative lifestyle. These laws currently exist in eight states: Alabama, Arizona, Louisiana, Mississippi, Oklahoma, South Carolina, Texas, and Utah (GLSEN, no date).

An annual attempt to pass a similar law in Tennessee has made news recently. Nicknamed the "Don't Say Gay" bill, the legislation has been introduced every year for at least 7 years. Though the wording seems to differ each time it is introduced, the basic premise is always the same: teachers are prohibited from discussing "any sexuality other than heterosexuality" in grades K through 8.

The 2013 version was particularly disturbing because it seemed to force school officials to "out" students suspected of being homosexual to their parents. The new provision would have allowed school personnel to intervene if they fear that an individual student is "engaging in, or may be at risk of engaging in, behavior injurious to the physical or mental health and well-being of the student or another person." Once the school intervenes, the bill says that: "Parents or legal guardians of such students shall be notified as soon as practicable of the circumstances requiring intervention" (Kempner, 2013b).

Again, what may be most disturbing about the law are the motivations of its lead sponsor, Republican State Senator Stacey Campfield, who made numerous homophobic comments in the press as the bill was being considered. He told USA Today that: "Being gay is not a dangerous activity. The act of homosexuality is very dangerous to someone's health and safety." When he called into a TMZ radio show the host asked him why we shouldn't teach young people how to protect themselves if they are going to engage in homosexual acts anyway. In response, Campfield compared homosexuality to heroin use, saying: "You know, you could say the same thing about kids who are shooting heroin. We need to show them the best ways to shoot up. No, we don't. Why do we have to hypersexualize little children? Why can't we just let little kids be little kids for a while?" In that same interview he explained (inaccurately by the way) that HIV rates are so high in Africa because "they are really into sodomy" and that it is virtually impossible to get HIV during heterosexual sex" (Kempner, 2013a).

There is no way we can declare the battle for gay rights over if men like this continue to get elected to make our laws.

Deliberate Discrimination

Unfortunately, Campfield's "Don't Say Gay" bill is not as potentially destructive as a law that was passed by the Arizona legislature in early 2014. The law was a blatant attempt to allow private businesses to discriminate against gays and lesbians. Several court cases in other states sided with gay and lesbian individuals who said they had been discriminated against by a private business that refused to serve them. For example, the New Mexico Supreme

Court said a photographer who refused to take pictures of a same-sex wedding violated the state's anti-discrimination law. When a baker in Colorado argued that serving gay customers violated his religious freedom because his religion opposes homosexual relationships, the Colorado courts did not buy it (Fuller, 2014).

In an effort to pre-empt such a decision in their state, Arizona lawmakers passed a bill that would allow business to refuse service if providing such service would conflict with deeply held religious beliefs. Supporters of the bill said it was not discrimination because in order to turn away customers the businesses or employees would have to show a "substantial burden on their sincerely held religious beliefs." Some supporters even argued that it was the businesses who were being discriminated against. The conservative Center for Arizona Politics helped push the bill forward. Its president told CNN News: "The Arizona bill has a very simple premise, that Americans should be free to live and work according to their religious faith. It's simply about protecting religious liberty and nothing else" (Sanchez and Marquez, 2014).

Backlash against the bill and the state was swift and groups around the country called on Republican Governor Jan Brewer to veto the bill. Protestors came to the Capitol holding signs such as "Civil rights trump religious wrongs," the National Hispanic Bar Association canceled a meeting of 2000 members it had scheduled in the state, and the NFL apparently began to look for an alternate site for the 2015 Super Bowl. Ultimately, Brewer succumbed to the pressure, vetoed the bill, and even chastised lawmakers for taking this on instead of working to solve other more pressing issues (Santos, 2014).

This veto does not put the discrimination issue to rest, however. Similar bills have been proposed in a number of other states including Idaho, Kansas, South Dakota, Tennessee, and Utah though none have gotten as far as the Arizona law (Fuller, 2014). What may be more disturbing is the number of court cases that are moving forward using a similar religious liberties argument. Many of the cases have to do with whether businesses that oppose contraception for religious reasons can be exempt from the requirement in the Affordable Care Act (commonly known as Obamacare) that insurance pay for contraception. If the courts rule in favor of broad-based religious liberties, it could pave the way for businesses to argue that they also have the right not to serve gay and lesbian clients because of their religious beliefs.

Worldwide Struggle

The struggle for gay rights is clearly not over in the United States but this country remain leaps and bounds ahead of so many others on these issues. In 2013, Russian President Vladimir Putin signed into law a provision meant to squelch gay rights activism. The law essentially makes it illegal to teach young people about homosexuality. As means of enforcement, it makes gay pride parades, protests, and events illegal, and fines anyone expressing pro-gay propaganda. In fact, anyone caught providing information on homosexuality to children could be fined heavily and foreigners who are caught violating this can be jailed for 15 days, fined the equivalent of $3000, and then deported (Kempner, 2013c).

Oddly, Putin argued that the purpose of the law was not to discriminate against gays and lesbians but to protect the country from declining fertility rates. He noted: "It is imperative to protect the rights of sexual minorities, but let's agree that same-sex marriage does not produce children" (Grove and Gutterman, 2013). Of course, the idea that restricting free speech about homosexuality will reduce the number of same-sex couples in future generations only makes sense if people believe that gays and lesbian are "recruiting" young people who would otherwise—if not exposed to propaganda—grow up to be heterosexual.

Despite this specious logic, it is unclear how much attention the international community would have paid to this law had it not been for the 2014 Winter Olympic Games which were upcoming in Sochi, Russia, at the time the law was passed. Many worried that gay athletes from other countries would be under threat of prosecution if they were open about their orientation and political beliefs. The International Olympic Committee (IOC) worked to get the reassurance of Russian officials that guests at the Games would be not be impacted by the law. Of course, some advocates pointed out that this focus was obscuring the real issue of how lesbian, gay, bisexual, and transgender (LGBT) Russians are treated every day (Palmer, 2013).

The focus on the Games cast a spotlight not just on the law, but also on the abysmal state of gay rights in that country. According to a Pew Research Center survey, about three-quarters (74%) of Russians said homosexuality should not be accepted by society. Overall, 16% of Russians said they believe homosexuality is acceptable, but acceptance is slightly lower (12%) among Russians over age 50 and slightly higher (21%) among those aged 18–29 (Reilly, 2013). Another survey by the Levada Center found that 85% of Russians disapprove of gay marriage, 34% think homosexuality is a disease, and 5% think gays should be "eradicated." Given these attitudes it is not surprising that LGBT people in Russia are frequent victims of violence and discrimination (Katz, 2013).

International attention to this issue has ramped up slowly in recent years. There were outcries when Uganda criminalized homosexuality, when Nigerian President Goodluck Jonathan outlawed gay rights organizations and his government began arresting people suspected of being gay, and when India's high court affirmed a criminal ban on homosexuality. In fact, the United Nations estimates that 78 countries around the world ban homosexuality, and in seven countries it is punishable by death. This has largely gone unchallenged by the international community until very recently. In 2011, the United Nations Human Rights Council passed a resolution, led by South Africa, that extended human rights principles to gays and lesbians around the world. While such a resolution shows support for gay rights around the globe, it is extremely difficult to enforce and these laws continue to exist relatively unabated (Sengupta, 2014).

The conclusion here is pretty obvious, like all civil rights and human rights struggles that have come before it and all that will come after, the battle for gay rights both in the United States and around the world has been long, slow, and intense and though much progress has been made (obviously more in some places than others), now is not the time to declare victory or let our guard down. The fight will go on, the pendulum will most likely swing back and forth, and hopefully in the end everyone will have the right to choose—free of discrimination and bias—who they want to love, have sex with, and marry, regardless of biological sex.

References

Coyle, M. (2010). The first case, 40 years on. *National Law Journal* (August 23). http://www.nationallawjournal.com/id=1202470861873?slreturn=20140212091930 (accessed August 8, 2014).

Fuller, J. (2014). The Arizona 'religious rights' bill—and where the fight might move next. *The Washington Post* (February 26). http://www.washingtonpost.com/blogs/the-fix/wp/2014/02/24/the-states-fighting-the-fight-between-religious-rights-vs-gay-rights/ (accessed August 8, 2014).

Gay Lesbian Straight Education Network (GLSEN) (no date). No homo promo laws. http://glsen.org/learn/policy/issues/nopromohomo (accessed August 8, 2014).

Gregory, S. (2013). Louisiana sodomy sting: How invalidated sex laws still lead to arrests. *Time* (July 31). http://nation.time.com/2013/07/31/louisiana-sodomy-sting-how-invalidated-sex-laws-still-lead-to-arrests/ (accessed August 8, 2014).

Grove, T. and Gutterman, S. (2014). Russia's gays fear more violence after brutal murder. http://www.reuters.com/article/2013/05/13/us-russia-gay-idUSBRE94C0AX20130513 (accessed August 8, 2014).

Hoffecker, L. (2005). Bush won't lobby for amendment. *Orlando Sentinel* (January 17). http://articles.orlandosentinel.com/2005-01-17/news/0501170143_1_same-sex-marriage-marriage-act-defense-of-marriage (accessed August 8, 2014).

Israel, J. (2013). Ken Cuccinelli's legal appeal and how he helped undermine Virginia's protections against adult sex with minors. *Think Progress* (April 3). http://thinkprogress.org/justice/2013/04/03/1816861/ken-cuccinellis-appeal-and-how-he-helped-undermine-virginias-protections-against-adult-sex-with-minors/ (accessed August 8, 2014).

Katz, A. (2013). Russia's anti-gay laws: How a Dutch activist got caught in the crosshairs. *Time* (August 5). http://world.time.com/2013/08/05/russia-faults-in-first-test-of-anti-gay-propaganda-law-but-future-remains-bleak/#ixzz2vlAzYldd (accessed August 8, 2014).

Kempner, M. (2013a). Baton Rouge sheriff arrests men for sodomy, despite law being struck down a decade ago. *RH Reality Check* (July 31). http://rhrealitycheck.org/article/2013/07/31/baton-rouge-sheriff-arrests-men-for-sodomy-despite-law-being-struck-down-a-decade-ago/ (accessed August 8, 2014).

Kempner, M. (2013b). Tennessee's newest "Don't Say Gay Bill" is worse than it ever was. *RH Reality Check* (February 7). http://rhrealitycheck.org/article/2013/02/07/tennessee%E2%80%99s-%E2%80%9Cdon%E2%80%99t-say-gay-bill%E2%80%9D-is-back-worse-than-before-as-its-sponsor-hits-ai/ (accessed August 8, 2014).

Kempner, M. (2013c). Russia's anti-LGBTQ law leads to protests, pushback, and a reminder of our laws here at home. *RH Reality Check* (August 7). http://rhrealitycheck.org/article/2013/08/07/russias-anti-lgbtq-law-leads-to-protests-pushback-and-a-reminder-of-our-laws-here-at-home/ (accessed August 8, 2014).

Lawrence v. Texas, 539 U.S. 558. United States Supreme Court. http://www.lambdalegal.org/sites/default/files/legal-docs/downloads/lawrence_tx_20030626_decision-us-supreme-court.pdf (accessed August 8, 2014)

MacKinnon, C.A. (2004). The road not taken: Sex equality in *Lawrence v. Texas. Ohio State Law Journal*, 65, 1081.

Moss, J.J. (1996). Bill Clinton interview. *The Advocate* (June 25). https://web.archive.org/web/20050208184130/http://www.advocate.com/html/stories/824/824_clinton_710.asp (accessed August 8, 2014).

National Conference of State Legislatures (2014). Defining marriage: State defense of marriage laws and same sex marriage. http://www.ncsl.org/research/human-services/same-sex-marriage-overview.aspx (accessed August 8, 2014).

Palmer, J. (2013). Russia must explain its anti-gay law, says International Olympics Committee. Reuters (August 9). http://www.huffingtonpost.com/2013/08/09/russia-gay-olympics-committee_n_3730925.html (accessed August 8, 2014).

Republican Party Platform (1996). *American Presidency Project*. August 12, 1996. http://www.presidency.ucsb.edu/ws/index.php?pid=25848 (accessed August 8, 2014).

Reilly, K. (2013). Russia's anti-gay laws in line with public's views on homosexuality. Pew Research Center (May 5). http://www.pewresearch.org/fact-tank/2013/08/05/russias-anti-gay-laws-in-line-with-publics-views-on-homosexuality/ (accessed August 8, 2014).

Sanchez, R. and Marquez, M. (2014). Arizona lawmakers pass controversial anti-gay bill. CNN (February 21). http://www.cnn.com/2014/02/21/us/arizona-anti-gay-bill/ (accessed August 8, 2014).

Santos, F. (2014). Arizona governor vetoes bill on refusal of service to gays. *New York Times* (February 26). http://www.nytimes.com/2014/02/27/us/Brewer-arizona-gay-service-bill.html?_r=0&module=ArrowsNav&contentCollection=U.S.&action=keypress&region=FixedLeft&pgtype=article (accessed August 8, 2014).

Sengupta, S. (2014). Antigay laws gain global attention; countering them remains a challenge. *New York Times* (March 1). http://www.nytimes.com/2014/03/02/world/africa/antigay-laws-gain-global-attention-countering-them-remains-challenge.html (accessed August 8, 2014).

Wolf, R. and Heath, B. (2013). Supreme Court strikes down Defense of Marriage Act. *USA Today* (June 26). http://www.usatoday.com/story/news/politics/2013/06/26/supreme-court-gay-lesbian-marriage-doma/2394621/ (accessed August 8, 2014).

INDEX

Klinefelter syndrome (XXY) 33–4

legal issues
  age of consent 283–92
  consensual sex 283–92
  Defense of Marriage Act (DOMA)
    76, 292–3
  'Don't Say Gay' bill 295–6
  gay rights 292–9
  'no homo promo' laws 295–6
  oral sex 291
  pornography 281–2
  rape laws 283–92
  sexting 281–2
  sodomy laws 294–5
Levitra (vardenafil)
  see also Viagra (sildenafil)
  testosterone 28
libido
  see also sex addiction; sex drive;
    sexual appetites
  drugs 135
  oral contraceptive pill 143–4
  transgender 53
lubrication 230
  menopause 93–4

married couples vs singles, sexual
    satisfaction 83–5
married sex
  rape 251–2
  sexual assault 251–2
  sexual satisfaction 83–5,
    87–90
masochism, female fantasies 197
masturbation 129–31
  circumcision 14, 18
  historical views 241–2
  partners 131
  pornography 254, 255
  prevalence 130
  sex addiction 241–2, 243,
    246–7
  stigma 130–1
  vibrators 120–1
  young people 99
matched sexual appetites 211–14
menopause, aging and sex 93–4
mental health, abortion 162–4, 166
meta-females (XXX) 34

NARTH (National Association for
    Research and Therapy of
    Homosexuality) 58
'no homo promo' laws 295–6

'off label' testosterone 28–9
oral contraceptive pill 141–6
  breast cancer 143
  fertility 143
  libido 143–4
  promiscuity 185–6
  side effects 142, 143–4, 145
  weight gain 144
oral sex
  herpes 179–80
  legal issues 291
  young people 98–100, 179–80, 264
orgasms
  clitoral 23–4, 93, 118–20
  faking 123–6
  G-spot 22–5
  'right way' 119–20
  simultaneous 117–22
  vibrators 120–1
orientation
  bisexuality 44–8
  gaydar 41–4
outside attraction 194–6
  emotional affairs 207
outside sexual relationships 203–9

pain during sex 127, 128, 229–34
Panax ginseng, aphrodisiac? 134
parenting, same-sex relationships 68,
    69–76
passion, vs sexual satisfaction 87–90
pedophilia 77–81
pelvic inflammatory disease (PID) 176,
    177, 231
  IUDs (intrauterine devices) 148, 149
penises 1–5
  bigger/better correlation 4–5
  body parts size correlations 1–2
  gay men 4
  size and pleasure 2–4
  size differences 1–2
  surgery 1
phismosis 37–8
PID see pelvic inflammatory disease
the pill see oral contraceptive pill